Oxford Socio-Legal Studies

The Social World of an English Crown Court

GENERAL EDITORS   Donald R. Harris   Keith Hawkins
Sally Lloyd-Bostock   Doreen McBarnet

Oxford Socio-Legal Studies is a series of books published for the Centre for
Socio-Legal Studies, Wolfson College, Oxford. The series is converned generally with the relationship between law and society, and is designed to
reflect the increasing interest of lawyers, social scientists and historians in this
field.

Recent titles in this series:

THE SOCIAL WORLD OF AN ENGLISH CROWN COURT

Witness and Professionals in the Crown Court Centre at Wood Green

PAUL ROCK

CLARENDON PRESS · OXFORD
1993

Oxford University Press, Walton Street, Oxford OX2 6DP

Oxford New York Toronto
Delhi Bombay Calcutta Madras Karachi
Kuala Lumpur Singapore Hong Kong Tokyo
Nairobi Dar es Salaam Cape Town
Melbourne Auckland Madrid

and associated companies in
Berlin Ibadan

Oxford is a trade mark of Oxford University Press

Published in the United States
by Oxford University Press Inc., New York

British Library Cataloguing in Publication Data
Data available

Library of Congress Cataloging in Publication Data
Rock, Paul Elliott.
The social world of an English Crown Court; witness and
professionals in the Crown Court Centre at Wood Green | Paul Rock.
(Oxford socio-legal studies)
Includes index.
1. Criminal justice, Administration of—Social aspects—Great
Britain.   2. Criminal courts—England—Wood Green (London)—History.
3. Witnesses—Social aspects—Great Britain.   I. Series.
KD7876.R6   1993   345.42'014—dc20   [344.20514]   93–16309
ISBN 0–19–825843–7

Set by Hope Services (Abingdon) Ltd.
Printed in Great Britain by
Biddles Ltd
Guildford & King's Lynn

For Chris and Caryn, who began it all

Acknowledgements

In being allowed to undertake research at all, I was fortunate not only to have received the help and advice of Martin Graham (a judge who sometimes sat at the Crown Court at Wood Green), the Lord Chancellor's Department, and Victim Support (and yet again of Helen Reeves, its Director) but also to have encountered a liberal and kindly Resident Judge who was well disposed to academic research, a forbearing Chief Clerk, and a friendly group of staff at the Crown Court at Wood Green. It could have been otherwise.[1]

I was fortunate, too, in the help I received from Robert Glass, the Branch Crown Prosecutor, and his staff; the police officers of the Hornsey and Tottenham divisions; David Adlington of the South-East circuit administration; Victim Support Haringey and Irene Rondell, its Chair; and numerous barristers (and the tenants of 4 Kings Bench Walk in particular).

The fieldwork was guided all the while from outside the court by Tim Gustafson, the National Co-ordinator of the Victim in Court Project, and I could not have hoped for a more supportive ally. It was guided from within by Geoff Spain, the Senior Probation Officer at the Crown Court. Elaine Player once told me that the probation officer is the field researcher's friend. Geoff Spain advised and befriended me from the first,[2] and it was his office that became my base and home territory in the Court before the Victim in Court Project was firmly established. I owe him a deep debt. After the formal opening of the project in April 1990, I began to badger Stephen Okafor, its busy co-ordinator, and his volunteers, particularly Emma Giovanni and Mac, for help and information, and I am grateful for their kindness and patience.

[1] My work followed in the wake of a report by a research and information officer of the Middlesex Area Probation Service (B. Hudson, 'Middlesex Area Probation Service Crown Court Survey: Summary of Results from the Crown Courts: 1987–1988', n.d.), which represented the Crown Court at Wood Green as exceptionally severe in its use of sentences of immediate imprisonment for the unemployed and Afro-Caribbean. The report was not popular in some quarters of the Court, and could well have discouraged the idea of further research.

[2] He became, in effect, my key informant, not only a mentor and confidant but 'a native speaker [who was] engaged to repeat words, phrases and sentences in his own language or dialect as a model for imitation and a source of information' (J. Spradley, *The Ethnographic Interview*, New York, Holt, Rinehart, and Winston, 1979, p. 25).

I should like to thank the Social Research Division of the London School of Economics, the Suntory International Centre for Economics and Related Disciplines (STICERD), and the Nuffield Foundation for their provision of research expenses, above all the costs of transcribing interview tapes; and Kim Lewis, Judith Russell, Fiona Morris, and S. Calvert for their work on the laborious task of transcription.

Throughout the field research I was conscious that a parallel evaluation project was in train. John Raine and Rena Smith of the University of Birmingham had been commissioned by Victim Support to ascertain the needs of victims and prosecution witnesses attending the seven Crown Court centres served by the 'Victim in Court' project, and to assess how well those needs were met and what the appropriate organization of a project should be. As part of that work, MORI undertook a substantial survey of witnesses appearing at the seven centres. The original intention had been to interview 100 witnesses from each court, a total of 700, but, in the event, 485 interviews were actually completed, 47 at Wood Green itself. Because there was a risk that the Court at Wood Green would be exposed to a surfeit of research, exhausting the goodwill of its staff, it was decided from the beginning that I would not duplicate that survey but would make use of it as a complement to my own field research. I am grateful to its authors for working with me in this fashion. From time to time, I shall turn to their surveys of witnesses at Wood Green and the other six centres.[3]

I am also grateful to Gordon Hindle of the Property Services Agency and to Tony Hennocq, the Court's project manager, for helping me to understand something of the architecture of the two courthouses; to Susan Zagor, who was a good companion and chauffeur; and to the people who read and commented on the book whilst it was in draft: Tim Gustafson of Victim Support, His Honour Judge McMullan, Stephen Okafor, Geoff Spain, Lord Windlesham, Michael Zander, and Lucia Zedner.

[3] There were a number of interim reports submitted to Victim Support. The principal report was J. Raine and R. Smith, *The Victim/Witness in Court Project: Report of the Research Programme* (London, Victim Support, Oct. 1991).

Contents

Introduction

The Social World of an English Crown Court completes a trilogy of works describing the origins and opening phases of a number of formal responses to the problems of victims of crime. The two earlier books, *A View from the Shadows*[1] and *Helping Victims of Crime*,[2] dwelt on policy-making in the governments of Canada and England and Wales. They touched on large processes at the centre of power in criminal-justice systems where knowledge about victims was generally second-hand, filtered by the politics of organizations pursuing their own, often diffuse goals. They described how the victim has been repre-sented variously as a number in surveys to measure the volume of crime, an opportunity to do good to offenders, a casualty of patri-archy, a hazard in law enforcement, an obstacle to penal reform, and an instrument of 'dercarceration;. Having formed a view of the grand politics of victims, it seemed a sensible next step to explore how those politics actually unfolded in one small and practical area. Going from the centre to the periphery, from the mediated to the immediate, from the general to the particular, could give old prob-lems a new appearance and allow the victim to assume yet another guise, that of prosecution witness.

This book is the result of taking just such a step. It examines the beginnings of one of the seven court-based demonstration projects to support victims and prosecution witnesses that were sponsored by the national association whose history had been traced in *Helping Victims of Crime*. It effectively starts in 1986, where *Helping Victims of Crime* ended. But it is more than a history of a victim-witness assistance scheme. The Court itself loomed even larger, more interesting, and more important as I followed Victim Support into Wood Green and tried to observe what befell witnesses. It became clear that the expe-riences of witnesses and the fate of their scheme could not be severed from the organization in which they were set. Witnesses are socially constructed, and the institution which shapes them is surprisingly obscure. It merits such sustained attention that the balance of the book has been changed to accommodate it.

Courts, and the Crown Court in particular, have been little exam-ined by criminologists, being part of the great *terra incognita* of British

[1] Oxford, Clarendon Press, 1986.   [2] Oxford, Clarendon Press, 1990.

criminology. Only a small portion of their workings has actually been mapped and those exploring them have tended to have quite set objectives in mind. There has been an insistent search for a latter-day North-West Passage in British criminology, a quest for answers to the penal crisis.[3] Much criminological research on the courts has attended (quite properly) to issues flowing from the overriding problems of prisons and the size of the prison population rather than from a regard for the court as an object of disinterested enquiry. It has seen the court principally as an imprisoning machine, concentrating on remands (Mary Tuck, then Head of the Home Office Research and Planning Unit, observed in her foreword to one study of the courts: 'there has been much concern of late about the size of the remand population'[4]), mitigation speeches,[5] and the effectiveness[6] and workings of sentencing.[7]

There has been virtually no analysis of the court as a complex social world. Little attention has been paid to the phenomenology of the trial. The moral careers of those whom court architects and administrators describe collectively as the 'public', the non-professionals,[8] the defendants, victims, and witnesses, have been somewhat neglected. There is, to be sure, a small corpus of work on the role of the 'public' in domestic and foreign criminal-justice systems, and I shall draw on it as this book advances.[9] But it *is* small, leading the Canadian soci-

---

[3] Peter Young has been moved to ask: 'why do criminologists pay so much attention to the use of imprisonment? to the analysis of its emergence? and to the ever-present penal (read prison) crisis? The answers to these questions may appear so self-evident as to cast doubt on the seriousness with which they are asked in the first place. Indeed, to pose these questions may seem heretical, in a minor way' ('The Importance of Utopias in Criminological Thinking', paper presented to the British Criminology Conference, 28 July 1991, 11).

[4] Foreword to R. Pearce, *Waiting for Crown Court Trial: The Remand Population*, Research and Planning Unit Paper 40 (London, Home Office, 1987), p. iii.

[5] See J. Shapland, *Between Conviction and Sentence* (London, Routledge, 1981).

[6] See S. Brody, *The Effectiveness of Sentencing* (London, HMSO, 1976).

[7] See e.g. J. Hogarth, *Sentencing as a Human Process* (Toronto, Univ. of Toronto Press, 1971); D. Moxon, *Sentencing Practice in the Crown Court* Home Office Research Study 103, (London, HMSO, 1988); D. Pennington and S. Lloyd-Bostock (eds.), *The Psychology of Sentencing* (Oxford, Centre for Socio-Legal Studies, 1987); C. Fitzmaurice and K. Pease, *The Psychology of Judicial Sentencing* (Manchester, Manchester Univ. Press, 1986).

[8] I shall make more of the significance of this dichotomy later in the book.

[9] See e.g. for Britain, D. McBarnet, 'Victim in the Box', *Contemporary Crises*, 7 (1983); J. Shapland *et al.*, *Victims in the Criminal Justice System* (Aldershot, Gower, 1985); for America, M. Knudten *et al.*, 'Will Anyone Be Left to Testify? Disenchantment with the Criminal Justice System', in E. Flynn and J. Conrad (eds.), *The New and the Old Criminology* (New York, Praeger, 1978); W. McDonald (ed.), *Criminal Justice and the Victim* (Beverly Hills, Sage, 1976); and for Canada, J. Hagan, *Victims Before the Law* (Toronto, Butterworth, 1983).

ologists Ericson and Baranek to write of the failure of the 'socio-legal literature' to focus on 'the perspective of the accused';[10] Shapland to observe how very rare is the research which 'explores the reactions of victims and of criminal justice personnel';[11] and Jackson and his colleagues to remark that 'there is little empirical research into the experiences of witnesses, defendants and jurors once they become involved in the criminal justice system'.[12] There have been gaps elsewhere. The 1981 Royal Commission on Criminal Procedure said very little about victims and witnesses.[13] When, in February 1992, the Royal Commission on Criminal Justice surveyed the Crown Court, it was reported that 'everyone involved in criminal trials at crown courts in England and Wales will be asked for their views on the workings of the system in what is believed to be the first full survey of its kind.'[14] Defendants and even, very exceptionally, juries were to be questioned about the conduct of cases. But to the great chagrin of Victim Support, and perhaps un-remarkably, 'everyone involved in criminal trials' did *not* include victims and prosecution witnesses. Prosecution witnesses were not everyone at all. And even when the experiences of the 'public' *have* been considered, it has often been without the assistance of empirical research. Work has proceeded on common-sense assumptions and second-hand reports about the phenomenology of victimization.[15]

This meagreness of research on witnesses in the Crown Court may perhaps be explained by the absolute thinness of British criminology;

[10] R. Ericson and P. Baranek, *The Ordering of Justice: A Study of Accused Persons as Dependants in the Criminal Process* (Toronto, Univ. of Toronto Press, 1982), 5.

[11] J. Shapland, 'Memorandum on the Victim and the Criminal Justice System', in European Committee on Crime Problems, *Report of the Select Committee of Experts on the Victim and Criminal and Social Policy* (Strasbourg, Council of Europe, 1983), 2. Similarly, J. Hagan remarked that, 'despite considerable journalistic speculation, we know very little about how victims respond to their experiences in the criminal justice process' ('Victims Before the Law: A Study of Victim Involvement in the Criminal Justice Process', *Journal of Criminal Law and Criminology*, 73(1) (1982), 317.

[12] J. Jackson *et al.*, 'Called to Court: Lay Perceptions of Criminal Justice in Northern Ireland', unpublished paper, 1–2.

[13] There is but a single reference to how delays in bringing cases to trial cause 'distress and inconvenience . . . to witnesses, victims and suspects' in the *Report of the Royal Commission on Criminal Procedure*, Cmnd. 8092 (London, HMSO, 1981).

[14] F. Gibbs, 'Opinion Poll Will Assess Courts', *The Times*, 17 Feb. 1992.

[15] See e.g. the otherwise worthy *Witnesses in the Criminal Courts* (London, Justice, 1986). Shapland has remarked how 'almost all . . . provisions [for victims] have been set up without reference to the experiences, thoughts or feelings of actual victims' ('Victims' Experiences of the Criminal Justice System', in R. Mawby (ed.), *Crime Victims*, Proceedings of a Conference in the South West Social Issue Series, Plymouth Polytechnic, 1986, 27).

by British criminology's overriding interest in the crowding of prisons; by the seemingly marginal intellectual and political standing of victims (Shapland reported that 'victims tend to feel forgotten and unwanted'[16]); and by the additional and important presumption that the Crown Court is a territory inhospitable to academic investigation.

There are two incidents remembered by criminologists. The first followed in the wake of allegations made in the 1970s that plea-bargaining was practised quite routinely in the English Crown Court. There was considerable agitation, lawyers protested, and the President of the Law Society himself scourged McConville and Baldwin, the authors of the report, questioned their academic competence, and insisted that the University of Birmingham, their parent body, should mount an independent investigation into the fitness of their work.[17] McConville and Baldwin were to be exonerated by that investigation; but criminologists are not used to such a stir, and it left its mark.

The second incident occurred when, in December 1981, the Lord Chief Justice, Lord Lane, refused to permit the continuation of a Home Office-funded inquiry into sentencing policy and practice in the Crown Court. The study had been undertaken by criminologists working in an established research centre who were concerned then, as their colleagues are concerned now, about 'the general level of sentencing and the pressure on the prison system'.[18] It was reported that the Lord Chief Justice had determined that the issues raised by the inquiry's pilot study were familiar enough to judges, that nothing useful would be gained by further research, and that, indeed, more work would only waste judicial time and public money.[19] The fate of the inquiry and the Lord Chief Justice's judgment were discussed by criminologists, who decided that Crown Courts were not welcoming places. It was supposed that no one could break into the courts if the staff of the University of Oxford Centre for Criminological Research,

---

[16] J. Shapland, 'The Victim in the Criminal Justice System: Final Report to the Home Office, October 1981', unpublished summary, 8. In America, the Homeric epithet for the victim is 'the forgotten person in criminal proceedings'. See e.g. R. Davis *et al.*, 'Expanding the Victim's Role in the Criminal Court Dispositional Process', *Journal of Criminal Law and Criminology*, 75(2) (1984), 492.

[17] See J. Baldwin and M. McConville, *Negotiated Justice* (London, Martin Robertson, 1977).

[18] A. Ashworth *et al.*, *Sentencing in the Crown Court*, Occasional Paper 10 (Oxford, Centre for Criminological Research, 1984), 2.

[19] Ibid. 64. Other, supplementary accounts circulated to explain why the inquiry collapsed.

working with Home Office money and support, could not do so. Pannick concluded that judges 'discourage sociological studies of their activities'.[20] A criminological taboo remained for a time and the few attempts made to breach it were not very successful.[21]

This book is an ethnographically based descriptive account[22] of the social world of an English Crown Court centre. Using much the same qualitative methodology that I have described elsewhere,[23] I began fieldwork in September 1989, spending lengthy periods observing the social life of courtrooms, the public and private areas of the courthouse, and the national and local committees superintending the Victim in Court Project. I tried to identify who figured in that life, what it was they were doing, and how they worked together. Expeditions were undertaken to deal with issues as they emerged. (Were women barristers more likely to comfort distressed witnesses? Did traditions pass from master to pupil concerning the treatment of witnesses? Did a distraught witness upset the staging of a counsel's performance? Did judges conceive it to be their duty to protect witnesses from distress?) Some of those questions may now seem naïve and ill-informed, but they had to be put before they could be revised or dismissed. They led to a continual reading of published and unpublished documents and the interviewing and re-interviewing of 'theoretical samples' of significant people. Fieldwork ended effectively in July 1990.

The Social World of an English Crown Court is a case study of a single institution. Ethnographic methods are intense. A sustained application of time and effort is demanded of one who tries to become familiar enough to ask the questions that complete strangers should not ask,[24] understand how the more idiomatic practices of an

---

[20] D. Pannick, *Judges* (Oxford, Oxford Univ. Press, 1987), 10.

[21] See J. Shapland and D. Cohen, 'Facilities for Victims: The Role of the Police and the Courts', *Criminal Law Review*, Jan. 1987, 29. Shapland and Cohen's postal survey of facilities for victims in the courts had to omit an examination of the Crown Court because the response rate of 13% was too small to warrant conclusions. The situation may now have changed. As I write, Roger Hood of Oxford University is studying the fates of different ethnic populations of defendants in the Crown Court and John Raine and Rena Smith of Birmingham University are evaluating Victim Support's Victim in Court Project.

[22] I have borrowed this phrase from P. Manning, *Symbolic Communication* (Cambridge, Mass., MIT Press, 1988), p. xiii. It seems best able to convey the approach I have tried to employ in this study.

[23] See 'A Natural History of Research on Policy-Making', in N. Fielding (ed.), *Actions and Structures: Research Methods and Social Theory* (London, Sage, 1988), 99–116.

[24] I was touched when, after a while, the chief security guard began calling me 'the professor in residence' and said, 'You work here too, you're one of us'.

organization form a working logic, grasp something of the way in which situated perspectives fold into one another, and produce what has been called 'thick description'. Such research has to be manageable, limited, and small. Although much of the book is an exploration of routine activity directed by the insider's recipe knowledge of how to conduct trials in *any* court, it does not pretend to generalize or compare far beyond what happened in a single court in a little under one year. In making that disclaimer, I have been encouraged by the very similar qualification which Feeley made about his own research on an American court:

> Most studies of the criminal process agree that the operations of the criminal courts are shaped by little-understood factors, and that decision are made as a consequence of an uncharted, complex, and interdependent set of relationships. Both of these factors militate against a comparative approach which by definition must *impose* at the outset a developed framework on the research.[25]

Kenneth Burke once observed that 'a way of seeing is always a way of not seeing',[26] and so it was with this research. Only some portions of the Crown Court loomed large as I pursued Victim Support to Wood Green. Questions emerged and changed as time passed, but they were informed always by a wish to understand the situated character of the prosecution witness. This book is not an exhaustive description of a Crown Court. It could not be so. Neither is it a lawyer's book, although it deals with law and advocates. It centres on processes affecting victims and those who testified on their behalf, touching the defendant only when the defendant touched them. It does not focus much on decisions about sentencing, bail, and remands. It has become, in effect, a broad analysis of the Crown Court at Wood Green as it developed within a more particular examination of the way in which conflict shaped prosecution witnesses' identities.

What emerged quite clearly was the importance of time and space in that process. And that is hardly remarkable: 'activity systems are inevitably organized in space and time'.[27] Time and space are themselves socially modulated, affected by those self-same 'activity systems' (phenomenologists would argue that 'time and space extend out from

---

[25] M. Feeley, *The Process is the Punishment* (New York, Russell Sage Foundation, 1979), p. xvi.

[26] *Permanence and Change* (New York, New Republic, 1935), 70.

[27] A. Rapoport, 'Systems of Activities and Systems of Settings', in S. Kent (ed.), *Domestic Architecture and the Use of Space* (Cambridge, Cambridge Univ. Press, 1990), 12.

the felt and embodied present'[28]). They are necessary and useful ways of framing an analysis of experience: in Stimson's words, they enable one to see as well as to listen.[29] And they are especially useful in describing the structured and wide-awake world of witnesses, where such features are much exaggerated. The difficult antagonisms of the trial process translate witnesses into people who are defined and regulated at every point by controls which lean heavily on the management of time and space for their effect.

Consider time. The importance of witnesses resides in their ability naïvely to defend recollections of events that may have taken place months or years before but lie recorded in statements reread perhaps only minutes before. Being a witness is, in part, a test of the ability to reconcile accounts produced at very different periods. Prosecution (and defence) witnesses must contend with artful questions intended to expose their veracity, character, and consistency. It is held dangerous for them to know too much in advance about the questions lawyers will ask and the answers which they will elicit. It is dangerous for them to compare memories with others about them. What they recall should be unsullied and entirely their own. It is dangerous for them to talk to lawyers because it should not be thought that they have been 'coached'. Yet it signifies little what they learn *after* testifying. Their knowledge will then have been spent. Released witnesses are like a bomb defused. Their sole remaining importance lies in the risk of contamination they present to the evidence of other witnesses as yet unexamined. There is a segregation of the innocent about to give evidence from the knowing who have already done so.

Consider space. Witnesses are permitted to enter certain parts of courthouses and not others, be exposed to some groups and not others, see certain events and not others, and the physical plan of the courthouse choreographs their behaviour appropriately. In the middle of my research, in April 1990, the influence of space on behaviour became even more salient as the Crown Court moved from a spartan 'crash building' to a modern *Palais de Justice*. Questions could be put about the effects of a newly designed environment.

Those three facets of a process, time, space, and conflict, seemingly sensed as one, best capture what besets the prosecution witness,

---

[28] J. Lewis and A. Weigart, 'The Structures and Meanings of Social Time', in J. Hassard (ed.), *The Sociology of Time* (London, Macmillan, 1990), 93.

[29] See G. Stimson, 'Viewpoint: Place and Space in Sociological Fieldwork', *Sociological Review*, 34(3) (Aug. 1986), esp. 641.

and they will become the themes of the chapters to come. The first chapter will describe the setting and work of the Crown Court centre at Wood Green. The following six chapters will each anatomize a separate but linked facet of the witness's experience, each being intended to build, layer upon layer and methodically, on what ran before. Collectively, they may capture some of the most important organizational and existential properties of the trial process. They will, in effect, represent the diagnosis. Chapters 8 and 9 talk of cure, reviewing the history and workings of an attempt to alleviate some of the pains of testifying. And the Postscript describes the long-term outcome.

1. The Setting: The Crown Court at Wood Green

Wood Green has always been the most ghastly Crown Court—'the bunker' is its nickname. But that being said, one of the things that always made it very good is the staff there—it's got a very good atmosphere and you just get on with it and do it. (A barrister speaking in 1989)

I shall begin at the beginning by describing a little of the formal history, setting, and organization of the Crown Court at Wood Green. It is necessary to open with a methodical procession through such structural matters because everything done within the Court was part of an elaborately planned division of labour. It will then be possible to turn to the special experiences of those who worked in the Court, visited it, and were brought to it for trial.

The Crown Court

The Crown Court is a new body. Although two prototype Crown Courts had been created in 1956 in Liverpool and Manchester to handle local work, the Crown Court proper became a national institution only in January 1972.[1] It was engendered by the Courts Act 1971,[2] that Act being a response to recommendations made in the 1969 report of a Royal Commission chaired by Dr Richard Beeching and established to examine and reform the administration of justice in general and the system of assize and quarter sessions courts in particular.[3] Beeching had been the chairman of the British Railways Board between 1963 and 1965, and he was celebrated principally for his 'modernization' of the rail network. Just as Beeching had reformed the railways, so he was to change the courts. His report described a 'patched',[4] antiquated, and fragmented network of courts

---

[1] For a brief history of the early internal debates about the reform of the superior court after the Second World War, see A. Bottoms and S. Stevenson, 'What Went Wrong?: Criminal Justice Policy in England and Wales, 1945–70', in D. Downes (ed.), *Unravelling Criminal Justice* (London, Macmillan, 1992), esp. 14–15.

[2] Ch. 23.

[3] Royal Commission on Assizes and Quarter Sessions, 1969, Cmnd. 4153.

[4] Ibid., para. 64.

that were not always to be found in centres of population where they were needed,[5] and were not in continual session.[6] It complained about overloading in certain areas and, in London especially, about long waiting lists and organizational inefficiencies. It proposed rationalization and change: to replace the localized, 'labyrinthine structure of assizes and quarter sessions',[7] there should be a new system and a new Court, the Crown Court, which would be marked by its 'convenience, quality and economy'.[8]

Formally, the new Court was to be regarded as a single national body of superior jurisdiction that could sit at any centre[9] and form as many courts at one location as necessary. It would be staffed by a new permanent bench of circuit judges[10] and administered as a whole, as a new Unified Court Service, by the Lord Chancellor's Department. But, because 'it would [have been] difficult . . . effectively to control the courts and offices in England and Wales . . . without delegating a great deal of control to regional or area offices',[11] there was also to be a devolution of power. There were to be six circuits, each having its own High Court judges acting as presiding judges, and each its own administrator and staff. Every centre, in turn, was to have a resident judge, attached judges, and judges moving about on circuit, a chief clerk, and administrative staff.

The Crown Court was a single court which exclusively heard all cases on indictment and triable before a judge and jury. However, partly in response to public upset at the maladroit handling of a succession of rape cases, its work was also graded into classes of importance dictated by the Lord Chief Justice and approved by the Lord Chancellor.[12] Not every case could be taken by every judge, and the Lord Chief Justice determined how the allocation was to be made.[13]

[5] Ibid., para. 74.

[6] Ibid., para. 75.

[7] I. Marriott and E. Simpson, *The Crown Court: A Preliminary Survey of the Scope for Computer Assistance* (London, Lord Chancellor's Dept., 1977), app. B, p. 1.

[8] Ibid., para. 49.

[9] By 1990, at the time of the fieldwork for this book, there were 71 main centres and 26 satellite centres managed from a main centre.

[10] By 1988, there were 82 High Court judges, 405 circuit judges, 627 recorders, and 413 assistant recorders in England and Wales; *Social Trends*, 20. (London, HMSO, 1990), 188.

[11] Lord Chancellor's Dept., *An Introducion to New Entrants*, (London, HMSO, 1985), 4.

[12] The Supreme Court Act, 1981, ss. 75(1) and (2), following directions given on 14 Oct. 1971 by the Lord Chief Justice.

[13] *Crown Court Manual* (London, Lord Chancellor's Dept., May 1990), 1.

The most delicate, explosive, and difficult cases were handled only by senior judges, the least demanding by recorders and assistant recorders, the part-time judges and judges in training who had to be barristers or solicitors of at least ten years standing.

There was a fourfold classification.[14] Class 1 was the most serious and included treason, genocide, piracy, and murder cases which had to come before a High Court judge. Class 2 cases included rape, child destruction, abortion, incest with a girl under 13, sedition, and manslaughter, and they were tried generally by a High Court judge, although they could be released by a presiding judge to a circuit judge. Class 3 cases could be tried by any judge, and included all offences triable on indictment apart from those specifically allotted to the three other classes. Class 4 cases were normally tried by a circuit judge, recorder, or assistant recorder, and they covered grievous bodily harm, robbery, and conspiracy as well as more mundane offences and offences 'triable either way' in the Crown Court or Magistrates Court. The four classes formed a flat pyramid: of the 90,000 cases committed annually to the Crown Court in the late 1980s, some 0.6 per cent of cases fell into Class 1, 1.2 per cent into Class 2, 3.3 per cent into Class 3, and 95 per cent into Class 4.[15] The vast bulk of Crown Court business consisted of burglaries, thefts, and assaults.

A hierarchy of offences was accompanied by an administrative stratification of the Crown Court centres into three tiers: in early 1990, at the time of this research, 24 first-tier centres[16] heard all classes of criminal indictment and High Court Civil and Family Division matters; 14 second-tier centres heard all classes of criminal indictment but no civil work; and 34 third-tier centres dealt with the 'less serious criminal cases only',[17] that is, cases falling under Classes 3 and 4.

The largest and busiest of the six circuits,[18] the South-Eastern, was so large that it had itself to be bifurcated into two divisions, London and the Provinces. It served a population of 17 million, handled nearly half the country's serious criminal cases,[19] and was staffed by

[14] This section makes use of *Judicial Statistics: England and Wales for the Year 1987* (London, HMSO, 1988), esp. 53.

[15] Ibid., table 6.3, p. 57.

[16] Based on *The Crown Court Review* (London, Lord Chancellor's Dept., 1990), vol. ii, app. A.   [17] Ibid. i. 4.

[18] See *An Introduction for New Entrants*, 5.

[19] e.g. in 1987, 255 of 565 Class 1 cases (45%) and 390 of 1,095 Class 2 (36%) cases were committed in the South-Eastern circuit.

just under half of the 400 Circuit Judges[20] working in England and Wales. By early 1990, there were eight Crown Court centres in London, seven being third-tier, one second-tier (the Central Criminal Court at the Old Bailey[21]), and none first-tier. All murders and almost all rapes were committed automatically from the London magistrates' courts to the Old Bailey, leaving the other court centres to deal with the other 98 per cent of cases, the great mass of mundane criminal business.

The Crown Court at Wood Green

Built on decrepit foundations, contending with a steadily growing volume of cases, designed to cover the breadth of the country, the new Crown Court swelled. In 1979, for instance, the Court dealt with 50,638 cases in England and Wales and with 10,482 in London; by 1988, those figures had increased to 106,524 and 19,004.[22] In 1972, the year in which it began work, Scott observed that 'the inadequacies of much of the court accommodation in England and Wales [were] little short of scandalous' and he prophesied 'a court building "boom"'.[23] So it was to be. Three years later, in 1975, an interdepartmental committee reported how 'the increase in the work of the higher courts' had been accompanied by an 'emergency building programme and the appointment of many judges'.[24] What was started then continued throughout the 1970s and 1980s. Staff of the Lord Chancellor's Department planned for an estimated 4 per cent annual increase in court business until the end of the century[25] and Crown Court centres and courtrooms mushroomed in proportion. One hundred new courtrooms were opened between 1980 and 1985[26] and 150 more by the end of 1988. Ninety building projects

[20] In late 1986, there were 182 circuit judges, 262 recorders, and 240 assistant recorders attached to the circuit; 'Circuit Profile No. 6: The South Eastern Circuit', *Your Court*, 2(1) (Oct./Nov. 1986), 9.

[21] 'When the Crown Court sits in the City of London it shall be known as the Central Criminal Court'; Courts Act 1971, ch. 23, para. 4(7).

[22] Based on Memorandum 3 submitted by the Lord Chancellor's Dept. to the Home Affairs Committee; Home Affairs Committee, *Crown Prosecution Service: Memoranda of Evidence* (London, HMSO, 1990), 44.

[23] J. Scott, *The Crown Court* (London, Butterworth, 1972), 47.

[24] *The Distribution of Criminal Business between the Crown Court and the Magistrates' Courts: Report of the Interdepartmental Committee*, Cmnd. 6323 (London, HMSO, 1975), 12.

[25] In fact, numbers of committals were in what was probably a temporary decline at the time of this research.

[26] *Your Court*, 1(1) (Oct./Nov. 1985), 10.

had been completed by the end of 1988, at a cost of £250 million.[27] Three new court centres at Truro, Coventry, and Norwich opened on one day alone in November 1988.[28]

The small, third-tier, six-courtroom Crown Court centre at Wood Green was part of that great wave of expansion. Conceived in 1977, it was housed three years later in what its architects called a 'temporary', 'crash', or 'emergency' building, intended later to be converted into the Court's administrative offices. It was set in the large site of a former school in North London, on a busy main road travelled by a number of buses, and near an underground station (the architect co-ordinating the project observed to a group of visiting journalists in March 1990, 'It's difficult to get good sites, one's always in competition with Sainsbury's, and it's very important to be near public transport'). The Court's first task was to act as an 'overflow court' for the Middlesex Guildhall, itself closed and being refurbished, and for the Crown Court at Snaresbrook. It then began to develop its own catchment area in the outer suburbs of north London, receiving committals for trial from the Enfield, Haringey, Barnet, Hendon, Hampstead, and Highgate magistrates' courts.[29] In a nondescript block in Lordship Lane, it had to wait like Penelope for ten years until it could move to the far grander and more complicated *Palais de Justice*[30] under construction behind the 'skilfully preserved Victorian façade'[31] of the former Royal Masonic School for Boys next door.

The business of the new Crown Court centre bore the threefold marks of its place in the geography of London, its role in the division of labour regulating the criminal-justice system, and the low security and small size of the cells and courtrooms of a temporary courthouse (a senior official of the Court said: 'security has something to do with it' . . . I mean the cells here are not very good'). The chief clerks of the local magistrates' courts having been instructed to commit their most serious cases to the Old Bailey, the outcome was that, as the local branch Crown prosecutor said, 'you won't get any murders.

---

[27] *Building for Justice* (London, Property Services Agency, 1989), 2.

[28] See *Your Court*, 4(3) (Feb./Mar. 1989), 6.

[29] Like all centres, it also continued to receive the occasional case transferred from elsewhere in London.

[30] Just as barristers labelled the old courthouse 'the bunker', so a barrister christened its replacement. In Feb. 1990 I overheard a lawyer asking a member of the Crown Prosecution Service, 'What are the facilities like in the new *Palais de Justice*? Is it nice inside?' The name seemed so apposite that I adopted it for descriptive purposes in this book.

[31] *Building for Justice*, 11.

You won't get many rapes. The majority of cases that go to [Wood Green] Crown Court are cases of dishonesty . . . This is an area where you see all kinds of crime: domestic offences, incest, public disorder, fights in pubs.' Wood Green received 1,683 new committals from magistrates' courts in 1989, 201 cases 'transferred in', and 549 cases carried forward from 1988. Of the 1,887 cases disposed of in that year, 1869 were Class 4 (99 per cent); 12 were Class 3 (0.6 per cent); and 6 were Class 2 (0.3 per cent). There was no Class 1 case. A senior official in the administration of the South-Eastern Circuit observed that the cases at Wood Green were generally of 'low calibre', reflecting 'the locality amongst other things . . . Generally, apart from this building [the Old Bailey] and Middlesex and Southwark, cases tried in the Crown Court are not very important.'

Table 1.1 makes it clear that the pattern and composition of offences tried at Wood Green were substantially the same as those to be found in the Crown Court as a whole. The Court's staple cases, more than two-thirds, were the Class 4 offences of assault, theft, and burglary. Only very occasionally would judges try cases of robbery, fraud, or sexual assault. What did distinguish the Court was its propensity to acquit. Wood Green was thought by many counsel to be a relatively lenient court, and its jurors working-class men and women not wholly unsympathetic to defendants. 30 per cent of Wood Green defendants, twice the national average, were acquitted in 1988.[32] Over a third of that number (35 per cent) were discharged by a judge, 15 per cent were directed to be acquitted, and 50 per cent were acquitted by a jury.[33] It was held by several counsel to be a little harder to obtain a conviction in Wood Green than elsewhere, and much harder to obtain a conviction for certain offences, and for assault on the police in particular.

Offences committed to the Crown Court centre were generally minor and diverse, refracting the conflicts, opportunism, and predatoriness of everyday life in the working-class suburbs of north London. Consider the indictments for trial on two very ordinary days in 1990. Twelve defendants were to be tried on a day toward the end of April. Defendants 1 and 2 were charged jointly with the theft of a cheque, with dishonestly receiving a cheque and with stealing

---

[32] Although it should be noted that the acquittal rate at Wood Green was no greater than at other *London* Crown Court centres: I am grateful to Judge McMullan for this point.

[33] Figures supplied by the Lord Chancellor's Dept.

TABLE 1.1. *Persons Tried for all Offences at Wood Green Crown Court, 1984*

	Total for trial	Not tried	Acquitted	Total found guilty
Violence against the person				
Wood Green	420 (21%)[a]	7 (4%)[b]	75 (42%)[b]	228 (54%)[b]
All courts	21,625 (20%)	646 (3%)	5,264 (24%)	15,630 (72%)
Sexual offences				
Wood Green	34 (2%)	2 (6%)	16 (47%)	16 (47%)
All courts	4,070 (4%)	85 (0.02%)	758 (19%)	3,227 (79%)
Burglary				
Wood Green	252 (13%)	5 (2%)	14 (19%)	151 (79%)
All courts	20,572 (19%)	256 (1.2%)	1,212 (6%)	19,104 (93%)
Robbery				
Wood Green	66 (3%)	—	13 (20%)	53 (80%)
All courts	4,029 (4%)	32 (0.8%)	554 (14%)	3,443 (85%)
Theft and handling				
Wood Green	685 (34%)	20 (3%)	213 (32%)	425 (65%)
All courts	30,402 (28%)	903 (3%)	4,595 (15%)	24,905 (82%)
Fraud and forgery				
Wood Green	125 (6%)	3 (2%)	18 (14%)	104 (83%)
All courts	6,632 (6%)	174 (3%)	685 (10%)	5,773 (87%)
Criminal damage				
Wood Green	50 (3%)	3 (6%)	17 (34%)	30 (60%)
All courts	3,144 (3%)	79 (3%)	577 (18%)	2,488 (79%)
Drug offences				
Wood Green	151 (8%)	6 (4%)	31 (21%)	114 (75%)
All courts	5,771 (5%)	105 (2%)	655 (11%)	5,011 (88%)
Other indictable (not motoring)				
Wood Green	112 (6%)	1 (1%)	35 (31%)	62 (55%)
All courts	8,022 (7%)	262 (3%)	1,830 (23%)	5,930 (74%)
Motoring				
Wood Green	101 (5%)	1 (1%)	30 (30%)	70 (70%)
All courts	4,311 (4%)	55 (1%)	417 (10%)	3,839 (89%)
Total of all offences				
Wood Green	1,961 (100%)	63 (3%)	597 (30%)	1,309 (67%)
All courts	10,578 (100%)	2,682 (2%)	16,546 (15%)	89,350 (82%)

[a] % of total offences. [b] % of offences of particular class.
Source: Home Office figures

£3,000, all from the same model agency; defendant 3 was charged with the theft of a radio cassette player and a holdall and with possession of an offensive weapon, a 'Swiss Army knife'; defendants 4 and 5 were charged with the burglary of two flats from which they were alleged to have stolen stereo systems, clocks, and a television, and the burglary of a pet shop, from which they had stolen dog food, dog chews, dog collars, and two calculators; defendants 6 and 7 were charged jointly with conspiracy to supply a controlled drug (315

grams of diamorphine) and with possession of drugs; defendant 8
with the theft of a purse containing £33; defendant 9 with the theft
and dishonest receiving of a building society account book; defendants 10 and 11 jointly with stealing purses and tights from one shop
and two jumpers from another; and defendant 12 with stealing a
wrench and spark-plugs from a garage.

Some five weeks later, on a day at the beginning of June, seven
defendants were to be tried: defendant 1 was charged on two counts
with assault occasioning actual bodily harm, on two counts of stealing
a wallet, a cash card, and a national insurance card, and the theft of
£90 belonging to a bank, on a fifth count of damaging a car, and on
a sixth of damage to a leather jacket; defendant 2 was charged with
the theft of three car wheels; defendant 3 was charged with an assault
on a woman, occasioning actual bodily harm; defendants 4, 5, and 6
were charged jointly with the burglary of two adjoining houses and
stealing a miscellany including four cigars, a ring, a sweatshirt, and
money, defendant 5 being charged separately with the theft of a
jacket; and defendant 7 was charged with dishonestly receiving a
'motor vehicle registration mark' believing it to be stolen.

Many Class 4 offences were serious enough but they did not
attract the gravest penalties. The judges of third-tier Crown Court
centres were not the most harsh. Very typically, they confronted
poor, disorganized, unskilled, young people committing commonplace offences. At Wood Green itself, the defendants sentenced
tended to be white, unemployed (51 per cent in 1987–8) men (92 per
cent in 1989) under the age of 25 (60 per cent in 1987–8).[34] Fifty-
five per cent or 1032 of those who appeared in 1989 pleaded guilty
and could expect a 'standard discount' in sentences of imprisonment.
The Court's sentencing policy was regarded by most judges and
staff[35] as quite liberal, and a distinct *frisson* would spread amongst

[34] Figures supplied by the Lord Chancellor's Dept. 6. According to figures supplied
by the Home Office, 27% of persons appearing for trial in Wood Green in 1988 were
aged between 17 and 20, precisely the same proportion as in all cases tried in the
Crown Court nationally.

[35] There was something of a competition between the probation staff of 3 courts to
win the highest proportions of community service and probation orders. Quarterly
returns were prepared to compare the rates of imprisonment and probation in Wood
Green, Isleworth, and Acton. In 1989, for instance, the senior probation officer's
returns showed that 9.6% of Wood Green disposals entailed probation orders in 1989
(compared with 10.8% at Acton and 8.0% at Isleworth); 9.8% entailed community
service orders (compared with 7.5% at Acton and 6.5% at Isleworth); 15.4% of sentences of imprisonment were suspended or partially suspended (compared with 15.6%

ushers, court clerks, probation officers, and others when that policy appeared to have been breached. There would be comment especially when assistant recorders and recorders, apparently unfamiliar with the Court and its ways, attached heavy sentences to unspectacular crimes. Any sentence longer than perhaps four years' imprisonment was taken to be severe enough to occasion talk that was excited both by a sense of awe at the power of the institution in which people worked and, from time to time but not invariably, by criticisms of judicial inexperience or an inappropriate punitiveness.[36]

The resident judge certainly took pride in his Court's reputation. When, in January 1990, *The Times* misrepresented the findings of a report produced by the National Association of Probation Officers and claimed that 69 per cent of sentences passed at Wood Green were custodial, depicting the Court as one of the most draconian of all,[37] he voiced dissatisfaction not only that his Court had been portrayed inaccurately but that the inaccuracy gave it an impression of undue severity. The court's senior probation officer, instructed to make immediate representations to the National Association, discovered that the incarceration rate reported for Wood Green had actually been confused with that for the Crown Court at Mold.

Table 1.2 shows that the Court did indeed resort to sentences of immediate imprisonment less often than the national average for almost all offences. Whilst the Crown Court as a whole imposed custody in about half the cases, Wood Green did so only in 38% of cases.

There was a marked affinity between the characteristics of offenders and those of the victims and bystanders who come to testify against them. After all, the two groups had tended to collide because they were very often members of similar populations discovered together in the same places and at the same times.[38] As in other

at Acton and 14.5% at Isleworth); and 24.8% involved sentences of immediate imprisonment (compared with 28.8% at Acton and 41.9% at Isleworth).

[36] On one occasion, for instance, an assistant recorder sentenced a man to a total of 4 year's imprisonment on 4 charges: 18 months, 18 months, 6 months, and 6 months consecutively for offences related to car theft. Staff in and about the courtroom registered surprise, considering that the sentences would customarily have been concurrent at Wood Green. The court clerk believed the matter unusual enough to gossip about it with counsel who entered the courtroom for the next case. It was rumoured that the assistant recorder had had his own car stolen.

[37] Q. Cowdry, 'Crown Court Prison Sentences 'Resemble a National Lottery', *The Times*, 22 Jan. 1990.

[38] See e.g. E. Fattah, *Understanding Criminal Victimization* (Englewood Cliffs, NJ, Prentice-Hall, 1991), esp. gh. 5, and S. Smith, *Crime, Space and Society* (Cambridge,

TABLE 1.2. *Sentences Imposed at Wood Green and All Courts in 1988*

	Total for sentence[a]	Absolute and conditional discharge	Fine	Probation	CSO	Immediate custody
Violence against the person						
Wood Green	231	13 (6%)	30 (13%)	13 (6%)	26 (11%)	89 (47%)
All courts	16,103	843 (5%)	1,648 (10%)	860 (5%)	1,488 (9%)	7,628 (47%)
Sexual offences						
Wood Green	18	1 (6%)	2 (11%)	4(22%)	—	8 (44%)
All courts	3,264	79 (2%)	119 (4%)	329 (10%)	47 (1%)	2,255 (69%)
Burglary						
Wood Green	211	3 (1%)	8 (3%)	33(16%)	31 (15%)	107 (51%)
All courts	20,250	364 (2%)	426 (2%)	2,387 (12%)	2,522 (12%)	12,394 (61%)
Robbery						
Wood Green	53	—	—	2 (4%)	5 (9%)	45 (85%)
All courts	3,443	13 (>1%)	27 (>1%)	131 (4%)	160 (4%)	2,985 (87%)
Theft and Handling						
Wood Green	452	36 (8%)	80 (18%)	52 (12%)	48 (11%)	148 (33%)
All courts	27,439	2,094 (8%)	3,119 (11%)	3,664 (13%)	3,3881 (12%)	10,120 (37%)
Fraud and Forgery						
Wood Green	106	9 (8%)	18 (17%)	10 (9%)	11 (9%)	19 (18%)
All courts	6,047	400 (7%)	531 (9%)	482 (8%)	509 (8%)	2,471 (41%)
Criminal damage						
Wood Green	33	3 (9%)	14 (42%)	14 (42%)	2 (6%)	7 (21%)
All courts	2,705	193 (7%)	214 (8%)	484 (18%)	292 (11%)	1,020 (38%)
Drug offences						
Wood Green	116	5 (4%)	30 (26%)	6 (5%)	3 (3%)	47 (40%)
All courts	5,138	183 (4%)	577 (11%)	343 (7%)	206 (4%)	3,028 (59%)
All cases						
Wood Green	1,392	80 (6%)	216 (16%)	131 (9%)	157 (11%)	523 (38%)
All courts	9,663	4,662 (5%)	8,272 (9%)	9,454 (10%)	9,961 (10%)	47,696 (49%)

[a] Includes cases sent by the magistrates' courts for sentence.
[b] Community service orders.

Source: Home Office figures.

Crown Court centres, the Class 4 offences committed by young, white, working-class offenders were prosecuted with evidence supplied by young[39] witnesses who were themselves largely members of the white working class. Seventy per cent of the small sample of Wood Green witnesses interviewed in early 1990 by MORI for the

Cambridge Univ. Press, 1986). M. Hindelang, M. Gottfredson, and J. Garofalo remark of the United States that 'offenders . . . are disproportionately male, young, urban residents, black, of lower socio-economic status, unemployed (and not in school), and unmarried. In our brief review of victim characteristics . . . it was seen that victims disproportionately share these characteristics'; *Victims of Personal Crime* (New York, Ballinger, 1978), 259.

[39] 33.3% of the MORI Wood Green sample were under 24 and another 53.3% were aged between 24 and 44; J. Raine and R. Smith, *The Victim/Witness in Court Project: Report of the Research Programme* (Oct. 1991), 6.

Smith and Raine evaluation were described as skilled and unskilled manual workers or as unemployed.[40] But there were rather fewer upper middle-class witnesses: only 4.3 per cent of the sample of those appearing at Wood Green were categorized as 'senior professional and managerial' compared with an overall average of 15.5 per cent of the sample of those appearing at Wood Green were categorized as 'senior professional and managerial' compared with an overall average of 15.5 per cent for the total survey population from the 7 Court centres.[41] Although the Wood Green witnesses were preponderantly white, three-quarters (76.6 per cent) of the centre's sample being described by Raine and Smith as 'UK White', Wood Green was distinctively more heterogeneous in the ethnic composition of its witnesses. The centre did, after all, serve Tottenham and its surrounding terrain, an area of heavy first- and second-generation immigrant settlement. Whilst 3.7 per cent of the witnesses in the overall sample were designated 'Afro-Caribbean, African, and Asian', the figure for Wood Green was 17 per cent. Wood Green was the only Court centre with a sizeable number of witnesses of Irish origin (4.3 per cent). Witnesses were split almost equally between males (48.9 per cent) and females (51.1 per cent).

The Crown Court at Wood Green may have tried relatively slight offences, but its attention to gravity and propriety was nevertheless very real (a circuit judge attached to another Crown Court centre observed that 'a criminal trial is, and ought to be, a formal and different proceeding'.[42]) The trial of any indictable crime was consequential because it could lead to imprisonment and a loss of reputation. It would take place before a judge and jury and its conduct would be measured, formal, and unhurried. Problems of evidence and proof could still arise in very much the same way as in trials for murder, rape, or arson. Yet it was also the case that the trial of a staple Class 4 offence was unlikely to be especially complicated or protracted. A member of the court's listing staff, responsible for the programming of trials and required to gauge their probable length, observed: 'we get . . . I suppose a relatively small number of witnesses . . . We have all Class 4 cases here . . . lots of the things we get are quite smallish crimes so we can be looking at things that

---

[40] *The Victim/Witness in Court Project: Report of the Research Programme* (Oct. 1991),. 7.

[41] The other Court centres were Teeside, Manchester, Liverpool, Preston, Newcastle, and Maidstone.

[42] His Honour Paul Collins, letter to *The Times*, 28 Apr. 1992.

have got, say, two to six fully bound witnesses.' As I shall show, the prosecution case in a standard trial for assault would probably have involved no more than brief testimony from the alleged victim, a bystander, and a police officer and agreed written evidence from a casualty doctor. Such a mix of relatively few 'fully bound'[43] witnesses, almost no expert witnesses apart from doctors called to attest to injuries, almost no documentary exhibits, and simple indictments affected the substance, structure, and pace of the Court's business.

Over half of trials (51 per cent in 1989) 'went short', as lawyers put it, defendants having elected to be tried but then deciding to plead guilty on the day. The average length of the 819 trials thus truncated in 1989 was 42 minutes. Wood Green's special role as a third-tier centre showed in the other 794 trials that were fought in 1989. The simpler the case, the shorter was it likely to be. It will be recalled that there had been no Class 1 case at all in that year. The four Class 2 cases that went to trial lasted an average of 13 hours and 30 minutes each, and the five Class 3 cases lasted for some 8 hours and 18 minutes each. The remaining 785 Class 4 trials lasted an average of 5 hours.

The centre was distinguished by the comparatively heavy volume[44] and brevity of its trials,[45] and it was correspondingly complex to administer. The Court's listing officer was known for his ingenuity in keeping courtrooms occupied (a judge talked about his office as 'superb'). He had devised a 'double-listings' system. On Mondays, Tuesdays, Wednesdays, and Thursdays, each uncommitted courtroom would be allocated a new trial to begin at a notional 10.15 a.m. That trial would usually be a 'fixture', a trial of some importance scheduled firmly in advance, perhaps on the application of counsel, because of the number of witnesses implicated, or the involvement of expert or child witnesses or the detention of the

---

[43] i.e. witnesses warned that they were obliged to attend trial and under threat of penalty if they failed to do so.

[44] It is difficult to estimate the number of courtrooms in use for criminal trials in the Crown Court as a whole. Courtrooms were continually being added and refurbished; County Court courtrooms were used occasionally for criminal cases and Crown Court courtrooms for High Court cases. Using the very rough estimate of upper and lower limits provided by the Lord Chancellor's Dept., the 6 courtrooms of Wood Green were between 5% and 20% busier than average.

[45] *Crown Court Feasibility Study* (London, Management Services Branch, Lord Chancellor's Dept., 1982), i. 12.

defendant in custody.[46] There would be a 'back-up trial' listed for the same time and the same courtroom, a trial of less importance 'which has not been fixed'. And there were other, minor trials, known as 'floaters' that were attached to no courtroom in the anticipation that a room would eventually fall vacant during the day as allotted cases collapsed or went short. The listing officer said: 'we find that usually one of them pleads or is stood out . . . so many trials aren't a trial when they come to court . . . on the whole it pays off.'

The outcome was that counsel, witnesses, police officers, and defendants seemed to be forever waiting, expectantly and often anxiously, for trials and news of trials. Their knowledge of the Court was constituted, in part, by an experience of long periods of inactivity outside courtrooms that would culminate in bursts of activity inside the courtroom itself. I shall discuss something of that experience of the organization of time in Chapter 7.

In the late 1980s there were some 6,000 practising barristers[47] in approximately 340 sets of chambers in England and Wales, the bulk being concentrated in 220 sets of chambers in London itself.[48] To impose order on the work of assigning prosecution briefs, the Crown Prosecution Service had, in effect, inverted the Lord Chief Justice's classification and devised its own method of grading barristers by the kind of cases they were believed capable of managing (after all, as a CPS law clerk working at the Court observed, 'If he's been at the bar for only two years, he's not up to doing a serious assault'). By the time the CPS began work in October 1986, counsel had been invited to join its 'prosecution list', had been reviewed by a committee, and had then been graded. Those whom the CPS designated grade 1 prosecutors were the most junior and grade 4 the most senior. Some 35% of the 3,000 barristers available to the CPS in London were classified grade 1 in early 1990. Thirty-seven per cent were grade 2,

[46] A CPS officer said: 'For a proper fixed date I'm looking for something crucial. I'm saying to them, This is a massive trial and it needs to be given a proper fixture. We've got a lot of witnesses coming along, a lot of private witnesses [i.e. not police officers] or witnesses travelling distances. . . . If I see anybody who is a doctor who is fully bound or a child who is fully bound then I would mark that case for a fixture. . . . Doctors have difficulties just being called to court on the spur of the moment. . . . The list officer will then either choose to take note of what I've said or ignore it.'

[47] The precise number in 1988 was 5944. See *Social Trends* (London, HMSO, 1990), 188.

[48] See P. Darbyshire, *English Legal System in a Nutshell* (London, Sweet and Maxwell 1989), 41.

described by the CPS law clerk as counsel called in the previous ten years who could try 'run-of-the-mill cases such as ABH [assault occasioning actual bodily harm]'. Only 5 per cent were identified as grade 4, and they were 'very serious counsel who can have anything'. There was a measure of discontent amongst barristers about the techniques and legitimacy of the grading process. Few professed to understand its workings and the manner in which it might be challenged.[49] There were thought to be anomalies and absurdities. One said: 'There is a certain amount of politics in this. It would depend on how much influence your own clerk [of chambers] has with the people who do the grading of barristers and I have heard it said . . . that it is difficult to get upgraded. We have some very senior people in these chambers who are very capable lawyers in their field but I don't believe we have anyone other than a grade 2.'

It was grade 1 and 2 barristers, rated the youngest and most junior by the CPS, who were most frequently to be seen prosecuting the Class 4 cases at Wood Green (a judge said, 'If you wish to see great advocacy, go to the Crown Court at Birmingham, not here'). Those defending would have been their equal or even more junior, although solicitors did not maintain any roll to equal the CPS list and relied more on their own networks (which are occasionally mediated by connections within the ethnic communities of north London[50]) and on the judgment of clerks of chambers. There were some 2,000 actions in Wood Green in 1989, consuming 1,366 days of court time, and almost every action involved more than one counsel. Unlike the stable and enduring social groupings that could coagulate around long-fought cases, there was a perpetual milling and flux of lawyers as they assembled and dispersed around the short cases at Wood Green. Counsel were forever flocking in and out of the Crown Court, travelling up the Piccadilly Line or by car, appearing in trials, making appeals against the findings of magistrates' courts (there were 137 appeals against conviction and sentence in 1989 and 100 against sentence only), requesting fixtures, attending to

---

[49] An officer of the CPS branch attached to the Court at Wood Green maintained that grading is reviewed regularly. A senior executive officer may sit in court and watch counsel in action, but more often a review would be based on an assessment of the way in which barristers received their briefs in the CPS office in the courthouse. Would they e.g. 'request bindovers too often, which is a cop-out just to get a fee? We'd see whether they're on the ball. Have they noticed admissions in the papers?'

[50] There are e.g. Greek or Greek-affiliated chambers which deal with Greek law practices.

matters of sentencing in Crown Court cases (sentencing would usually be deferred for probation and other reports, requiring counsel or
their colleagues to return to deal with the sentencing of their clients
only) and to matters of sentencing transferred from the magistrates'
courts (124 defendants were so committed in 1989), and applying for
bench warrants (112 warrants were executed in 1989). They said
again and again, 'I just go in and go out.' Some would know one
another and the Court staff. Some, indeed, would become 'regulars',
identified by name or nickname. But most were strangers, part of the
mêlée that congregated daily. I shall discuss those matters too.

Class 4 cases fought by a great number of different junior counsel
were tried quite typically by a quantity of relatively junior judges
who had themselves formed part of the rapid expansion of the
Crown Court. No High Court judge sat in any of the Court's six
courtrooms in 1989. Sixteen different circuit judges presided over trials in that year, sitting for a total of 780 days and for periods that
varied between 4 days and the 173 days sat by the resident judge.
Filling the gaps between periods served by circuit judges were 16
recorders and 13 assistant recorders, who sat for a total of 419 days,
some for as little as 5 and some for as much as 55 days in the year.
Again, although no Lords Justices or High Court judges sat at the
Centre, in this pattern Wood Green was not substantially different
from the Crown Court at large (see Table 1.3).

TABLE 1.3. *Days Sat by Judges and Recorders in 1987*

Type of judge	All Crown Court	Wood Green
Lords Justices	3 (>1%)	—
High Court judges	2,776 (4%)	—
Circuit judges	49,411 (70%)	1,030 (71%)
Deputy circuit judges	955 (1.3%)	—
Recorders	10,636 (15%)	232 (16%)
Assistant recorders	7,293 (10%)	186 (12%)
TOTAL	71,074	1,448

The Crown Court is a modern institution and its circuit judges
were, in the main, newly made. The resident judge of Wood Green
had himself appointed to the bench in April 1980. Of his fellow
judges sitting in 1989, one had been appointed on the same day as
he, and one before him, in 1977. But the others were, on average, of
just over two-and-a-half years' standing, two having been appointed
in 1989. The recorders serving at the Court were also in the main

newly made, being, on average, of but three years' standing.[51] With
the exception of the two or three most senior judges who could be
entrusted with rapes and other Class 2 offences, appointments to the
bench at Wood Green were all quite recent and knew themselves to
be so. One said of the range of cases he confronted, 'I am a junior
judge as I have only been recently appointed. . . . Murder doesn't
come here. Rape you have to be designated and of course you have
to spend some time as a circuit judge before you are designated. I
would deal with practically everything but grave [cases].'

Conclusion

The Crown Court at Wood Green was a small, third-tier, six-court
centre set in the outer suburbs of London, managing a considerable
flow of the lesser offences of burglary, assault, and theft. It was new,
having been founded in 1980, and its staff and judges were also new.
In the distribution of its cases, the age of its defendants, the seniority
of its judges, and many other matters, it was quite typical of the
Crown Court at large. What made it special was that, before its
removal to the grand *Palais de Justice* in April 1990, it enjoyed a reputation as a friendly, dingy, crowded court where convictions were
rather more difficult to secure and sentences tended to be light. Let
me turn now to the trials which were the Court's central project.

---

[51] Based on *Hazell's Guide to the Judiciary and the Courts* (Henley-on-Thames, Hazell,
1990), 18–20.

Part I

Defining the Witness

2. Trials as Conflict

'I've known a bomb disposal officer faint in the witness box because he can defuse bombs but he couldn't give evidence.' (Detective constable)

The trial was at the heart of the Court and its very reason for being, the drama about which events turned, its conflicts, controls, and dangers saturating every identity and association. So important was it that no sense can be made of the larger organization and work of the Court until it has been examined. Turning to it first, I must delay the task of describing some other important matters, in particular the role and character of the professionals who worked on the trial. The staff and users of the Court will remain rather spectral figures until Chapter 4, but they cannot be given much substance and flesh until I have conveyed a sense of the place of the trial within their life. As I proceed, recall that I am concerned always with events and experiences as they affected prosecution witnesses. There will be almost no discussion of the examination of defendants, verdicts, sentencing, and mitigation. I shall start by giving a portrait in miniature of the trial process, and will then return to dwell on some of its principal features.

Trials are ceremonial, disciplined, and staged, and they unfold in set order. Participants come forward at their proper times to perform their stylized parts. Every appearance must be choreographed precisely and unambiguously. Were that not so, there could be allegations of misconduct and appeals for retrials. One judge serving at Wood Green observed: 'Trial by jury has become, as a result of decisions by the Court of Appeal, an inordinately fragile process which may have to be aborted on the most (apparently) trivial pretexts and . . . the result of which can be overturned for the most (apparently) trivial irregularities.' Individuals, many of them ill-versed in court procedure, would not know what was expected of them: their behaviour had to be tightly structured. And there could be a larger confusion. As I shall show in the next chapter, a number of trials could well be on the move through the courtroom at the same time, one trial being under way as the jury on another were 'out', deliberating about their verdict. There could follow a series of complicated alternations in which the team composing one trial gave way to that of the other as juries returned to ask questions and announce verdicts. Without the most exact discipline, there could be a jumbling together of the participants in quite separate actions.

Trials were done to formula. The logic of accusation and defence under the adversary system required such a strict sequence of standardized events that a trial at Wood Green could have taken place at any other Crown Court centre in England and Wales (once counsel remarked to a court clerk: 'The trouble is when you're in court, you can't remember whether you're in Southwark or Wood Green'). Tight prescriptions ordered how charges were to be put and answered, a case would be made, and a defence would be presented. So it was that counsel and judge entered and the defendant would be asked in a set form of words how he or she would plead: 'A—— B—— you stand indicted for that you, on the —— day of —— [e.g. stole]. . . . How say you A—— B—— are you guilty or not guilty?'[1] If the plea was not guilty to all or some of the counts, if the trial was 'effective', as lawyers would say, a panel of jurors would then be assembled and sworn, each affirming or swearing 'by Almighty God that I will faithfully try the defendant[s] and give a true verdict according to the evidence'. Each detail of that little ritual would also be minutely regulated: a juror who did not read the oath correctly would probably be required to read it again. A juror who took the oath but did not hold the bible correctly might be required to start again. Jurors would be charged with set words about their duties: 'Members of the jury, the defendant A—— B—— stands indicted for that he, on the —— day of —— [e.g. stole] . . . To this indictment, he has pleaded not guilty, and it is your charge to say, having heard the evidence whether he be guilty or not guilty.'

The prosecution always opened, and it was the duty of the prosecution always to explain the burden of proof ('you must be satisfied so that you are sure'), the nature of evidence ('evidence is what you hear from witnesses under oath'), and the task of the Crown ('at the very outset one has to be clear that it is the prosecution that brings the case and the prosecution will have to prove it. . . . I have a duty to introduce the case to you and to introduce the issues . . .'). A prosecutor would invariably list the principal figures who were supposed to have played a part in the events alleged in the indictment, and the testimony they were expected to offer would be so previewed

[1] Taken from P. Morrish and I. MacLean, *Crown Court Index* (London, Longman, 1989), 343.

and edited that it was given context and connection ('you will hear from X who will say . . . and then you will hear from Y . . .').

Prosecution witnesses would then be called serially, and in the order anticipated in the opening, to be examined by the prosecution. There could be no leading questions of one's own witnesses, a leading question being one that was framed to suggest the answer desired. Counsel would resort instead to a succession of little prompts that were intended to take the witnesses through their history incident by incident: 'And what happened next?' 'And then what happened?' Such examination-in-chief would characteristically be accompanied by a solicitous and encouraging manner ('The first thing you try to do is to make them at home. . . . It's your witness and you try and make sure he's at home'). Questions would be asked gently, politely, and in a conversational tone. It was supposed that witnesses would appear to lay their own naive recollection of events before the jury for judgment (although, as I shall show, it was the lawyers' hope and expectation that they would actually do something rather different and recapitulate their written statement, what lawyers called 'the proof').

Prosecution witnesses would then be turned over to a questioning that was neither gentle nor conversational. The chief purpose of the defence was to extract information and impressions that were favourable to the defendant and unfavourable to the prosecution. They sought to discredit the prosecution witnesses and their testimony, making them seem, as Morison and Leith put it, 'fragile'.[2] Wider questions and leading questions were permitted under cross-examination. They would be asked with some show of acting, artfully, incredulously, and often fiercely. At a set point in cross-examination, usually in the final stages, counsel might work themselves up to a climax, simulating a sternness of manner and goading the witness (Mazengarb called that phase 'slamming' and remarked that 'the time to slam a witness . . . is towards the end'[3]). They would repeatedly accuse witnesses of falsehood: 'You're lying. The whole thing is a tissue of lies, is it not?' (One counsel said, 'There is a certain pathos to repetition which can be very effective in cross-examination, particularly if you've got a witness who's not answering the question'). 'Slamming' would be the one last push

---

[2] J. Morison and P. Leith, *The Barrister's World and the Nature of Law* (Milton Keynes, Open Univ. Press, 1992), 144.

[3] O. Mazengarb, *Advocacy in Our Time* (London, Sweet and Maxwell, 1964), 190.

made before retiring, a push that might just expose battered witnesses and force them to admit that they had been untruthful all the while ('it can damage the witness beyond repair, or destroy him'[4]). It was in counsel's instructions that an opponent's witnesses were liars or mistaken, and therein lay their mandate to allege mendacity. But even more stemmed from an adherence to instructions. Counsel might wish to display how vigorously they were doing their work, how great was the structured antipathy between a witness and the defendant, and how very absurd the accusations against a client should seem to be disinterested observer: 'You show you are angry as you would hope that an official bystander would be angry, had they in fact confronted the situation seen through the eyes of defence counsel's instructions . . . "I think this is preposterous. I stand as an official bystander shocked by this allegation." That's pretty effective.'

Witnesses would be re-examined by the prosecution to repair whatever damage may have been done under cross-examination. That complete, the prosecution case would have been presented. It would be followed as a matter of course by a space in which the defence could call their own witnesses to be examined and cross-examined in like fashion.[5] Closing speeches were then made; the judge would sum up; the jury might or might not deliver a verdict; and there could follow speeches in mitigation, reports, and sentencing if the verdict is guilty. Let me now elaborate and analyse this portrait in detail.

The Adversarial System

It is important neither to belittle nor yet to exaggerate the conflicts of the trial system. On one level, the contested trial was palpably adversarial: Weinreb called it 'a highly ritualized struggle between good and evil, the State and the Malefactor.'[6] and Neubauer argued that 'the basis of criminal law can be summarized in two words, human conflict'.[7] There was an antagonism that was so commonplace, widely presumed, and routine in the courtroom that it is almost nec-

---

[4] M. Hilbery, *Duty and Art in Advocacy* (London, Stevens, 1946), 35.

[5] The defence does not always produce witnesses and it is not required to do so, although there is a widespread recognition that, as a barrister put it, 'often one doesn't call a client [i.e. the defendant] for very good reasons'.

[6] L. Weinreb, *Denial of Justice* (New York, Free Press, 1977), 98.

[7] D. Neubauer, *America's Courts and the Criminal Justice System* (Pacific Grove, Calif., Brooks/Cole, 1988), 16.

essary to be reminded of its significant features: that trials were fought by two opposing sides ('fight', 'side', and 'opponent' being words in common use), one prosecuting and one defending, and each having its own retinue and clients; that the system was conceived not as an inquiry into the final truth of a matter but as a struggle, a 'trial of strength',[8] between two competing, partial, and incomplete cases made out in public by advocates; and that judge and jury acted as arbiters rather than as inquisitors, necessarily leaving much that was unquestioned, unsaid, and unresolved.

The perennial issue was whether the Crown could prove its case to the satisfaction of jurors, not establish what might 'really' have happened. It was not how protagonists in their 'natural attitude' understood and presented their problems, but how matters could be reconstructed for purposes of a successful prosecution.[9] 'Dispute' perhaps best captured the character of such trials. Mather and Yngvesson defined a dispute as 'a particular stage in which conflict between two parties . . . is asserted publicly—that is, before a third party', and, they continued, 'at a fundamental level, the transformation of a dispute involves a process of *rephrasing*—that is, some kind of reformulation into a public discourse'.[10] Disputes involved the deployment of a public language (a 'specialized legal discourse'[11]) and a narrowing of conflicts to formulate the few pivotal allegations that organized the presentation of a case.

A case was a deliberate simplification that obscured some issues, giving luminosity only to what were called the 'facts at issue', the facts that were deemed to be causally related to the commission of the offence. It was so constructed that it tended to strip away volumes of context and history (a recorder told a jury in his summing-up at Wood Green: 'the background to the incident is not the concern of the Court today. What is of concern is what took place on [a certain date]'). It was designed to ignore many of the tangled social relations, hurts, incidents, motives, and emotions that could be woven into personal disputes, concentrating on but a few matters.[12]

---

[8] P. Devlin, *The Judge* (Oxford, Oxford Univ. Press, 1979), 54.

[9] See A. Sarat and W. Felstiner, 'Law and Social Relations: Vocabularies of Motive in Lawyer/Client Interaction', *Law and Society Review*, 22(4) (1988), 739–40.

[10] L. Mather and B. Yngvesson, 'Language, Audience, and the Transformation of Disputes', *Law and Society Review*, 15(3) (1981), 776, 777.

[11] Ibid. 783.

[12] Thus W. Felstiner, R. Abel, and A. Sarat observe that 'the early stages of naming, blaming and claiming are significant . . . because the range of behaviour

It was intended to shed greyness and ambiguity, severing the ties with what de Waele and Harré once called the 'unfolding processes'[13] of social life, amplifying the differences between protagonists, focusing on the circumstantial and situational, and offering a stark argument for fault-finding and judgment. A member of the branch CPS staff serving Wood Green said: 'our system is not designed to test the truth of anything. It's about pragmatics and fairness.'

At the core of a prosecution case were pointed allegations about wrongdoing, immorality, and mendacity whose acceptance would almost certainly lead to public disgrace and punishment. I have remarked how trials moved routinely, almost mechanically, through set stages. In their opening speech, prosecution counsel would make it evident to the jury that they were presenting what was, in essence, a chain of *assertions* about the offence, the victim, the defendant and the connections binding them together. In one very typical case, the prosecutor began by stating: 'The Crown say that this was an attack and it also says it was an unprovoked attack . . . again the Crown say that . . . piecing the picture together, the witnesses for the Crown will say . . .' Note that the prosecution did not claim: 'This is what happened' but 'This is what the Crown *say* happened'. The prosecution case was a *thesis* to be defended in an argument that was substantially rhetorical.[14]

So the adversarial system brought it about that, even though they frequently alluded to what were called the 'facts of the case', the prosecution would, in effect, tell juries that they should not listen to what they said as if it were unproblematic and unchallenged. On the contrary, a prosecutor's speech was to be received as a piece of interpretation with which to frame *allegations* ('The suggestion in the prosecution evidence is that no-one had any business to hit Mr X . . . I don't know whether it will be suggested that it didn't happen like that. It may be that it will be said that it wasn't Mr Y who did it'). Those allegations were a contestable construction placed on what may have been the rather murkier and muddlier events of the experienced world.

they encompass is greater than that involved in the later stages of disputes, where institutional patterns restrict the options open to disputants' ('the Emergence and Transformation of Disputes: Naming, Blaming, Claiming . . .', *Law and Society Review*, 15(3) (1981), 636).

[13] See J. de Waele and R. Harré, *Personality* (Oxford, Basil Blackwell, 1979).

[14] See Morison and Leith; *The Barrister's World and the Nature of Law*, 5.

An opening statement would suggest to the jury what questions they might consider as the trial proceeded ('I don't propose to say more now than will enable you to make sense of the evidence when you hear it. When you hear the evidence, you will know what to listen for'). It would typically be described as a relatively slight thing, a preamble that should be brief,[15] especially in the kinds of case tried at Wood Green. It was presented as what could be expected of one who was paid to be persuasive, a suggestive account that was not self-validating: 'You will decide the case on the evidence, not on counsel's speeches.' To become more, it was said, the prosecution case required substantiation of a special kind, evidence, and that could emanate only from one authority, witnesses of the facts in question ('What I have told you is not evidence. It is an outline. Evidence is what you hear from witnesses'). Evidence was the report of those who purported actually to have seen and heard what was alleged to have happened.[16] It elaborated and underpinned a case. It was memorable. Evidence was recorded by the shorthand writer, whilst opening statements were not. I shall describe evidence more fully below.

The prosecution would routinely promise to furnish witnesses to testify on behalf of each component stage of a version of events ('At that point, the defendants sought to assault X and you'll hear something about that. . . . To summarize, and you'll hear the evidence . . . and you'll also hear . . . You'll hear, members of the jury, that the defendants were employed . . . You'll hear that the defendants were interviewed and I'm not going to go into those interviews at length. You'll hear from the police officers who did the interviews'). That then was the prosecution thesis, an explanatory frame of accusation to be girded by oral testimony from bystanders and participants on the scene at issue.

It was the job of defence counsel to supply a rival way of explaining what had occurred, what might be called the antithesis, although that term was not used in the courts. The defence case did not have to be as solid or imposing as that of the prosecution. It was an attack that sought chiefly to so puncture the impression achieved by the prosecution and prosecution witnesses that it became difficult for the

---

[15] See Mazengarb, *Advocacy in Our Time*, 146.

[16] The prosecution may well decide not to call witnesses damaging to their case but they should disclose their names to the defence. See C. Emmins, *A Practical Aprpaoch to Criminal Procedure* (London, Financial Training Publications, 1987), 105.

jury to be sure of what had been said and, indeed, of what may have happened (and, in the relatively sealed world of the courtroom,[17] where stories and their tellers were all there was to judge, doubt did not seem very difficult to introduce). The defence would employ argument and questioning to reveal inconsistency, error, improper motives, forgetfulness, and falsehood in prosecution witnesses. The questions would often be searching. One counsel said: 'Anything that tends to mask the reality about the witnesses is hostile to the adversarial process. It should be stark. The choices that [the jury] have should be stark. The compulsion to tell the truth should be there.' The questions would probe minor contradiction after minor contradiction: 'You have to deal with things in detail, first of all to prevent anybody from saying that you didn't do that, but also ideally of giving a different account of even small details, raising a doubt as to the prosecution case . . . because [the jury] have been told they have to be sure.'

Almost as a matter of course, counsel would, as a judge put it, so 'blackguard' the witnesses that they were no longer believable. Under cross-examination, victims and prosecution witnesses could be asked about matters touching on their 'title to credit': their way of life, their associations, their past convictions, their disinterestedness, and their integrity.[18] They could be vilified and shamed as they defended, in public and perhaps for the very first time, testimony about matters that were painful, embarrassing, and once personal. (Victim 20,[19] for instance, had been questioned about events before she had had a miscarriage: 'He was going on about me and X . . . she was pregnant at the same time, going out together buying baby clothes. That upset me because I don't like talking about it.') At stake, wrote Ericson and Baranek, was the protection of valued aspects of identity.[20] Prosecution witnesses certainly experienced questioning by defence counsel as an assault on their identity. Those for whom

[17] A journalist, recalling his experience as a juror at Wood Green, wrote about 'a sense of watching a case from a position of fresh innocence, through a glass that filters out some of the surrounding "reality"' (H. Young, 'An Indictment of Justice', *Guardian*, 1 Feb. 1992).

[18] See *Archbold: Pleading, Evidence and Practice in Criminal Cases* (London, Sweet and Maxwell, 1988), 484.

[19] A total of 33 victims were interviewed between Jan. and June 1990, 16 before the move to the new courthouse and the inauguration of the victim-witness project, 17 afterwards. They have been numbered in the order of interview.

[20] See R. Ericson and P. Baranek, *The Ordering of Justice: A Study of Accused Persons as Dependants in the Criminal Process* (Toronto, Univ. of Toronto Press, 1982), 205.

public face was important (and it is important for most of us[21]) found it harrowing (Victim 6 called it 'nerve wracking . . . I was shaking inside'). The techniques deployed were precisely those used by the prosecution in cross-examination of the defendant, and they seemed to put prosecution witnesses themselves on trial. Victim 20 told me after cross-examination, 'They made me feel like a criminal! It's the last time I'll come to court.' And Victim 17, a victim of assault by a cabdriver, said the worst about her routine cross-examination, in which she had been accused of lying, taking drugs, being drunk, and being provocative, was

Being called a liar all the time, being accused of causing the affray. He asked me if I had been drinking . . . I knew what [defence counsel] was trying to do. I'm not stupid. When he said I was smoking cannabis, that's when I went, 'No way! This is getting out of hand!' I just felt that I was the one being proved wrong. . . . How can he imply we were doing something with absolutely no proof!? How can he do that? Can he do that, suggest that we were taking drugs when we weren't? It's total rubbish! What was really upsetting was trying to convince them I was telling the truth. That's not fair.

In promoting that antithesis, and to sow uncertainty in the jury's minds, the defence might produce their own witnesses, who could be 'blackguarded' by the prosecution in turn.[22] Defence witnesses' motives, credibility, and creditability could be exposed to public examination, and that would be disagreeable for them too. A judge reflected: 'A close investigation of people's motives and actions may be very uncomfortable for those investigated.' So it was that advocates laid their tales and tale-bearers before jurors, inviting them to place a favoured construction on facts, arguments, and witnesses and deliver a verdict. The result, Pannick argued, was a choice between different constructions. 'The reality is that the adversary process of a trial more than leaves the truth mysteriously hidden, covered over by the evasions and half-truths of competing contentions.'[23]

Trials were intended to culminate in the unambiguous victory of

---

[21] For the importance of face, and particularly of presenting oneself as 'hard' in the everyday life of young working-class males, see P. Willis, *Common Culture* (Milton Keynes, Open Univ. Press, 1990), 103.

[22] Such discrediting was not disfavoured. Those in the prosecutor's retinue tended to regard defence witnesses with some suspicion. A police officer reflected: 'A lot of prosecution witnesses are there because they were in the wrong place at the wrong time a year ago, whereas the defence witness is there because they were a mate of the defendant's in the boozer.'

[23] D. Pannick, *Judges* (Oxford, Oxford Univ. Press, 1987), 53.

one side or the other (unless, of course, there was an appeal), and very grave matters were at stake for those involved, the people formally called the 'alleged' defendants and victims. There was, on the one hand, liberty and reputation and, on the other, a vindication of wrongs. Trials supplied competing stories about the past, reconstructing all the indeterminacy and muddle of everyday life into what McConville once called 'opposing distortions'.[24] Juries would be given bleak choices between innocence and guilt, truth and falsehood, this or that account. Over and over again, they might have before them two quite plausible descriptions of the 'same' episode. Over and over again, they would be invited to choose between the credibility of one story and its train of witnesses and that of another. Only one version could prevail, and obstacles to its acceptance had to be explained by simple, corrigible error or dishonesty, not by the ineluctable ambiguity of a social world where multiple truths coexisted.[25]

Whatever lawyers and professionals might argue outside the courtroom,[26] witnesses tended to take it that defeat signified that they had been disbelieved, that they had been taken for liars. And that was not a view discouraged inside the courtroom itself. Of one very routine trial, the prosecutor said to the jury, 'It's quite clearly a case of whom you believe. If you believe the defendant, then . . .', and a judge summed up in another such case: 'There it is, members of the jury, that's the evidence. That's the evidence on which you've got to decide this case . . . The prosecution say that unless you find all these police are telling lies, you'll have to find the defendant guilty.' Being publicly cast as tellers of untruths engendered distress. A barrister reflected that 'those who give their evidence orally are the most vulnerable. They don't expect their credibility to be challenged'. One witness, Victim 16, said: 'What really upset me was trying to convince them I was telling the truth. That's what upset me.' And another, Victim 1, said: 'I thought it would be straightforward. They kept asking me questions and trying to put them the other way

---

[24] M. McConville, 'Justice in the Dock', *Times Higher Education Supplement*, 8 Feb. 1990.

[25] See M. Pollner, 'Mundane Reasoning', *Philosophy of the Social Sciences*, 4(1) (1974).

[26] That argument characteristically took the form that failure to win a prosecution case reflected the heavy burden of proof, a burden that demanded that juries must be *sure* about the defendant's guilt. Witnesses were not necessarily to be seen as liars. Rather, it was said, the jury had probably been unable to arrive at a state of certainty about a case.

around. It got confusing.' Even police officers who gave evidence regularly said, as one sergeant said, 'I don't think you ever get used to it . . .'

In delivering a verdict, there could be nothing of legal consequence between guilt and innocence (unless it was reintroduced *afterwards*, when greyness could be invoked by the defence in mitigation). After all, that was probably the chief purpose of the trial, to give an unambiguous and decisive resolution to disputes that could otherwise have continued interminably. The Court was the non-partisan third party confronting the dyad of victim and offender, accuser and accused, the party hitherto untouched by quarrels and passions.[27] And the prosecution's task would be confounded and the defendant would be aggrieved if the Crown tried to persuade jurors so that they were sure that a defendant might just *probably* be guilty. Certainty was the prosecution's province, doubt that of the defence. Whatever epistemological dilemmas might arise, the prosecution's simple polarized choice was a harder test to pass, and it could be argued that it was almost certainly better for purposes of justice: juries could not declare the defendant and victim both complicit in what had happened; the victim could not be just a little guilty or the defendant also wronged.

'The complexities . . . are usually not apparent . . . because police and prosecutors structure their accounts of cases to fit into accepted legal categories. These categories are simple, often dichotomous (guilty/not guilty; sane/insane; intentional/not intentional; reckless/not reckless; voluntary/-involuntary) and deny the ambiguities and uncertainties of the world of experience.[28]

Only occasionally would lawyers protest about the starkness of such choices. In only one instance did I hear an advocate publicly criticize the feeding of a confused relationship into the adversarial system, and that was on the eve of the trial of a man on assault charges related to domestic violence. The defence counsel remonstrated with the prosecution that neither defendant nor victim was clearly blameless: 'This is the sort of case where the judge should take the two and bang their heads together!'[29] But the prosecution was adamant.

[27] See G. Simmel, 'The Triad', in K. Wolff (ed.); *The Sociology of Georg Simmel* (New York, Free Press, 1950), 146–7.

[28] M. McConville *et al.*, 'The Case for the Prosecution' TS, n.d., 22.

[29] And it should be noted that that counsel had a reputation in the court for being unusually emotional and theatrical in her conduct.

'We're fighting,' she said. All contested trials were called 'fights'. Ushers would ask counsel if a trial was to be a fight. The use of battle language was not fortuitous.

Conflict was not merely a matter of form. Although trials have been described in the vocabulary of a sporting contest, as if they were game-like, they were often stuffused with the intense passion and pain of their civilian protagonists. There was an anger that could be ignited more than once as the Court reunited those who had fought, exploited, wronged, vilified, and oppressed one another; set them against each other again in public; interrogated them; judged them to be truthful or untruthful; exonerated or condemned them; and then inflicted punishment. And that anger was sometimes quite tangible. Crown Court buildings were the occasional targets of political and personal attack, being designed to withstand vandalism and bomb blasts.[30] They were witnesses to commotion as people hurled abuse at one another, furnishing a latter-day Greek chorus to comment on the performance of witnesses and defendants, and crying out in shock, lamentation, or triumph at verdicts and sentences. Those appearing in Court had often to be physically restrained and kept apart.[31] I shall describe just such a running display of wrath in the next chapter. Yet, on another level, conflict was quite controlled, and much of the remainder of this book will provide a description of just how it was made safe.

Very few lawyers and staff appeared surprised at outbursts. It was not considered professional to evince surprise at very much at all. The extraordinary anger and discomfort of witnesses, victims, and defendants were ordinary enough matters to those who worked in the courts every day. That is part of the business of being a professional, to translate the private and exceptional troubles of others into the recurrent and unremarkable materials of a specialized craft. (There were, nevertheless, moments that made counsel and other professionals apprehensive. One barrister told me of the lawyer's nervousness whenever a defendant was asked to examine a weapon.)

In effect, the antagonisms of private individuals were taken up and mediated by professionals who worked with the standard forms of conflict but did not experience its volatile contents as their own. It was not *their* distress and humiliation that counsel paraded before judge and jury. A barrister said: 'The professionals aren't allowed to

---

[30] See 'Liverpool Crown Court', *Construction*, July 1979, 30.

[31] See K. Manasian, 'On Trial', *Interior Design*, Apr. 1981, 20–1.

show emotion, it's a big claim to make, but in fact they generally don't get emotional.'[32] In such a separation of form from content, of professional composure from the layman's anguish, counsel, staff, and others traced two domains: the calm, disciplined world of the insider and the wilder, angrier world of the civilian. That is a theme I hall pursue more than once, and especially in Chapter 5. Insider and outsider was the great organizing opposition of the Court.[33] Insiders necessarily shared a closer intimacy than any possible with an outsider. Whilst civilians moved in and out of the courtroom in great numbers, often never to be seen again, sometimes not even to be remembered (a judge remarked that 'witnesses are the fodder of the courts'), insiders were likely to meet day after day. They might know one another elsewhere in other courts, in police stations or chambers. They might begin to recognize one another, learn something about one another, and form patterns of dependency and collaboration that transcended the special features of an evanescent case. There was, observed Ericson and Baranek of the Canadian courts, a 'stake in future relationships that must be kept in mind in conducting transactions'.[34]

As they worked together in trial after trial, as counsel were seen sometimes defending, sometimes prosecuting, so the embedded adversarial roles of the trial system became detached from the selves of those who played them. Advocates were not to be confused wholly with the animosities they dramatised. They were, as the saying goes, 'only doing a job'. A probation officer remarked, 'They are just playing parts. They are lawyers just playing parts. It's a great big game with rules to be observed!' And, in doing that job, it would not do to lose the good will of an usher, a court clerk, or a colleague when so much in the courtroom rested on a friendly co-operativeness that was itself based on trust. A barrister said:

One is obviously going to be pleasant to ushers and so forth on a mercenary level because if you want your case on quickly, then one will do . . . But having said that—and it may sound a trite thing to say—but I always try and work with counsel as well . . . I always try and make it as friendly as possible so you can have a laugh, simply because it's your working environment.

[32] A barrister was reported to have said of a trial lawyer's performance in the American case of William Smith, 'She became too emotionally engaged. The more professional you are, the more you keep that under wraps.' 'Kennedy's Verdict on Kennedy Case', *Sunday Times*, 15 Dec. 1991.

[33] As it is of the criminal justice system at large. See e.g. M. Young, *An Inside Job* (Oxford, Oxford Univ. Press, 1991), esp. 111.

[34] *The Ordering of Justice*, 14.

In the courtroom itself, there were endemic good manners that eased fraught and antagonistic relations that were always teetering on collapse. One counsel committed to defence work remarked, 'It can be quite civilized, counsel working very hard for their side whatever it be, but we are all supposed to play by a set of rules . . . There is no point in us getting into an argument . . .' Judges and counsel would say the most disagreeable things in the most agreeable way, the substance of conflict being presented in the forms of polite breeding.[35] Defendants were addressed by proper title and, until they were convicted, were always called 'gentlemen' and 'ladies'. Counsel did not menace witnesses bodily as their colleagues sometimes did elsewhere, in North America and Australia for example. They were rooted to their own small space in counsel's row, remaining physically remote from those whom they interrogated, reinforcing not only their own appearance of authority but also the formality and impersonality of their discourse. There was a tight control over the kind of talk that was permitted, and over the taking of discrete turns to speak in particular. People could usually be heard clearly, decorously, and one at a time. Their speech did not often collapse into shouting matches, although it sometimes seemed on the verge of doing so. And all that discipline and courteousness were enforced by judges.

In one case, the judge told a defence counsel to take his hand out of his pocket when he addressed the court. In another, counsel was repeatedly corrected in the courtroom itself, the judge telling him, 'Do things properly, it's not agreeable' and 'I may say, Mr X, that I would be grateful if you would take particular care to address witnesses with courtesy'. Witnesses themselves were rarely reproved. *They* were not expected to be disciplined or self-controlled. On the contrary: for reasons that I shall explain below, a candid, unbuttoned display of self could advance the Court's purposes.

Evidence

Trials centred on evidence, and evidence itself was conceived to be a very special form of knowledge.[36] Quite literally, evidence was what

---

[35] Giving a different inflection to much the same point, M. Feeley observed of the American court: 'Language in the courtroom is extremely arcane and formal, and it can easily accommodate the most bitter denunciations and sarcasm in a way that does not unduly strain the rituals of court procedures' *The Process Is the Punishment* (New York, Russell Sage Foundation, 1979), 68.

[36] Justice remarked that 'without witnesses all the other people part in a criminal

made matters evident, a fact that induced in the mind a persuasion of the proof of the existence of some other fact.[37] It was yet more precisely defined in the courtroom itself, being knowledge properly obtained and usually brought on oath[38] before judge and jury by those who claimed directly to have seen or heard matters bearing on the events in dispute, by the 'witnesses who have perceived the facts in question'.[9] It could emanate only from those who were, in effect, emissaries from the world of events being scrutinized (a judge admonished one barrister by saying. 'The object of cross-examination is to elicit answers, not to give evidence. You know that very well'). Evidence was judged by a common-sense, empirical epistemology that asserted the existence of a domain of unambiguous phenomena independent of human knowledge.[40] Judgments in trials, it was argued, should turn on attempts to assess claims made about the direct observation of an autonomous world of fact.[41]

Although statements could correspond to objective facts,[42] it had also to be recognized that they rested on observations and observers that were themselves quite possibly fallible. Witnesses were prone to lapse, error, and deceitful reporting. Since observation and memory were held to be the 'twin pillars of knowledge',[43] powers of sight, hearing,[44] and recollection could all be properly questioned in the courtroom. It was commonplace to hear a counsel say: 'You have forgotten so many things; maybe you forgot this too?' Some people, indeed, were considered inherently unreliable, instances being children or people with defective intelligence.[45]

Lay evidence was supposed to consist of reports about a direct

trial . . . would be left with nothing to do: only the witnesses, with their unique knowledge, can prove the facts on which the entire trial turns'; *Witnesses in the Criminal Courts* (London, Justice, 1986), 1.

[37] See W. Best, *The Principles of the Law of Evidence* (London, Sweet and Maxwell, 1922), 6.
[38] Not everyone was obliged to take the oath: e.g. young children not thought mature enough to appreciate the significance of oath-taking might be exempted.
[39] R. Cross, *An Outline of the Law of Evidence* (London, Butterworth, 1980), 1.
[40] See P. Waddington, 'Justice Seen to Be Undone', *The Times*, 24 May 1990.
[41] See J. Jackson, 'Two Methods of Proof in Criminal Procedure', *Modern Law Review*, 51(5) (Sept. 1988), 550–1.
[42] See W. Twining, *Theories of Evidence: Bentham and Wigmore* (London, Weidenfeld and Nicolson, 1985), 13.
[43] See Jackson, 'Two Methods of Proof in Criminal Procedure', 550.
[44] See R. Walker, *The English Legal System* (London, Butterworth, 1985), 635.
[45] See M. Zander, *Cases and Materials on the English System* (London, Weidenfeld and Nicolson, 1988), 357 ff.

observation of the physical and social world, not with speculation. A lay witness's surmises were not material. Neither was the history or larger context of an observed incident (a defence counsel said to the defendant on one occasion, 'Don't go into detail. Go into the brief facts'). What witnesses reported about other people's utterances was not material: under the hearsay rule, those people themselves should come forward to attest to their knowledge or else it should remain silent.[46] Witnesses could sometimes be stopped quite abruptly from testifying when it appeared that they were alluding to the remarks of others.[47] (A judge intervened during testimony on one occasion to say: 'You're not allowed to say what X said to you because we've got certain rules of evidence.' On another occasion, counsel said: 'What she saw you can't say. What we're interested in is what you saw. Let me ask the questions.')

What any witness could have seen of the facts was small. The English criminal law tended to restrict testimony to a description of activities set inside discrete episodes of time and confined to the doings of visible protagonists.[48] All else was supposition, and lay witnesses were not to be trusted with suppositions: 'a belief based on inference or impression is an opinion; a belief based on direct perception of a fact capable of precise perception is not an opinion . . .'[49] It was expert witnesses, skilled in their judgement, who were entitled to opinions, not laymen and women.

The outcome was ironic. Since lay knowledge was considered most imposing when it was recent and uncontaminated, it was best to question witnesses, not about their actual recollections of events, events that had occurred some time before, but about the statements they had made to the police in the immediate aftermath of an incident.[50] Witnesses would be given their statements to 'refresh their memory' as they waited outside the courtroom. They would frequently be requested to reread their statement as they stood in the box, and they would then be asked, 'That was the statement you made when matters were fresh in your memory?'

[46] There are exceptions to the hearsay role, e.g. admissions and confessions.

[47] See D. McBarnet, 'Victim in the Box', in W. Chambliss (ed.), *Criminal Law in Action* (New York, Wiley, 1984), 330.

[48] See J. Shapland, 'Memorandum on the Victim and the Criminal Justice System', in *Report of the Select Committee of Experts on the Victim and Criminal and Social Policy* (Strasbourg, European Committee on Crime Problems, Council of Europe, 1983), 7.

[49] Walker, *The English Legal System*, 653.

[50] See Ericson and Baranek, *The Ordering of Justice*, 6.

Those written statements were artefacts. Police questioning had given them a shape, relevance, and coherence at times inconsistent with mundane experience. Such a statement was purposive, it anticipated the prosecution that might ensue, and it was concerned with the evidentiary requirements of the trial. It was phrased in a legal discourse of facts, truth, and evidence; strained out an immaterial moral discourse of blaming, relationships, and motives;[51] and portrayed the victim himself or herself as 'a shadowy, passive, innocent figure partaking in a discrete encounter with the offender'.[52] There was, said Shapland, difficulty in actually 'fitting the victim's testimony into this pattern'.

On arrival at court, witnesses would discover that they were not actually expected to remember all the details of very distant happenings. They would be told that they would be tested on statements furnished by the police instead, and they usually took pains to memorize them. A barrister said: 'Generally speaking, alleged victims and their witnesses give evidence in accordance with their [statement]. . . . Witnesses are allowed to see their statements. One would expect them to give evidence in accordance with their statements.' It was considered most important that that should be so. Witnesses' statements were part of the bundle prepared by the barrister's professional client, the CPS or the defence solicitor. They were familiar and expected; and chief amongst them, as I shall explain below, was 'the proof', the clinching statement that said, in the words of one barrister, ' "I saw him do it" or "he told me he did it" '. It was the proof that was the key to a case, and it had to be brought before the court in examination in chief. Counsel wished for no departure from a pure recitation of the proof, no elaboration, invention, or digression.

In questioning their own witnesses, counsel wanted no surprises ('The golden rule is you ought never to ask a question that you don't know the answer to'). What *would* disconcert a lawyer would be 'when they answer a question with an answer that I didn't expect'. Answers given in examination were supposed merely to confirm what one already knew: 'you hope that you get out the evidence that you want, and that's really your case, having produced your witness, having gone through the witness evidence, you sit down.' One counsel said:

[51] See S. Merry, *Getting Justice and Getting Even* (Chicago, Univ. of Chicago Press, 1990), 112–13.

[52] Shapland, 'Memorandum on the Victim and the Criminal Justice System', 9.

Given that you accept that your instructions that the prosecution witness statement is true, your job as counsel is to try to get out of the witness as much of the truthful facts contained in the statement as you can, excluding things that are inadmissible but of course taking into account the fact that usually the statement was made when the matter was fresh in the witness's mind, and by the time you have got to the Crown Court, maybe months or a year on, and the witness may not have refreshed his or her memory from the statement and may have forgotten bits of it.

However, there was a problem: the examination of one's own witnesses could not be 'leading'. Questions were not allowed obviously to drive their answers. The extraction of the proof from a friendly witness was an oblique and sometimes delicate exercise. A seasoned counsel said:

I would have, I hope, as much control as I can. I would exercise control over the witnesses, i.e. how the story is told and try and make sure the story is told how I wanted it. But I wouldn't in any way impose on him or her. I would try to make sure they didn't know they were telling me how I wanted it told, as opposed to how they wanted it told.

So it was that those witnesses who sought to be independent and eschew their statements would occasion apprehension. They were rogue elements: 'If he says, "I'm confident", I get a bit worried because you never know what the results might be. But I mean, if he says, "I'm confident, I can do without the statement", then there you are.'

In the courtroom, standing in the box, witnesses would almost invariably be confronted by contradiction. There were two memories under examination. One, ill-organized perhaps, turned back to events last observed directly several months or a year or more ago. The other, more tidy (often too tidy) referred to a typewritten account seen minutes before. Between the two was what a judge called 'the normal deviation of witnesses from their statements'. Opposing counsel would repeatedly play on that deviation because it was a prime opportunity to inject doubt. After all, if witnesses contradicted themselves, some part, and perhaps the whole, of their evidence might be deemed untrustworthy. Victim 20 recollected how, she had been given her statement whilst waiting to give evidence, 'but it didn't do any good because I forgot it. They were trying to wind me up, saying certain things were in my statement, but that was a year ago. I can't remember. It is so long.'

Remedial work might subsequently have to be done in the re-examination of one's own witnesses: 'if your witness gives particular evidence which doesn't fit in with their statement, you either have to take the view that you're stuck with it, or you have to ask permission from the judge for the witness to see his statement to refresh his memory again, although that's a difficult exercise if he's already done it outside the court.' But evidence remained a peculiar entity, not at all what it seemed or what was expected in the lay world. The part played by the statement, McBarnet remarked, 'might be seen as somewhat defeating the public presentation of a witness's testimony on oath as only what he *directly* experienced'.[53]

The insistence that evidence was produced legally led to the exclusion of certain information obtained in breach of such statutes as the Police and Criminal Evidence Act. Judges at Wood Green daily disallowed statements secured by the police. They insisted on a formal caution being administered, a contemporaneous written record being taken (a judge said, 'Anything up to 28 days will do'[54]), and the presence of a solicitor when requested by the defendant. If evidence was the juridically useful recollection of unambiguous facts, strains were imposed on the police witnesses who gave it. One police inspector reflected:

Giving evidence was always an ordeal because barristers sought a consistency and recall that could not realistically be produced so it was necessary to embroider, not lie or fit up, but put a gloss on what was said. The worst thing was the literally truthful police officer because it then became very difficult to co-ordinate one's own replies with his. The worst man I ever worked with had been a Jehovah's witness who gave absolutely straight answers to every question. He would not say that notes had been taken 2 hours after the interview but 8 days. He placed me in a spot because I had once said 2 hours and had been confronted with the inconsistency. He had subsequently been transferred to the mounted police. The mounted police never make arrests.

---

[53] McBarnet, *Conviction: Law, the State and the Construction of Justice* (London, Macmillan, 1981), 96.

[54] I was advised by another judge that ' "contemporaneous" . . . means what it says and never anything else. Different considerations apply to whether notes may be used by witnesses to "refresh their memories" when giving evidence. To obtain leave to do so, such notes need not be contemporaneous, as long as they are made within a period after the recorded event which permitted of accurate reflection, and were made "as soon as practicable" after the event. I am quite astonished that anyone should regard 28 days as allowable, unless in fantastically unusual circumstances.'

Most important of all, perhaps, was the principle that a recollection brought forward as evidence should be the witness's own, not some foreign construction insinuated by others. It was held that evidence had to be a special form of uncontaminated intellectual property, a memory of direct observation, not what others had suggested might have happened. It was open to discrediting if it could be shown that another had materially affected what was said. (To be sure, there was the stark anomaly of the defendants who were an audience to all that was said about them; but there was a strong insistence on a counter-ing principle, the principle that, as a judge put it, 'it is an important right [that] you can't be tried in your absence'. If the defendant was thought to have tailored his or her own evidence as a result of hear-ing testimony, it was said, 'you can cross-examine him to that effect'.)

Cross-examination would accordingly turn around whether wit-nesses had discussed the case with others, overheard others discussing the case, or, worst of all, had been 'coached' or influenced by one who actually knew what others had said or asked in the trial itself.[55]

Witnesses were warned not to talk about their evidence.[56] (A CPS law clerk remarked. 'Of course people talk, but the point is not to be seen talking.') As a matter of course, an opponent's counsel would ask them whether there had been talk about the case with other 'civilians': 'How much conversation was there between you and your [family or friends or associates] about this incident before you made this statement?' They might be told rhetorically, 'You've been warned from time to time that you'd have to come to court, so it's been on the horizon and there has been discussion about it all', or 'You see, you didn't see what had happened that night. You listened to what other people had told you and tried to piece it together

---

[55] It should be noted that jurors, too, were subject to a special epistemology that insisted that their minds should not be sullied by knowledge unregulated by the judge and the rules of evidence, or by prejudice born of a prior acquaintance with the coun-sel, defendant, or victim. There were very tight controls over those with whom the jurors could mix in the courthouse. They were effectively segregated from all but the usher, doubling as a jury bailiff, and those meeting in the disciplined world of the courtroom itself. Jurors would be told on their induction at Wood Green: 'You must say if you know anyone in the trial, a barrister or a defendant. It's no good going halfway through a trial and then the trial folds.'

[56] See *Witness in Court* (London, HMSO, 1988), the leaflet prepared by Victim Support and the Home Office and supposedly sent by the police to every witness called to give evidence: 'It is much better not to talk to anyone about the evidence you will be giving in case you are asked about this in court. If you have discussed the case with other people you might find when you get into court your evidence is doubted.'

afterwards?' (In this instance, the victim assented.) Since it was almost inconceivable that witnesses had not, in fact, had some prior discussion of the offence with others, accusations of contamination were easily confirmed. Much evidence could be represented as no longer an artless memory but a jumbled concoction of a witness's and others' knowledge.

As a matter of course, discharged witnesses and witnesses in the middle of examination would be warned not to talk about the case with anyone. Requests were made that they should segregate themselves by not dining, travelling, or sitting together (although it must be remarked that those requests seemed frequently to be unheeded).

Contact with a police officer, a social worker, or lawyer could be even more damaging (a counsel said: 'If they talk they will take on the ideas and suggestions of someone else'). Those professionals were, after all, not innocents but the knowing, who were well aware of the kinds of knowledge that could do the most harm to a case. Hilbery argue that 'a man skilled in law and experienced in Court work may know just the little difference in the evidence which would make it suffice for success. If he sees and talks to the witnesses he may . . . suggest to the witnesses what their evidence ought to be if the case is to be won.'[57] Whilst those attached to criminal justice agencies might exercise a special care, there was also a constant wariness about the risks of overly intimate relations with witnesses in waiting. A police officer was overheard to say gingerly to a witness seated next to him, 'I'm not really supposed to talk to you but you can ask *some* questions.'

Relations and encounters between witnesses and others were monitored continually by staff and professionals, and suspicions about the possible contamination of evidence could well lead to the making of formal representations and the mounting of attacks in cross-examination. One of the judges sitting at Wood Green observed that 'defence counsel would have a field day in cross-examination' if there had been prior talk about evidence. Protests might be made. Thus a counsel said that, if he saw a victim and prosecutor together for any length of time, 'I would in fact have a word with him and want to find out why, as a matter of courtesy. If I wasn't satisfied, then I would raise it with the judge.' And, indeed, in October 1989, I did observe a barrister reporting his anxiety about having seen witnesses

[57] *Duty and Art in Advocacy*, 11.

who had just given evidence 'milling around' with those waiting to do so. The judge observed that a police officer was supervising the witnesses outside the courtroom but that he would 'have a word with them'. In the Crown Court at Belfast, such suspiciousness led defence counsel publicly to accuse a witness of having been 'well coached'.[58]

There was a perennial fear amongst counsel of seeming to collude and coach. Improper contact with lay witnesses was thought capable of damaging a naive and untutored mind: 'A witness may understand information from you that he/she shouldn't really know.' After all, it was counsel who could anticipate better than anyone the pattern of a trial and the questions that might be asked: 'There should be no contact between the questioner and the witness so as to suggest what the answers are going to be.' The very idea of conversation was regarded with abhorence:

> It would be most undesirable if I was seen talking to a prosecution witness, and this sort of thing does happen, and the defendant or one of his representatives should see me doing that and thereafter some question should be raised in court about my having done so. You have no idea the effect, the sort of dramatic effect that this potentially has on the court process and on the jury's mind.

The Principle of Orality

Evidence was given orally in the Crown Court.[59] Zander argued that 'the principle of orality has always been at the heart of the trial, partly because of the dominant role played for centuries by the jury'.[60] Trials were public disputes in which argument and evidence were adduced in full hearing before judge and jury and recorded by shorthand writers. Everything that could be put into speech *was* spoken (photographs, maps, and other items that resisted translation into talk were submitted as *exhibits* that had nevertheless to be 'proved in the normal way' by a witness's verbal acknowledgement). Orality converted the manifold documents and statements of a counsel's brief

---

[58] See J. Jackson *et al.*, 'Called to Court: A Public View of Criminal Justice in Northern Ireland', unpublished TS, 5.30.

[59] There are no juries and shorthand writers and no operating principle of orality in the magistrates' courts. Much that would be outspoken in the Crown Court is the subject of little inaudible conferences between lawyers, justices and clerks. Documents are often read quietly and not aloud in those courts.

[60] *Cases and Materials on the English Legal System*, 345. Note, too, the comment of Devlin that 'the centrepiece of the adversary system is the oral trial' (*The Judge*, 54).

into speech delivered by lawyers and witnesses. Even the written records of interviews between police officers and witnesses, defendants and victims were declaimed *verbatim*, usually by officers and counsel who took turns to enact the parts of interrogator and interrogated. Agreed, written evidence from expert witnesses, most typically a doctor's statement about a victim's injuries, would be read out to the court word by word (a judge told the jury in just such an instance, 'You're now about to hear a statement being read. Please treat it as evidence given from the witness box'). Gestures and identifications made in court were described out loud 'for the transcript'.

The principle of orality had necessary but taxing consequences for the delivery of evidence and the experience of being a witness. The first such consequence I have already listed. It was that each speaker was supposed to have a distinct and protected turn,[61] uninterrupted by others, and clearly audible to judge, jury, and shorthand writer. A judge remarked:

I have to hear absolutely everything and if I am going to hear everything, I have to ask them to repeat their answer . . . I am also concerned with the jury, so I ask the members of the jury whether they can hear or not, and I say to them that 'if any of you cannot hear, you must raise your hand'.

A second consequence was that, evidence being thus audible, nothing was allowed to remain tacit, elided, discreet, or *sotto voce*. A prosecution witness who muttered something to an usher was told, 'Please, anything you say should be said out loud so that it can be taken down.' *Everything* had to be said out loud, the shaming, the private, or the indifferent, and it had to be said loudly. At the beginning of trials, judges would characteristically tell the jury that 'witnesses do not sometimes speak up. You must signal to me by raising your hand or in some other way if you cannot hear.' Thereafter, they would try to ensure that the jury could hear. They would ensure that the shorthand writer could hear. They were concerned about their own ability to hear. Witnesses were forever being told to speak more loudly, especially in the acoustically deficient courtrooms of 'the Bunker'. They were instructed 'to speak much louder than that. You'll have to pick up your courage and shout at the wall'. The court was not a place for modesty or for the little face-saving stratagems by which people conventionally manage the disclosure of embarrassing matters. Witnesses had, in effect, to trumpet what they almost certainly wished to state

---

[61] See J. Atkinson and P. Drew, *Order in Court* (London, Macmillan, 1979), esp. ch. 2.

quietly or not at all, adding strain to a performance already strained: 'If you don't shout out there's no point in your being here.'

Witnesses were obliged to call out words and phrases that they might not normally choose to use at all, flouting taboos of language. (In one very typical example, a witness under cross-examination had reluctantly to repeat what her assailant had said to her: 'She said "Shut your fucking gob", if you *want* me to repeat it.' In another instance, counsel asked, 'Do you remember what you said?' and received the reply, 'My exact words? "I don't do shit like that."') The Court was audience to all the violent doings and language of the bedroom, street, and public house, witnesses having to recite the heedless and profane speech of angry relationships.

Witnesses had to direct their speech awkwardly, not at their questioners, the counsel, or judge a few feet away, but at a jury sitting at some distance across the courtroom. They would be interrogated by one but were expected to throw their reply to another: 'It's very natural for you tor turn to me but would you to turn to face the jury and speak up?' and, again, 'I would like you to face the jury. Forget about me. They must hear what you say. Loud, please, and slowly.' And: 'We can't have a private chat, you must throw your voice.' The kinds of matter discussed in testimony were normally those confided in a whisper to one very near, and there were ensuing tensions between the demands of intimate disclosure, on the one hand, and those of the formal communicative style appropriate to 'public distance', on the other,[62] between the conventions of everyday speech and those of the court. It is hardly remarkable that witnesses had forever to be told to speak up. Even experienced police officers found the requirement to look away from counsel difficult to comply with: 'I find it very difficult not to speak back to the person who is speaking to me', said a detective constable.

The place from which testimony was given, the 'box', was set prominently to the fore of the court, near the judge and prosecution counsel, in full view of the jury and the defendant. (Prosecution witnesses frequently claimed that defendants silently menaced them as they testified: 'I could see him out of the corner of my eye watching me', said Victim 19.[63]) Confined to the box, standing up (being

[62] See E. Hall, 'Silent Assumptions in Social Communication', in R. Gutman (ed.), *People and Buildings* (New York, Basic Books, 1972), 141.

[63] The most recent generation of courtrooms are designed to prevent jurors and defendants and the public from menacing one another by gesture or grimace. The

allowed to sit was a special dispensation of the Court), often ill at ease, the witness was a conspicuous object to be examined closely by eye and ear as each answer was given in turn. Demeanour and deportment provided a moving non-verbal commentary on credibility and steadfastness:[64] 'We look people in the eye when we talk to them, and when they're talking to us, we look at their lips', said a barrister. Counsel welcomed their physical distance from witnesses. It enabled them to judge reactions as questioning and testimony unfolded:

In some of the courts the witness box is next to the jury box. The jury can see the face of the witness. That is terribly important because so often we decide whether somebody is telling the truth not actually on the answer that's given but in the way it is. Very often you can tell by the expression or the hand movement even of a particular witness. I think it is crucial to see the witness.

A witness's bearing was then itself taken to provide a non-verbal commentary both on character and credibility, and it was not a little useful to reveal how witnesses responded to the stress of examination. Such a disclosure could, in turn, underscore quite different points as counsel examined and cross-examined individual witnesses at various stages of the trial.

Consider self-control. A witness's manifest self-control in the box could be read as the mark of an ability to discipline the emotions, and *that*, in its turn, might be thought to show how very restrained and unprovocative such a one was likely to be at other times and in other places. The contained witness would make a weak candidate for representation as a victim who had recklessly brought on his or her own assault, and the issue of self-defence could be of critical importance in certain cases. After all, the ideal of a responsible

courtrooms of the Crown Court at Newcastle upon Tyne, for instance, shield jurors from the public gallery. There is no shielding of the witness box.

[64] Mazengarb, in his advice to counsel, said: 'Attention can be paid to the following indicia of a perjurer: (a) an excess of zeal in giving evidence . . . (b) an uneasiness of manner shown in the way he shifts his hands, or body, from side to side (the shifty witness); and also if while standing he gives the witness box a slight kick; (c) an unwillingness to meet the gaze of the Court or to look into the eyes of the opposing advocate; (d) a laboured or cautious manner of speaking which is suggestive of the fact that he is repeating what he has been told, rather than stating facts within his own knowledge . . . (e) a trembling of the body, sweat on the forehead, and an obvious desire to get his evidence over as soon as he becomes embarrassed under cross-examination' (*Advocacy in Our Tim*, 200–1).

individual is at the very core of law.[65] And other matters could be involved: trials are about morals and deserts as well as law. Juries were sometimes thought to believe that certain victims, shown to be the kinds of people they were, were really entitled to no protection under the law. As one barrister said, 'Very often you may feel that you have—as a prosecutor or defender—the jury with you—because sometimes the jury may feel, "Well, she's [the victim's] getting what she deserves", rightly or wrongly, you might sometimes feel that a verdict was based on that.'

Witnesses themselves would often try to stay contained. A favourite method of dealing with stress was to 'hold my hands down' and press the fingernails into the palm or back of the hand. Police officers had been trained to refrain from direct eye contact with defence counsel, looking instead at the judge or jury, but almost all maintained, in effect, that such a tactic flouted the normal silent rules of communication and could not be sustained for long. One sergeant said: 'I would suggest that in trials which don't last for very long. If you're in the box for half a day or a day, at the end of it you face the counsel—it's I think normal—it's quite difficult to go through a third person doing anything, well I've found that I do that anyway.'

Yet a contained witness could also fail to carry conviction. Counsel argued that police officers often made poor witnesses because their delivery appeared rehearsed and monotonous, without any show of emotion: the good witness was supposed to break down in the box at some point. Indeed, a *lack* of composure could be read as the only proper response to the harrowing business of remembering a painful past and bringing it back to life. When witnesses remained impassive, inferences could be made about the substance and impact of the events they described.[66] Tears and anger underwrote sincerity: 'You would let it happen', said a counsel talking about examination-in-chief, 'because I mean if she wants to sob or he wants to bang his

[65] See M. Wiener, *Reconstructing the Criminal* (Cambridge, Cambridge Univ. Press, 1990), 54.

[66] See A. Robinson, 'Rape Story All Judges Must Read', *Daily Mirror*, 20 Sept. 1990. The story to which she refers is that of Jill Saward, a rape victim, whose very composure encouraged a judge to imagine that the trauma to which she had been exposed was 'not so great'; J. Saward, *Rape: My Story* (London, Pan, 1991), 133. Journalists will routinely comment on a defendant's impassivity when sentences are delivered, as if it signified a heartlessness rather than the state of numbness that often accompanies the closing stages of a trial. See the report titled 'Father Is Jailed for Murder of Daughter', *The Times*, 31 Nov. 1991.

fist, then I'm not going to stop them, because in one way it underlines your case, it's useful.'

In other contexts, and under cross-examination especially, a witness's emotionality in the box could do him or her a disservice. Counsel tended to try to excite it quite deliberately to reveal one who had such poor self-control that he had probably responded immoderately to earlier provocation.[67] The very embarrassment of a witness who was ill at ease could aid one's case. One barrister observed that the guilt of people accused of 'heat of the moment' crimes could be revealed by their ill-temper under cross-examination. If they behaved badly on trial, it would be implied, they might well have behaved badly towards a victim or a defendant in the past:

I tend to ask questions of the witness, initially some of them quite harmless and really not to the point, in order to gauge the length of a witness. If they are testy witnesses—for example, I remember a really splendid case, where there was a chief inspector. In fact, my opponent warned me that I was going, as it were, to have real difficulties with him, almost initially, any sort of minor point of challenge, he lost his temper. So, when it came to the actual build-up I got angry, and it was what I wanted because he just exploded!

Tears, embarrassment, and anger might also be the signs of controls collapsing as guilt, certainty, or perjury were exposed by cross-examination. Witnesses could be made to 'blush with shame'.[68] On one occasion, I was told, a victim 'burst into tears because she appreciated that she might have made a mistake. The second victim did exactly the same. And both of them admitted that they might have been wrong and that's why they burst into tears.' I shall return to the rigours of cross-examination below.

All those matters would be brought to the jury's attention, presented quite explicitly as proper tests to be applied in assessing veracity. Judges would invite jurors to consider how witnesses had acquitted themselves. After all, the witnesses' behaviour in the box was a powerful clue to their behaviour outside the courtroom. It was evidence about evidence. A recorder remarked in his summing-up: 'You alone are judge of the facts. You must decide which evidence you will accept and which you reject. You heard the evidence given and have had an opportunity to witness the way in which it was

---

[67] For the spectacular effectiveness of a deliberate attack on a defendant's self-control under cross-examination conducted in an American murder trial, see B. Porter, 'Mind Hunters', *Psychology Today*, Apr. 1983, 52.

[68] Mazengarb, *Advocacy in Our Time*, 201.

given.' And, in another case, the judge said of the defendant, 'the fact that the defendant has been sitting in the dock should not affect your judgment of the defendant's evidence. It is how be behaves in the witness box that is important.'

A fourth consequence of orality flowed from the inability of a recording machine or pencil to make much of testimony that leaned on gesture, inflection, or irony for its meaning ('You're shaking your head. For the benefit of the shorthand writer, you mean "no"?'). One witness was reproved for employing a sarcasm that would carry an altered meaning in transcription. Everything disclosed had to be bald, literal, and unambiguous, transformed into stark assertions that robbed speech of the tricks and devices that added nuance, cloaked feeling, and preserved face.

A fifth consequence was that witnesses were not allowed to proceed at a pace greater than the capacity of judge and shorthand writer to note what they said. Most judges took painstaking, long-hand notes to aid the preparation of their summings-up, although one worked quite deftly at the keyboard of a small electronic type-writer. Shorthand writers, qualified to work at some 225 words a minutes, recorded testimony that was delivered, one estimated, at about 160–80 words a minute. It was their joint needs that dictated the rate and continuity of delivery. Testimony could not flow spontaneously and unchecked. It could not move at its 'own' unprompted speed. Witnesses were not always allowed to forget their difficult and intimidating surroundings to become engrossed in what they said. They could be continually interrupted by pleas of 'Will you tell this slowly please because it's got to be written down?'; 'Wait a minute because there must be a report of what goes on'; 'Take it slowly, take it slowly'; 'Pause, stop, because it's all being written down'.

It followed that being a witness was to experience a minute control of every move and utterance. Counsel, judges, and ushers were ceaselessly steering, admonishing, and coaxing. One counsel said:

The first thing I tell a witness is to speak up and where to address the answers to, because they always try, the temptation, the understandable temptation, is that they will always try and have a chat with you. I mean you have got to overcome that. And, as far as speed is concerned, you have to realise to most people giving evidence, it's something completely new and rather traumatic, and you will, you do get these very volatile witnesses, so you do have to do it and get them to slow down. So what you do is keep your eye on the shorthand writer . . .

Even the shorthand writers would very occasionally make wry faces, interject 'It's too fast', or ask a witness to repeat what had been said. The cumulative impact could be quite disconcerting. The most seasoned witnesses could be disconcerted. One police officer remarked:

When I was a beat officer I appeared many times and when I appeared it's sheer abject terror. You've been called. You walk through the court and every eye is on you. You step in the box and someone thrusts something at you—you see the card and you can't even read it. Then it calms down a little because you've got the prosecuting counsel who tries to calm you down. And then the judge says the jury can't hear you. Then the next thing is that you feel confident again and you get into your flow and the judge says you're going too fast. The judge is writing everything down. They write in long hand. You've got these interruptions being slung at you. Then your confidence goes and the judge says, 'I've told you before. The jury can't hear you. Keep your voice up' . . . And that is the easy part of it.

Stagecraft

A sixth consequence of the principle of orality worked on the gulf between insiders and outsiders that I have already introduced. If the application of the principle bewildered witnesses by its exhortations and admonitions to interrupt their speech, to speak loudly and brashly, slowly and discontinuously, in little reportable phrases, and facing away from their questioners all the while, the effect on advocates was quite different. When all attempts to win the jury were oral, the oral had to be winning. Orality encouraged a certain theatricality of manner.

Almost every lawyer was adamant that the flamboyant historics of a Patrick Hastings or a Sergeant Sullivan had disappeared from the courts. Marshall Hall would undoubtedly have been regarded as something of a ham in trials of the Class 4 cases of Wood Green.[69] One judge observed:

There is hardly any acting done. All the atmosphere these days is against it. I mean, that's because the population is generally well-educated and they

[69] John Mortimer recalled that his father had told him about how Marshall Hall had been 'preceded into court by a clerk bearing a pile of clean handkerchiefs, a carafe of water and an air cushion. When the prosecution evidence became awkward, he would blow his nose, a sad trumpet, on one of the handkerchiefs. If it became worse he would knock over a glass of water. If it became really damning he would slowly inflate the cushion and then the jury had eyes and ears for nothing else' ('Playing to the Jury', *The Times*, 22 Apr. 1992).

know if somebody is acting and they come down like a ton of bricks on any insincerity. So it is quite different from the Edwardian or Victorian period when several cases took the place of popular theatre in a sense . . .

But, if advocacy was no longer rank melodrama, it did continue to demand a more understated acting. It was impossible to regard it simply as a projection of everyday methods of argumentation into the courtroom. It was couched in its own legal language, and accompanied by a certain stagecraft. A barrister said of the courtroom: 'I think it's a special kind of stage. I do think that having some kind of atmosphere, which may be the same thing as a sense of drama, and at the same time, a sense of stage management, is important.' In effect, counsel felt themselves to be playing a part in which they deployed special forensic techniques. And, from time to time, they did more by embodying and enacting some of the conflicts of the trial. They could simulate the outrage of the injured community or the falsely accused who was mute in the dock:

It's highly staged because of this scenario. It goes back to that everyone has a role and everyone's placed in this particular state. The amount of acting that you do is almost directly proportional to how much is required. A lot of cases are very laid-back and there is no acting involved at all. A fraud case, for example, which is just documented after document. Apart from some humour, to keep the thing alive, there is no acting. But if you have police officers who are accused of lying or civilians who are accused of lying or bad conduct, an element of artificial heat is generated by counsel in parts of cross-examination. Not all of it. But those parts that it's important to emphasize or to express the rage of your client's case. But it's simulated rage, or ought to be.

Counsel had a theatricality that embraced a loudness of voice, a thespian's gestures, and a physical presence (the architect who designed the new courtrooms claimed, perhaps not with complete seriousness, that the seats in the counsel's row were built on the presumption that barristers were all 6 ft. 6 in. tall). They wore wigs and robes that could be flung, trailed, or draped for dramatic effect. They had been apprentices in a craft that celebrated stories about great dramas and the masters of advocacy.[70] Barristers were at the centre. They stood out against the rest and they were intended to do

---

[70] See McBarnet, *Conviction*, 18. See e.g. Mazengarb's references to Shaw and Marshall Hall in *Advocacy in Our Time*, 34, 40, and references to Patrick Hastings, Sergeant Sullivan, and others in D. Napley, *The Technique of Persuasion* (London, Sweet and Maxwell, 1983), pp. xi, 1, 10.

so. The new courtrooms of the *Palais de Justice* were furnished with pale woods and decorated in whites and light pinks and purples that were designed expressly by their architect to make the black garbed counsel seem especially prominent.

It should be noted that all this theatricality was reasonably controlled. Professional emotionality was not allowed to be unreined and it certainly was not supposed to appear anything other than counterfeit to the knowing eye.[71] There was no florid manner in court beyond gestures of face and voice and the little movements that were allowed within the right space of counsel's row. Counsel did not flounce or gesticulate overmuch. They did not bodily approach those giving evidence, loom over defendants and witnesses, or move to deliver documents and exhibits to juries, judges, defendants or witnesses. In even the most punishing attack, they would remain immobile, emphasizing how very disciplined and formal was their display of emotionality and conflict. A recently appointed judge remarked of some of the older courtrooms in other centres: 'From the point of view of counsel, you were almost too near the witness. I remember pouring her a glass of water and that kind of thing. The separation and remoteness which is part of the formal atmosphere of a trial was missing.'

Counsel kept their distance. Any other course would have been thought ill-mannered and brazen. It would have distracted attention from the face and voice of the witnesses giving testimony and imperilled the order of the courtroom (one barrister said, 'We are not like Perry Mason, we don't stride up and down the court room . . . the jury must concentrate, and it is desirable that they concentrate on

---

[71] I shall argue in a while that there were obvious signals emitted to show that the apparent mood of certain parts of cross-examination was spurious. Yet there was a clear problem caused by the states that counsel needed to induce in themselves in order to perform at all: it was not easy to appear in court and not easy to behave aggressively for any length of time. Counsel talked of having to work up pressure in themselves ('particularly in those cases where it's all police evidence, suggesting a police officer is a liar is a fiarly strong accusation, and it does help, or certainly for me personally it helps, if there is a little bit of adrenalin behind it'). That condition was not very different from a more authentic emotionality. One barrister said, 'It's very difficult to tell when people are play-acting or not. Because part of our job is to communicate their frustration or the rage of their client, whether they are prosecuting or defending, by and large defending . . .'. And a perceptive probation officer observed: 'With everyone, the defendant, counsel, judges, you get the same slightly temperamental, nervous attitude, quite noticeable, before they [go into court] . . . and then they relax afterwards . . . so tempers are liable to explode all over the place, as if they were in the theatre.'

the witness and not on the antics of counsel'). It would have risked opprobrium amongst colleagues and judicial rebuke.[72] The suspicion that counsel actually did lose their temper, that their anger was felt, could be most damaging to reputation.

It was as if every move was calculated, and that very calculation added to effect. Counsel tried to be audible but not too loud; to be well-modulated in their delivery but not obviously mannered; to be clear and pleasing to the ear ('an ugly voice is a great handicap'[73]); to speak 'felicitously' ('avoid the monotony of everyday conversation and develop a facility for using colourful expressions and allusions'[74]), and to be effective in the use and pitch of their voice so that it 'express[ed] the mental attitude, whether it be quiet confidence in the right, or high-minded indignation at the wrong'.[75]

Looks and bearing were cultivated.[76] After all, it was the task of counsel to convince by word and gesture, and persuasiveness would be lost by a manner that conveyed hesitation, uncertainty, disorder, or absence of purpose. Counsel were invariably, indeed sometimes showily, well dressed in neat suits and impeccably clean shirts that displayed flashes of gold at the cuff and wrists. Their hair was kempt. The men were clean-shaven or, very occasionally, they sported well-groomed beards and moustaches. Theirs was an appearance of self-control and organization that symbolized many things. It was a visible subscription to the decorum and good order of the courtroom, a subscription that was policed by judges[77] and the Bar Council.[78] Lawyers were seen to have 'that primary essential—command of [themselves]':[79] it was as if they were advertising that *they* were in control; *they* knew what they were doing; *they* were able to detect the truth or falsehood of what witnesses said to them. Perhaps, too, their appearance was an iconic representation of a particular way of talking about the social world, an orderly world of neatly visible bound-

---

[72] When, in an usher's absence, counsel delivered papers to a judge himself, he said, 'I hope you don't mind my stepping forward. It looks as if I've just come back from America.'

[73] Hilbery, *Duty and Art in Advocacy*, 26.   [74] Mazengarb, *Advocacy in Our Time*, 28.

[75] Hilbery, *Duty and Art in Advocacy*, 26.

[76] for an example of a general manual for the practice of stagecraft, see Mazengarb, *Advocacy in Our Time*, esp. 24–48.

[77] I have been reminded by Rosie Kerslake, herself the wife of a barrister, that, in some courts, judges would tell improperly dressed advocates: 'I cannot hear you'.

[78] See General Council of the Bar, *Code of Conduct for the Bar of England and Wales* (London, 1989), 26.1.

[79] Mazengarb, *Advocacy in Our Time*, 141.

aries and distinctions where things could not be ambiguous and relations were clear.[80] It was an invitation to see matters as unequivocal, organized, and certain.

The speech of counsel was studied, clear, and articulate in the main. It was the formal speech of public men and women accustomed to being heard and reported at a distance, well-modulated, with an idiom and pace that conveyed authority[81] (a judge remarked to a witness, 'We forget that people aren't accustomed to shouting. We are. We spend all our time talking to people who are twenty or thirty feet away'). It was not often counsel who were asked to slow down, pause, or repeat questions by judge or shorthand writer (although, to be sure, witnesses did sometimes request counsel to do so). It was not counsel who seemed muddled or hesitant in thought. On the contrary, they were audibly in control. Counsel were the interrogators and witnesses the interrogated, and they could press hard when they chose: Victim 18 said she had been 'scared': 'He kept pressuring me, and saying, "you're lying, you're lying", and that was just what made me break down.' When witnesses attempted to turn round and catechize counsel themselves, when, perhaps, they retorted, 'How do you know what happened, you weren't there?' they were either ignored or told firmly that it was the lawyers who were the questioners, not the questioned. Counsel were not in court to answer witnesses ('Just answer the question', they would say).

Counsel made repeated use of their own local courtroom rhetoric, working with formulaic words and phrases that seemed to resonate with assurance and conviction (at least on the first time of hearing); phrases that could intersperse other questions and observations; dent an opponent's witnesses; provide a kind of architecture for talk, marking the climaxes, beginnings, and endings of question sequences; and be deployed, it may be presumed, when they flagged or wished to collect their thoughts.[82]

Thus cross-examination would lean on the reiterated question, put over and over again and more aggressively, in a manner quite alien

---

[80] See M. Douglas, *Purity and Danger* (London, Routledge and Kegan Pual, 1966).

[81] W. O'Barr observed that 'rhythm and pace are important. . . . [do] not . . . bore the jury with extreme slowness, [do not] break the pace of the examination, especially when surprised . . . use silence strategically, and . . . speak more slowly when complicated facts are being presented'; *Linguistic Evidence: Language, Power and Strategy in the Courtroom* (New York, Academic, 1982), 36.

[82] See D. Tannen, *Talking Voices: Repetition, Dialogue, and Imagery in Conversational Discourse* (Cambridge, Cambridge Univ. Press, 1989), 48.

to mundane conversation (it was as if the righteous anger of counsel grew at each unconscionable refusal of the witness to be truthful). It would contain questions parading as sure statements: 'You see, what happened, I put it to you officer, was this . . . wasn't it?' It would end when counsel lifted their eyes to stare at the witness and issue a flat, recipe-like contradiction of all that had been said: 'The simple truth of the matter is . . . [otherwise] is it not?' People in everyday life do not conventionally talk of simple truths. Neither do they deny another's claims in so bold a fashion. They do not often gaze aggressively. Such harshness could be disquieting, eliciting either an angry riposte or a faltering reply that could look a little like shiftiness.[83]

Counsel would represent a witness's testimony as contrived and partisan: 'Why, according to *you* were you meeting him?' they might say. 'Let's go back to your version', they would say wearily and sometimes incredulously, as if that version, beggaring sensible belief, needed only a little more rehearsal to expose its fragility. They would suggest that disputes about evidence were to be attributed solely to a witness's reluctance to admit the truth, asking after a denial, 'You won't accept that?' as if it were simple stubbornness that prevented acquiescence. They would proceed as if the mendacity or wrongdoing of an opponents witness were so evident that it required no independent demonstration. Accusations would be slipped in and proved by fiat: in one ordinary instance, a defence counsel asked a police officer, 'Having been abusive to him, did you . . .' as if the abusiveness itself was not in doubt. Witness's denials were never acknowledged but would either be disregarded utterly or meet with a faintly disbelieving 'Yes' as if that were enough to dispose of the matter.[84]

If counsel were stereotypically smooth, articulate, and well-groomed, witnesses appearing at Wood Green tended to be informally and poorly dressed (men were often ill-shaven and almost never wore neckties), faltering and ill at ease in public. Sometimes they could not be heard or understood at all, prompting a judge to say on more than one occasion, 'I'm afraid I can't hear a word of that'.

---

[83] Such accusations against others are unusual because they are privileged and have no counterpart outside the courtroom. See S. Bedford, *The Faces of Justice* (London, Collins, 1961), 20.

[84] Counsel may, of course, be right. Witnesses *do* lie, spectacularly so on occasion, e.g. the case of a trial for conspiracy to pervert the course of justice that resulted in the conviction for perjury at Newcastle upon Tyne Court of 26 Crown Court witnesses in 1991. 18 of those witnesses were sentenced to imprisonment. See *The Times*, 21 Nov. 1991.

David Napley advised counsel that the 'witness should remain under your control' and counsel themselves to 'constantly keep your emotions under control. Never lose your temper, or you will assuredly lose your case, your dignity and your client.'[85] Counsel were, in short, performers whose composure and command could contrast quite tellingly with that of the ruffled civilian: they were the managers, not the managed, the cool, not the heated.[86] And social class elaborated features of the divide. In appearance, at least, counsel tended to be upper middle-class,[87] white[88] men[89] earning fairly well[90] whilst witnesses were preponderantly working-class and not infrequently unskilled or unemployed. Whatever their origins might have been, the style of barristers was almost invariably patrician. It was as if something of the gap between gentlemen and plebeians, between officers and other ranks, entered the relations between counsel and witnesses. More than

---

[85] *The Technique of Persuasion*, 123, 110.

[86] A. Hetzler and C. Kanter remark of the American court: 'upon entering the courtroom, the differences between the actor's [*sic*] court costumes or styles of dress were striking. Those in uniform were the formal dispensers of power . . . For those not in uniform, style of dress dictated their respective status. The lawyers usually wore high quality suits . . . In almost all cases the defendant represented the lowest status in terms of quality of dress. He rarely wore a suit and was often dressed in loud colors. . . . Each change towards color and lower quality seemed to parallel changes from "actor to acted upon", from power to weakness'; 'Informality and the Court: A Study of the Behavior of Court Officials in the Processing of Defendants', in S. Sawyer and E. Sagarin (eds.), *Politics and Crime* (New York, Praeger, 1974), p. 77.

[87] For some rather dated material on the social origins of barristers, see R. Abel, 'Comparative Sociology of Legal Professions', in R. Abel and P. Lewis (eds.), *Lawyers in Society*, iii (Berkeley, Clif., Univ. of California Press, 1989), 114. Abel informs us that, in 1976, more than half of the Bar had attended public school and three-quarters had fathers who had worked in managerial or professional positions. More recent material suggests that the social-class recruitment of the legal profession is undergoing change, and that the Bar is becoming rather more open. Whilst Abel reported that a third of the Bar in 1976 had graduated from Oxford and Cambridge, N. MacErlean states that that figure had dropped to a fifth by 1991; 'Class Barrier: The Bar's Berlin Wall?', *The Lawyer*, 5(38) (Oct. 1991), 10. I am grateful to Robert Reiner for his help with this point.

[88] A study commissioned by the Bar and carried out in 1987 and 1988 showed that under than 1% of senior counsel were from the ethnic minorities. See *The Times*, 19 April 1990. In 1989, half of all chambers had no ethnic-minority tenants, and 53% of non-white barristers were to be found in just 16 sets. See *The Times*, 8 Oct. 1991.

[89] 21.1% of barristers were women. See *Women in the Professions: A Report from the UK Inter-professional Group* (London, Law Society Shop, 1990).

[90] See 'Barristers Advertise Counsel at up to £1,000 a Day', *The Times*, 31 Mar. 1990. In 1990, the standard CPS rates for counsel were £190 for the first day and £130 for 'refreshers' thereafter. Silks (Queen's Counsel) would negotiate their own fees, but few appeared at Wood Green. In the financial year 1988–9, the CPS laid out £42,670,000 in counsels' fees. *Crown Prosecution Service Annual Report* (London, HMSO, 1989), 11.

once, barristers looked like the calmly reasonable, successful, and confident representatives of a rational order who were effortlessly superior to the ungainly and emotional creatures coming to be judged and give evidence.

Indictments

Imagine the participants of a trial assembled. The first matter of consequence laid before them all would be the bill of indictment.[91] The indictment was the wager thrown down, the written accusation of crime, that had to be proved by the prosecution and rebutted by the defence. It was a perfect encapsulation of the adversarial system.

The indictment was a formal document, prepared by Crown Court officers, signed by a court clerk, and incorporating the charges brought by the Crown against the defendant. It was based on statements and depositions sent to the Crown Court on committal from magistrates' court.[92] Each offence listed in an indictment was a 'count' that had to be laid out in a separate paragraph and contain a statement of the offence, the statute infringed, and particulars of '(i) the party indicted, (ii) the party injured, and (iii) the facts and the intent that are necessary ingredients of the offence'.[93] A specimen indictment is presented in Fig. 2.1.

The indictment performed different services. It contained the charges that the defendant was required to answer in person and on arraignment by the court clerk, pleading guilty or not guilty to all or some of the counts. Many trials at the Crown Court at Wood Green would be prefaced by anxious enquiries and deliberations about whether they would 'stand out' or be 'effective'. There could well have been preliminary negotiations between lawyers, the CPS,[94] and defendant about pleas, an 'indication' perhaps having been obtained from the judge about likely sentences.[95] It was understood that there

---

[91] It will be recalled that the Crown Court has exclusive jurisdiction to try indictable offences.

[92] See *Magistrates' Court Act 1980*, ch. 43, s. 19. For a general treatment of committal see R. White, *The Administration of Justice* (Oxford, Blackwell, 1985), 69 ff.

[93] *Kenny's Outlines of Criminal Law*, 19th edn. (Cambridge, Cambridge Univ. Press, 1966), 595.

[94] Such discussions could chiefly be for dramaturgical purposes. A barrister told me that it was always possible to say that one must take instructions, speak to a CPS representative, and say, 'You don't want me to accept a plea in this case, they haven't a leg to stand on', and then return and say, 'I am instructed not to accept a plea'.

[95] Seeking an indication was part of a delicate transaction that, since the case of Turner (R. v. *Turner* [1970] 2 QB 321), had to avoid all appearance of formal plea

INDICTMENT   No. 890000

IN THE CROWN COURT AT WOOD GREEN
THE QUEEN -V- JOHN SMITH

JOHN SMITH
is charged as follows:-

Count 1

STATEMENT OF OFFENCE

THEFT, contrary to Section 1(1) of the Theft Act 1968

PARTICULARS OF OFFENCE

JOHN SMITH on a day between the 1st day of July 1989
and the 2nd day of August 1989 stole a cheque belonging
to George Brown.

Count 2

STATEMENT OF OFFENCE

HANDLING STOLEN GOODS, contrary to Section 22(1) of
the Theft Act 1968.

PARTICULARS OF OFFENCE

JOHN SMITH on a day between the 1st day of July 1989
and 2nd day of August 1989 dishonestly received stolen
goods namely a cheque belonging to George Brown
knowing or believing the same to be stolen goods.

T.Green
Officer of the Court

Dated the 27th December 1989

Fig. 2.1.

would be a standard discount on prison sentences for a guilty plea, and that a plea of guilty on one count or for a lesser count[96] might encourage the prosecution to let other counts 'lie on the file in the public interest' or be awarded a formal finding of 'not guilty' because of the 'slightness of the matter'. Just over half the defendants appearing in the Crown Court at Wood Green pleaded guilty, less than for the Crown Court as a whole (but comparable enough with other London centres).[97]

The other service of the indictment was to map out the prosecution case, specifying exactly what it was that had to be proved in court. Barnard called an indictment a series of answers to the questions: 'Who, when, where, did what to whom?'[98] That who, when, where, what, and whom were the matters that the prosecution had to cover piece by piece as they 'opened' the indictment by addressing the jury and directing their minds 'to the main questions in dispute . . . tell[ing] them what evidence [they] proposed to adduce, and . . . explain[ing] its bearings upon the case'.[99] If an indictment was, as Matthew Hale put it, 'a plain, brief, and certain narrative of an

bargaining. Counsel would consult judges in chamber who could go no further than inform them whether, whatever the plea, they would imprison the defendant and might say that they have in mind a certain sentence were he to be found guilty. The Turner case established that counsel should advise defendants about their plea and indicate that this is likely to affect their sentence; defendants were supposed to have freedom to choose their plea; there should be free access to discussion between counsel and judges, preferably in public; the length of sentence judges might impose were to be irrespective of plea; and the essence of that discussion should be made known to the defendant. A judge at Wood Green said: 'What it really comes to is this, that there's no objection to a judge indicating to counsel that, for instance, whatever the outcome of the case, and whether it proceeds as a trial or a plea, he will not be sending the defendant to prison. . . . So usually what a judge is saying to counsel is, "I won't be sending him to prison in any event, trial or fight or plea", or alternatively he may say, "I am not going to give an indication".' The whole process is guarded by what a counsel called 'careful' speech and 'formulae', and 'it is now a policy that the judge has a shorthand writer or somebody taking notes when he sees the counsel'. Indications seemed to be secured in about one-sixth of the cases. For a brief discussion of the development of 'Indications', see R. Brandon and C. Davies, *Wrongful Imprisonment* (London, Allen and Unwin, 1973), 59.

[96] e.g. a defendant was arraigned and pleaded not guilty to a count of assault occasioning actual bodily harm. His counsel moved to talk to him, the court was read out again, and he said 'Not guilty, guilty to common assault'.

[97] According to the 1990 Report of the Lord Chancellor's Working Group on Pre-Trial Issues, in 1989, 71% of defendants committed for trial eventually pleaded guilty in the Crown Court as a whole. The comparable figure for the Crown Court at Wood Green was 55% (a figure, it should be noted, that was relatively high for *London*).

[98] D. Barnard, *The Criminal Court in Action* (London, Butterworth, 1974), 70.

[99] *Kenny's Outlines of Criminal Law*, 611.

offence committed',[100] the duty of the prosecution was to restore detail, supply a story, and, above all, produce the witnesses whose narrative statements had been collapsed, compressed, and given legal form in the charges.

Prosecutors were usually understated in their opening address. They were supposed to begin by reminding the jurors that they were disinterested Ministers of Justice who had no duty to win at any costs. They merely assisted the jury in arriving at 'the truth'. They would then characteristically proceed to tell jurors quite explicitly that the indictment was, in the words of one prosecutor, the 'what and the who of the [offence]'; offer what amounted to a plotted version of the counts, transforming them back into a tale with characters; and then undertake to prove the charges with the assistance of oral evidence: 'Those are the facts that will be given by the witnesses.'

In effect, the indictment laid out a programme of work,[101] a series of 'procedural steps',[102] that would be undertaken by the prosecution. In one minor case of indecency, the prosecution informed the jury: 'I have to prove that the defendant made an assault, and second that the assault would be considered by right-minded people to be indecent, and you are the right-minded people, and the third is that the defendant intended the act.' In a more serious case of assault, the prosecution said:

At the very outset one has to be clear that it is the prosecution that brings the case and the prosecution will have to prove it. . . . I have a duty to introduce the case to you and to introduce the issues. . . . The first thing the prosecution will have to prove is that it was this person who caused the injuries . . . The attack was witnessed in part by Mr X and you will be hearing from him. . . . The next matter the prosecution will have to prove is that a wound was caused and a wound is simply a breaking of the skin. The third element that the prosecution has to prove is that if there was a wound it was done unlawfully. It wasn't done by accident. It wasn't done in self-defence or any of those matters. The fourth matter is very important and that is that the defendant intended the GBH [grievous bodily harm]. That is really serious injury. You can find out intent by looking at all the circumstances. You may come to the conclusion that he intended the injury if he used a weapon . . .

---

[100]   2 Hale PC 169.

[101]   In explaining that programme of work to a jury, counsel were often obliged to simplify quite difficult problems. Lucia Zedner commented: 'I am struck by the need for the prosecution to translate criminal laws into something comprehensible to jurors—in the process riding roughshod over the complexity and highly contested nature of concepts like "intent".'

[102]   Barnard, *The Criminal Court in Action*, 10.

Instructions

Accompanying the indictment and statements in the brief, and relayed to counsel alone, would be instructions prepared by the defence solicitors or the CPS, and they were supposed to guide lawyers as they restored content, context, and detail to the bare bones of the charges.[103] Instructions could be meagre indeed, but they were supposed to give a gloss on witness statements, explain the case for the indictment, and point counsel to its principal strengths and weaknesses.

A typical set of prosecution instructions might be some few hundred words long and it would not be generous in detail. It would proceed by offering a 'preamble' stating the charges, the date of the committal from magistrates' court, and the terms on which the defendant was remanded or released on bail. Its major portion would lay out the 'brief facts' of the case in narrative form, highlighting particularly damaging or pertinent admissions made in interview. 'We try and convey to counsel the facts which particularly tended to show the defendant's guilt', said one of the instructing CPS officers at Wood Green. She continued: 'Instructions were usually a sort of précis, [saying] something like' As can be seen from so-and-so's statement'). She would rarely discuss her instructions with counsel before the case (counsel might change at short notice anyway) and any conversation would be on the telephone; she rarely observed the counsel she had instructed prosecuting cases in court; and she would not expect to be able to recognize her instructions in what counsel actually said: 'Counsel reads his instructions, or not as the case may be, and then goes ahead and reads the case himself and puts it forward in his own way, I think.'

Defence instructions varied in length from the copious to the invisible. They too would begin with a preamble about the charges, committal, and conditions on which the defendant awaited trial. But they would also affirm the defendant's claims of innocence ('Mr Smith strenuously protests his innocence and wishes to enter a plea of not guilty') and they might offer a gloss on what had happened, including a running commentary on the witness statements. In an assault case, for example, the victim might be described as having been provocative himself. He could have had a history of violence. The

---

[103] See S. Blake, *A Practical Approach to Legal Advice and Drafting*, 3rd edn. (London, Blackstone, 1989), 41.

instructing solicitors might reflect that counsel would be 'interested' in the independence of certain potential defence witnesses, or in the possibility that a prosecution witness was unreliable ('He is a man known to use violence and had just been released from prison'). There might be information secured from the prosecution about convictions recorded against prosecution witnesses. All that would be the material of a potential defence.

Counsel were supposed to be bound by instructions. They were not to put any allegations that were not specified[104] ('What you are not entitled to do is put something definitively to a witness unless you are instructed'). On occasion, they would flag to their professional colleagues that they *were* following instructions meticulously: 'You are giving a signal to the judge and to your opponent that this is what you are putting on your client's instructions.' Defence counsel would do so particularly when they made their most forceful, angry, contentious, or disagreeable points. It was then that they seemed to distance themselves a little from the substance of their utterances and from a difficult role, by beginning, 'I must put it to you' or 'I suggest': 'If you use those two terminological introductions then the probability is that you are acting on instruction.' But it was quite evident that instructions were often not generous enough to prepare counsel adequately. Counsel would work on the materials provided by the trial as it unfolded, exploring inconsistencies and contradictions in the testimony of opposing witnesses, and they could move out beyond instructions to embark on what were called 'fishing expeditions': 'You can fish, quite legitimately as long as the judge doesn't interrupt.'

The Proof

Most important of all the statements in a brief was what lawyers called the 'proof'. The proof was what one barrister described as the 'nub of the case'. It was the pivotal statement or set of statements by witnesses claiming, in the typical prosecution case, to have seen or heard the offence as it occurred, perhaps actually having witnessed

---

[104] 'A barrister may only adduce evidence obtained from or through his professional client. He must not devise facts which will assist in advancing his client's case,'; General Council of the Bar, *Code of Conduct*, 22.10.

the offenders committing the offences against the victims,[105] and, in the defence case, that there was provocation or that the defendant was elsewhere at the time and place of the offence.[106] In the neat form of a witness statement, shaped by the pattern of police interrogation, anticipating what would be done by lawyers, such a proof would very probably be direct and unambiguous, containing what the prosecution needed to use in its case before a jury. The proof was not 'spontaneous' or artless. It was organized by a very practical agenda, focus, and terminology.[107]

What follows is an excerpt from a typical enough proof provided by a man whom I shall call Jones, the victim of an assault committed in a public house and tried at Wood Green. It was completed in hospital some five days after the assault had taken place:

I noticed as I went into the pub that Mr Smith was in there talking to someone in the public bar. I bought a drink and went from the bar to the games room. I did this to get out of his way. After a short time . . . Mr Smith came through to the games room where I was. When he walked in I was going to go back into the public bar to keep out of his way. As I turned my back towards him to leave, he called out, 'Jones, I want to speak to you'. I turned round to face him and as I did he punched me in the face with I think his right fist which caught me on my left eye. Then he punched me again on the right side of my face and I fell to the floor. As I was going down and as I was down I was hit and I think kicked several times about my head and body by Mr Smith . . .

If that written statement could be recapitulated orally and before judge and jury, much of the work of the prosecution would have been done. 'Getting a witness up to proof' was a matter of establishing the 'nub of a case' publicly in court. The proof was quite clearly a pragmatic thing, bearing very precisely on the requirements of a successful prosecution. As McBarnet argued, what was required was 'a partial account (in both senses) limited to the "facts of the case" as defined by law and strategy rather than by the victim's perception of his or her experience'.[108] Prosecutors did not want over-co-operative

---

[105] One legal dictionary defines 'proof of evidence' as 'the collection of statements taken by witnesses . . . before a trial which represent the evidence which each side hopes to produce in court in order to prove its case'; *Harrap's Dictionary of Law and Society* (Bromley, Harrap, 1989), 226.
[106] Indeed, there is a phrase that solicitors 'proof a witness' to describe the key interviews conducted by the defence. See J. Mance, 'Mock Justice?', *Counsel*, Mar. 1990, 15.   [107] See McConville *et al.*, 'The Case for the Prosecution', 101, 139.
[108] 'Victim in the Box', 330.

or fulsome witnesses. They did not want ambiguity in testimony: that would be sought by the defence. (Mr Jones of the Wood Green statement was alleged to have been swearing, and smelling of alcohol in Smith's own statement to the police. That contention would have formed very little part of a constructively phrased prosecution proof and, indeed, it played no part.) Prosecutors did not want excessive, confusing detail bearing on victims, their history and motives. It was sufficient that victims confirmed orally that the offence had been committed and without undue provocation.

Victims were not called to say 'what really happened'. That was not germane. They were summoned to testify clearly about material issues only, and do so by orally repeating the written proof as faithfully as possible. The favourable witness was one, said a counsel, who would 'say in court what they have said in a statement to the police. The prosecution proceed on the basis of what a complainant or a witness says to a police officer which is reduced to a statement form.' Examination in chief consisted largely of drawing the proof out of witnesses line by line. A counsel remarked:

'There would be no way I would have access to that witness other than through the proof, and then all I would be able to do in the trial would be to lead the witness through the evidence, to take the witness through, without doing so, if you see what I mean. I can't lead her. I have to say, 'And what happened next?' and hope that what she answers is what's in the proof.'

And judges, aware of what was being done before them, aware that a written document was being reproduced orally in the courtroom, might from time to time actually ask counsel in the middle of their questioning what page in the written statement they had reached.

The Good Witness

Proofs were recounted by witnesses who would then be tested by the opposition, and their character and performance bulked large in the unfolding trial. I have already stated that it was a consequence of the principle of orality that witnesses should be seen and heard so that their veracity could be judged.[109] Indeed, it was a presumption that

---

[109] 'as a general rule a witness . . . should give his evidence orally in court. The jury can then see him, hear him and decide how trustworthy he is'; Emmins, *A Practical Approach to Criminal Procedure*, 108.

witnesses were tendered as people capable of being believed,[110] and it was most unorthodox for them to be impugned by their own counsel. On the contrary: witnesses would be commended to the jury by the side that called them.

The victim was the prime witness in many of the routine prosecutions of Class 4 cases at Wood Green. A barrister said:

The victims are usually called first for a number of reasons. First, because usually, chronologically, they are the beginning of the story. Second, because you don't want to keep them waiting longer than necessary. And thirdly, because much of the evidence turns on what they have to say and—again an extreme example—there may be no other evidence. So that if they break down in cross-examination, that's the end of the case.

As the prime witness, the pivot of the prosecution case, the victim was almost automatically challenged by the defence about his or her veracity, disinterestedness, integrity, knowledgeability, way of life, reputation, and associations.[111] Juries would be invited to consider his or her truthfulness and they would be repeatedly reminded of the importance of a plausibile delivery and demeanour. The manner in which witnesses had acquitted themselves was a standard topic in any judge's summing-up. Each witness might be described in miniature, although that description could actually be quite threadbare. Consider one very ordinary summing-up in a very ordinary trial:

The victim was taciturn and young. Sometimes you may think it was difficult to get him to answer head on. Well, you must draw your conclusions from that. Then there were the police officers, they were rather young and inexperienced perhaps, but is the criticism of them fair? . . . You saw the defence evidence, you could see what he said and what you made of him. So there it is, members of the jury, who do you believe and who don't you believe?

If the credibility of witnesses was critical, so, by extension, was their eligibility for casting in the narrative that a lawyer proposed to develop. Out of what may have been grasped initially as the ambiguous murk of reported experience, a murk that could be interpreted in many different ways, counsel were required to prise out, define, and fix the characters of the parties in a trial.[112] Bennett and Feldman

---

[110] See Cross, *An Outline of the Law of Evidence*, 287.   [111] See *Archbold*, 490.

[112] S. Merry remarked that 'the same event, person, action, and so forth can be named and interpreted in very different ways. . . . Each naming points to a solution [to a problem]'; *Getting Justice and Getting Even*, 111.

observed that 'jurors are bombarded by lawyers with invitations to stereotype defendants, victims, and witnesses.'[113] In effect, counsel made use of simple moral types, personifications of the virtues and vices that lend motive and meaning to plots. If the victim did indeed appear to be an innocent being who had had no part to play in his or her misfortune,[114] if the defendant did seem malevolent, the prosecution case would prosper. That moral character was not given *ab initio*: victims could not be deemed self-evidently good or innocent and defendants bad or guilty. It was only the prosecution that alleged that they were so, and the prosecution had to flesh out such allegations. Indeed, it was precisely the aptness of such characterization that could be in contention in a fought trial.[115]

Yet, because the character, motives, and mental state of witnesses were often opaque and little known, impenetrable even to searching exploration, counsel tended sometimes to refrain from making direct reference to the moral character of their witnesses, turning instead to a more transparent surrogate, the reasonable man, 'an extraordinary actor homunculus', who could be contrasted with 'the real actor'[116] for purposes of exposition.

For the purposes of conducting a defence, and so long as the case was being contested, the defence was professionally required to believe that the prosecutor's characterization was inaccurate and that the defendant was as innocent as he or she claimed to be.[117] Consider the stance taken by a solicitor who disagreed with arguments that radical lawyers should refuse to represent defendants on rape charges:

[There are] a number of startling assumptions. In the first place, there is the reference to the defence being 'disputed by the victim'. What victim? The woman only becomes 'a victim' once the defendant is convicted. . . . It is also taken for granted that in any conflict of evidence between the defendant and the woman, it is the woman who must be speaking the truth. No

---

[113] W. Bennett and M. Feldman, *Reconstructing Reality in the Courtroom* (London, Tavistock, 1981), 60.
[114] See N. Christie; 'The Ideal Victim', in E. Fattah (ed.), *From Crime Policy to Victim Policy* (Basingstoke, Macmillan, 1986).
[115] See McBarnet, 'Victim in the Box', 334.
[116] M. Scott and S. Lyman, 'Accounts, Deviance and Social Order', in J. Douglas (ed.), *Deviance and Respectability: The Social Construction of Moral Meanings* (New York, Basic Books, 1970), 104.
[117] See W. Boulton, *A Guide to Conduct and Etiquette at the Bar* (London, Butterworth, 1975), 69; and Mazengarb, *Advocacy in Our Time*, 80–7.

woman, it is asserted, would ever say she had been raped if she had not been. This is palpable nonsense.[118]

Almost as a matter of course, victims would be represented by prosecutors as hapless and unsuspecting, as unwitting actors in their own tragedies, and it was that portrayal that had to be undone by the defence. Defence lawyers would routinely try to turn matters on their head, transforming victims and their supporting witnesses into villains or fools.[119] Thus, the victim in an assault case would frequently be cast by the prosecution as blameless and by the defence as provocative, drunk, or angry ('The position is that . . . you had a lot to drink and were extremely annoyed with him'). The victim might be as culpable as the defendant. (A barrister said, 'There is a famous opening . . . in an affray case and it was the shortest opening that one can think of in an affray: "Members of the jury, an affray is a fight in a public place between a large number of people . . . In the dock stand the winners and I'm now going to call the losers one by one to tell how they lost".') The victim might be accused of having lied about an incident ('The truth of the matter is you are lying through your teeth'), of having exaggerated ('A lot of this is spite', said a defence counsel), or of having incited the offender. The victim might have been impelled by greed:

There's no doubt he suffered serious injury. As a result [the victim] is able to apply for criminal injuries compensation, quite rightly. Quite right that someone does not have to be convicted [for the victim] to be paid. Did [the victim] know that? Is that what he thought? Does not that colour his motives a little bit? . . . If you're a bit suspicious but not at all sure, you'll have to give a verdict of not guilty.

In deciding whether to prosecute at all, then, the CPS were obliged to consider the moral character of the witnesses in the case. Might they have a 'motive for lying', were they 'forgetful or motivated to exaggerate', were they open to attack by the defence on the grounds of their 'credibility'? In their instructions to prosecute, said a member of the CPS attached to Wood Green, they would 'flag things like whether there were any witness problems'. One very real

---

[118] M. Mears, 'Rape and the Radical Lawyer', *Law Society's Gazette*, 12 (28 Mar. 1990), 16.
[119] According to O. Klapp, villains and fools are 2 of the 3 major social types available for purposes of casting: there is the hero and there are 'villains and fools [who] are negative models, respectively of evil to be feared and hated, and absurdity to be ridiculed'; *Heroes, Villains and Fools* (Englewood Cliffs, NJ, Prentice-Hall, 1962), 16.

problem for the prosecution, but not for the defence,[120] was that it was almost certainly the case that witnesses would be known only to the police, it was on police knowledge that the prosecution would have to rely: 'If the police told us that "we think so-and-so would make a good witness", we would tell counsel that, or if this person might turn out to be a lousy witness, we tell counsel that as well.' The CPS and the prosecutors they briefed at the Crown Court at Wood Green had to learn about witnesses at second hand, through documents, statements, and police reports only. Unlike their colleagues elsewhere, in Holland[121] or Canada,[122] for instance, they could not see, interview, or prepare the witness. To be sure, a rough stereotype could be applied ('You can certainly guess something about their background'). The police themselves, for example, were assumed to have a uniformly monotonous and unpersuasive manner of delivery,[123] but the lay witness moving towards the box was generally a dimly defined entity whose conduct was unpredictable.[124]

---

[120] Defence solicitors would routinely comment on their client's and other witnesses' potential impact as a witness. One told me: 'My instructions to counsel would enclose . . . any thoughts I might have on the client and what sort of witness the client might make', and another would reflect on his client's 'background, and his history and his attitude—the way he is responding to things'. Solicitors appeared unwilling to make flat recommendations that counsel should or should not call their clients to testify, but would nevertheless make broad hints ('I haven't pushed the point, I have left it, but counsel should be aware of that and make his tactical decision').

[121] See J. Wemmers and M. Zeilstra, 'Victim Services in the Netherlands', *Dutch Penal Law and Policy*, 3 (June 1991), 4.

[122] e.g. in Manitoba witnesses are told: 'Before court begins the lawyer calling you as a witness will likely meet with you to review your evidence'; *Victim/Witness Assistance* (Manitoba, Attorney-General), n.d. In addition, see L. Axon, *Preliminary Evaluation of the Etobicoke Court-Based Victim/Witness Project* (Toronto, Attorney-General of Ontario, 1988), 17–18; and *Victim/Witness Assistance Program User Satisfaction Report* (Toronto, Ministry of the Attorney-General of Ontario, 1989), p. ii, where it is noted: 'from the perspective of the police and Crown Attorney's interviewed, the program results in more confident victim/witnesses who are better prepared to testify in court.' An Ontario Crown Attorney told me: 'We'd be lost without witness prep. We need it to make good witnesses.' When accosted about the kinds of reservation which his British counterparts would voice about such matters, he replied that, if the defence counsel asked, 'Did you speak to the prosecution counsel?', 'The answer should be "Yes", and when asked "Did you discuss the evidence?", the answer should always be "Yes", and if "What did he say?", "Tell the truth!" '

[123] One counsel talked about how easy it was to discredit police officers in cross-examination: they used notes, prepared their notes collaboratively, did not tend to read their statements beforehand to refresh their memory, and were wooden in delivery, he said.

[124] D. Neubauer remarked that American prosecution counsel found incompetent witnesses to be their chief probalem; see *Criminal Justice in Middle America* (Morristown, NJ, General Learning Press, 1974), 118.

Barristers found it difficult to define clearly the constituents of a good witness.[125] Desired traits presumably included a capacity to display appropriate emotion and conviction by intonation and bodily and facial gestures. Good witnesses should be clear, audible, measured, succinct, forthright, and honest in manner.[126] One counsel said: 'The most convincing witness is always the most straightforward, honest witness who's patently telling the truth.' Another talked about 'somebody who has a clear recall and doesn't get flapped easily, who doesn't make mistakes, somebody who is accurate and consistent'. In one case that I observed, the witness was described spontaneously by the prosecution as 'excellent' because he was a disinterested bystander who had given strong, loud, and decisive answers, looking counsel straight in the eye all the while, and saying emphatically that he had 'no doubt at all' whenever he was asked how confident he was about what he had said. It was very much those traits that barristers tried to coax out of the witness in the box before them, and that was a difficult enough operation, involving delicate manœuvres formulated rapidly *in situ*. A judge observed: 'There is always an element of risk, and there are all kinds of assessments and decisions being made which are not [apparent] to somebody listening [unless they had read] the papers in the case first.'

I have argued that prosecution counsel would have created a rough working typification of the witness from the documents in the bundle: 'I would have got a picture of them in my mind from their statements which could be right or could be wrong.' They would then have to establish how that typification should be applied and modified as the interrogation actually unfolded: 'When I see them in the witness box and listen to them, I would make some assessment about how I'm going to handle them.' Being unable to lead their own witnesses, they would nevertheless try obliquely to prompt them to reproduce the proof ('Your job as prosecuting counsel is to put the facts, as the prosecution witnesses say them, before the court'), in

[125] Most counsel agreed that it was difficult to describe a good witness. One referred to a 'combination of accurate recollection [and] absence of, so to speak, disingenuousness', but he continued, 'It's terribly difficult. When you meet anybody you know, what are those things that strike you about them and lead you to conclude that they are either trustworthy or not?'

[126] The Crown Counsel Victim Witness Services of the Ministry of the Attorney-General of British Columbia laid stress on very diffuse traits in its witness-preparation training programme. Listed as 'issues of witness credibility' were body language, facial expressions, being consistent in testimony, verbal communication, and physical appearance. Workshop Outline, COVA Conference, Calgary, Alta., 17 May 1989.

chronological order ('What happened to him/her, how it came to happen, and what happened afterwards), pithily ('It does help to be concise'), audibly ('making sure that the jury hears'), slowly, and step by discrete step ('We will want to investigate these matters one by one', said a counsel in court). Evidence should be given economically, with little that was ambiguous, unanticipated, and expansive, because that could disconcert the prosecution and permit an opponent later to feed on uncertainty and doubt. But it was important also that that evidence should appear neither rehearsed and unspontaneous ('If you're too concise it can sound a bit like a pre-memorized statement') nor shorn of the minor particulars that can confer verisimilitude "What often gives somebody credibility is remembering silly little details, stupid little things like they wore yellow or that sort of thing").

Narratives

Witnesses relayed stories and bits of stories that were given structure and plot by counsel. It was the plausibility of a narrative, the manner in which it made sense of the 'facts', the witnesses, and the evidence, that was presumed to weigh in the jury's minds. Yet there was a difficulty. Counsel knew very little useful about jurors. After all, no research can be conducted on deliberations in the jury room,[127] counsel were debarred from becoming jurors themselves, and there could be no informal conversation between juries and barristers. Jurors were to be avoided as witnesses were. They, too, were the innocents who should not be exposed to improper knowledge without control and surveillance,[128] and they were largely inscrutable in consequence.[129]

Jurors might sometimes laugh or make facial or other expressions in response to particular lines of argument and questioning. They

[127] One of the few stipulations imposed on me by the Lord Chancellor's Dept. was that I should not interview jurors at Wood Green. The inviolability of the jury room was to be waived exceptionally in 1992 to allow the Royal Commission on Criminal Justice to question jurors about their views on trials and the trial process.

[128] On one occasion, in Jan. 1990, a barrister reported to the judge: 'The space outside this particular court is very limited indeed. It is very difficult to have a confidential discussion. I did in fact have such a conversation last night and a lady came around the corner. She might have overheard us although it was phrased in esoteric language. I asked her who she was and it turned out she was a member of the jury. I thought I ought to bring it to your attention.'

[129] See Morison and Leith, *The Barrister's World and the Nature of Law*, 152.

might emit yet more subtle gestures, subliminal signs, that constituted what one barrister called 'an aura'. But there was little more. One barrister said, 'you obviously don't know what happens in the jury room—there are idiosyncrasies which we really can't understand.' And another observed, 'The problem for counsel whether you're prosecuting or defending is that he doesn't know what the jury is like. And juries, as far as one can make out, are quite different.' One counsel concluded, in effect, that there was little practical purpose in concerning himself with how the jury were responding to his performance:

Personally very little of my time is spent wondering how the jury is going to react to a question . . . I don't even . . . for most of the time, I'm hardly aware the jury is there, personally that is. It's me, the witness and the judge and I see very few other people in the court.

Jurors were a black box, an entity receiving information and emitting decisions, whose internal workings were obscure.[130] Counsel had to supply their own rough-and-ready model of those workings, and they did so by following the empirical epistemology that I have described. For pragmatic reasons, and perhaps for want of anything better, the jury were thought to employ common sense in their reasoning. Trials were grounded in lawyers' repeated appeals to the jury's common-sense knowledge of the social world. Jurors were *told* to use common sense in judging the facts. At the conclusion of one routine case, the assistant recorder told the jury: 'When you retire to the jury room, you bring with you your secret weapon, your common sense.' Over and over again, counsel would invoke common sense and its companion subject, the reasonable man. They would say, for example, that 'it's only common sense that when a man is attacked he should defend himself'.

The repeated allusion to common sense could be regarded as little more than making the best of a bad job, flattering the inexpert good judgement of laymen and women. But it can also be defined as

---

[130] Interestingly enough, the journalist who had sat on a Wood Green jury pronounced on the enigmatical character of *counsel's* performance. Counsel were bafflingly obscure to him: 'This is not a straightforward unfolding of the story, but one which is marked by obscure silences and mysteriously unput questions. Slowly you sense you are getting a case from which the procedural formalities exclude the search for total truth. At moments one wants to scream at the barrister to ask the obvious question and one could never be sure in this case why he hadn't asked it'; Young, 'An Indictment of Justice'.

something more substantial. Common sense may be represented, in part, as an objectification of the practical knowledge that motivates, explains, and organizes mundane experience. It may well be riddled with ambiguities and inconsistencies (as all applied reasoning must be), but it is probably as reliable a stock of interpretations as any. After all, common sense is more thoroughly put to the test than any other, and it does offer direct access to the mundane reasoning of others on the social scene.[131] It has to be truthful on pragmatic grounds because it is what people must presuppose about one another to get on with their practical affairs. It is *common* sense. Without a working presumption of its existence, people would be thrown back on their own inner subjectivity.

We have . . . to keep in mind that the common-sense constructs used for the typification of the Other and of myself are to a considerable extent socially derived and socially approved. Within the in-group the bulk of personal types and course-of-action types is taken for granted . . . as a set of rules and recipes which have stood the test so far and are expected to stand it in the future.[132]

Common sense and the reasonable man supplied a grammar of the plausible motive, the appropriate response, and the characteristic interconnectedness of things, which was summoned time and again in the courtroom. It was a logic that showed how the world was, how people generally behaved, and what was going on all around them. It was in effect a fund of interpretive formulas that conferred order on narratives and it was especially useful when knowledge of others was slight and mediated, based, as barristers' knowledge so often was, on paper reports hastily perused. Into common-sense narratives could be inserted the victim, the defendant, police officers, bystanders, and all the other supporting players. Prosecutors could then deploy the stock typifications of common sense to tell their brief, accusatory stories.[133] Defence counsel could, in their turn, draw on much the same knowledge and typifications to tell rival exculpatory stories about what had 'really happened'. As Bennett and Feldman observed, 'the criminal trial is organized around story-telling'.[134]

---

[131] See J. Douglas, *American Social Order* (New York, Free Press, 1971), 8–9.

[132] A. Schutz, *Collected Papers* (The Hague, Martinus Nijhoff, 1962), i. 19.

[133] See e.g. G. Abrahams, *According to the Evidence: An Essay on Legal Proof* (London, Cassell, 1958), 6.

[134] *Reconstructing Reality in the Courtroom*, 3.

Stories provided a means of locating and explaining the central action and actors.[135] They were given in miniature by lawyers who attempted to tie events and people plausibly together. They were parasitic, dependent in some measure on the motivated accounts given by lay protagonists and participants whose evidence was being tested in the courtroom itself. They stemmed from instructions, from statements, and from the testimony that unfolded before lawyers as examination proceeded. They were simple, even crude, because there was almost never time or information enough to develop themes and give them originality. At bottom, and perhaps as a consequence, they drew on themes from a much larger reserve of embedded knowledge about recurrent patterns of action, about good and evil, mishap and adversity, causality and chance.[136] They were formulaic.

Time and again in the routine Class 4 cases of the Crown Court at Wood Green, the same plots seemed to be exposed, plots that were familiar to the point of being a little hackneyed to insiders, but perhaps rare enough to sway a jury. Those plots hinged on the standard sequences of action that Wachs, in another context, has called the folklore of crime-victim stories:

Why is it that when two different people get mugged at different times on different . . . street corners, their stories are amazingly similar in style and structure? By identifying the traditional nature and features of stories, we can try to understand how stories are composed and how they are used by tellers. . . . [There are] common themes, character types, and . . . internal features, structure and stylistic details.[137]

Such simple thematic properties of story-telling recurred across very different contexts. They were the means by which people could grasp what had happened and convey it to themselves and others.[138] They were the means by which defendants themselves explained their conduct. Standard defences welled up, it may be presumed, from the

---

[135] See J. Shotter, 'Social Accountability and the Social Construction of "You"', in J. Shotter and K. Gergen (eds.), *Texts of Identity* (London, Sage, 1989).

[136] See R. Jackall, *Moral Mazes: The World of Corporate Managers* (New York, Oxford Univ. Press, 1988), 172–3.

[137] E. Wachs, *Crime-Victim Stories: New York City's Urban Folklore* (Bloomington, Ind.: Indiana Univ. Press, 1988), 59–60.

[138] Ken Plummer, for instance, remarks that 'many "victims" of sexual violence have started to tell the same formal story . . . there is a striking commonality to the tales I have read and heard'; 'Telling Sexual Stories: From Modern Narratives to Late Modern Narratives', paper presented at the Conference on Sexuality and [Post] Modernity, Univ. of Copenhagen, 11–13 Dec. 1989.

reservoir of justifications that people conventionally deployed to make sense of their life and actions,[139] and defence counsel were obliged to proceed as if they believed what they had been told.[140] Lawyers searched documents and interviews for their story-like properties, which they could then talk into life through examination and cross-examination.[141]

Consider the case of the trial of a man charged with wounding with intent and of possessing an offensive weapon, a knife. It was a small enough case. It did not last very long, attracted no interest from the public or the press, and raised no points of law. I shall dwell on it because its very ordinariness makes it interesting. What was alleged, particularly by the defence, was exactly what an experienced lawyer or spectator might have expected, but it was certainly not what the victim in the case expected. Let me call him Evans.

The case itself was a 'floater', to be tried, perhaps, on a Monday morning in late 1989, and the prosecution counsel had received the papers three days before, at 6.30 on Friday evening, at a time when he was waiting to take part in a major fraud case. He read them at 11 p.m. on Sunday night. Before the trial opened, at 9.30 a.m., the defence and prosecution counsel met without apparent design in the barristers' mess and gossiped about general and particular matters, the character of the judge who was to try the case, and, more circumspectly, about the defendant, the defence, and the witnesses in the case. There was agreement that the case would turn on matters of identification, and that the defendant himself might well 'get out of hand' under examination. He was described as dangerous, and his counsel said he rather hoped he would not remain at liberty.

The trial opened at 11.15 and it was short. Each of its components was short. The prosecution opening lasted for 15 minutes, and it told the jury about the use of a lock-knife that had been used with an intent to wound: 'The Crown says if you possess a lock-knife which is capable of causing a wounding, that is an offensive weapon.' A little narrative was supplied to frame the case: a couple who had been drinking left a wine bar to sit in a park 'for half an hour', and

---

[139] See R. Samuel and P. Thompson, introd. to *The Myths We Live By* (London, Routledge, 1990), esp. 10.

[140] See General Council of the Bar, *Code of Conduct*, 24.3. Zander remarks that it is recognized that strain can lead defendants to make wild allegations; see *Cases and Materials in the English Legal System*, 352.

[141] See D. Maynard, 'Narratives and Narrative Structure in Plea Bargaining', *Law and Society Review*, 22(3), 475.

had then telephoned for a taxicab. The car had arrived and Evans and his girlfriend tried to enter it, but the defendant 'who, it is fair to say, say the Crown, was very drunk and abusive', tried to prevent them from doing so: 'a knife was plunged into [Evans's] cheek, dislodging a tooth.' After wounding his victim, the defendant made off, the cabdriver took Evans to hospital, and the matter was reported to the police. The defendant was subsequently arrested and recognized in an identity parade. The case would turn on identification: 'The defence have served notice of an alibi—you know what that is, but we can't assume anything in these courts . . . The issue in the case is probably clarified by the alibi notice—was it the defendant who did it or was it someone else? The Crown's case is that two witnesses identified him.'

There was a more detailed explanation of the counts contained in the indictment itself, jurors being pointed to those portions that the prosecution wished to emphasize: 'Intention is the serious part—you will have to listen to the evidence and establish whether the defendant actually sought to do serious harm. The Crown must prove that he has no lawful authority to carry that knife, or no reasonable excuse.'

The actual presentation of the case then followed the larger logic of the trial ritual and the lesser logic of a properly constructed narrative.[142] By and large, prosecution cases are structured chronologically in Aristotelian fashion.[143] (A lawyer, not involved in Evans's case, observed: 'You would, for your own benefit, reconstruct [the events] in a chronological order, and set them out in a little chronology, however short that may be, and then, when you introduce the facts to the jury, set them out in a straightforward fashion, which obviously is chronologically, but not always.' Another lawyer, also uninvolved, called such a chronology 'the order of common sense'.) the temporal sequence of the case would be mirrored in the order in which the witnesses were called ('It would usually dictate the calling of witnesses, because obviously you want to unfold the story in a sensible fashion'). And examined at the very beginning, the linchpin of the routine assault case, would be the victim: 'The general rule in

---

[142] Only occasionally would that order be disrupted by e.g. the early examination of an expert witness who was deemed too busy to be kept waiting for his or her proper turn.

[143] 'Cases have beginnings, middles, and ends, while problems often do not'; Merry, *Getting Justice and Gestting Even*, 88.

any assault case is that you call the victim first . . . generally they are the person about whom it revolves and in that sense you get them in first.'

That, then, would be the structure of the case. The victim who was 'at the beginning of the story', Evans, had been sitting outside the courtroom for two hours, having arrived at 10 a.m. to wait nervously with his girlfriend until the officer in the case had come. The police officer had spent perhaps ten minutes with him: 'He told me to talk loudly. "Be careful whatever you say".' Evans had been given his statement but nothing had been said about the trial itself: 'He just said stick to your statement.' No one else had spoken to him; he had known nothing about trials and about who would ask questions; and he had been nervous and worried.

Evans was called at 12.00, to be placed under instant and continuing control by counsel: 'Speak up and throw your voice to the back of the room. Address your answers to the jury. . . . I'll take you through your evidence bit by bit. It'll be a lot easier.' From that point, he was encouraged to recount what had happened stage by stage, questioned by a counsel who did not 'lead' but who prompted each new answer, asking 'What next?' at intervals. It was his story that his girlfriend had decided to go home: 'How were you going to get home?' 'I made a 'phone call for a cab.' The taxicab was to meet the couple at a telephone booth: 'As you waited, did anything happen?' (At that point, the shorthand writer protested at the speed of the witness's delivery, and counsel said, 'Now pause, because I can see the shorthand writer's already starting to give up'.) The defendant was then said by the victim to have appeared, drunken and abusive, and he reported how he had remonstrated with him: 'I said, "go away please. I don't want no trouble".' 'Did he say anything in particular?' He said, "I'm going to stab you".' The taxicab had arrived, and it was entered by the victim's girlfriend, but Evans himself had been unable to move: 'He was swearing and holding the door.' Evans had been stabbed: 'The scar on your cheek—is that of any interest to us?' 'Yes, that was the wound, I got nine stitches.'

Evans was prompted to furnish a meticulous description both of the defendant's physical appearance (his height, colour, and complexion) and of the identity parade that had been organized: it *was* the defendant who had been pointed out to the police inspector, he affirmed. He had no doubts about the matter. Examination-in-chief had lasted for 16 minutes, having substantiated the tale told by the prosecution: an unprovoked and bloody attack had been launched by a stranger on an unwitting and unprovocative man.

Defence counsel rose at 12.21 and explored a string of alternative explanations through questions put in cross-examination, questions grounded in the defendant's own allegations about what had happened. The victim was alleged to be lying: 'Are you making some of this up as you go along?' 'No.' Evans was asked to look at his statement 'out of fairness'. Why was there an inconsistency between the statement and the testimony just given in reply to the prosecution? 'Now you say he said, "I must stab you".' 'No, he was going to stab me.' 'Now, would you like to look at your witness statement? Does it say, "He said 'I am going to cut your throat'"?' 'Yes.' ' "I remember that he said he would cut my throat." There you're telling the police that he said that early on. Why couldn't you remember that?' 'I was in pain. My memory is clear now.'

Evans was alleged to have provoked the defendant. It was alleged that he had known the defendant before and spoken to him in the wine bar: 'Did you say anything that could have been offensive?' 'No.' 'Did you say something that might have been intended to be innocuous but might have offended him?' 'No. My girlfriend was pregnant at the time. I didn't want no trouble.' 'Did you know the man? Was this an old score, an old argument?' 'No.'

Evans was alleged to have had designs on criminal injuries compensation: 'Are you having to making a claim to the CICB in this case?' 'Yes, sir.' 'Is it your view that you need to identify someone to make that claim?' 'Did you pick on the first person you saw in the identification parade?' 'No.' 'There was only one person in the ID parade who remotely resembled your description.' 'Yes.'

There was an allegation that the evidence had been coached and prefabricated: 'I suggest that you and your girlfriend discussed the evidence you were going to give in this case, and you're embellishing your tale so that the wrong man is going to be convicted and you're going to get compensation.' 'I couldn't miss him.'

The allegation was made that visual conditions had been so poor that the victim could not have seen what he claimed to have seen: 'What was the lighting like at the time of the incident?' 'Where was the street light in relation to the [telephone] box?' 'This was late at night, wasn't it?' 'This all happened pretty quickly.' 'And it was pretty dark.' 'You can only have had a fleeting glimpse at the person.' 'You're not at all sure you picked out the right man?' It was suggested that the victim had been drinking heavily and was too confused to have seen clearly. Cross-examination lasted for 19 minutes.

At 12.40, prosecution counsel undertook re-examination to repair some of the damage that might have been done. He established that the incident may have lasted for minutes, that the assailant had been within a foot of him all the while, that he had looked at the assailant continuously. Re-examination lasted for 4 minutes.

The victim declared afterwards that he had felt 'a bit bad' when questions were put, he had felt 'shame, being in public', he had been examined longer than he had expected, and he was 'shaken'. After his girlfriend had herself testified, the two left the court, not to return. They did not stay to witness the examination of the defendant, closing speeches, the summing-up, verdict, or sentence, and that was typical enough of many prosecution witnesses. They had been accused of cheating, plotting, drunkenness, vindictiveness, quarrelling, muddle, and mendacity, and it had all been undertaken as a matter of course and in a few minutes.

A unique offence, offender, and victim had been subjected to a round of formulaic defence attacks (and the prosecution would have turned to do the same to the defendant). Defence and prosecution counsel do not devise utterly new forensic methods for every trial in the Crown Court at Wood Green, Acton, Southwark, or Snaresbrook. They rely on standard stories, stories in which they may actually have little trust themselves: 'Counsel are only putting a case. You don't believe in your case. You suspend belief. You are simply a vehicle for putting a case.' The succession of diverse stories floated in the case of Evans's assault were certainly not tendered with great conviction. Yet, however wooden their delivery may have appeared to the professional and insider, they were disturbing enough to the newcomer, the witness or juror, who knew nothing of courts, and that was what made them effective. A victim in another case remarked: 'I didn't think he would be trying to make stories up . . . I was confused. He would ask me something, and then something completely different. [Some of the questions] came out of the blue. I was shocked.'

The most common defence story of all was that the prosecution and its witnesses were simply lying. One counsel remarked: 'On your instructions, they must be telling lies or that they might possibly be making a genuine mistake', and, if they *were* lying, the defence argument would follow without difficulty: one barrister said: 'The defence to an assault is usually fairly standard—it wasn't me, or he started it'[144] (it will have been noted that both had been floated in the trial of Evans's assailant). If an assault had taken place in a public house, the victim had been drunk and provocative. If it had occurred a long time ago, the victim would have forgotten what had taken place. A barrister said:

> I think it's a standard repertoire really. I mean if something happens at night and it is in a darkened street, then usually, especially or particularly if identification is an issue, then you would really start off by asking the witness to describe the lighting in the street that night, to ask him also to describe innocent things, like the clothing that hadn't been referred to.

Those routines were not always represented as mere *ad hoc* devices or concoctions. Lawyers tended to talk about them as if they mirrored the very patterns of life itself: one solicitor, discussing the preparation of defence instructions, referred to 'recurrent situations' in everyday life and another to a 'recurrence of the same type of activities' and to 'variations on the same theme'. It was as if it was not only the stories that were reiterated again and again, but the matters they described. (The legal authority, Thomas, certainly assumed that that was the case. He claimed confidently that 'the overwhelming majority of offences which come before criminal courts arise from factual situations which conform to a recurring pattern'.[145]) But the stories would have been coaxed out of defendants as statements were taken, and it may be presumed that certain stories were held to be more useful and telling than others.[146] Experienced defendants would have heard and seen what passed for an effective defence.

It will have been noted, too, that the defence in Evans's case did not sustain any one line of attack for long. On the contrary: he was manifestly 'fishing', searching for his opponent's weak points.[147] It was not his job to build a firm narrative structure himself: he was required only to undermine the prosecution's case. Many defences followed that line. They cast a wide net in their search for the one or two sources of doubt that might enter a juror's mind and bring

---

[144] To be sure, some of those defences might be perfectly sound. In many fights, the victim may be regarded merely as the one who went to the police first. M. Wolfgang observed of murder that 'it is probably only chance which results in one becoming victim and the other an offender'; *Patterns in Criminal Homicide* (Philadelphia, Univ. of Pennsylvania Press, 1958), 265.

[145] D. Thomas, *Principles of Sentencing: The Sentencing Policy of the Court of Appeal Criminal Division*, 2nd edn. (London, Heinemann, 1979), 30.

[146] See Sarat and Felstiner, 'Law and Social Relations'.

[147] See Napley, *The Technique of Persuasion*, 90.

about an acquittal. And what was also significant was that there were weak points which neither defence nor prosecution were willing to exploit: Evans had been married, and it was with his pregnant mistress that he had been making love in the park (it is not remarkable that he should have confessed to feeling ashamed); the defendant had just been released from prison after having served a sentence for another offence of violence. But these matters were not disclosed at all. In the end Evans's assailant *was* convicted, but the jury were given generous reasons to doubt if they had wished to do so.

Conclusion: The Witness as an Object in Conflict

Let me summarise. The public identity and private experience of the prosecution witness are manifestly forged in conflict. Becoming a witness at all stemmed from entanglement in a conflict or problem that led to the Court as a 'last resort'.[148] Witnesses were brought, willingly or unwillingly, to testify to the conflicts that had seen or experienced, and to relieve problems and emotions. Trials were devised to revive and sustain an old anger, fuelling it quite deliberately for purposes of interrogation and judgement.

Yet victims discovered that their role was not mirrored by any special standing in the trial. It was not properly their trial at all and they were at best 'alleged victims'. Their word was not assumed to be true. They were to be put on view so that their truthfulness and probity could be assessed publicly. They may perhaps have confronted the defendant again for the very first time since the original offence. They were attacked publicly. It was thus unremarkable that anxiety and anger welled up when situations became especially charged, when stories were being recounted (Merry argued that, because 'problems . . . are so emotional . . . people themselves are likely to get out of control, to violate the rules of appropriate behaviour in court'[149]), when the offender and victim came too near one another (one defendant burst into tears in the waiting area outside the courtroom, crying out about Victim 20, 'I know what she's like! She'll start all over again! She'll wind me up!'),[150] when statements

---

[148] See R. Emerson, 'On Last Resorts', *American Journal of Sociology*, 87(1) (July 1981).

[149] *Getting Justice and Getting Even*, 14.

[150] Occasions have arisen when prosecution witnesses have been too fearful to offer testimony. See J. English, 'The Case for Judges' Rules', *Police Review*, 30 June 1989, 1318–19; T. Shaw; '15 Months in Jail for Witness Who Refused to Testify', *Daily Telegraph*, 13 June 1989; and 'Pickles Censured for Jailing Woman', *Guardian*, 21 June 1989.

were contradicted or mocked, and when trials came to a head as defendants were discharged or sentences were delivered.

It was the adversarial system in particular that translated witnesses into objects in conflict. It was dedicated to pitting the testimony, credibility, and reputation of victims and defendants against one another.[151] Witnesses unknowingly came to be assailed in court, and to be seen and heard closely as they were assailed. They confronted a form of trial by ordeal in which their claims to knowledge and veracity were subjected to organized and sustained attack by professional adversaries. For practical purposes, it was their steadfastness in the face of a belligerent cross-examination that established the public truth or falsity of what they claimed. Dunstan argued that questions so asked could not be described as simple requests for information. To the contrary, they were produced and treated as 'accusations, counter-denials, displays of disbelief'.[152] Indeed, a dictionary of law defined the purpose of cross-examination as the discrediting of witnesses and the exposure of flaws in their stories.[153] Cross-examination was waged as if to unmask those with false pretensions to knowledge, and it worried away at any semblance of contradiction, inconsistency, deceit, and error. It played on the expressions, gestures, and demeanour that seemed to betray the cheat and the liar. Witnesses were people whose very moral status was in contention.

In their attempts to discredit an opponent's witness, there was little that counsel were not allowed to say. To be sure, *some* limits were observed. Lawyers were restrained by what they called the 'tit-for-tat' principle, a principle that dictated that, if the past convictions and other matters affecting the reputation of an opponent's witness were introduced in evidence, opponents were allowed to do the same to one's own witnesses in their turn.[154] Lawyers did not care to 'alienate the jury' by appearing to bully witnesses ('You don't want to rub the jury up the wrong way—if you have got a victim who has suffered, a sure way of getting your client convicted is to bully the victim'), although what transpired in the jurors' minds could not always be gauged, and counsel formed different opinions about their sensibilities. (Some, indeed, argued that the jury was best forgotten

---

[151] See McConville, 'Justice in the Dock', 14.

[152] R. Dunstan, 'Contexts for Coercion: Analyzing Properties of Courtroom "Questions" ', *British Journal of Law and Society*, 7(1) (Summer 1980), 64.

[153] *Harrap's Dictionary of Law and Society*.

[154] See *Archbold*, 517.

when a case was being made.) Lawyers could be reproved by judges for unintelligibility; for unseemly speech;[155] for irrelevance[156] ('Is this of any relevance? We're not discussing charges of criminal damage'); for 'wasting the court's time' ('I think the jury can form their own impressions. We're going back over old history'); and for being unduly offensive or vexatious in their questioning.[157] (Judges would tell defence counsel, 'I think that draws the line clearly enough' or 'The jury have a picture now', or ' "I think the jury have got the point. There's no point in labouring it. I think they got it five minutes ago" when they considered that allegations had become oppressive.) They might have intervened occasionally when witnesses were distressed, asking perhaps, as one judge asked, 'How are you doing? Would you like a glass of water?' But judges did *not* conceive it to be their duty generally to defend witnesses against the telling questions that could be vital to a client's case: one recorder told me: 'It's not our business to protect witnesses. That's not our business at all.' And a judge said:

I think one must realize that the defence counsel is there to defend and to press home such points as he can [but] as a matter of doing the job, he shouldn't embark on a sort of general attack, [an] unlimited attack on the character of a witness.

Judgements about what constituted an unwarranted or unlimited attack would be contingent, tending to be bound, as so much complicated legal argument is bound, by reasoning devised to contend with the complexities of the concrete case rather than by the application of general and abstract principles:[158]

It is very difficult without seeing the context. It could be quite legitimate advocacy, it could be mere timewasting, it could be being positively bloody. Much would depend on precisely what the circumstances are.

Besides, judges would not know what counsel's instructions are, and counsel are obliged to follow instructions:

I wouldn't know what the instructions are. . . . It is very unwise for a judge to wade in too quickly. A lot of these questions may be being put, and they

---

[155] In the 19th c., judges acquired the new duty to control displays of improper emotion in court. See Wiener, *Reconstructing the Criminal*, 66.

[156] See *Archbold*, 484.

[157] See Cross, *An Outline of the Law of Evidence*, 288.

[158] See K. Hawkins, 'On Legal Decision-Making', *Washington and Lee Law Review*, 43(4) (fall 1986), 1161–1242.

should be, on instructions. The instructions may be bizarre, and they may rebound on the chap who gives them, but that is his funeral.

Counsel were given great latitude within those restraints, and victims and other witnesses were very often distressed about the imputations that were made about them. As a matter of course, and in the most ordinary trial, gravely wounding allegations would be put to witnesses. I have already listed the many allegations made by the defence in the case of Evans. In yet another quite routine case of assault on a woman, doubts were cast on the victim's truthfulness ('There was no fist smashed in your face. You made it up'), her language ('You said, "Fucking go away", is that not so?'), her aggressiveness ('You raised your palm, is that right?'), her self-discipline ('You had gone berserk when he walked out on you'), her sobriety ('The position is that . . . you had a lot to drink and were extremely annoyed with him'), and her conduct ('You were making abusive phone calls to [the defendant]'). In his closing speech, the defence counsel called the alleged victim 'a spiteful, bitchy woman with a drink problem'. No lawyer with whom I discussed those imputations appeared to find the defence strategy untoward. It was, they declared, very much the standard line of argument they would have taken themselves. In effect, lawyers in London resort to the operating typifications, the 'normal crimes', described by Sudnow as part of the practical work of the criminal courts of California.[159] Witnesses are translated into routine categories and then subjected to the routine attacks that those categories warrant.[160]

There is one other sense in which witnesses were objects in conflict. Evidence was at the epicentre of the trial, and it was treated in such a way that the witnesses who delivered it became epistemological innocents who had to be shielded. Before testifying, witnesses were not to be exposed to improper knowledge. After testifying, they were not themselves to contaminate others in waiting. The undischarged witness had to be protected against the corruption that could stem from almost anyone who had business with the trial.

---

[159] See D. Sudnow, 'Normal Crimes; Sociological Features of the Penal Code', *Social Problems*, 12 (1965).

[160] R. Emerson makes very much the same point in his *Judging Delinquents*. Users are described as 'making pitches' in the courtroom which defer to the court's local interpretations and conceptions of moral order. Pitches are strategies that rely on a shorthand knowledge of the salient characteristics of the trial; *Judging Delinquents* (Chicago, Aldine, 1969).

Such a state of innocence had its dangers. Lawyers, judges, jurors, and staff kept their distance from prosecution witnesses for fear of appearing to conspire, collude, and coach. Witnesses were isolated, instructed not to talk with anyone about their evidence. I shall return to a discussion of how conflict kept them at bay in other chapters.

3. Trials and Anomie

> Radical separation from the social world or anomy constitutes . . .
> a powerful threat to the individual. He become anomic in the
> sense of becoming worldless. . . . The socially established nomos
> may thus be understood, perhaps in its most important aspect, as a
> shield against terror. The ultimate danger of . . . separation is the
> danger of meaninglessness. (P. Berger, *The Social Reality of Religion*)

The trial was an agonistic process, a process of struggle which tested
witnesses as their identities and stories were thrown hard against one
another. So abrasive could that central collision become on occasion,
so important and distinct were its consequences, that it merits one
last glance before I move on to discuss the social relations that
played around it. There are problems still to be explored, and the
best way of presenting them will be through the medium of a case
study. In this chapter I shall reassemble some of the principal events
of a single trial,[1] presenting them as the interacting parts of an emergent whole, and viewing them, like *Rashomon*, in the round. It is not
possible, desirable, or necessary to narrate everything that happened
in detail, but I shall look closely at a few events and at the questioning of two central prosecution witnesses in particular.

I had no early knowledge of the trial and I could not have selected
it in advance for study. Like Evans's case, it was not considered
memorable and, indeed, it was not very different from others. It
attracted no interest from lawyers or journalist. The staff of the
Court did not single it out for comment. And it was that very ordinariness which made its emotional pitch, pathos, and theatricality the
more remarkable.

This case study should illustrate a number of matters. It will be
my sole opportunity to provide a dense, continuous, and linked
description of a single piece of activity in the Court, and it is for that
reason that I shall reproduce some extensive passages of talk between
counsel and witnesses. In so doing, I hope to convey something of

---

[1] I was invited by a judge to sit next to him in the next trial that would be heard in
his court. In the event, I observed events as they unfolded, spoke to the principal prosecution witnesses, the judge, and defence and prosecution counsel, and examined
papers. I have changed names, dates, and events sufficently to preserve anonymity but
not so greatly as to distort the substance of the analysis.

the phenomenological texture of a routine trial for assault at Wood Green. The case study will demonstrate the choreography of the adversarial system. But, more important, perhaps, it should also show how very savage allegations can become; how the ordeal of an alleged defendant can blur into the trial of an alleged victim; how visions of the world can become so radically opposed that they seem not to meet at all; and how, in the pitting of one angry witness against another, social reality can begin to dissolve into a kind of meaninglessness, best described as anomie,[2] in which all sense and order are lost and witnesses talk instead of each others' madness.[3] That is certainly the state described by Scott and Lyman:

Confusion and a state of anomie may arise when one interactant cannot fathom any meaning from the other's behavior and thus is left in a state of diffuse anxiety and fear. Such is likely to occur when the interactants employ entirely different and mutually impenetrable universes of discourse and gesture.'[4]

That virtual collapse into the chaos of anomie took place in the trial that I shall describe in this chapter. The dispute became so transformed, and the disputants grew so apart, that witnesses no longer professed to understand one another and were reduced to expostulating about the absurdity of one another and of the trial itself. They had laced themselves, their relations, and their narratives together in ways that made the public and personal one;[5] staked valued identities and reputations; engaged in what Goffman once called aggressive acework;[6] launched images of self and action against one another in a clash of vituperation and disbelief that elicited pain, bewilderment, and anger; and became, in consequence, like the inhabitants of Babel who could no longer 'understand one another's speech' (Genesis 11: 7).

---

[2] P. McHugh treats meaninglessness and unintelligibility of purpose as characteristic of anomie; see *Defining the Situation* (Indianapolis, Bobbs-Merrill, 1968), 51–3.

[3] Such accusations are especially likely when no proper sense can be made of the other, and behaviour appears 'strange, bizarre, and frightening'; T. Scheff, *Being Mentally Ill* (London, Weidenfeld and Nicolson, 1966), 32.

[4] M. Scott and S. Lyman, 'Accounts, Deviance, and Social Order', in J. Douglas (ed.), *Deviance and Responsibility: The Social Construction of Moral Meanings* (New York, Basic Books, 1970), 97.

[5] See A. Shuman, *Storytelling Rights: The Uses of Oral and Written Texts by Urban Adolescents* (Cambridge, Cambridge Univ. Press, 1986), 25.

[6] 'By *face-work* I mean to designate the actions taken by a person to make whatever he is doing consistent with face. Face-work serves to counteract "incidents"—that is, events whose effective symbolic implications threaten face'; E. Goffman, 'On Face-Work', in *Interaction Ritual* (Harmondsworth, Penguin, 1972), 12.

Anomie was easily induced in the courtroom. However hard counsel may have tried to adduce relevant evidence about the 'facts in the case', what they were actually attempting to reconstruct was an invisible,[7] inaudible, often defunct (perhaps never extant) world outside the courtroom that could be approached only mediately and never without oral and written testimony. The courtroom, remarked Goodrich, was 'blind to the outside like an archive or a bunker, its reality [was] exclusively within'.[8] Phenomenologically, it may be said, testimony was all. It was free of the conventional sensate world in which an audience could move about independently and probe and ask questions. It was sustained chiefly by itself and its hearers' feeling for the possible, and it was inevitable that it had much that was solipsistic in consequence. The imaginations of lawyers, civilians, and jurors were the only region in which cases could be judged. And those imaginations had to be somewhat artless: John Mortimer has written about the occasional innocence of the advocates who work 'isolated in the strangely unreal world of law courts'.[9]

Advocates persuasively arguing a case could easily spin webs of meaning that attained a solid and objective enough appearance (as Bedford observed of one trial, 'The facts appeared to point in one direction. They nearly always do until one's heard another side'[10]). The speech that counsel deployed was not very different from that of the most ardent truth-teller, and it was often difficult to choose between them. *They* also used language which came before its audience to be heard and considered and, in that hearing and consideration, in a common experience of the things said, in the power of language to stimulate and to give form, the ideas described could become phenomenologically concrete themselves. Kwant once observed that it is important not to 'emphasize the bond between language and existence so much that the proper character of speech is denied'.[11] A major part of that proper character is that speech is *sui generis*: it possesses its own independent power to organize and confer meaning. Its 'opaqueness, its obstinate reference to itself, and

---

[7] It is perhaps significant that a frequent comment made by counsel about the courtrooms in the new *Palais de Justice* was that it was good to see daylight. A central shaft permitted some natural light to percolate through one frosted window in the corner of the room.

[8] P. Goodrich, *Languages of Law* (London, Weidenfeld & Nicolson, 1990).

[9] 'Playing to the Jury', *The Times*, 22 Apr. 1992.

[10] S. Bedford, *The Faces of Justice* (London, Collins, 1961), 16.

[11] R. Kwant, *Phenomenology of Language* (Pittsburgh, Duquesne Univ. Press, 1965), 32.

its turning and folding back on itself are precisely what makes it a mental power; for it in turn becomes something like a universe, and it is capable of lodging things in this universe'.[12] Language, in other words, seemed able to eclipse the subjective and the immediate by 'provid[ing] knowledge about realities which not only transcend[ed] the current experience of the individual, but also [were] practically, if not also in principle, inaccessible to him'.[13]

How was one to discriminate between an account that was truthful and a clever facsimile of the truth produced by one who may not have known whether he was, in fact, not really telling the truth? After all, the amateur truth-teller could actually be less convincing than a skilled barrister. Jurors and spectators might not have regarded the apparently authoritative professional as a deceiver, and counsel tried strenuously to seem authoritative and truthful. And lay witnesses, police officers, and defendants themselves had the strongest of motives to convince their audience. The result was that court-rooms were transformed into a kind of critical limbo in which uncer-tainties and half-beliefs abounded. The oddest stories were floated in the courtroom that *might* just have been true, and spectators, judges, jurors, and counsel had no reliable and independent means of ascer-taining whether or not they were so. A judge wrote of judges that they had 'no magic x-ray eye to decide what is true evidence and what is false—that is the jury's province'.[14] Indeed, when so much was at risk, it would have been prudent to take the odd story very seriously indeed. All hearers could do was turn to other testimony, to a direct observation of the testifiers, to their common sense, and to their general experience of the social world.[15] But a good story-teller could overcome every such check, and there remained an ineluctable and pervasive sense that the world of trials was not quite firmly anchored, that barristers worked professionally to beguile their audi-ence, that things could sometimes be other than they seemed, and that, on occasion, social reality itself was in suspense.

[12] M. Merleau-Ponty, *Signs* (Evanston, Northwestern Univ. Press, Ill. 1964), 43.

[13] A. Schutz and T. Luckmann, *The Structures of the Life-World* (London, Heinemann, 1974), 249.

[14] Letter from His Honour Lyall Wilkes to *The Times*, 22 Mar. 1991.

[15] Scott and Lyman observe that knowledge and judgment in the courtroom are formed 'under extremely onerous conditions—absence of direct observation, conflicting statements, and a situation in which the accused has a vested interest in establishing an excusable or justifying intent'; 'Accounts, Deviance and Social Order', 113.

Many disputes lurch from crisis to crisis, each lurch inducing a sense of anomie as disorder and conflict throw people's truths out of joint with one another. The most acute of all transitions can be accompanied by what Merry called 'catastrophic shifts in meaning', shifts that tend to occur when 'prolonged periods of stasis [are] followed by rapid, catastrophic change'.[16] The movement of disputes to Court could mark just such a significant transformation of conflict. It was a turning-point that made private antagonisms public, required a formal accounting to be made before strangers, and it supplied a new and graver context for the interpretation of acts, identities, and relations. Anxiety and anger could mount as the prospect of a trial loomed nearer. Merry wrote how 'the intensity of emotion at the point of confrontation was related to the long period of building tensions'.[17] That idea of a catastrophic shift in meaning captures much of the tenor of the trial that I shall describe.

The Trial of John Grey: The First Day

Preliminary Matters

The defendant, whom I shall call John Grey, had been arrested in, say, November 1988 and charged with the offences of threats to kill, criminal damage, and assault occasioning actual bodily harm on two women. He pleaded not guilty at committal proceedings in the magistrates' court and was remanded in custody. In time, he was committed for trial at the local Crown Court centre at Wood Green, it having been noted that Grey's offences were Class 4. Grey was awarded legal aid (he was unemployed and in receipt of supplementary benefit, and it was observed that he was in danger of being sentenced to prison not only because of his previous convictions but also because the alleged offence entailed the use of a weapon) and he was refused bail by the magistrates, who argued that he might commit further offences.

In March 1989, Grey's solicitors were approached by the Crown Court listing officer[18] who asked about 'the type of plea anticipated or known; how long the case is expected to last and the name of the counsel conducting the case'. The Court anticipated that the hearing would be listed within eight weeks. In that month, too, at a special

---

[16] S. Merry, *Getting Justice and Getting Even* (Chicago, Univ. of Chicago Press, 1990), 95.
[17] Ibid. 95.
[18] The exact duties and roles of all such staff will be described in the next chapter.

bail application in the Crown Court at Wood Green, Grey was released from prison because there were 'no sufficient reasons given to refuse bail'. He was told that he should not communicate with the principal prosecution witnesses or go within 100 yards of their home.

Those involved in the case were warned to attend court for a trial that was fixed for hearing on 19 July 1989 but, in the event, John Grey failed to surrender to bail and a bench warrant was issued, to be renewed and executed finally in October, John Grey being returned to prison. There followed a delay in which the imprisoned Grey tried several times to change his solicitors. His trial did not actually begin until 6 March 1990, some sixteen months after his arrest.

Prosecution evidence was based chiefly on statements taken from the two principal witnesses, whom I shall call Jane Brown and Janet Green, in November 1988, immediately before the arrest. Jane Brown's two-and-a-half page signed statement was, in effect, the narrative version of a transcribed interview. Instead of being a bald script that alternated questions and answers (a copy of which was also presented in the trial 'bundle'), it reconstructed and paraphrased the actual speech of interrogation to tell a story as if in the first person and using short, plain sentences.

Jane Brown's statement recalled how she had moved to live with her friend Janet Green in Crouch End, north London. In September, she had started seeing Grey and stayed with him intermittently. Their relationship had deteriorated within three weeks: 'He started hitting me. He used to slap me about the face if I would answer him back. After a while he was assaulting me regularly. . . . He used to become violent if I answered him back, argued with him and when I told him . . . that I was going to leave him.' Matters came to a head in November 1988, she said, when she had stayed with Grey at his flat and had been told to make his breakfast in his microwave oven. He had attacked her when she did not manage to operate the oven:

He punched me in the stomach. We argued and I told him that I did not want to go out with him any more. He picked up a knife, held me against the wall and held the knife to my throat. He then asked me again if I wanted to go out with him. Of course, out of fear, I said, yes. He then got the knife and slashed my right cheek with it. I have a cut two inches long and two other small cuts around it.

John Grey was said to have warned her that any more talk of her leaving him would lead to further woundings. He took Jane Brown back to Janet Green's flat, where she discovered that, to compound her problems, Green had left a note telling her to quit. Jane Brown packed her possessions and left to stay with her sister. Next day, she discovered that Janet Green had also been assaulted and the flat ransacked: 'As I walked into the flat, I saw that Janet had a badly bruised face and I also noticed that her telly was badly smashed.' John Grey was said to have telephoned and 'told me he would come down and kill me, Janet and Jeannette [Janet's child]. I believe that he would kill me if he ever met me again. I feel very frightened because of his size and what he has done to me in the past.' That was the core of Jane Brown's statement.

Janet Green's own statement related how she had been living alone with her daughter in Crouch End until Jane Brown had come to stay with them in January 1988. When Jane Brown and John Grey began going out together, Jane Brown 'would hardly ever stay at my flat. . . . I was aware that JOHN was beating her up. I know this from what she has said to me and from the injuries to her that I have seen. Whilst this was going on, she also began to owe me money for bills etc. and I decided that she must vacate my flat by 17 November.' Janet Green recounted how, in the evening of 14 November, she had been at home with another friend and their children when

JOHN came to the door. . . . I told JOHN that whilst he was in my flat he could take Jane's possessions with her. He went into JANE'S bedroom. . . . I went to JANE'S room. I was met at the door by JOHN, he was being aggressive. He was punching and kicking me. He told me that some of his tapes were missing. I told him that I had taken JANE'S television into my room to make sure that she paid me the money she owed. He pushed me into the front room. He pushed me on to the floor and kicked me about ten times to my head and body. He then kicked my television so hard that it completely disintegrated. He then continued beating me. [My friend] was still in the room, was holding my daughter Jeannette. JOHN pushed the two of them over on to the floor. He then went into the kitchen and came back into the room carrying a butter knife, which had a four inch blade on it. He held the knife in front of my face and said, 'I want you to dare me to use the knife, I want some blood, I will kill you with it.' He said, 'Come here.' I said, 'JOHN, don't order me about.' He then punched me very hard on my nose and dragged me into my bedroom. . . . He held the knife up and said to all of us, that if anyone moved he would kill us. Shortly after that he walked out of my flat.

There had followed telephone conversations between John Grey and Janet Green in which she had been told that 'I was dead if anything happened to JANE and he was going to get me and my child with a lot of people. I take this threat very seriously as I am sure he is capable of doing it.' That was the core of Janet Green's proof of evidence.

Two other written statements from prosecution witnesses, two from hospital casualty officers, and five from police officers were included in the bundle of committal papers prepared for counsel.

John Grey himself had been arrested on 18 November 1988 and had been interviewed by the police. He admitted having had an argument with Jane Brown but was reported to have said that the allegations about threats to kill 'were rubbish, I didn't do that'. He denied punching Jane Brown. The injuries to her cheek had been caused by his fingernail: 'I was just arguing with her and I scratched her accidentally, it was a total accident.' He had, he was reported to have said, hit her on the first occasion 'because she threw an ornament at me . . . I hit her on her arm a couple of times or so.' He had gone to Janet Green's home in Crouch End to see if Jane Brown was there but allegations about anything else would be answered in court: 'I tell the full story when I get to Court. . . . The girl is lying and I know why. I'll explain all that at the right time. . . . The right time is at the Court.'

Prosecution counsel had been instructed to act in the case at 'the last minute' and had read those statements and proofs 'over night'.

I can say I got the flavour of it. It was quite a nasty domestic violence case . . . It seemed to me, reading between the lines (you will appreciate I was just there to prosecute a case) but it was a case where the chap had really gone in very heavy on women he had no respect for at all.

The Trial

Grey's case was a 'fixture', listed simultaneously and in competition with another, lesser trial for the same courtroom at 10.15 and with several 'floaters' hunting freely for courts. Having been remanded in custody, Grey was awarded primacy in the competition for judge and courtroom (it was noted in the advance warned list issued in late January that he was in prison). Imprisoned defendants came first, but their trials often faltered and failed, and those attached to other cases lived in the muted hope that fixtures will 'go short' (through a guilty plea) or be 'ineffective' (for want of papers and people). Those matters would take time to resolve themselves, and there was always a great deal of anxious bustle before it is clear whether or not a fixture *will* start.

Trials began in a state of muddle and incomplete knowledge. (One judge observed in interview. So many different people are involved. All sorts of things can go wrong.') Counsel, police officers, solicitors' clerks, and CPS staff scurried around each morning before 10.00 to establish who had arrived in the courthouse and whether they had been successfully identified by those who sought them (many witnesses and defendants, after all, would have been known by name alone). I shall describe in Chapter 6 how the casts of different trials were to be seen at the beginning of the day struggling, like Plato's severed lovers, to come together and become 'effective'. It would not have been certain until the very last minute that every witness, police officer, counsel, defendant (and indeed, on occasion, recorder) had converged simultaneously on the courtroom as they were required to do if a trial was to proceed.

There was, in any event, the almost inevitable flurry of other matters to be dealt with before the condition of Grey's case could be inspected in the courtroom. There was unfinished business from before. The judge began at 10.22 by concluding the last few minutes of summing-up in a trial that had spilled over from the previous day. The jury from that trial retired directly at 10.26, to reappear periodically like a jack-in-the-box throughout the hearing of Grey's own case. A defendant from yet another case appeared to be sentenced and a probation officer waited in attendance. A pair of counsel from the fourth, twin trial continued to haunt the courtroom in the hope that Grey's trial would abort and that various police officers and witnesses would emerge in time to make *their* case effective.

At 10.41 a tannoyed summons was relayed around the building for all parties in the case of Grey. At that very moment, Grey himself was with his counsel in the cells in the bowels of the building, the first meeting they had had. 'How long will this take', the judge asked the prosecutor, 'if it ever gets started?' He was told by the prosecutor that two police officers were awaiting news of the private prosecution witnesses, and a CPS law clerk was dispatched to discover what had become of them; 'It's a bit late in the day, isn't it?' observed the judge. One of the barristers in the second listed case in waiting informed the judge: 'I'm in the same lamentable situation. I'm waiting for police officers. I waited outside but there is no one there.'

When his trial did open eventually at 10.47 on 19 March 1990, Grey was arraigned on five counts: two of assault on Jane Brown occasioning actual bodily harm, one of assault on Janet Green occasioning actual bodily harm, one of making a threat to kill, and one of criminal damage to Green's television; he pleaded not guilty to them all. But proceedings still could not move forward immediately. A prosecution witness had yet to appear; the police officer who had taken contemporaneous notes at the time of the incident (the 'scribe') was on compassionate leave and another officer was certified sick as a result of a bicycle accident. The judge enquired, 'Why are we all here if there's no prospect of getting on with the case? It's extremely serious to have two young women, if their account is to be believed, who have had a most distressing experience, should come and then be sent away.

Grey's own counsel, Jonathan White, was himself in a state of unreadiness. He was to tell me afterwards that he had 'got the case late the day before. I had never seen the client.' A thirty-minutes adjournment was requested, White declaring in court that he was in 'some difficulty. I've only just met Mr Grey and I've taken instructions.' There were, he explained to the judge, discrepancies between his written instructions and 'what I've just been told by my client' and he needed further clarification. He said later:

> There was a certain amount of ambiguity in the version which was on paper, but when I went through it with him he, as it were, filled in the gaps and made it make sense, so the way I was reading it was probably not quite as accurate as I would have wanted him to read it. Once he gave me the context for each paragraph, then I was okay. . . . It took me a good 45 minutes to go through the evidence he had given the solicitors so that we were all confident that I was going to represent him on the basis that he required.

Judge, prosecution, witnesses, and jury were obliged to wait. They had no choice in the matter. The judge was powerless to move the trial along: he could not forbid counsel to consult his client. He had simply to wait. One of his colleagues observed in interview: 'As a practitioner, you run around saying, "My God, we are on tomorrow, we have got to do this and this!" but as a judge you say, "If they are not bloody well ready, I am not doing it and I will come in when I am wanted".'

Whilst John Grey was being interviewed by counsel and his case was being adjourned, there was some discussion with the other counsel who were dogging the courtroom about the prospects of their own case, the second trial that had been listed for the same court-room and the same time. After all, it was still possible that an alter-native trial would have to be found if the missing witnesses rendered Grey's case 'not effective'. But a barrister in that rival trial was him-self not at all 'sure whether we can go on'.

The judge retired to chambers to discuss the confused state of the day's business with the listing officer. He was, he said, anxious to take the case of Grey because the witnesses were waiting. But, for the moment, he was offered and accepted the taking of a plea in the case of another defendant, Jones, a matter that detained him for a few minutes only. Counsel, defendant, and probation officer in Jones's case converged on the courtroom. It lasted but a new min-utes: the judge took the plea, requested a social inquiry report, and adjourned the case for four weeks.

At 11.41, all the parties in the case of Grey were called once more and they trickled back into the courtroom. One of the first to do so was the prosecution counsel, who reported that a missing police officer could attend after lunch. Defence counsel then entered the courtroom, moved to the dock, and resumed his conversation with John Grey ('Mr White, have you returned to court to take part in this trial?' he was asked).

Counsel made immediate applications. The defence was refused a request to sever the five charges on the grounds that the offences had taken place on different days and that hearing them simultaneously would be prejudicial. There was a successful application from the prosecution to release an expert witness, a doctor, whose evidence would not be contested. By 11.45, the case looked as if it might at last begin and the court clerk and the listing officer were informed that the other listed trial would have to be consigned to another court. With no little irony, it was explained to the counsel acting in the case of Grey that I was there 'to see the efficiency with which the court proceeds'.

Fifteen 'jurors in waiting' were escorted into the courtroom at 11.49 to be empanelled. Grey was told that he could object to the jurors as they were being sworn and he did, indeed, challenge the very first two. They were, he thought, familiar but he could not say why. The thirteen remaining members of the panel in waiting returned again to their retirement room whilst the two suspect jurors and Grey were quizzed by the judge about their possible connec-tions. One objection was allowed, bringing a black juror onto the otherwise all-white jury and that, thought the lawyers, had probably been its purpose. The remaining jurors in waiting returned to be sworn. One had evident difficulty in reading the oath, a matter that might have presented difficulties to a more pedantic judge and certainly in cases where a juror's literacy would be at issue, but the judge signalled to the clerk that he was content and the jury was considered sworn.

At 12.06, the indictment was read out, the jury was charged, and the trial edged forward a little. Yet, within a minute, at 12.07, the jury in the first case passed a note to the judge making it known that they sought information, and Grey's jury were told to leave once more. Their query answered, a satisfied first jury retired again at 12.15, leaving Sean Black, the prosecutor in the case of John Grey, to open. Black's was a modest, truncated account, containing the bare bones of a case that conformed to McBarnet's description of pleading as a motivated interpretation: 'It is not just edited into a minimal account—a microcosm of the incident—it is an account edited with vested interests in mind.'[19] John Grey's attacks were the product of a thoroughly trivial and unmotivated incident, Sean Black said. His opening took 10 minutes:

What I say is not evidence . . . these matters, so the Crown say, occurred some time ago. . . . Brown will say that she was assaulted, and assaulted she was, because you will see the evidence of the doctor who examined her . . . So medical evidence exists as to that first matter. . . . [There was] some trivial, so the Crown say, incident which led to an assault. . . . For no good reason, the Crown say, the defendant inflicted violence. She was seen by a doctor . . . and you won't be seeing the doctor because again this is agreed evidence.

The Examination-in-Chief of Jane Brown

Sean Black had said of his strategy, 'In a small case like that, really it dictates itself. The victims came first in the case, chronologically, and that's what I did there.' The two victims were called one by one and in the order outlined in the opening. Black proposed only to establish that they had been assaulted in the manner described in the indictment and by John Grey, the named defendant: 'I have just got to satisfy them that he assaulted them, whacked them, without any lawful . . . self-defence or whatever.' All else was immaterial.

[19] D. McBarnet, *Conviction: Law, the State and the Construction of Justice* (London, Macmillan, 1981), 17.

Jane Brown herself was the first victim in chronological order and she was called first to testify, at 12.30. John Grey began to stare hard at her as soon as she entered and he continued to do so during her entire testimony. Sean Black's questions were, in essence, a standard succession of little cues that took Jane Brown through her proof, as if line by line: 'Help us please with what you remember happening since you got up that morning', 'What happened next?', 'Where did you go?', 'When that happened, what had you done, had you said anything or done anything?' Brown's recitation of her evidence replicated much of the written statement that had been recorded some sixteen months before, and it concluded with the claim that 'he said if I ever did that again he'd cut me up some more'. She was interrupted only once by Black's request that she should 'pause there, take these matters slowly', but the judge, an adept taker of notes, remonstrated, 'It's alright, I'll tell you when I need you to slow down.'

Cross-Examination

Examination-in-chief had lasted for 18 minutes and it had confirmed a straightforward tale of a hapless woman and a bullying man. Cross-examination began at 12.48 and *that* supplied an utterly new and different frame for the reading of events, people and acts. The allegations were of course predictable and familiar to the defence and the defendant who had constructed them (although it will be recalled that there had been some anxious consultation about what was to be said and how consistent it would appear), but they must have disconcerted outsiders who had had no forewarning. They bemused the prosecution counsel: 'It did surprise me really. When you have been in this game even for a shorter time than I have, nothing surprises you, but I think it did surprise me to the extent that a lot of counsel would not have conducted the defence case in. that way. But if those are his instructions, that's what he's got to do.' Whether they really surprised the prosecution witnesses was the pivotal issue of the trial. They certainly professed great surprise. One was to say afterwards: 'He came up with such silly questions. . . . everything [Grey] told them he made up. It's all lies. He's such a good liar, I just can't believe it!' The cross-examination of prosecution witnesses in the case of John Grey may well have stirred up one of the catastrophic shifts of meaning so graphically described by Sally Merry.

The defence counsel, Jonathan White, remarked afterwards that he was obliged to follow his client's instructions 'absolutely, word for word. For example, if the client told me that the Martians landed in his back yard, I have to put that to the relevant witness.' On those instructions, the prosecution witnesses were 'pretty nasty, lying individuals [who] were hardly likely to agree with what I said if I asked them nicely'. It was for that reason, he said, that he 'was fairly robust and aggressive with the witnesses'. He was only the mouthpiece of his client:

You go into court and represent your client in a way that he would do himself were he able to do so, if he had the skills you are supposed to have. I underline the word 'supposed'. A lot of barristers won't . . . the majority of barristers won't be aggressive. What they will do is take the safest course of action because a lot of judges don't like aggressive barristers.

On his instructions, Jonathan White had been told that Grey

Had been framed by these lying jealous women. You can't walk into court and treat them like ladies and be polite to them. Within reason, you have to make it plain that this is where you stand and if you are quite nice and polite to them, it won't have any effect. People like that don't react in any way that you want them to if you are nice to them. It's as simple as that. You have to be able to fire questions at people and be able to make them think, and one of the benefits in some ways that barristers have is a quick mind, and you hope that your opponent is not as quick as you.

White began that consciously aggressive, quick, and disarming cross-examination by attempting to established the moral character of the prosecution witnesses. Jane Brown was, he alleged, sexually lax: 'You met the defendant at a tube station and within a few days you slept with him. You slept with him every night until the Wednesday.' She was shiftless, poor, and dependant. 'Are these domestic details relevant?' asked the judge and was told that, indeed, they were. Cross-examination resumed with a piece of scene-setting:

JONATHAN WHITE. Isn't it right to say you were staying more often than not with Mr Grey?
JANE BROWN. Yes.
JONATHAN WHITE. Why?
JANE BROWN. Because I'd had a bit of a tiff with Janet.
JONATHAN WHITE. Why?
JANE BROWN. Because I was behind with my rent.

Some other similar matters were considered, and then the blanket accusation, absolutely routine in cross-examination, was made that the witness was lying. It was an accusation designed not only to shock the witness, satisfy the client, and signal an attack but also to prepare the path for an alternative construction of events, a different story:

JONATHAN WHITE. Your evidence so far: 'There was a note from Janet asking me to leave her home. She did not like me being with John and I was behind with my rent.' Why was there no reference to the injury?
JUDGE. Is this all relevant? Mr White, get on with the trial.
JONATHAN WHITE. You're lying through your back teeth from beginning to end.
JUDGE. She did say she had left because she was behind with her rent. I may say Mr White that I would be grateful if you would take particular care to addresses witnesses with courtesy.

The beginnings of a different story were then presented, and their origins in White's instructions were flagged by the tell-tale word 'suggesting'. This was not White's speculative account, but Grey's, not some fishing expedition launched by White, but Grey's own explanation voiced vicariously by his professional representative:

JONATHAN WHITE. I am suggesting there was something far more serious going on between you and Janet than you have told us about. . . . Do you know what the word 'charlie' means in the vernacular?
JANE BROWN. It's the slang name for coke.
JONATHAN WHITE. Coca Cola?
JANE BROWN. Cocaine.
JONATHAN WHITE. How do you know that?
JANE BROWN. Because I read leaflets.
JONATHAN WHITE. I put it to you that you were selling cocaine for Janet.
JANE BROWN. Are you putting it to me as a fact?
JUDGE. No, counsel was following instructions and asking you whether you were covering the rent by selling cocaine.
JANE BROWN. No I wasn't.
JONATHAN WHITE. You had lost your job, and you had no money coming in, unless it was from selling cocaine which you deny.

Cross-examination broke at 1.05 for lunch, the witness being instructed by the judge not to discuss the case with anybody for fear of contamination and interference: 'I'm going to tell the CPS to tell you not to eat with anyone in the case.' She was later to be seen weeping in the company of police officers outside the courtroom. There was agreement amongst the professional insiders working in the Court that the case was 'beginning to hot up'. There was also some trepidation that testimony about cocaine-dealing might lead to police proceedings. It was thought that the witnesses should be warned to be careful about what they said. The CPS law clerk remarked that the case was complicated because the victims were vulnerable to discrediting, having convictions for perjury, and that might well be a matter raised by the defence.

At 2.07, the court returned to discuss whether directions should be given to the jury in retirement about a majority verdict and, said the judge, after four hours it was enough to recall the jury and so instruct them.

All parties in the case of Grey were recalled at 2.11, Jane Brown returned to the box at 2.14, and the defendant immediately complained that a spectator, her boyfriend, sitting in the public part of the courtroom, was menacing him. The boyfriend, it was claimed, was making gestures and leaking information to those in wait outside. Questioned, he said he knew Jane Brown but not John Grey. He was excluded to ensure that the defendant 'had a fair trial and feels that he is having a fair trial'. No professional participating in the trial believed that such menaces and leaks were occurring in earnest but it was imperative to manage matters with a scrupulous show of care. Cross-examination resumed finally at 2.21, and it combined what the prosecution called 'planting the seeds of doubt' with the continuing construction of a competing narrative. The jury were invited to regard Jane Brown and Janet Green as deceitful, conniving, drug-pushing lesbians who were not to be trusted in court and whose tendency to provoke was all too evident:

JONATHAN WHITE. Is it right you have had some lesbian relationship with your friend Janet?

JANE BROWN. No!

JONATHAN WHITE. I suggest that you gave Mr Grey that impression.

JANE BROWN. No.

JUDGE. Well, there it is, Miss Brown. You don't need to go any further.

[. . .]

JONATHAN WHITE. I put it to you that it was his idea that you go to hospital, and that when you arrived you lied about what happened.

JANE BROWN. Yes.

JONATHAN WHITE. You said a statue fell on you.

[. . .]

JONATHAN WHITE. You had a heated argument. You picked up a crystal ashtray and half-threw and half-hit him.

JANE BROWN. No!

JONATHAN WHITE. Because you're quite violent yourself, apart from being a liar.

JANE BROWN. No!

JONATHAN WHITE. And he raised his arm to restrain you and that was why you were bruised.

[. . .]

JONATHAN WHITE. You were facing being behind with the rent and received criticisms all round and being only human you overreacted.

JANE BROWN. No.

JONATHAN WHITE. You argued every day about getting a job.

JANE BROWN. No.

JUDGE. Did Mr Grey have a job at the time?

JONATHAN WHITE. And then the situation got so bad that you succumbed to temptation?

JANE BROWN. What temptation?

JONATHAN WHITE. You were offered the opportunity by your friend Janet to sell drugs, to sell cocaine, and that would have taken care of the rent.

JANE BROWN. No.

JONATHAN WHITE. But Mr Grey objected to this.

JANE BROWN. No. He objected to nothing because it was a pack of lies.

JONATHAN WHITE. The pack of lies is from your mouth.

[. . .]

JONATHAN WHITE. He said if you sold drugs, he would leave you.

JANE BROWN. No.

JONATHAN WHITE. There was a big argument between Janet and Mr Grey, because Mr Grey said you were not going to sell drugs.

JANE BROWN. No.

JONATHAN WHITE. And a grudge grew up between Janet and Mr Grey.

[. . .]

JONATHAN WHITE. . . . and there was an argument in which Janet said you ate all the food without paying.

JANE BROWN. No!

JONATHAN WHITE. . . . This so-called argument on the 14th was totally based on your lack of responsibility in life.

JANE BROWN. I wouldn't put it like that if you don't mind my saying. I get a punch in the face because I didn't know how to use the [kitchen].

[. . .]

JONATHAN WHITE. You're talking rubbish, aren't you?

[. . .]

JONATHAN WHITE. You couldn't heat up rissoles.

JANE BROWN. You don't eat rissoles for breakfast.

JONATHAN WHITE. Well I don't.

JUDGE. Well, I think we can get along without going into all this.

[. . .]

JONATHAN WHITE [*referring to Jane Brown's injury*]. You're lying from beginning to end.

JANE BROWN. That's your opinion. That's what we're here to decide.

[. . .]

JONATHAN WHITE. You had an argument about your being irresponsible. You were behind with the rent, out of a job and about to sell cocaine.

JANE BROWN. No.

JONATHAN WHITE. He said he didn't want you to have his child.

JANE BROWN. I didn't want his child. [*John Grey looks at her with something of a grimace.*]

[. . .]

JUDGE. Haven't we been through all this? Have we to go through it all again?

JONATHAN WHITE. The fact of the matter is that the defendant was concerned for your welfare?

JANE BROWN. After he threatened to kill me, he was concerned about my welfare!

[. . .]

JONATHAN WHITE. Janet alleged that you'd take her cocaine.

Police officers, members of the 'law and order unit',[20] entered and sat at the back of the court, having been given prior warning that the jury in the parallel trial had agreed on a verdict and that it would be useful to 'show uniform' as staff put it, the time of sentencing always being especially heated. At 2.49, the jury in retirement did indeed send a note to the judge and Jane Brown, still in the box, asked whether she could sit down. As she did so, she mouthed 'Liar' obviously and theatrically to John Grey, who was conversing with his solicitor. At 2.55, a majority verdict was announced and the cast of the earlier trial reconvened: the defendant, counsel, a probation officer, and a police 'antecedents' officer all trooping in to displace the members of Grey's trial. At 3.07, Grey was released until the morrow. The rest of the judicial day was given over to sentencing the defendants in the parallel trial amidst visible distress, reproaches, and tears in the public gallery.

The Trial of John Grey: The Second Day

At about 10.20, at the beginning of the second day, the participants in Grey's trial were scattered about the courthouse, waiting for the trial to resume, within distance of the courtroom but at a wary

---

[20] For more detail see the discussion of the police presence in court in Ch. 4 below.

remove from one another. Jane Brown was on her own, no one speaking of her or coming near here, a witness isolated and unapproachable in the middle of examination, a woman in purdah. Janet Green sat with a police officer in one small anteroom. The defence counsel, Jonathan White, waited alone in another. A CPS law clerk and prosecution counsel conferred in the hall. Staff gossiped about the case, and it was evident that the prosecution witness had earned some sympathy. One probation officer said that the defence counsel was 'notorious for his rudeness. He's been even ruder in other courts. He's notorious.' Another remarked that allegations about the witnesses' lesbianism were 'purely malicious and gratuitous. It's clear that his client is malicious and that the defence should exercise his professional discretion in putting those points.' The judge himself could do 'nothing except listen to the points made'.

The trial resumed at 10.43 after the hearing of a bail application. At 10.45 the jury entered, Jane Brown was recalled and cross-examination resumed and ended within a minute. Brown was released after perfunctory re-examination at 10.48, asking whether she could stay in court and being allowed by the judge to do so.

The Examination-in-Chief of Janet Green

At 10.50, Janet Green was called and sworn. The opening questions of examination-in-chief centred on her relations and quarrel with Jane Brown, forming an invitation to recite the 'bare facts of the case' as the prosecution saw them. Although she spoke quietly, Sean Black did not ask her to talk more loudly, and it was the judge who ascertained that jurors were having difficulty hearing her: 'Would you speak up so that those ladies and gentlemen under the clock hear you?'

Examination-in-chief turned to the day of the assault. It took Janet Green little by little through her proof of evidence:

SEAN BLACK. Were you at home?
JANET GREEN. Yes, I was.
SEAN BLACK. Did someone arrive at your property?
JANET GREEN. John Grey did.
[. . .]
SEAN BLACK. Going into Jane's bedroom, what happened?
JANET GREEN. I felt John's hand on my face.
SEAN BLACK. What did he do?
JANET GREEN. He grabbed me. Punched me. Hit me with his foot and his fists.

[. . .]

SEAN BLACK. After that, what did he do?

JANET GREEN. He continuously beat me up with his fists. Bumped me on my
nose. [*The defendant stares hard at her all the while.*]

[. . .]

SEAN BLACK. Did John have anything in his hand?

JANET GREEN. A butter knife. He held it to my face and said, 'I dare you to
tell me to use it. I want some of your blood.'

[*Jane Brown in the gallery whispers a melodramatic 'He's mad' and looks sternly at Grey.*]

[. . .]

SEAN BLACK. What state were you in at that time?

JANET GREEN. I was in pieces. I was physically . . . Two black eyes. Fractured
nose. Scars to my left and right shoulder.

SEAN BLACK. I think you went to hospital.

JANET GREEN. Yes, that's right.

[. . .]

JANET GREEN. He said if anything happened to Jane, he's going to kill Jane
and my daughter.

It was then that Black decided to turn to the difficult problem of
the uncertain creditability of his own witness. Black proposed to
introduce the defendant's history of convictions for attacks on women
but, under the 'tit-for-tat' rule, his own witness's conviction for perjury would almost certainly be disclosed by the defence in retaliation.
And, indeed, White certainly intended to allude to that conviction
himself. An opponent's conviction for perjury was too valuable to
forego. He had consulted Grey on the matter and secured his agreement ('Oh yes, he knew the situation. I told him what would happen'):

We challenged their credibility . . . obviously if one has been found guilty of
perjury in the past that's material. Clearly material when she said, even
though she was there to lie, she agreed she was lying . . . it was all relevant
to our case at the time. It was even more relevant because I knew my
client's previous convictions would be introduced . . . The tit-for-tat rule, as
the court described it. If you impugn a character via prosecution witnesses,
as it were, then your own character is at risk.

It was thus that Black planned a pre-emptive attack. He would be
the first to reveal Green's past and work to neutralize its power completely to discredit her. He told me later:

I had to. It would have come in, in that case. His previous convictions were
going to go in, so I'm afraid the prosecution witness has no protection under

the law. . . . I take the view that it really takes the sting out of the defence point. It's got a double edge. I think your Crown's case is stronger if it is dealt with by the Crown advocate before . . .

So it was that Sean Black asked Janet Green, his own witness, publicly in court about her convictions. She herself could not have known that such a question was coming. She had not been briefed ` by counsel or police. On the contrary: any such briefing would have been grossly unprofessional, perhaps enough to abort the trial. She said later that she had been unprepared and upset. Her earlier convictions were, she thought, remote and forgotten, no longer at issue. She was a different woman. The police, she said,

Gave me my statement to read and they wouldn't tell me what [Grey] had been charged with apart from ABH, and they didn't tell me that my previous convictions were going to be brought up. I fail to see the relevancy to this case. I'm not ashamed of it. It's something that happened years ago. I had my reasons for it. . . . That was eighty-two, eighty-three, seven or eight years ago, and in that time I've worked, I've got my own flat, kids. You know. I am very independent.

Examination-in-chief proceeded thus:

SEAN BLACK. I have to put this to you for completeness. You have appeared in court before, with two convictions.
JANET GREEN. That's right.
SEAN BLACK. You have an offence of perjury in which you gave a false alibi for a defendant in a rape trial.
JANET GREEN. Yes.
SEAN BLACK. Who was that defendant?
JANET GREEN. He was my ex-boyfriend.
SEAN BLACK. And you were put on probation for two years. More recently, for an offence of theft, you were fined £40 and ordered to pay costs. . . .
[. . .]
SEAN BLACK. The offence of perjury is lying on oath. Have you lied this morning?
JANET GREEN. No. I have not.

The Cross-Examination of Janet Green

Cross-examination began at 12.18 and it was experienced as an assault, Jane Green feeling that 'I knew that they were trying to break me down. It was like a dream. I wasn't expecting this from John Grey!' Her earlier conviction for perjury was introduced immediately, just as Black had foretold:

JONATHAN WHITE. If you had been asked in 1985 were you telling lies what would you have said?

JANET GREEN. I would have said, 'Yes, I was.'

JONATHAN WHITE. Oh I see, if you went to speak on behalf of the defendant.

JANET GREEN. I was scared and beaten up by my boyfriend.

JONATHAN WHITE. I see.

[*He was, he said, 'cross-examining up hill and, down dale, trying to work it all out' at this point. He had improvised as he had gone on, trying to discover telling points. 'For example, the point about her moving out so quickly . . . the one about Jane moves out of Janet's flat without even finding out whether or not she could stay longer, even though she's given three days to move, and even though she should have been given a minimum of four weeks, that arose almost out of nowhere. It wasn't suggested to me by the client. It was something that became apparent as we went through the evidence. At the time it fitted in with what he said. It came from nowhere.'*]

JONATHAN WHITE. You left a note for Jane. She had fallen behind with her rent. You stood in relation to her as a landlady. Are you aware that the minimum notice you have to give someone of eviction is 4 weeks? Is that something you are aware of?

JANET GREEN. No.

[*John Grey stares hard at her. Janet Green said later, 'It made me much stronger because, although he was staring at me, it was like he was trying to look at me or make me break down with his feelings. But I couldn't because after what he had done to me with his fists, his hands, and his foot, it didn't make any difference.'*]

White then resorted for a while to the routine allegation, made in almost every piece of cross-examination, that the witness was lying.

JONATHAN WHITE. You're not telling the truth, are you?

[. . .]

JONATHAN WHITE. I'm going to put this to you quite clearly, Miss Green. You are lying from beginning to end?

JANET GREEN. No, I'm not lying.

[*She was to say later, 'He's got forty or fifty convictions and he's trying to make out I'm the bad character because I've got a conviction for perjury!'*]

JONATHAN WHITE. Let's go back to the beginning. Were you quite close friends with Jane Brown? Were you like sisters?

JANET GREEN. More like cousins.

JONATHAN WHITE. Was there ever any sexual relationship between you and Jane Brown?

JANET GREEN. Not when I have a two-year-old child and I was four-and-a-half months pregnant.'

[*She remarked later, 'They were talking about lesbians but it's very obvious, to put it plainly, what turns me on and it's not a woman! I have got a kid of two and I'm four-and-a-half months pregnant!'*]

JUDGE. Is this relevant? Can we move on?

JONATHAN WHITE. Well, your honour, it is relevant.

JUDGE. Well, move on to something else.

JONATHAN WHITE. Have you ever had a relationship with Mr Grey?

JANET GREEN. Me? A relationship?

JONATHAN WHITE. Because you accused Mr Grey of using you.

JANET GREEN. God, where do you get these questions from?

JUDGE. I'll tell you where he gets these questions from. The instructions of his client. He is obliged to put them if he asks them courteously. So if you would just answer 'Yes' or 'No'.

[. . .]

JONATHAN WHITE. There came a point when Jane Brown no longer worked as a care assistant. Why?

JANET GREEN. Jane Brown was being beaten up.

JONATHAN WHITE. Every day? All of the time?

[. . .]

JUDGE to JONATHAN WHITE. Just listen to the answer, Mr White.

[*It may have been observed that the judge, intervened on a number of occasions, and particularly when the moral character of witnesses was being scrutinized at length. Both Jonathan White and Janet Green subsequently called the judge 'very fair'. Janet Green remarked, 'I've got no complaints about him.' White himself observed, 'I must say that the judge handled every point admirably. There's no question about it. I know he interrupted but judges do that on a regular basis. It's really a question of communication between the judiciary and the bar. It's right that judges have to control what goes on in their courts, and quite properly most of the time they do so.'*]

JONATHAN WHITE. What you're saying is a pack of lies, in all fairness, isn't it?

JANET GREEN. No, it's not.

JONATHAN WHITE. The fact of the matter is that you'd reached an agreement with your friend, Jane Brown, that she would go out and sell some charlie.

JANET GREEN. Charlie!

[*She laughs. Sean Black believed that such incredulous laughter actually enhanced Green's credibility: 'I thought that she dealt with it well enough herself, really. Just laugh, she really did laugh.'*]

JONATHAN WHITE. Laugh a bit more! Let's have some acting!

JONATHAN WHITE. You were approached by the defendant that you had asked Jane Brown to sell drugs for you and he didn't want you to do that.

[*Janet Green asked later, 'What woman with a two-year-old kid, logically, and four-and-a-half months pregnant, logically, what woman is going to be on cocaine!? It doesn't really make sense!'*]

[*It was at that point that Jane Brown stormed out of the public part of the courtroom, shouting when the allegations were made that Grey was going to rescue her from selling cocaine: 'Lying, lying, he's mad!' The judge told a police officer to make sure that she did not speak to anyone else.*]

JANET GREEN. No. No.

JONATHAN WHITE. That's why Jane left so promptly before even seeing you on the 14th.

JANET GREEN. No.

JONATHAN WHITE. Let's examine what you say happened in relation to this alleged attack . . . He grabs you by what?

JANET GREEN. The neck.

JONATHAN WHITE. I see. Then what . . .

[. . .]

JONATHAN WHITE. Was he kicking you hard?

[. . .]

JONATHAN WHITE. I see. How many times?

[. . .]

JONATHAN WHITE. . . . Why is it, then, that your chest, abdomen and neck were all normal in examination?

JANET GREEN. I don't know. All I know is that I had kicks on my head and stomach.

JONATHAN WHITE. You were exaggerating. You were seen by a doctor . . . I want to put this very gently to you, you are lying about the extent and nature of your injuries.

JANET GREEN. No. I'm not lying.

JONATHAN WHITE. And you're also lying about who caused those injuries.

[. . .]

JONATHAN WHITE. So who else caused this attack?

[. . .]

JONATHAN WHITE. Your honour, my client did not cause these injuries. Your honour, I'm closing very quickly to the point.

JUDGE: I'm glad to hear it.

[. . .]

JONATHAN WHITE. And then it was said that Jane is going to be kidnapped. And Mr Grey said nothing better to her.

JANET GREEN. No. No.

JONATHAN WHITE. And then there was a telephone call to Mr Grey to say, 'We've got Jane.

Cross-examination ended at 11.41. There was but one minute's re-examination. Green then joined Brown to sit in the public part of the courtroom where they offered a continual commentary, audible and inaudible, on the remainder of the trial. In particular, they laughed incredulously and noisily as Grey himself gave evidence: Green said later, 'Everything he told them he made up. It's all lies. He's just such a good liar, I just can't believe it. That's why I had to laugh. I just couldn't believe it. I thought, this can't be real.' The judge was obliged to instruct the two to sit where they would not be visible to the jury. Their reactions were distracting, he said. Sean

Black was himself displeased by the laughter and by Brown and Green's English counterpart to a Greek wailing. Their misbehaviour may well have prejudiced the jury: 'the reason why he was acquitted [on some counts] was that they didn't conduct themselves very well after they were released, sitting there . . . I sent the officer over to one to say I think they might as well get out.'

John Grey's Testimony

I do not propose to relay the rest of the examination of the other prosecution witnesses, although it should be noted that they were punctuated by loud expostulations from the defendant and the two chief prosecution witnesses, who sat in court all the while. It would, however, be useful to recapitulate some of John Grey's own testimony, because that will not only give a balance to the prosecution case but show how trials can pitch one story against another. Grey was called at 12.52, and the dock officer sat near him as if to signal his dangerousness. White, his own counsel, began by examining Grey's character, reading his 'antecedents' aloud and attempting to neutralize their import:

JONATHAN WHITE. Preliminary points—you are not a man of previous good character; you left school without qualifications, and then you began a career of criminality.

JOHN GREY. That's correct.

JONATHAN WHITE. 15.4.82—juvenile court for theft. Did you plead guilty or not guilty?

JOHN GREY. Guilty.

JONATHAN WHITE. Stole a handbag in Brixton. ABH. 'Will you tell the jury whether you pleaded guilty or not guilty?

JOHN GREY. Guilty.

JONATHAN WHITE. Will you tell the court what you did?

And so it went on, White reciting Grey's previous convictions one by one and catechizing Grey about how he had pleaded:

JONATHAN WHITE. So to every offence there listed except the one in . . . you pleaded guilty. And in relation to the present matter, you plead?

JOHN GREY. Not guilty.

The Court resumed at 2.10 and defence counsel examined Grey about his relationship with Jane Brown. He quite visibly followed Grey's written statement as he did so, and the judge followed it too. Grey emerged as a man concerned about a slattern's moral and economic welfare:

JONATHAN WHITE. About her falling behind with rent, what did you say to her?

JOHN GREY. I said that she should do something about it, go for a job or income support.

The first alleged assault, it was to appear, was no assault at all but an innocent attempt to ward off Brown's own angry and unreasonable attack on him, an attack prompted by his remonstrations:

JOHN GREY. I had an argument with her, just about her laying about, not doing nothing really . . . I can't remember the exact words she said, but I said she was irresponsible. She was lazy. She tried to throw the ashtray at me and I tried to defend myself by punching her arm away.

JONATHAN WHITE. Would you agree that you did strike her arm. Why did you strike her arm?

JOHN GREY. Because I tried to block the ashtray.

[. . .]

JONATHAN WHITE. Did you ever argue with her about not making money for herself?

JOHN GREY. Yes, of course. I thought she could do much more for herself. She wanted to stay in bed all day and have intercourse and
. . .

JOHN GREY. She got a note from Janet saying she would have to start doing some work for her next Monday. And the work was selling charlie for her. . . . I said if she does it, then that's it, it's finished between the two of us. So she went and told Janet that she wasn't going to do it at all.

John Grey was actually a latter-day Gladstone who had been trying to rescue Jane Brown from a moral fall into drug-pushing:

JONATHAN WHITE. You at this point were threatening to leave Janet if she started selling cocaine. You went around and started taking your clothes from Janet's place.

JOHN GREY. Yeah.

[. . .]

JONATHAN WHITE. How did Jane feel about you?

JOHN GREY. She loved me.

Grey was depicted as an attractive man who did not have such a desperate need for any one woman that he would use violence to retain her.

JONATHAN WHITE. Were you so infatuated with her that you would threaten her with a knife if she wanted to leave you?

JOHN GREY. Nah. Nah.

JONATHAN WHITE. It's been suggested that when she said she wanted to leave, you became very angry and threatened her with a knife.

JOHN GREY. No, definitely not. . . . there was an argument. I put my hand around her chin. She pulls her face away and there was a scratch, a little graze.

JONATHAN WHITE. Did you have sharp nails? [*Grey shows his nails to the jury.*]

JONATHAN WHITE. How did she react?

JOHN GREY. She didn't go crazy. She just said, 'You bastard' or something like that.

John Grey was something of a Lothario who had slept with many women, with Janet Green as well as with Jane Brown:

JONATHAN WHITE. It's alleged that you kicked and punched Janet several times about the body and that you destroyed a television in her flat.

JOHN GREY. That is total rubbish and she knows that it is total rubbish.

On the day after the alleged assault on Brown, Grey asserted, he had received a 'very threatening' telephone call from Janet Green and two men, one of whom said that he would come down and take the 'coke': that other boy said, 'We've got your girl here anyway, you'd better come, anyway' and she came to the phone and said, 'You'd better come up anyway.' But John Grey was one who could look after his own:

JONATHAN WHITE. In response to these threats, what did you say?

JOHN GREY. I tried to make them think twice. They said they were coming down to out me, my mother and sister. I said if they do it, like an eye for an eye, I know where they live.

Examination-in-chief ended at 2.50 and cross-examination began with the task of recasting the defendant's moral character yet again. Grey was not really a kindly moral guardian at all but a shiftless, criminal ne'er-do-well who preyed violently on weaker women.

SEAN BLACK. What work do you do?

JOHN GREY. I did some labouring, I was a DJ.

SEAN BLACK. What was the longest you've ever had a job?

JOHN GREY. About six months.

[. . .]

SEAN BLACK. You've got fifteen convictions for dishonesty-related offences and six convictions for theft from the person.

JOHN GREY. Yeah.

SEAN BLACK. Always from women victims.

JOHN GREY. Yeah, they were.

SEAN BLACK. If I was to suggest that suggests you have no respect for women, what would you say?

JOHN GREY. I wouldn't go around hitting them.

[. . .]

SEAN BLACK. How tall are you?

JOHN GREY. About six foot one.

SEAN BLACK. You're quite a fit young man.

[. . .]

SEAN BLACK. You told Jane Brown that she wasn't doing anything too constructive with her life.

JOHN GREY. Yeah.

SEAN BLACK. Would you say you were doing anything constructive with your life?

[. . .]

SEAN BLACK. You took her to hospital.

JOHN GREY. Yeah.

SEAN BLACK. Feeling guilty about the injury?

[. . .]

SEAN BLACK. There was no ashtray incident. That was mere invention on your part.

JOHN GREY. I blocked it.

SEAN BLACK. In fairness to you, I draw your attention to page 5 of the interview—'I hit her on her arm a couple of times or so.' How many times did you hit her?

JOHN GREY. Once.

SEAN BLACK. It says a couple of times or so.

Black then resorted to the expedient of all cross-examiners, the 'slamming' that Mazengarb had described. Black repeatedly and angrily accused John Grey of lying. It may not have advanced the jury's understanding of the case but it did attempt to unhinge the defendant, it created a certain theatrical urgency, and it served as a catharsis for Black himself. At that point, Black had lost some of his moral distance from the case and he was quite genuinely annoyed: 'I can't remember what I said, 'pack of lies' or 'balderdash', whatever it was, but I thought he really had sold us a pack of nonsense, lies, and I was getting a bit irritable by then, and I wasn't going to go through his whole account.'

SEAN BLACK. I'm not going to dwell on the cocaine aspect of the case. I suggest it's all hogwash and beside the point.

[*Black was to dismiss the allegations of drug-pushing as a mere 'smoke-screen' that was a distraction to the main thrust of the case. He took it that the judge did not really wish him to pursue them: 'I know the areas the judge want[ed] me to put and that wasn't one . . . it was wholly irrelevant.'*]

JUDGE. I do wish you wouldn't use offensive language of this kind. We all know what hogwash is but it might affect sensitive witnesses . . . and it raises the temperature of the court unnecessarily. I did raise the matter with Mr White . . . you meant he was telling lies, a pack of lies.

SEAN BLACK. . . . she says you punched her in the stomach.

JOHN GREY. I never punched her at all.

[. . .]

SEAN BLACK. It's at that point you picked up the knife.

JOHN GREY. Over her leaving me? She's not the only woman in the world.

[. . .]

SEAN BLACK. Can I suggest to you that you did it because you have a short temper?'

[. . .]

SEAN BLACK. I'm putting it to you that you put a knife to her face.

JOHN GREY. It was a scratch. Just a scratch! I do wish you had a doctor's evidence.

SEAN BLACK. And you say it was an accident with an overgrown fingernail?

JOHN GREY. I put my hand on her face and she turned away quickly and that is how the scratch occurred.

[. . .]

SEAN BLACK. Got a clear recollection of that visit that afternoon? Can you remember it clearly?

JOHN GREY. I'll try.

Black and Grey became embroiled in something of a pantomimical altercation in which allegations and denials were traded back and forth, Black insisting on the accuracy of his allegations and Grey as adamantly denying them. Many episodes of cross-examination degenerate into just such an exchange of 'oh yes, you dids', 'oh no, I didn'ts', without making discernible progress. Grey certainly conceded nothing. But the repeated making of impassioned points might have impressed jurors that the prosecution, too, was trying to do its job and that it had its own fervent conviction in the truth. And some allegations might have lodged themselves in the jury's minds.

SEAN BLACK. You see, I put it to you it's all lies. It never happened in the way you said.

[. . .]

JOHN GREY. Why should I assault Janet Green?

SEAN BLACK. 'I'm not here to answer your questions, sir.

[. . .]

SEAN BLACK. Kicking. Remember kicking her?

JOHN GREY. No. I didn't touch her.

SEAN BLACK. Punches. There were punches as well.

JOHN GREY. No.

[. . .]

SEAN BLACK. Can I tell you that you were not telling the truth about that and remind you that you destroyed the television as well.

JOHN GREY. Most definitely not. I never did that.

SEAN BLACK. It's not right to say that you slept with Janet Green.

JOHN GREY. Why should I lie about that?

[. . .]

SEAN BLACK. Can I suggest you were brandishing the knife in the way that you've heard?

JOHN GREY. Why should I do that?

[. . .]

SEAN BLACK. Can I suggest to you that you're a very violent man?

JOHN GREY. Most definitely not. I did put my hand to her face but it was no more than that.

[. . .]

SEAN BLACK. These girls made these complaints because you did behave violently in the way that you've heard.

JOHN GREY. They're . . . one hundred per cent liars, one thousand per cent.

Cross-examination ended at 3.20. The judge concluded that it had been all rather muddled. Black should not have asked repeated and probably fruitless questions about whether what Grey had said was a pack of lies but should have gone straight to the story about the cocaine. The defendant was an arrogant young man and it would have been a simple piece of cross-examination. There had been a weak prosecution and a rude defence. A lot of gratuitous mud had been thrown.

In his closing speech, Sean Black observed to the jury: 'You have to decide questions of fact about the rather sorry state of affairs that took place in this flat . . . Where you have witnesses who give such different accounts, I suggest to you there are ways of judging what they say. One is to look at things that are not challenged.' And he continued by alluding chiefly to the undisputed medical evidence about the injuries sustained by the victims. That could not be doubted, he said. Indeed, the defence had not challenged it.

Jonathan White himself concluded:

At the end of the day, it's a fairly simple matter . . . it's the Crown that brings this case and it's the Crown that must prove this case. . . . You have to say to yourselves, what facts can I be sure of . . . Is it true to say that what the doctors saw amounts to the evidence'. I have to say it does not. The physical evidence given by doctors does not square with what the witnesses said. I suggest that these young ladies had ample reasons to lie. You may think Mr Grey had ample reasons to prevent Miss Brown selling drugs. And knives. There seem to have been a lot of knives. One against her throat and another to the cheek. He seems to have been knife-happy. It's a bit hard to believe, isn't it? These allegations framed in this indictment are only words. Allegations made by people are very easy to make but difficult to disprove.

The judge's summing-up began at 4.02 and continued to the next day:

I'm only going to give you a very brief summary of the evidence because you've all been sitting there and it's been a very brief case. In this case, both sides are saying the other is lying from beginning to end. Witnesses come before juries not only so that the jury can hear the evidence but so that the jury can see them, sum them up, assess them, and you're asked to bring that skill into the jury box. . . . The first witness was Jane Brown, the victim, the alleged victim, in counts 1 and 2. What you think of her is very important to the case. She says one thing. The defendant says another. You have to make up your mind to see whether what she says is true . . . The defence says it's all part of a hate campaign arising out of this mysterious background of cocaine and so on . . . Jane Brown said that she was at his mum's house, she spent the night there, they argued, she answered back and he didn't like that and he punched her. . . . She was cross-examined about the matter and said that was how it had happened . . . You may think that the argument is absurd because she continued to stay with him because of the way people in such relationships behave. . . . The defendant says, 'We had an argument, she was [*reading his notes*] laying about, she was hanging about all day . . . I got heated and said she was irresponsible and lazy, she had an ashtray and I punched her arm out of the way . . .' So there we are, we have the defence saying that she had an ashtray and he punched her arm out of the way. Well, members of the jury, you have to consider whether that was the truth of the matter . . .
You will recall no doubt the sight of Miss Brown in the witness-box, you will recall the sight of Mr Grey in the witness-box. No doubt small women do sometimes hit big men . . . Was it reasonable for a man to hit her more than once? Was it reasonable self-defence? That in itself could be a basis of a conviction of assault. . . . Now you see you've got to look back on what was happening and bear in mind the nature of the feelings people had at the time . . . It was put to Miss Brown it was all nonsense. Nothing of the sort happened . . . You have to ask yourself what you think of the two stories. You have to ask yourself what you make of Miss Brown's account of the

matter. And here we come to the general background of the matter. One has the disagreeable accusation that she is a lesbian, of drug-trafficking, that she is a layabout, of sexual promiscuity, of not paying her fair share, and matters of that sort. It is important to remember, members of the jury, that questions are not evidence. Evidence is given by witnesses. Evidence is what is said in reply. The fact that the question's been asked doesn't mean that it's true. And you have to bear that in mind when questions are thrown about pretty freely. . . . You may remember the extraordinarily self-righteous questions, if I may say so, that were put on behalf of the defendant . . . No doubt she was a layabout. People of that age often are. But what that has to do with the events in question is another matter . . . She said, 'It was not true I sold cocaine for Janet'.

And that raises the whole matter of cocaine. It is part of the defendant's case that Janet Green was proposing to go into the cocaine business and was going to recruit Jane Brown . . . There again, members of the jury, you have to weigh these matters up. Because it was, after all, these young women who went to the police. It was not the defendant who went to the police to say these dreadful matters are going on. Do you think these women would go to the police and invite the police to investigate what's going on? . . . The mere fact that a person is telling lies does not mean that he is guilty of the offences with which he is charged. . . . You have also to consider whether Miss Brown has exaggerated the extent of her injuries . . . The fact that the victim knew what 'charlie' meant did not mean that she was involved in selling it—a lot of people in the court know the meaning of that word. No doubt counsel does. It was alleged she was not a woman of good report. She had been guilty of perjury in an earlier . . . but she said when she gave evidence in this court she was not telling lies. The fact that someone was guilty of crime is relevant to your view of them, but it is not realistic and fair to say that if they have previous convictions, they must be telling lies now . . . she said, 'It was quite untrue I had a lesbian relation with Miss Brown, quite untrue that I had sex with Grey. . . . My belly was bruised and swollen.' And that is something the defence draws your attention to because there is no medical evidence about swelling. . . . Hostage-taking . . . sadly, those things may well go on, ladies and gentlemen of the jury, but does the person who complains about hostage-taking go to the police to complain about the assault? 'And why', he said, 'if I wasn't involved with her, should I threaten her if she said she would leave me' . . .

Antecedents—remember this, will you, you mustn't use details of a person's convictions to say, 'Well, he's got a lot of convictions so he must be guilty' . . . this is put before you to enable you to assess the character and his believed ability, about boy scout talk of pulling your socks up and irresponsibility and things of that sort . . .

Summing-up ended at mid-day on the third day of the trial. The jury returned at 2.45 with guilty verdicts on counts 3 (the assault on Janet Green) and 4 (damage to property), and not guilty on counts 1, 2, and 5. Grey was sentenced to nine months for assault and three months for damage, the sentences to run concurrently.

Strategies and Styles

There was much commonality between the two barristers' experience of the trial. Both had received their cases, in their own words, 'at the last minute'. Both had known nothing and had seen nothing of the central figures in the case before they encountered them in the courthouse on the day of the trial itself. They had to form rudimentary, second-hand impressions of actors and actions, based on working typifications and stocks of professional knowledge that framed the interpretation of statements and instructions. (The prosecutor, for example, remarked, 'I live five minutes from where it all happened. I live in Muswell Hill . . . so I know the road where they all live.') They made very rapid readings of their bundles, resolving a line of argument to pursue as they appeared in the trial the following day, and some of that line was formulated *in situ*, the questioning being, as defence counsel put it, 'up hill and down dale'. They were both unable to correct or investigate the anomalies and imperfections of their bundles: the prosecutor was dissatisfied with the state of the medical evidence ('there are inconsistencies in the medical evidence . . . but you always get these points: someone says "I was hit here" and there is no mark'), and the defence was concerned that Grey was so dismissive of everything that had been said ('I was a bit worried that he was rubbishing everything that had ever been written that he was supposed to have said and done, and I was beginning to wonder whether or not I was going to be embarrassed professionally'). They both professed to be quite neutral in their stance towards the central conflict of the case and the protagonists who had animated it (the defence counsel said, 'My own personal judgment was totally irrelevant'), but anger had evidently been unleashed at certain points, and particularly when witnesses refused to budge from what counsel believed were absurd positions.

Both counsel were a little wary of 'their' own witnesses, and both were a little uncertain about exactly what *had* transpired between them all. The prosecutor remarked, 'In that case, there may have been something, knowing what goes on in that neck of the woods . . . They were young girls and I wondered what they were up to, those girls. I'm sure they are no strangers to criminal activity, and I thought it might be more to do with street life than drug-dealing.'

The defence was not so much concerned with the truthfulness of the account he had to tender but with its consistency and resilience in court: 'The only rule is that you have to be able to convey a logical argument, one put to you by way of instructions from your client. That's all there is to it.' His duty was to 'represent [my] client's interest, and obviously you bear in mind the words he's used to describe what happened. You make sure you convey the meaning he has conveyed to you, but you also do it with a style acceptable to the jury that's not going to put you in so much trouble with the judge that you end up being reported to the Bar Council.'

Keith Hawkins proposed that legal reasoning is given order by 'decision frames' that are 'the means by which meaning and relevance are given to information, for information as such does not automatically prompt a particular decision, and it involves organizing, selecting, and omitting "facts"—as well, of course, as interpreting them.'[21] It was in that sense that both lawyers gave a frame to their selection, interpretation and presentation of the materials they were to put to the jury.

The Prosecutor

The prosecutor, Sean Black, had understood the case to be a simple, unpleasant piece of domestic violence. His instructions had been thin: 'They had consisted of statements, really very few. That's the proof, I don't have a word statement from the victim. I just have their statement.' But he 'did get the feel of the case really. A case like that, you wouldn't get . . . I can't even remember what sort of notice I had about it. I certainly wouldn't have known anything about it before the day before. It wasn't one of my own cases, like some cases I have prosecuted, I get in weeks before hand so I can look at it.' It had been 'a very straightforward case from a prosecution point of view . . . a case where the chap had given a right good hiding to women he had no respect for at all.' He had been hampered in demonstrating the injuries to Brown and Green because, although he had seen photographs taken immediately after the event, they 'weren't in an admissible form; I didn't have the person who had taken them, and I didn't have a statement from them'. Having received the papers only hours before the case was to begin, it being 'a last-minute case', he could not do much to rectify the problem, and 'the case was made very much weaker by the state of medical evidence'. The poverty of the medical evidence probably accounted for Grey's acquittal on some accounts, Black imagined. His case had not been strengthened by his own witnesses:

Just young girls, no strangers to the courts themselves, I didn't think they were the best of witnesses. I do remember having to ask them to speak up. Usually a sign that people aren't telling the truth . . . Their evidence didn't have the conviction you would have expected about it.

Black had established the defendant's character quite successfully ('He was so dismissive . . . at that point about him mugging, and [it]always being women walking down the street, no respect for women, and I think it spoke for itself'). Grey's defence had been thin, unexpected, and substantially beside the point. The allegations about cocaine were a mere distraction that were not only undeserving of serious consideration but were quite tangential to the central charge of assault. The story was so transparently absurd that

I didn't press them very hard about [it] which I suppose in some ways might have seemed a bit flimsy. But I took the view he really wasn't telling a word of truth. It was self-evidently flimsy and wholly irrelevant in my eyes. . . . At the end of the day, we were there for three assault counts, and you won't find that in the book as a possible defence for assault.

He might have made the point that cocaine was 'actually a very expensive drug, class A, and you don't get nineteen-year-old girls dealing in cocaine . . . I thought they were a bit young for that, but you never know, people get younger and younger.' Yet, in retrospect, the drugs allegation was quite unimportant in helping the jury 'decide the guilt or innocence of that defendant'. He had undertaken not to explore the allegations of sexual liaison, lesbian or heterosexual, that had been made by the defence: he could not cross-examine his own witnesses ('I mean the people to be cross-examined about their sexual inclinations or whatever were the people who were [accused of those matters]') and forcing the defendant on the issue would have been without profit: 'I could have asked him "What is your evidence about that?" but I could just hear it now, the judge would have said he was not happy at all when that was being [aired] . . . it really was mud-slinging.')

He had himself decided to be understated in his management of the case. The defence had been 'rude—I wouldn't have adopted that style. . . . I didn't have the same histrionics . . . but I am told I am a very low-key prosecutor, which usually has the desired effect, actually.' Whilst the defence had worked on a broad front, trying to 'plant seeds of doubt', 'that's not my game'. It was the job of the prosecution to satisfy the jury that 'he assaulted them, whacked them, without any lawful excuse'.

Defence Counsel

The defence counsel, Jonathan White, had also taken the case at the 'last minute'. Grey had been an angry client: 'He felt anger towards these two women. Certainly he felt that they had fitted him up.' White had himself felt quite disinterested about the case and its protagonists: he was merely following instructions, and those instructions were that Brown and Green were nasty liars. Such instructions warranted an aggressive stance, a stance whose sole liability was its capacity to alienate the judge ('Judges don't like cocky barristers'). White was something of a neo-Darwinian, a man whose instincts were to defend ('Prosecuting is not something I do often') and whose view of the courts was that of a feral predator: 'It's a question of territory. You've got to remember that all barristers and all judges are human, we are all animals, and in court we have animal instincts. . . . When the judge sums up, he is the man in charge and he wants it to be clear in everybody's mind that he is in charge.' But the judge in Grey's case was 'very fair'.

White considered the prosecutor to have been insufficiently probing in his interrogation of witnesses:

He did say it was all hogwash. He didn't examine, which is the difference between what I did and what other advocates would do. He put to the defendant without cross-examining on each point, he put that each proposition was a lie. He just more or less left it.

White himself had been clearly instructed that the prosecution witnesses were untrustworthy, scheming women who should be handled with a measure of controlled ferocity:

Those two witnesses, the two girls, were lesbians, they were drug-pushing, or at least potentially so, influenced by men from their backgrounds, and had fitted [Grey] up. He had been framed by these lying, jealous women. You can't walk into court and treat them like ladies and be polite to them.

The Witness

And what of the defendant and those lesbian, lying, promiscuous, shiftless drug-pushers themselves? The defendant had declaimed from the box that the women were 'one hundred per cent liars, one thousand per cent'. Let me review how one of them described her experience of the trial. Janet Green, it will be recalled, had reported her assault in November 1988. She had been visited by a Victim Support volunteer in the immediate aftermath of the crime, but the volunteer had not herself been a victim of violence in the past, and she 'really wasn't much help, because when you haven't experienced something, you don't know how that person is feeling. You can try and feel but you don't know how that person is feeling. . . . I appreciated the fact that they came and were concerned about me, but it wasn't enough.' She had then, she said, heard nothing for over a year; there had been a silence until the very eve of the trial itself. Arriving at Wood Green, she had been met by the police officer in the case who had taken her to the waiting area outside the courtroom: 'He just sat me down. I wasn't getting no response from the prosecution.'

She had made an overture to Sean Black, but 'I believe he couldn't talk to me because it would have caused confusion in the court. They would have thought he was telling me things. He said that, not in so many words, but you could see that's what he was saying.' (Black himself observed, 'I did speak to them rather more than I usually do . . . before they had given their evidence, only because they had to wait outside for quite a long time. Really, just to explain to them why and when they were likely to be called on. I never talk about the case to them. You're not supposed to.') Janet Green had been aggrieved by such exclusion, and her sense of outrage had been exacerbated by the actual pattern of questions pursued by the prosecution. She construed the examination of her past as an attack by her 'own side':

The next day . . . I came in and called a police officer and said, 'I am not satisfied with this, what you lot are doing, you're not doing the job right. Everyone's on this guy's side. He is obviously trying to make me look a liar because I have got a previous record. That was years ago'. The police tried to explain to me that the solicitor [*sic*] couldn't talk to me and explain things to me until I had gone into the box and come out, which I still couldn't understand, because he is meant to be on my side. I felt rejected and thought that I should be getting some support as I am four-and-a-half months pregnant. The prosecution shouldn't be able to slander me.

Janet Green said that her actual experience of testifying had been distressing: 'I was in shock. It was unreal' (it should, however, be recalled that she had testified more than once before.) She was frail, being in a moderately advanced state of pregnancy and disquieted by the proximity of John Grey. She had neither expected the prosecution to introduce her convictions nor anticipated the pattern or effect of the defence questions: 'The lies he said were so brilliant, I am worried he's going to get off' (this was said before the jury returned a verdict). She had taken great exception to Grey's own testimony: 'Anyone can pick up a bible and swear. He's done it. He picked up the bible and knows he's lying. It's like an insult to pick up that bible and swear you are going to tell the whole truth. He's lying through his teeth.' The only explanation she could give for those lies was that Grey was ill: 'I felt sympathy for him. He needs help. He needs medical attention. He needs to be locked up in an asylum and get help because he is schizophrenic. . . . When I went back in there, I was listening to him and lies that he was telling the court, I heard it for my own self!'

She felt that she would have liked to say more: 'I had no opportunity to do that.' She would have told the court about 'how this has disturbed my child. She doesn't go up to men. She doesn't like men to come to me. She is protective of me because I have been beaten up. She finds it disturbing.' She would also have said 'that this has left me wary. I never been able to seriously think about getting involved in a relationship, though I am four-and-a-half months pregnant. I am scared that I will be beaten up at the end of the day. Men can just turn, and this is what this guy's done. He's turned.'

Summary and Conclusion

A rather stormy series of incidents occurred in November 1988, and those caught up in them had made their reports, more or less fulsomely and publicly to the police and, in one case, privately to a succession of solicitors. Those reports were interviews recorded by police 'scribes', transformed into narrative by officers, signed by the participants who thereby became a new entity, 'witnesses', and translated into the foundations of a case. The lawyers prosecuting and defending the case read their bundles hurriedly and at the last minute, forming only the most cursory sense of its protagonists and plots. They imposed different frames. One, the prosecutor, required only the central, simple, situational, and circumstantial details that would give a little flesh to the counts on the indictment. He sought to have no more than a basic argument about an identified man hitting and kicking identified women unlawfully. All else was immaterial. The other, the defence, demanded a more or less coherent exculpatory story from his client, a story which he did not need to believe himself but which should have a reasonable prospect of credibility in public. Neither lawyer had plumbed what 'actually' happened in the case, neither had really tried to do so, and neither was obliged to do so. There was very little law in what they argued (although a technical submission to sever the indictment had been made). Neither was there forensic evidence or significant expert testimony. The case was one of story against story. So many are.

Victims, defendant, and witnesses then converged to become players and audience, as counsel gave shape to their tumultuous, charged, and complicated experiences, a shape secured through the questions and speeches made during a brief and continually interrupted trial. It is evident that such a process did not serve to vindicate the witnesses' alleged wrongs, nor was it directly supposed to do so. It was devised to do a different job, to test the charges on the indictment.

The defendant was accused of assault and criminal damage, but the prosecution witnesses who came to testify against him were accused of very much more: of lying, sexual aberration, provocation, slovenliness, and drug-pushing. The criminal record of Janet Green was paraded before the Court. No doubt some of what was alleged by the defence was well enough grounded. No doubt the defendant did have a story to tell, a story invoking the themes of denial, self-defence, and self-justification. The prosecution witnesses may well have lied (one had certainly lied in the past). But what was said about the victims was, they claimed, unheralded and unexpected, and its public character shocked them quite markedly. They declared that they found their principal accuser irrational and absurd.

Brown and Green became defensive, indignant, and confused. It was they who had to adjust. They claimed that they felt frightened and alone, unsure of what was happening and in need of symbolic assurance. No one had seemed materially to acknowledge or assist them. Janet Green said: 'I think it would be nice if the prosecution or someone who's on your side could be there to help you through the case, talk to you, say, "You're doing very well", because it is a horrible thing for a victim to be up there.'

4. Trials as Practical Work

> Students of the criminal-justice process have already given much
> time and attention to the question of which model of complex
> organization makes sense of the court . . . and they have had little
> success in answering it. (D. Maynard, *Inside Plea Bargaining: The
> Language of Negotiation*)

I have discussed trials and the conflicts which were at their core. Let
me now take the next step and show how they were translated into
the work of different professionals, insiders and outsiders, and how,
in turn, they created the four concentric and overlapping social
worlds that I started to describe in Chapter 2 and shall continue to
describe in Chapters 5 and 6. An analysis of that work will continue
throughout the rest of the book, and a number of arguments introduced here (and particularly those concerning space and time) will be
elaborated at greater length in their own separate chapters.

I intend at this point merely to marshal the staff of the court and
show how they treated prosecution witnesses. One cannot advance
any further towards understanding the process of becoming a witness
unless that ensemble of waiting staff, each with his or her discrete
task and set of practices, has first been introduced. Witnesses were
work. They were formed in work. They were looking-glass selves[1]
that reflected and defined the actions of officials. They were, in short,
aspects of professional activity. Whilst witnesses encountered staff as a
personification of the Court, staff encountered witnesses as problems,
resources, opportunities, and constraints, in short, as practical
objects.

The Social Structure of the Court

Practically, the court was a contradictory enterprise. It pivoted
around an adversarial system that was, observed Skolnick, arguing
about its American counterpart, 'like the sporting event in that it
presupposes an underlying ethic of genuine conflict. Furthermore,
as in all institutions based on conflict, there is a perception of

---

[1] See C. Cooley, *Human Nature and the Social Order* (Glencoe, Ill., Free Press, 1956),
184.

"deviance" when actors who are supposed to be genuinely antagonistic begin to co-operate.'[2] People were adversarial, yet they had also to work together to engage in conflict, and there were widely ramifying conventions about how their relations should be conducted. The political result was that the court was translated into a coalition of formally hostile powers that maintained a careful distance from one another. Within the courthouse could be discovered the representatives of a collection of notionally independent bodies whose relations were continually negotiated[3] and often tenuous. The CPS, probation service, police, counsel, and others were in the court but not quite constitutionally of it. They met in the courtroom, transforming the organization that housed it into what might be called a 'rendezvous institution'. Neubauer wrote of the very similar American courthouse:

> The criminal courts consist of separate institutions without a hierarchical system of control. There is no central authority. A judge cannot reward a clerk, a prosecutor or a public defender who performs well. The courts are not a central organization. Each of the courthouse regulars is a representative of a sponsoring organization, which in various ways monitors their activities, hires them, fires them, and rewards them.[4]

Fig. 4.1 represents the social structure of the Court centre. The focal conflicts, practices, and etiquette of the trial process tended at once to act centripetally, drawing organizations into the courthouse, and centrifugally, scattering them away from one another and from the court buildings themselves. Agencies kept a wary physical distance from one another and the Court. The CPS, for example, maintained a base within the courthouse, but its principal offices were to be found in a separate building several hundred yards away, its geographical distance advertising a symbolic independence. The CPS, it was claimed, should not be regarded as integral to the court bureaucracy at all. It was a thing apart.

---

[2] J. Skolnick, 'Social Control in the Adversary System', *Journal of Conflict Resolution*, 11(1) (March 1967), 52–3.

[3] See A. Strauss, 'Interorganizational Negotiation', *Urban Life*, 11(3) (Oct. 1982). I have been told of how coalitions and patterns of influence at other Court centres could generate very different structural configurations. In some centres, for instance, the branch Crown prosecutor worked closely with the listing officer, circumventing the authority of the chief clerk. In Wood Green itself, the branch Crown prosecutor stated: 'We only have the power to persuade. We don't have any say in [listing matters].'

[4] D. Neubauer, *America's Courts and the Criminal Justice System* (Pacific Grove, Calif., Brooks/Cole, 1988), 99.

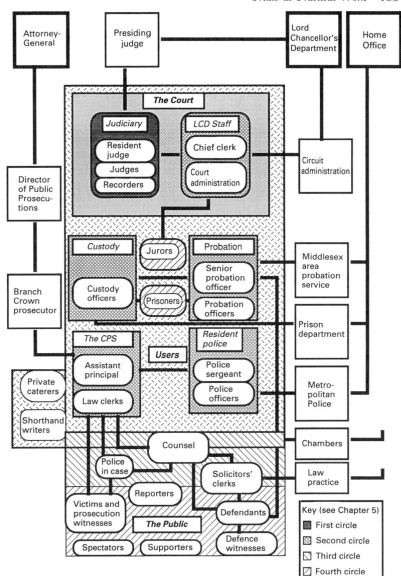

Fig. 4.1. *The Administrative Organization of the Crown Court Centre at Wood Green*

Only the administrative staff and judiciary were set quite unambiguously within the social and physical fabric of the Crown Court itself and there, alone, they attempted to maintain the neutrality of a body that was intended to rehearse and contain, but not to join in conflict.

Let me deal with those bodies first before I proceed to discuss what were called the 'court users'.

The Court Staff

The Management Support Division of the Lord Chancellor's Department, reviewing the work of the Crown Court in 1990, identified 'six core functions': pre-trial, jury management, listing, trial, post-trial, and determinations.[5] The work was intense, involving a flow of some 2,000 cases a year at the Crown Court at Wood Green. There was continuous pressure to reduce the time spent by defendants awaiting trial and time spent in custody especially. Fig. 4.2 shows how each 'function' had its attendant staff and hierarchy

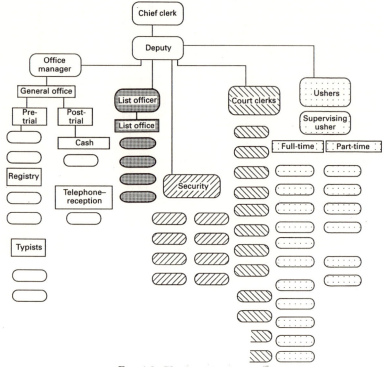

FIG. 4.2. *The Court Administration*

[5] Management Support Division, *Crown Court Review*, i: *The Report* (London, Lord Chancellor's Dept., 1990), 5–6.

and how all were controlled by the chief clerk. It also shows how very few were the staff working at the centre.

The Chief Clerk

The chief clerk conceived his principal duty to be getting cases to trial:[6] 'The reason the Court exists is to list cases, to get cases on, that's the prime function of the Court, of the administration.' But he was involved additionally in tending the small bureaucracy that made that possible. He appointed, managed, and promoted staff. He represented the court to the circuit administration and to powerful bodies around him. In so doing, he was, in effect, a baronial power complete with a fief and subordinates, a power surrounded by other baronies with *their* territories and personnel. He organized relations with the 'users' that were embroiled in the trial process, users such as the CPS and the Probation Service, that occupied sectors of his court, paid no rent or other charges,[7] and 'lay outside the court's effective control'.[8] He could not manage or order them. His was a more complicated role: 'We do talk to them on a regular basis to find out what their specific problems are and we try to help as far as we can . . . with defence solicitors and with CPS . . . it's largely a diplomatic exercise, listening to people.' He had followed the practice adopted by many of his colleagues in other Court centres. To bring the users and administrators together, to inject some order, he had instituted a regular Chief Clerk's Meeting to review the problems of what had become a working condominium of powers: 'It's a fairly informal sort of arrangement.'

The chief clerk also liaised continually with the resident judge, another baronial figure, the most permanent and senior judicial figure in the court and the person bearing the greatest and most obvious authority. There was in that relation another source of play and ambiguity in policy-making. Those who administer public organizations are quite frequently required both to manage and to serve

[6] The chief clerk of another Crown Court wrote to the Chairman of a victim support scheme in June 1987, 'The Court is not concerned with the actual Prosecution of the case. All it does is to provide a means whereby the case can be tried.'

[7] The Lord Chancellor's Dept. had decided that levying charges on users could lead to a complicated and ultimately worthless series of calculations in which demands for the cost of space and equipment would be countered by a sheaf of demands to remunerate users for the services they provided the Dept. Probation would start charging for social inquiry reports, the police for protection and details of 'antecedents', and all would come out of substantially the same central, tax-generated revenues.

[8] Ibid. 20.

professionals of high social standing and great public visibility. Their control may be less than sure. Just as hospital administrators enjoy an equivocal relation with consultants and university administrators with academics, so the character of the connection between the court's administration and its judiciary could not be neatly resolved. The resident judge was not called a manager, and he was not supposed to manage, but he was, in many matters, the titular head of the court and the man with the greatest public influence. Things done in his Court would bear on him and his reputation directly. In practice, there was a division of labour. The chief clerk delivered cases to the courtroom and the judges dispatched them once they had arrived: 'The judges are largely responsible for the work that gets before them in court and getting rid of that, and we do have a monthly consultation, in fact, on cases which are getting a bit stale, what action we can take to bring those up.' And the resident judge himself said:

Undoubtedly it is [the chief clerk] who is the administrative head of the court. The extent to which I found myself involved in administrative matters, that is, administrative matters directly concerning the court, is really simply the function of the inevitable consultation and co-operation that there must be between the Resident Judge and the chief clerk. . . . [But] I think I would expect my word to have considerable weight in relation to the functioning of the court. On the other hand, in relation to certain matters, for instance staff, that's totally outside my sphere and one might be asked to express a view but one is not expected to prevail necessarily.

That seemed to be the style of the place. In what I shall proceed to describe as a small institution, an institution whose members knew one another by name, prided themselves on being part of a 'team' or a 'family', had developed elaborate interdependences, and differentiated sharply between insiders and outsiders, there were traces of what Burns and Stalker once called 'organic bureaucracy'.[9] In many matters, the court retained a flexibility of practice and role. A number of staff, and the senior staff in particular, displayed a market aversion to procedures that were regarded as large, cumbersome, and overly formal, and that aversion was to become apparent later when efforts were made to adorn the Victim in Court project with the panoply of a full-blown steering committee that contained representatives from almost all the bodies that touched on victims and the volunteers who helped them.

The chief clerk's world was functionally and spatially concentrated. He dealt with the judges, the circuit administration, heads of the agencies called 'court users', and his own staff. His office was a fastness in the back regions lying behind locked doors marked 'private'. He had no practical commerce with witnesses. He was not obliged to do so. Witnesses were not his affair and he did not 'see' them in any consequential sense. He was not 'seen' by witnesses. He wore no gown or wig or uniform. Witnesses and other outsiders frequenting the courts would not have known who he was and what he did as he moved about the public areas of the court in civilian dress. They did not speak to him unless it was as to another stranger in a strange building. They were 'unpersons' one to another. I shall deal with some of these matters again in a later chapter.

Listing Staff

'Some people describe me as the most powerful person in the Court. I might dispute that,' said a listing officer.

Getting cases to trial was the central business of the Court, and the man who organized it was the listing officer: 'In conjunction with barristers' clerks [he was] responsible for the planning and programming of the court time table.'[10] Each new case committed to the Crown Court was numbered, coded, indexed, and set in a running list to be appointed its time for trial. There was a continual work of matching witnesses, defendants, police officers, judges, and courtrooms. Listing decisions had to encompass estimations of the probable duration of the case, the number of defendants, the number of witnesses, the availability of expert witnesses, the involvement of children or elderly witnesses, and the length of time the defendant had been committed. They were influenced by the size of courtrooms free at particular times and by the availability of judges of an appropriate grade. They were 'beset by unpredictable variables and subtleties, especially in the couple of days before a case is heard and hectic telephone activity, especially with solicitors and bar clerks, result[ed]'.[11] They were driven always by the imperative that a defendant had to appear in court within 56 days of committal from the magistrates' court (waiting time being a strategic 'performance indicator' for the courts[12]).

[9] See T. Burns and G. Stalker, *The Management of Innovation* (London, Butterworth, 1955).

[10] Lord Chancellor's Dept., *Crown and County Courts Standards and Design Guide*, 1985 with amendments (henceforward *The Guide*) (London, LCD, n.d.), amendment 15, Sept. 1989.

[11] I. Marriott and E. Simpson, *The Crown Court: A Preliminary Survey of the Scope for Computer Assistance* (London, Lord Chancellor's Dept., 1977), 5.3.2.

[12] See Standing Commission on Efficiency, Lord Chancellor's Dept., *The Crown Court: A Guide to Good Practice for the Courts.* (London, HMSO, 1990), 5.

The listing officer existed in a world of crises and rapid decisions, a world of cases collapsing, being adjourned, and going short. He was forever patrolling courtrooms, bobbing in and out to monitor whether cases were viable (whether, as the lawyers put it, there was 'a fight'), a courtroom was about to fall empty, or a new time would have to be found for trials being postponed. Court clerks would telephone the latest intelligence about cases straight from their courtrooms to his office. He embarked daily on a labour of Sisyphus as he shuffled business from courtroom to courtroom (a counsel reported at one point to a judge, 'I've spoken to your list officer and he is beset, as all list officers are, with difficulties'). He retained a sang-froid amidst continually impending chaos. I have already described his patent double-listing and floater stratagem, but even that would fail from time to time. On occasion, not one of the centre's six courtrooms would be in session, no trial being robust enough to start. I shall enlarge on the precariousness of cases in a later chapter, but it should be noted how very vulnerable they were to problems set by disappearing witnesses, defendants, and victims, changes of plea, evidence not yet obtained and badly prepared, indictments badly drafted, the illness of judges, and the elusiveness of police officers. Characteristic cries were to be heard in courtrooms at about 11 a.m. every morning: 'Nobody knows what's happening!', 'Three cock-ups in three cases!', and 'We're ready to say we're not ready'. 'Twenty to twelve,' the court clerk said one morning, 'and we've done nothing! Nothing!' and counsel replied to her, 'Ah, but it's the style in which you do nothing!'

Cases committed by magistrates' courts were 'logged in' by the listing office and then placed on to a 'warned list' of cases likely to be heard after some 4–6 weeks: 'People need time to prepare cases, basically', said one of the listing officer's staff. The warned list would name the probable week in which a case would appear ('Everybody knows that it can come up any day that week'), although there would invariably be a 'runover period' the next week, every week being at once a new warned-list week and an overlap week from the proceeding list. The warned lists were sent to the CPS, defence solicitors, and thence to police crime support units to ascertain officers' leave and the availability of 'civilian' witnesses. The centre's Class 4 cases did not typically attract crowds of witnesses, but there were frequently enough impediments to a trial to oblige the list office to 'dewarn' a case and 'rewarn' it later. The largest cases of all, perhaps twelve a month, would be discussed by lawyers and listing office staff together at monthly 'tea parties' 'to decide on a date that everybody can agree'.

In the actual warned week itself, said a member of the listing staff, defence solicitors and the CPS 'are just basically awaiting a phone call so the day before when we're compiling the list, we ring out the cases to all relevant parties.' 'Because I don't really know what's going to happen during the day', it would only be late in the preceding day that the listing officer would know what tomorrow's business might be. Daily, he would 'do a [provisional] list usually immediately after lunch: it goes then to the CPS [for counsel], to the police [for witnesses], to the probation [for reports], and prison service [for defendants], and at the same time one of my staff rings every single solicitor [for witnesses and counsel] who is in tomorrow's list, giving them advance notice.' At 4 p.m. there would be one last list, the 'final list', sent to the police, to the CPS, to a set of 'linked chambers' in the Temple, and to room 6 in the Royal Courts of Justice.

Resort to the 'linked chambers' and room 6 was just "part of tradition, it's a benefit to the Bar, but not to the Court". A number of the busier sets of criminal chambers had formed a pool, each affiliating itself to a linked Crown Court centre whose provisional and final lists they received each day, the final lists being photocopied and exchanged with clerks from the other linked chambers in a little ritual in the yard of Temple Court. In turn, in Room 6, in the dusty depths of the Royal Courts of Justice, in the late afternoon, could be seen a huddle of barristers' junior clerks representing chambers excluded from the 'linked system', copying names from lists pinned on boards.

In the expectation that a third of the cases would be 'stood out', a third 'go short', and a third 'effective', cases would be double-listed (fifteen per cent of trials were 'fixtures' and 57 per cent 'trials' between December 1988 and November 1989) and floated (28 per cent were 'floaters'). It was a system that 'does work very well' (although a CPS law clerk declared that Wood Green was 'notorious for too much listing', that is, for listing more trials than the courtrooms would bear). Between December 1988 and November 1989, 34 per cent of trials were actually 'effective', 26 per cent went 'short', and 35 per cent had other outcomes (they were 'bound over', led to a bench warrant being issued to compel the attendance of witnesses, and the like). Only 5 per cent were released for want of a free courtroom. A total of 83 days during the 12 month period were declared by the list office to be short, i.e. of under 4 working hours, in that year. See Table 4.1.

TABLE 4.1. *Analysis of Listing; December 1988 to November 1989*

	Results			
-	Effective	Pleas	Released no room	Other
Fixtures	154	49	—	65
Trials	332	300	34	344
Floaters	118	122	60	208

The listing office dealt with judges, court clerks, counsel, and solicitors. It was a little more accessible than that of the chief clerk. After all, it had to be reached by visiting professional outsiders, counsel, who sought to make or break fixtures. The office remained unequivocally in the court's private back regions but it faced outwards, stationed on the margins, adjoining the public areas of the courthouse and approachable by those who knew about such things. Relations between the listing officer and counsel would be direct enough in the courtroom itself, but they became indirect outside, signifying the divide between the staff inside the administration and the professionals without. Counsel and others were discouraged physically from entering the office itself. In both buildings, dealings were generally perfunctory, transacted across a boundary that signified the separation between the Court's private and public spaces, and called by court designers 'over-the-counter' business.[13] In the Bunker, that boundary was quite literally a hinged counter that could be lifted to permit passage; in the *Palais de Justice*, it was thick glass of a kind to be found in banks and building societies.

Like the chief clerk, the listing officer and his staff wore no gowns, wigs, or special insignia (although he would have had a clipboard). They moved about the courthouse in civilian dress, inspecting the progress of trials and channelling their flow. They would also have seemed 'unpersons' to civilians and witnesses, mistakenly identified as fellow witnesses, solicitors, detectives, or probation officers. Their knowledge of witnesses was always mediated, a feature of trials reported by lawyers, never intentionally given flesh in face-to-face meetings. The occasional enquiry or telephone call from a witness

---

[13] *The Guide* stated that 'there is some "over-the-counter" business with members of . . . the legal profession. . . . [A]ccess from public circulation . . . is required . . . to the listing office by the legal profession' (ss. 11.1, 11.2).

would be fielded back to a solicitor or the CPS, the prosecution wit-ness's indirect representative *faute de mieux*; they would not be allowed to lead to a prolonged exchange. The listing office had no practical interest or stake in witnesses: 'Obviously we like people to deal with their representatives, through the solicitors. But victims don't have representatives, [so] we refer them to the Crown Prosecution Service if there's any problems.'

Court Clerks

If it was the listing officer who consigned cases to courtrooms, it was court clerks who attended to the practical business of trials when they arrived:

As a court clerk you are responsible for the general administration of the actual court, preparing the judge's papers so he has all the information that is necessary, making sure that the details of the defendant are there, whether he's in custody, on bail, conditions of bail, his age [for sentencing]. All these things we need to know before we go into court.

Court clerks managed the courtroom:

We are the link, in effect, between the court in its fuller sense, and the judge and the administrative side behind that. So you put the two together basi-cally. In court, you are liaison, if you like, between the judges [and] the bar-risters . . .

Clerks ensured that all the parties in a trial were present, arraigned defendants, prepared orders, liaised with the listing office and counsel about the progress and probable lengths of cases, and completed a record of the court proceedings.[14] They represented the administra-tion in the courtroom, sitting below the judge, facing out towards the body of the court, acting as its eyes and ears, searching for signs of trouble and reacting to problems as they arose. It was their 'whisper telephone' that linked the courtroom with the world outside, commu-nicating intelligence, summoning counsel and witnesses, and calling for help in need.

The work of court clerks oscillated between bustle and inactivity. The first preparations for trial would be energetic indeed, as clerks enquired about the presence of counsel and defendants, witnesses, papers, and evidence. They would ask each pair of counsel in turn, 'Will it be a fight, gentlemen?' But trials were precarious, prone to

---

[14] Based on *Crown Court Review*, ii: *Appendices*, 24.

die stillborn, and an early bustle would characteristically dissipate into uncertainty and then inertia. Matters could be held in suspense as counsel went to the judge in chambers, seeking 'indications'. There could be protracted private deliberations between lawyers, '*voir dires*', to ascertain the admissibility of evidence and witnesses, and periods of anxious quiescence as missing witnesses were sought.

I have observed how the social life of the centre was organized in large measure around waiting for trials and news of trials. Court clerks 'frequently spend considerable lengths of time waiting for court to commence, perhaps because a defendant or witness has failed to appear or for one of a number of reasons'.[15] Like any other professional caught in inactivity, they would search for diversion and an end to tension, bantering gently with counsel, shorthand writers, police officers, and ushers as the long mornings dragged by. In doing so, they softened the harshness of a courtroom given chiefly to reproducing conflict, emotionality, and anger.

Court clerks dealt with judges, staff, counsel, and witnesses. They were the administration's face to those who had come to trial. They were supposed to be visible, distinct, identifiably part of the Court. They wore a gown and special bands. They could be recognized by outsiders, and they were sometimes approached. The courtroom was their distinctive sphere, and it was there that they were immobile and open to engagement as they conferred with counsel, police, and others. Yet their relations with witnesses were rather circumscribed, almost inadvertent, because witnesses were not fully their responsibility and it was not with witnesses that they were required to deal. They might answer questions when the court had not started or had risen. They might tell an usher to offer tissues and water to witnesses in distress when a trial was in motion. However, it was evident that they were physically, structurally, and symbolically remote from the public, seated deep within the well of the courtroom in an area whose topography mirrored their role and relations. They were near the judges, users, and staff but distant from the parts occupied by witnesses and civilians. As I shall show in Chapter 6, they were set inside a zone forbidden to all but staff (although no signs or markers made that unambiguously evident), and witnesses could reach them only by shouting or gesticulating.

Court clerks were reticent as soon as they quit the courtroom.

---

[15] Ibid., i. 10.

They were at their most mobile and elusive at those times, seeming always to be in well-advertised transit to somewhere else. They understood themselves to be part of an organization whose neutrality was vulnerable in a charged and divided world. They were surrounded by conflicts that could damage their standing, conflicts they should not encourage or feed with leaked knowledge. Accusations could be levelled about interference in the trial process. Their impartiality could be impugned. One court clerk reflected, 'The difficulty is that we try to have minimal contact because you have to be seen to be correct and not have any influence on anybody', and another said, 'We have to keep aloof. As far as the public are concerned, we have little or no contact at all directly, in the sense of a one to one basis . . . you don't have contact with witnesses or people of that nature.' Court clerks maintained that it was the ushers who treated with witnesses: 'The usher is the point of contact.'

Clerks had very few dealings with witnesses and witnesses knew little of them. They were part of a mass of insiders and officials that merely bewildered the witness-in-waiting. They were part of the confusing spectacle of a courthouse in which everyone but the witnesses appeared to understand what was afoot.[16]

Ushers

Ushers prepared the courtroom and they mediated physically and symbolically between what happened inside it and the wider world outside, between the judge and the court clerk, on the one side, and the larger universe of counsel, jurors, and witnesses on the other. Their job was 'running the court and seeing that the judges have their court run smoothly'. (A judge said, 'A good usher is one whom you don't notice. Ushers are noticed only when things go wrong.') They repeatedly traversed the boundary between the courtroom and the public areas, relaying information about counsel and cases to the court ('I check that counsel are there, find out what the length of time the case is going to be, whether it's going to be effective as a trial, or a plea or a standout'), bringing news about trials to those waiting outside, and summoning those required to join the trials within. They would patrol that boundary, challenging outsiders who had ventured into the court, checking that no witnesses listened improperly to testimony before giving evidence themselves. One said,

[16] See P. Goodrich, *Languages of Law* (London, Weidenfeld and Nicolson, 1990), 190; and Maynard, *Inside Plea Bargaining*, 32.

'We try and ensure that no potential witness goes into court while the court is going on. That is most important. We don't want a retrial.' And another said, 'I know a good few of the [police] officers, I'm not bothered about them because they should know. But I do bring it to their attention if required. When anybody comes into court, I ask them, "Are you due to give evidence in this case?" If they answer "Yes", I ask them to leave forthwith.'

Ushers crossed and policed another important boundary, that between the court and the jury room, summoning, escorting, and empanelling jurors, protecting jurors from outsiders and outsiders from jurors (the job of the usher, acting as jury bailiff, was 'to prevent improper entry to/exit from Jury Retiring Suite'.[17] They moved back and forth between groupings conventionally denied direct contact within the courtroom itself. Judges, court clerks, jurors, witnesses, defendant, and counsel worked through the ushers: 'We liaise between the public, the bar and the judge, we act as a sort of link. I am the link between the judge and anyone else. You've seen the practical things I do, swearing in the jury, taking the pleas, taking the verdicts . . .' They would pass glasses of water to those in the trial, to witnesses, jurors, and counsel but, significantly, not to outsiders, to coughing journalists or public spectators. They would offer distressed witnesses a chair or tissue (placed on the usher's table would be copies of the Bible and the Koran, a box of tissues, and water and glasses under a protective cloth). They could act as interpreters (one Scottish usher was sworn in to translate the broad Scots of a young witness[18]).

Ushers had dealings with judges, court clerks, witnesses, counsel, and jurors. They, too, wore black gowns that made them visible to outsiders. They joined the worlds inside and outside the courtroom but, like the court clerks, the courtroom was their sphere. Within it, witnesses were summoned, challenged, sworn in, and shown exhibits. Elsewhere, outside that domain, witnesses were a source of danger. Witnesses were thought to be at risk of becoming overwrought. The trials in which they were engaged could become endangered: 'One remark could be mistaken or blown out of all context, so you've got to be really on your guard and realize what you're saying.' Witnesses were not to be conversed with casually lest ushers were accused of coaching, interference, and the leaking of information: 'We're not

[17] *The Guide*, 5.3.   [18] *Guardian*, 22 Feb. 1990.

allowed to give advice to members of the public. The actual case that is going on is taboo.'

Like the court clerks, ushers, above all, represented a court that was emphatically neutral in a setting riddled with conflict, and they maintained a symbolic and physical distance from witnesses. One usher said, 'I couldn't sort of be seen standing chatting to [prosecution] witnesses, enjoying their favour, because of the defendant.' And another said, 'We obviously can't speak to them about the trial. You can't say anything. I'll only speak to them if they need something or they need to speak to somebody but nothing to do with the trial. You know, nothing at all.' They sought to display a conspicuous disinterestedness in the proceedings. They may have joshed with one another, police officers, counsel, and court clerks in the long hours of waiting that supported the life of the Court, but as soon as the solemn proceedings began, the ushers receded and became solemn themselves. They signalled that they were not embroiled in the conflicts of prosecution and defence. They were to be seen as apart, impassive, offering no visible commentary by gesture or word: 'You've got to be neutral. You can't take any side what so ever. . . . You've got to sit there. Impartiality—I mean, sometimes, it's hard [to remain impartial] when something's has been said in court and it's funny [and you can't laugh yourself].'

Witnesses were not, therefore, really thought to be in their care, because care might betoken partiality. It was the job of the professional adversaries to look after their own: 'The CPS usually takes on things like that. On the prosecution side, the CPS have all the dealings with their own witnesses, and police have their own. Defence-wise, probation are usually on hand and are very, very good. They can settle things down.'

Yet ushers, the members of the court staff who had the most frequent transactions with witnesses, who saw witnesses when they were most often in distress, found it difficult to maintain a distance at all times. To be sure, some were too busy, too vulnerable, or too inured to risk entanglements with witnesses. One said he would not intervene if he saw a witness in distress because of 'pressure of work, more or less. I haven't got time to work out what it's all about anyway.' But others were softer: 'If you do, like, have feelings towards somebody, well, I try not to show it, but I try to treat them all with care and sympathy, no matter who they are'; and a colleague remarked,

Anybody that looks lost or bewildered by it all, we try to sort it all out and make them at ease. . . . We're approachable, let's put it that way. Somebody sees the cloak, officialdom, they come up and ask us, 'Is this the way to a certain court?', obviously then we would stop and point them out to where they want to go. If we see this person in distress or anything like that, then we try to assist [but] we're not allowed to give advice to members of the public.

Inside the courtroom, the usher would act the part of an anonymous servant who fetched, carried, and escorted unobtrusively and without fuss. Their contact with the witness would be discreet and businesslike. Outside the courtroom, encounters would typically be brief, cheerful, and to the point, never unnecessarily protracted. It would not be with ushers that witnesses could linger. The ushers and reception staff of Wood Green were well-regarded by witnesses. 91 per cent of the Raine and Smith sample of witnesses declared them to be friendly (compared with 75 per cent for the witnesses from all seven courts surveyed).[19]

Security Staff

The Crown Court centre was regarded as a place of danger. It was a place to which those defined by the State as dangerous and difficult were brought for trial and sentence. It forced nervous and often angry adversaries to wait next to one another in close company and for long periods; it pitched them at each other in the courtroom; it made public judgments about their character and veracity; it exonerated or condemned them; and it imposed penalties that were thought by some to be harsh and others to be a vindication. The core conflict of the trial received eager attention from what the security staff called 'followers' or 'the support teams', groups of relations, friends, and allies who formed claques that could applaud or condemn each stage of what happened. Little clusters of supporters might be seen warily eyeing one another in the common waiting areas. There could be turmoil when juries announced their verdict[20] and, above all, when sentence was given. A CPS law clerk remarked that 'the dangerous time is the sentencing'.

[19] J. Raine and R. Smith, *The Victim/Witness in Court Project: Report of the Research Programme* (London, Victim Support, Oct. 1991).

[20] In Apr. 1992, for instance, 12 supporters were reported to have been sentenced to 'a night in the cells for contempt' after a 'noisy outburst of pleasure after a jury at Newcastle upon Tyne crown court found John Barclay . . . not guilty of wounding two men in a brawl'; *The Times*, 3 Apr. 1992.

The prevailing ambience of the public areas of the courthouse was actually one of quiet nervousness, people sitting in cowed huddles, whispering one to another and smoking incessantly. Violence was rare but it seemed always to threaten, and those many hazards did create an omnipresent sense of danger. Staff preserved memories of spectacular events in the past. They could learn about events in other Crown Court centres.[21] They would gossip about the disquieting events of the day, any incident being reported and magnified, amplifying what all knew, that the courthouse was a place where conflict was repeatedly imported and enacted in trials where it could sometimes barely be controlled.

It was the security staff who were supposed to prevent that animosity escaping restraint:

Duties included the opening and closing of buildings, internal patrols, car parking checks, searching baggage and directing or escorting court visitors. . . . Problems are many and varied, the more serious involving incidents of knives and replica guns being taken into court buildings causing alarm and concern to staff and other court users. The Crown Court by its nature attracts a number of undesirables some bearing grudges against the judiciary, police or staff and any perceived lack of security affords opportunities for these people to inflict harm and damage.[22]

Security staff would be the first to arrive in the building in the morning and the last to leave at night. They would inspect those entering the building, looking through their bags and belongings. They would patrol the public areas, working, as the senior security officer said, 'just for the sake of law and order, peace, security'. They would scan a volatile public for signs of unrest: 'Aware, this is the things, the awareness of it, you know. I do stress this with my chaps when I'm training them through, is to be aware all the time.' They would move from one courtroom entrance to another, checking what was happening within. Armed with their own lists, they would con-

---

[21] e.g. *The Times* carried reports of a number of disturbances at Crown Court centres that succeeded one another very closely in time. See 'Court Rampage', 2 July 1991, 'Cells Protest', 11 July 1991, and 'Prisoners Overpower Guards and Escape', 13 July 1991. The first report recorded how 'police overpowered 12 prisoners on the rampage in Middlesborough law courts who had caused £10,000 of damage. The trouble began when a local man awaiting sentence on violence charges attacked a policeman who was escorting him to the lavatory.' On 4 December 1991, *The Times* reported how a man was stabbed to death in the public parts of the Crown Court at Swindon.

[22] *Crown Court Review*, i. 51.

centrate on those courtrooms where sentences were to be delivered ('When a heavy sentence or an unexpected sentence comes down—short fuses, it boils over. Again you can, with experience foresee this, swamp it, get some uniform up there. That tends to quiet it down before it starts'). They would be visible where affrays were being tried ('We know what sort of case it is, probably. When it's violence and affray. You get a lot of problems with affrays'). They would hover where large crowds of supporters were to be seen ('The support teams we call them. We find out what court they are going to. We keep an eye on it'). They would look out for a few notorious local families. 'You get to know them,' said a security officer; 'we look on the lists for the names and make a point if we know the names to look for in that court.' They would respond to clerks' and ushers' requests at difficult moments. 'Obviously we look for [danger] ourselves, especially in a district like this. . . . You do get a lot of disruptive elements in this area.'

Security staff were few, most were middle-aged, and they acted, in practice, as the first line of defence. Their task was to guard the public spaces in and around the courthouse: 'The responsibility of the court is the security, not the police. The responsibility of the police is inside the six courtrooms. We deal with all the public areas, all areas except inside the courts.' They had no special powers of arrest but they could detain people 'if we wanted to'. Should matters go awry in those areas, however, they would turn to the small group of police officers who were stationed permanently in the building, and to the other uniformed officers[23] who had come to testify about cases or to act as 'antecedents officers' giving information about a defendant's convictions and history: 'If there is a disturbance that bubbles up before we get some help from Hornsey Control, we call pull officers in.'

Security staff wore uniforms not unlike those of the police. Some, indeed, had retired from the police. They dealt with the police, ushers, and the public. Their special regions were the public parts of the courthouse and, typically, they were the very first staff encountered as they checked witnesses entering the building. They might be asked about the location of trials, lawyers, and police officers. They might

---

[23] Plain-clothes officers, detectives, in court to give evidence were self-evidently incapable of 'showing uniform' and would not be the first to intervene in the event of disorder. Uniformed officers, as a detective sergeant put it, 'can act the role of a police officer . . . I would get a uniformed officer out there who is completely separate from the whole thing and he's in uniform.'

well be the first to see witnesses in distress as they toured the building's public spaces. In all this, they would play an ambivalent part: acting alternately as a source of help and as an agent of formal control.

Like their colleagues, they believed themselves to represent a court that was above the conflicts of the trial, and they sought to advertise their neutrality: 'You've got to be completely unbiassed, obviously.' Like their colleagues, they saw a protestation of neutrality as a way of defusing the anger of what were often angry people. Like their colleagues, too, they did not wish to release knowledge about the controlled world of the courtroom to people milling about in the spaces outside. ('It's just general security. It's not wise to gossip about what's going on in the court.') They were alert to the risks presented by the prurient who might exacerbate antagonisms ('Human nature being what it is, you will find that they're interested in child-molesting cases, that sort of thing, and we don't broadcast this at all, we don't tell them') or by the curious. They were guarded in their dealings with the public 'for general security's sake. The public really expect it from us, they will ask you questions, but they don't really expect you to give them a thorough answer.'

It remained always their principal task to regard civilians as sources of trouble to be treated with suspicion. They were 'aware all the time'. That was what they were paid to be. It was not their business to look after prosecution witnesses or to give them comfort. That was the work of the police: 'You haven't got the time to sort of nursemaid people. If you think they are very distressed, we're into the Police Office and inform them.'

Yet, again, precisely because they were visible in public space, an obviously authoritative agent of the court, accessible because they were conspicuous as they stood still and surveyed the passing scene, they were subject to numerous requests for assistance. Security staff could see and be seen by troubled witnesses. Sometimes they became supportive despite themselves, transformed into a version of the 'philosopher, friend and guide'[24] who might assist the beleaguered witness. Security and assistance could merge. At the end of a case, for example, they might escort victims out of the back door, away from the 'one or two of the support team . . . [that] hang about outside'. Security could give way to compassion. Staff might, very rarely,

[24] For a parallel situation, see E. Cumming, I. Cumming, and L. Edell, 'Policeman as Philosopher, Friend and Guide', *Social Problems*, 12(3) (winter 1965).

give witnesses sanctuary in their own office (an exceptional step whose significance I shall explain in a later chapter):

I've had them sitting in here. They know they're here, there is an officer in uniform, it helps them. They've told somebody who says, 'Okay, my dear, you sit there and we'll fetch you a cup of tea.' I'll make them tea here, you know. It's not done in most courts. This is my personal public relations.

The Receptionist

The telephonist-receptionist was a temporary member of staff throughout the period of research, a 'Kelly girl', and she was placed conspicuously at the very fore of the court, the second person to be seen when the public entered the courthouse building. She was yet another pair of eyes and ears working for the Court, surveying the mill. Before April 1990, her position in the Bunker was behind a glass window in the main 'concourse area', a busy space where crowds congregated each morning to search for other members of the teams that coagulated around trials: defendants for solicitors, counsel for solicitors and police officers, police officers for prosecution witnesses, solicitors for defence witnesses. After April 1990, hers was a solitary position at a reception desk thrust prominently out into the entrance hall of the *Palais de Justice*. There she answered the telephone and fielded direct enquiries from counsel, police officers, and witnesses about the whereabouts of places and people. She operated a tannoy system that reverberated its messages in duplicate around the building.

She wore no distinctive uniform, but signs and location made it clear what she did, that she worked for the Court and could be approached by outsiders. The transactions she managed were bunched: intense, sometimes frenetic activity in the mornings when new trials began would be succeeded by quieter periods in the afternoons when nothing much seemed to happen. So visible and prominent was she, stuck out in the entrance hall, that all the staff, public, and professionals who traversed the court's public spaces passed her repeatedly and exchanged pleasantries as they did so. She became something of a star in the process. Her reception desk was an obvious rendezvous for those who arranged to meet, for those who lingered to watch the passing scene, and for those who protected the courthouse. Security staff and police, above all, would gossip with her at some length each day as they eyed those entering the building.

The receptionist dealt with numerous witnesses each day. She encountered them at first hand across her desk and at second hand by telephone, and she was manifestly sympathetic to them. Indeed, she hoped one day to become a victims support volunteer. But there was little she could do, immobile and busy as she was, locked into place, always on the switchboard, never having ventured into a courtroom. At best she could tell witnesses where their trials would take place and how they might find the police room.

The Judiciary

I have already touched on the judges and recorders of the Crown Court at Wood Green. They formed the other firmly embedded hierarchy, part of the Crown Court, iconic of it, a very metonym. When judges spoke of the Court they meant themselves.

Court judges were required to be barristers of ten years' standing or recorders of three years' standing.[25] They not only dealt with the more serious cases (although not murder) but undertook a quantity of civil work in the County Court.[26] They presided over trials, attempting, as one Wood Green judge said, to get them off 'the ground with pace and dignity, and particularly with pace'. They determined the law before counsel and jury, especially in matters affecting the admissibility of evidence and in summing-up at the conclusion of trials. Very generally, said Lord Denning, they should listen to all the evidence, interfering only to clarify neglected or obscure points; see that advocates behaved and adhered to the rules; exclude irrelevancies and discourage repetition; make sure they understood the advocates' points; and make up their minds where the truth lies.[27] One of the judges based at Wood Green described his work:

The role of the judge first is to preside at the trial and to see that the rules are adhered to—the rules of procedure—then he deals with all questions of rule that arise in a number of stages. . . . In the course of the trial . . . he has to move on to questions of admissibility of evidence, he has to rule at the end of the prosecution case whether there is a fit case to go to the jury . . . and he sums up at the end.

The judicial role was quite circumscribed. Eisenstein and Jacob

---

[25] Courts Act 1971, s. 16.

[26] See C. Emmins, *A Practical Approach to Criminal Procedure* (London, Financial Training Publications, 1987) 42.

[27] In *Jones* v. *National Coal Board* (CA, 1957) quoted in P. Darbyshire, *English Legal System in a Nutshell* (London, Sweet and Maxwell, 1989), 95.

said of the American judge: '[He] does not rule or govern, at most he manages, and often he is managed by others.'[28] Judges could not appoint or dismiss staff or users. They could do little to reward or punish staff or users, although they might require them to give an account of themselves when things went awry and they could pass judgment on the competence of their performance as they interjected and summed-up. In trials, they were not obliged publicly to ascertain the truth or falsity of evidence, although they might invite juries to reflect on inconsistencies and improbabilities in accounts given by witnesses and defendants. They could not examine or cross-examine witnesses. They could not summon independent witnesses themselves. They were supposed not overly to interfere in cases. They could not determine much of the flow and frequency of cases that came before them. Many of the parties involved in trials lay outside their effective control and were often reluctant participants at best. There was little that judges could do to get trials to court: 'There are more ways of trials not starting than there are ways [of starting] . . . There are usually a number of people who'd much rather be somewhere else, and also there are a lot of people deeply indifferent to it. Obviously one can't initiate very much. One can't go and find defendants and witnesses. All one can do is try to stimulate the ones that can in various ways.'

Judges saw witnesses in only the most formal and regulated circumstances. Access to the Court's secluded inner regions was controlled, and most controlled of all were the approaches to judges' chambers. Clerks, ushers, and counsel were permitted there but witnesses could never come 'backstage'. Witnesses were 'seen' only in the firmly disciplined forum of the courtroom itself, their appearances orchestrated in full view. They came in great numbers before judges and juries to be seen and heard giving evidence. That was all. A judge said: 'You never see witnesses, you never see a defendant, except in court.' Another said, 'We have no dealings with them outside.' Anything else would have been taken as improper, almost scandalous. There could be no contact that was not managed, public, and formal.[29] Judges and witnesses were kept firmly apart.

[28] J. Eisenstein and H. Jacob, *Felony Justice* (Boston, Little, Brown, 1977), 37.

[29] So it was that, under the rules formulated in 1955 by Lord Kilmuir, then Lord Chancellor, a judge was supposed not to make public utterances outside the courtroom: 'So long as a judge keeps silent, his reputation for impartiality remains unassailable; but every utterance he makes in public, except in the course of the actual performance of his judicial duties, must necessarily bring him within the focus of criticism.' Cited in *The Independent on Sunday*, 10 May 1992.

Social distance was preserved by the conspicuous and courteous even-handedness with which judges treated witnesses and defendants: witnesses were always addressed by proper title and always with politeness (it was counsel who occasionally behaved roughly and were treated roughly by judges in public, although one judge could be abrupt enough with defendants). Relations between judges and civilians were very largely ordered, calm, clear, and exact.

Physical distance was enforced by the vigilance of ushers, who would not allow witnesses to encroach too near. It was guaranteed by the very design of the courtroom and its furniture (I shall describe in Chapter 6 how, between the well of the court and the area containing the clerk's table and the judge's bench, was a space known as 'no man's land', a prohibited terrain where people could not venture). The judges' bench was set on a terrace high and isolated above the courtroom. (Some alarm was expressed at the design of the new courtrooms after April 1990. Ushers were scandalized: 'Witnesses can almost *touch* the judge as they go into the box!') Judges were not allowed to penetrate very far into the public world.

All this confirmed the constitutional and functional independence of the judiciary. Judges were apart from the legislature and executive,[30] required to shed other appointments that might entangle and compromise their judgment.[31] They were above conflict, disinterested regulators, not a contending party.[32] Like the administrative staff, outsiders came to them with conflicts in which they had no formal part. There could be no unregulated contact between witnesses and a judge recognizable as a judge. (Interestingly, when judges very exceptionally moved into the public areas of the courthouse, wearing 'civilian' dress, they took themselves to be virtually invisible, unidentifiable as judges: 'They wouldn't recognize you. They just see a chap in a raincoat with a briefcase.' It was only when they were robed and wigged that they were subject to such major constraints.)[33]

---

[30] See R. Walker, *The English Legal System* (London, Butterworth, 1985), 230.

[31] See O. Mazengarb, Advocacy in Our Time (London, Sweet and Maxwell), 47.

[32] The empirical research on courts, including this study, suggests that contestants tend to see judges as just such a disinterested party. See e.g. R. Ericson and P. Baranek, The Ordering of Justice: A Study of Accused Persons as Dependents in the Criminal Process (Toronto, Univ. of Toronto Press, 1982), 183.

[33] One circuit judge wrote to *The Times* to say, 'I sit in a medium-sized town, trying criminal cases almost day in, day out. You would be surprised what an effective disguise wigs and robes make. The result is that when I do the "ordinary" things that judges are not thought to do because they are so out of touch with life, I am not recognized.' David Hodson, 5 May 1992.

What they could do, from time to time, was ask the usher to offer distraught witnesses a tissue, a glass of water (one lawyer called it 'the magic water'), a chair, or a brief adjournment.[34] But, as a matter of course, judges also expected that counsel would be hard and witnesses upset. Trials were intended to be uncomfortable and probing, and distress was their natural companion. A witness's lack of control might bring about the disclosure of important matters otherwise suppressed. It might signify how close barristers were to important discovery. It might be a sign of rage as liars were unmasked. Counsel could not shrink from inflicting pain. Neither could judges take a partisan role or interfere unduly with counsel as they proceeded quite properly to drive the witnesses who came before them. That was the job of advocacy, a job that judges had themselves undertaken in the past, a job they knew and understood, and judges should not obstruct it: 'Defence counsel has to defend and if the witness is there he is likely to be severely cross-examined.' It was the business of judges to preside impartially, ensuring that the proceedings had a decorum; that witnesses could be heard, understood, and recorded; that evidence was permitted and relevant; and that time was not wasted.

Prosecution witnesses acknowledged that impartiality.[35] Judges were seen to be above the hostilities that were staged before them. They had a civility of manner very different from that of defence counsel. From time to time, they would curb the incivilities of the defence. The prevailing epithet applied to the judiciary was that they were 'very nice', Victim 4, a 16-year-old witness, and Victim 5, a 13-year-old, said independently of the judges in their cases that they were 'really nice'. Victim 18, a young victim of assault who had undergone a particularly harrowing cross-examination, remarked that the judge had been 'pretty fair, I like him', and she remembered how grateful she had been when he had ordered an adjournment. 58 per cent of the witnesses in the Raine and Smith Wood Green sample who had testified called the judge in their case 'helpful' and 'concerned' (only 12.5 per cent called the judge 'unhelpful'); 63 per cent called him 'sensitive'; and 67 per cent called him 'patient'.

---

[34] Witnesses attending Belfast Crown Court were reported to feel that judges afforded them more protection than prosecution counsel. See J. Jackson *et al.*, Called to Court: A Public View of Criminal Justice in Northern Ireland', unpublished TS, 7.8.

[35] So, it has been reported, do defendants in many courts: e.g. in Canada it appears that defendants accord judges legitimacy as an unbiased umpire; see Ericson and Baranek, *The Ordering of Justice*, 183.

The Users

Administrators and judges together formed the Court, and they presented themselves as above the faction and clamour of conflict. About them, their relations fluctuating and sometimes ambiguous, were the well-named Court 'users', the more markedly partisan professionals who were not of the Court itself yet who made use of it, were physically in the Court yet not quite constitutive of it. The Lord Chancellor's Department may have given the CPS, probation service, prison service, and police equipment, telephones, photocopiers, and, above all, their own spaces within the courthouse (possession of a dedicated space was taken by administrative staff to be one of the criteria of membership of the inner social world of the Court, a matter I shall pursue in Chapter 6). But the users' standing and allegiance were not really the same as those of the judges and court administration. Theirs was a loosely coupled connection. The senior probation officer, one such user, occupying offices in the courthouse and attending the chief clerk's meetings, said, 'Remember I'm on the sidelines. I'm not a civil servant and I'm here simply because the Court is good enough to have me here and to make me an honorary member of the team.' I shall enlarge on the significance and character of such loose-coupling in the next chapter.

Users were agencies and the representatives of agencies with a formal and acknowledged part to play in the bringing and prosecution of trials. They tended to be publicly and structurally identified with one or other of the parties in the conflict, although theirs was necessarily a professional alignment, a matter of paid employment rather than personal passion, supposedly governed by a calm discipline and moderated by a web of restraining ties.

Users tended to eschew an appearance of emotion and partisanship although they could indeed be wary, and were sometimes carping, about one another. In a sense, theirs was a mundane job of work,[36] and they characteristically invested themselves less in winning and losing than in seeming to acquit themselves competently in the eyes of their colleagues. After all, counsel would say, many trials were simply not winnable and no judgment could be made about a failure to succeed.

---

[36] See M. Mileski, 'Courtroom Encounters: An Observational Study of a Lower Criminal Court', *Law and Society Review* 5(4) (May 1971), 473.

Yet there were exceptions to disinterestedness. There were the first daunting cases of a barrister's, police officer's, or probation officer's new career in which the novice felt tested and exposed.[37] There were poignant cases of rape or child abuse which could not but excite feeling. And there were offences which touched on the wider political or ethical loyalties of certain users, raising them above the standing of yet another routine Crown Court case.

All the users collaborated in and around the trial, but a few must take analytic precedence because their work was concerned directly with victims and prosecution witnesses. Let me begin with the CPS.

The Crown Prosecution Service

The CPS was established under the Prosecution of Offences Act of 1985[38] as an 'independent prosecuting body'[39] staffed by some 1,200 lawyers[40] and responsible for all police-initiated prosecutions.[41] Crown prosecutors had the same limited rights of audience as solicitors,[42] permitted to appear only in the magistrates' courts and never in the Crown Court itself.[43] Crown Court prosecutions had to be entrusted to independent counsel briefed by the CPS. To the chagrin of many members of the CPS,[44] there were no dedicated English and Welsh prosecutors equivalent to the procurators-fiscal of Scotland, the Crown attorneys of Canada, or the district attorneys of North America. The branch Crown prosecutor observed, 'Our own lawyers don't have the right to appear in court. In Scotland, they do things better.' In matters affecting the Crown Court, the role of the CPS was to regulate, choose, brief, and service cases behind the scenes and largely away from the public gaze.

The CPS had divided England and Wales into 31 parts, 3 in

[37] See E. Hughes, 'Institutional Office and the Person', in *Men and Their Work* (Glencoe, Ill., Free Press, 1958), 58–9.

[38] Prosecution of Offences Act 1985, c. 23: 'An Act for the establishment of a Crown Prosecution Service for England and Wales . . .'

[39] See 'Crown Prosecution Service's Submission', in Home Affairs Committee, *Crown Prosecution Service: Memoranda of Evidence* (London, HMSO, 1990).

[40] See the article by Allan Green, the Director of Public Prosecutions, 'Not Guilty as Charged', *The Times*, 23 Feb. 1990.

[41] Some prosecutions were inaugurated by other bodies, e.g. Customs and Excise, the Post Office, and large department stores.

[42] Defence solicitors were observed to make ribald comments about a CPS solicitor working in one of the magistrates' courts that committed cases to the Crown Court at Wood Green: they said the last thing they would want to do is work for the CPS.

[43] Prosecution of Offences Act 1985, s. 4.

[44] See 'Crown Prosecution Service's Submission', 28.

London itself, each area being administered by a branch under a Crown prosecutor, and each intended to be autonomous in most matters[45] but bound by a code and required to achieve consistency in prosecution policy. Area 2 was London North, an area based on police divisions and their attendant magistrates' courts,[46] corresponding roughly to four London boroughs.

Area 2's branch Crown prosecutor was a solicitor who had specialized in defence work, had then moved to work in the legal branch of the Metropolitan Police and thence to the office of the Director of Public Prosecutions, the head of the CPS. In this, he had much in common with his fellow branch Crown prosecutors. He and many of his senior staff[47] had served as police prosecuting solicitors before October 1986, when the CPS began, and they worked with networks of acquaintance and stocks of knowledge unbroken from the past.

Decisions to prosecute in the Crown Court were governed by several criteria and by two general principles above all, sovereign tests 'laid down by statute'. One invoked the 'public interest': 'Hard to define but it is easy to recognize when it jumps up and bites you in the leg. There's the victim's private interest and that of the police. We're receptive to views but Parliament gave us the duty to make up our minds whether to prosecute.' There was no single interpretation of the public interest.[48] Judgments invoking it turned on assessments of the triviality and gravity of an offence, its 'staleness', the 'realistic' prospects of obtaining a conviction, and the fitness of an offender to plead. They turned on the usefulness of initiating prosecutions when a defendant was already incarcerated or was about to be tried on other, more serious charges. They considered whether it would be 'oppressive' to prosecute defendants who were 'peripheral' to the main case, very ill, very young, or very old. They might exempt, for instance, a young first offender who had engaged in unlawful sexual intercourse with a willing partner.

The other test was 'evidential sufficiency': 'reliable evidence—has a person been clearly identified?' The code demanded that questions

---

[45] 'It is intended that decisions on prosecutions in the great majority of cases will be taken in the local offices'; *Proposed Crown Prosecution Service: The Distribution of Functions between the Headquarters and Local Offices of the Service* (London, HMSO, 1984), 1.

[46] Chiefly those at Tottenham, Enfield, Highgate, Barnet, and Hampstead.

[47] The assistant principal law clerk, responsible for the direct management of affairs in the courthouse, was one instance.

[48] See A. Sanders, 'Incorporating the 'Public Interest' in the Decision to Prosecute', in J. E. Hall Williams (ed.), *The Role of the Prosecutor* (Aldershot, Avebury, 1988), 33.

should be asked about whether there was enough credible testimony from creditable witnesses to sustain a case:[49] had the evidence had been gathered properly under the provisions of the Police and Criminal Evidence Act, what sort of impression would witnesses make, were they all available and competent to give evidence on the day, was there a possible conflict between eye-witnesses?[50]

It should be remembered that those decisions were almost invariably mediated, paper arguments made on the basis of second-hand, written reports and statements supplied by the police, and only very occasionally on a direct observation of witnesses themselves in the magistrates' courts. The staff of the CPS would see very little of witnesses before they came to Crown Court, unless it was in the ever-rarer preliminary procedure, known as 'old-style committal proceedings', in which a case was tested in miniature before the justices to gauge how robust it would prove in a full-blown Crown Court trial.

In late 1989, the branch CPS occupied two sites. One, a large office block set quite conspicuously at a distance from the courthouse, contained some 30 lawyers who vetted cases, drafted indictments, and prepared briefs. It was under the direct control of the branch Crown prosecutor, who rarely visited the courthouse a few hundred yards away, who '[didn't] take part in the chief clerk's meetings, [was] no part of the court administrative structure and didn't want to be'. The other site, set physically inside the courthouse itself, was a 'room to prepare necessary casework'. Operating from it and managed by the head of the Crown Court section, an assistant principal law clerk (who *did* attend the chief clerk's meetings), was a 'court team' of some 9 'CPS representatives', 'para-legals, as it were', 4 established and 5 trainee law clerks servicing the counsel who prosecuted the cases. The law clerks were allocated 2 courtrooms each, and they were forever scurrying back and forth between a pair of prosecuting counsel engaged in different cases, the 'CPS room', the police room, and photocopying machines. Their place in the courtroom was immediately behind counsel, a mirror of the defence solicitor's clerk who serviced the other side, passing papers, checking queries, chasing documents and witnesses.

I have explained that prosecution counsel were not permitted to

---

[49] D. McBarnet writes of the need for the prosecution to make a case using admissible evidence, proving intent, employing a minimum standard of sufficient evidence for a conviction, and in a way that would convince a jury; see *Conviction: Law, the State and the Construction of Justice* (London, Macmillan, 1981), 102.

[50] Based on *Crown Prosecution Service Annual Report* (London, HMSO, 1989), 46.

talk directly to their witnesses. Problems touching on conflict and the control of knowledge transformed contacts between lawyer and witnesses into a source of intellectual contamination, a danger to avoid. The particular epistemology at work in the Court made it imperative to protect the artless innocence of a witness's impressions. Just as defence counsel were obliged to speak to their private clients at second hand through their formal clients, the briefing solicitor, so prosecuting counsel spoke to witnesses principally through CPS law clerks and the police. It was the law clerks who mediated relations between those who could otherwise damage one another.

Yet the law clerks had a difficulty. It was only police officers coming to court, infrequent attenders or even strangers perhaps, who could identify the prosecution witnesses in a case. At the beginning of any trial, in the space of perhaps thirty minutes, the participants in a case could be seen searching anxiously and sometimes frenetically for one another: counsel for their police officers, law clerks for police officers, police officers for witnesses, witnesses for police officers. In that half-hour, law clerks attended counsel acting simultaneously in two separate cases. They were supposed to ensure that indictments, statements, and papers ('the bundle') were complete and ordered. They established the presence of all the police officers and witnesses appearing in the cases. They distributed expense claim forms to witnesses. They seemed forever to be in motion at the beginning of every morning. One of those supervising them said: 'My staff would like to do more but we don't have the time. To be honest we don't even know our witnesses. They're just a name.'

A protagonist with a complicating mandate to retain an independence of other agencies,[51] to prosecute only in the public interest, and to refrain from pursuing cases at all costs, the CPS had an ambiguous relation with the personal victim. It represented the State, not individual victims, in its dealings with defendants. The role of the victim was to suffer and then attest to the injuries to person and property that were translated metaphysically into an attack on the community as a whole (Hagan observed, of the very similar position in Canada, that 'the effect [has been] to largely remove the victim from the criminal-justice system'.[52] The CPS did not warn witnesses

---

[51] See D. Gandy, 'The Crown Prosecution Service: Its Organization and Philosophy', in Hall Williams (ed.), *The Role of the Prosecutor*, 11.

[52] J. Hagan, 'Victims Before the Law: A Study of Victim Involvement in the Criminal Justice Process', *Journal of Criminal Law and Criminology*, 73(1) (1982), 12.

(that was the job of the police), it had no power to summon them or interrogate them, and its staff had almost no prior conception of how witnesses would behave. Its only contact with the victim was as a witness seen first at court to give evidence, and there were major limits on what could be said and done when that contact *did* take place. The CPS did not wish to be accused of tutoring witnesses about how they should give evidence: 'We don't talk about anything of the case obviously. We just talk about the expenses and, perhaps, if they are very nervous, we might say what they should expect in court—there will be people sat here, and that's a jury . . .' Very generally, the law clerks 'were just there with the forms'. Defence counsel 'wouldn't want to see us having conversation in depth—we tend to walk past [victims], if I have met them before, I will say "hello, how are you?" and then I will go straight on to court.'

Knowledge of victims was largely second-hand and fleeting, part of a flurry of activity, confined perhaps to 'no more than a "good morning".' Very rarely would the junior law clerks have contact with victims, even with victims in distress, said a supervising officer, 'and it's very often too late. We know only if police officers tell us and we don't know the police officers well. Only if we see them on a regular basis, only if they arrest a lot of people.'

Yet the CPS *did* have some personal dealings with victims, *did* take responsibility for the payment of their expenses, and *did* need them for successful prosecutions. It represented them *faute de mieux* in a number of the places where agencies met and discussed the criminal-justice system.[53] It would sometimes consult them about accepting pleas to a lesser charge, and particularly when a defendant elected to be bound over. Its law clerks were expected to 'speak to civilian witnesses about general matters to put them at ease, for example about when they are likely to be called or the layout of the courtroom'.[54] They would sometimes take charge of witnesses. On one occasion, in December 1989, for example, the CPS took the 6-year-old victim of an indecent assault to the rest room, but 'it wasn't satisfactory because we had no one to sit with her and chat to her or help. She had her mother with her but mum can't always allay fears. She doesn't know what's happening.'

---

[53] At a time when Victim Support began to adopt the treatment of prosecution witnesses as an issue, an official of the CPS wrote to Victim Support in 1986: 'I can assure you . . . that the Crown Prosecution Service is aware of the important role played by witnesses and that, so far as we are able, the Service will seek to represent the interests of witnesses.'   [54] *The Crown Court: A Guide to Good Practice*, 18.

Much would depend on when the encounter took place in the life cycle of the trial. Little attention could be given to witnesses in the busy time when the preliminary work before a trial was being done. More could be accomplished when the trial was under way, witnesses were accounted for, and counsel seemed content with the state of their papers. More important, perhaps, witnesses who had been discharged were not vulnerable to the accusation that they had been coached by a law clerk. So it was on one occasion that a law clerk could be seen spending a considerable period comforting a distraught witness who had rushed out of a courtroom in tears during the middle of a trial. As a matter of policy, she said, she would, 'after the examinations and they are released . . . go out if they are upset and make sure they are okay, and I will chat to them then'. But she also said:

All of us, we like to try and say hello to the witnesses and tell them a bit about what will happen—'You will be called in, just wait here for now'—but [we have not much time] at all I'm afraid because . . . when you are between two courts . . . we have a part heard in the morning plus two extra trials listed, so we have a total of six things that we have to be aware of and we're fetching and carrying all the time.

The CPS did not undertake to look after victims and prosecution witnesses. Formally, the branch Crown prosecutor maintained, victims were the responsibility of the police. It was the police who first responded to witnesses, maintained contact during the period that elapsed between offence and trial, warned witnesses about the approach of the trial, and came to court to give evidence and manage the conduct of the case. A law clerk said:

I think the police officers are much closer to them as they actually do meet them, perhaps met them on the occasion when the offence arose, they meet them here again and they might recognize them, and then, because they are witnesses, all witnesses together, they obviously go and have tea together, whereas we don't. We shouldn't do that.

Fifty-six per cent of witnesses were reported by Raine and Smith to have found the CPS staff helpful and 73 per cent declared that they were 'friendly'.[55] The witnesses I interviewed talked about very brief encounters in which they had been given expenses claims forms

---

[55] Raine and Smith, *The Victim/Witness in Court Project*, 13.

and had, more rarely, been told about matters such as the delays that plagued trials. Even so, the law clerks did not and could not warn them about much of what was to come: Victim 16 said that the law clerk in her case had been 'really nice, but she hadn't said how I was on trial [under cross-examination]'.

The Police

Police officers were to be found everywhere: giving evidence in court, waiting and gossiping outside court, talking in the canteen, saunter-ing through public space, or closeted in the police room. Some were obvious enough in their uniforms, others less so in civilian dress, but they seemed manifestly at ease, moving slowly in an institution whose proceedings were themselves unhurried, displaying a studied familiar-ity with the Court as a place of routine work, suggesting by their demeanour that it was not *their* troubles that the Court was about to expose.

They formed two clusters. One group of officers was large, its members changeable and unfamiliar, defined more or less firmly as outsiders. They were the 'officers in the case', men and women who were based physically outside the Court, often detectives, who had come to see to the prosecutions they had themselves investigated; supply the CPS with papers, exhibits, and statements; give evidence at trial; and check the presence of their own 'civilian' witnesses, fur-nishing them with copies of the statements that 'refreshed' their memories. They were a large group indeed, composed of officers who might well be unknown to one another, the staff, and the Court.

Alone of the professionals, they would probably have had a previ-ous acquaintance with prosecution witnesses.[56] They could well have seen them at their most distressed. They might have done something to repair the sense of symbolic disorder that can arise in the immedi-ate aftermath of crime.[57] They had probably warned them about the impending trial and 'point[ed] out the court . . . show[ed] them the rough layout of the court . . . explain[ed] to them the procedure at court'. They were the only professionals who could be recognized by witnesses, and witnesses would be told to seek them out on arrival at court. They often chaperoned witnesses inside the building itself,

---

[56] Not all the officers in the case would have known witnesses; e.g. senior officers could well have delegated the taking of statements to junior colleagues.

[57] See C. Fischer, 'A Phenomenological Study of Being Criminally Victimized', *Journal of Social Issues*, (1984), 40(1), 170–1.

particularly when defendants were near ('As long as we are with our witnesses, they get the impression, and the right impression, that we are taking care of them'). They visited and revisited witnesses during the hours of waiting that preceded trials.

The other officers were a group of some four police (and two civilians) who worked in two special court-based units, were known to the staff, and lodged in the court building itself. It was most important that they had such a possession of the rooms that marked out staff considered to belong physically and symbolically to the Court's social world. It signified that they were insiders rather than outsiders. At the beginning, in the cramped space of the bunker, those offices had been confined to one modest site on the ground floor. Housed together, the two court-based units worked effectively as one until they were removed to the more commodious *Palais de Justice*. After April 1990, they occupied rooms on separate floors, and differences of personnel and function were more emphatic.

The first unit, a 'police liaison unit' nominally under an inspector but actually under a sergeant in 1989–90, ferried information back and forth between Court, police, and users. It notified crime support units in police stations about trials newly listed; visiting police officers about trials and civilian witnesses; the CPS about witnesses; counsel about police officers; civilian witnesses about police officers; and judges about defendants' records or 'antecedents'. The unit was a relatively sheltered place where people were to be met and knowledge was to be had, a 'sort of meeting-place, to find out who's here', the sergeant said. It became, by extension, a rendezvous or entrepôt where professional acquaintances were renewed and gossip exchanged, and where officers could unbutton themselves before returning to the more demanding outer world. An officer who frequently attended the Crown Court said, 'You can walk in and know nobody, you can walk in and perhaps see somebody you haven't seen for five years. I think it is taken as being a meeting-place, where you can meet old colleagues.' It was, in short, a home territory inside a public building, and I shall return to the significance of such places in the next chapter.

The second, the 'law and order unit', was responsible for the 'maintenance of security or "Law and Order" in the building'.[58] Its officers worked in loose concert with the security staff, 'showing uniform' where it was needed and 'prevent[ing] disorder and [ready] to

[58] *The Guide*, amendment 8.1b.

be called upon by the judges if there is any'. The officer in charge said, 'One of our laid down jobs is keeping the peace and being at the judge's command in case there is anything they need you for.' They patrolled the building, and most particularly the potentially turbulent areas adjoining courthouse and courtroom doors, eyeing defendants, witnesses, and support teams. As they moved about the courthouse, conveying information and 'going to various departments . . . I suppose in doing this you are patrolling'. Their office was set by the main entrance, next in line to that of the security staff, and it acted as a second check on those who came and went: it was a 'presence at the front entrance'. The Sergeant in charge could often be seen at his doorway, surveying the crowds of passing civilians, looking for known faces, 'supporters' teams', and signs of trouble: 'My professional eye is trained for that. One never knows where trouble is coming from.'

In difficulty, the 'law and order unit' room would provide a secure and protected space in which vulnerable prosecution witnesses could be hidden until the time came for them to testify. The occasional rape victim and the more frequent child victims of indecency would be hidden there, out of the curious or menacing gaze of public and defendants:

If there is a case where there is some sensitivity and the victim feels threatened by the defendant or people like that, then we will provide somewhere such as this office to keep them in. . . . This is really the one room that is free and can be guarded.

Police officers were regarded as the natural chaperons, indeed the allies of prosecution witnesses. They both sought convictions and they both had a stake in witnesses acquitting themselves well.[59] So it was that the police warned, met, accompanied, settled ('just generally try[ing] to put them at ease'), and briefed their witnesses with statements and advice. (One said, 'I tell witnesses that they will probably be quite fiercely cross-examined, and that they've got to be prepared for it really', and another, 'I like to explain to them that they will be questioned by both counsels, prosecution and defence, and defence will be questioning them, trying to protect their client. So they are

---

[59] There were exceptions. Officers patently did not support one prosecution witness involved in a protracted and bitter affray that had culminated in the victim lodging a complaint to the Police Complaints Authority. Police evidence in the case was actually rather more sympathetic to the defendant.

not to be expect that it will be an easy ride.') Victim 20 talked about how his officer had said, 'Don't worry about it, it isn't as bad as you think. You say what you saw and you will be alright.' There were patterned routines. One officer would corral his witnesses together for protection: 'If there are several of them [I] get them as a group and hopefully they feel safer as a group. Take them to the canteen and buy them a cup of coffee.' He would also 'tell them what was going to happen [because for them] it's the unknown, what's going to happen, they've seen it on television, but I think that's people's only experience'. That would be standard enough: the greeting of witnesses, the buying of coffee, the concern about safety, and the provision of information. Another officer who frequently attended the Court at Wood Green said he would 'show them the layout of the court, and then I will give them a cup of coffee basically. It's early in the morning and I think they quite appreciate that. . . . If I can't sit with them, I will ensure that somebody is looking after them.' And another said:

'I personally see them, maybe not necessarily first but near to the front, and speak to them, tell them exactly what's happening and get them a cup of tea or whatever, and then speak to counsel . . . Once I've spoken to prosecution counsel, and he will probably want to speak to the defence counsel as well to find out the position as regards to that particular case, and then I would go back and speak to witnesses and tell them what the position was.

But relations between officers and victims could also be stiff, constrained and potentially compromising. After all, it is part of the business of becoming a professional to steel oneself to the suffering of the client. The victim's distress was, in effect, the police officer's everyday work, and a certain distancing had to ensue: 'I think you can detach yourself as doctors do.' Detachment inhibited too full an exploration of the victim's anxiety and anger. And some police, particularly those younger and less experienced, had to contend with their own nervousness. Testifying in Crown Court was almost certain to be a disagreeable experience in which officers would be exposed to the savagery of what counsel called 'plod-bashing'. The police were unusually concerned about face, and they resented being called liars in public. Yet they had to appear calm, composed, and professional, neither emotional nor engaged, impassive before attack:

I find that sometimes our credibility can be questioned because the most horrendous allegation can be made to an officer who simply says, 'No sir'.

Whereas your average member of the jury, if he thought I was giving evidence and that man made that allegation to me, I would go mad. But you can't be seen, you may be thinking, 'Awful', but you simply have to say, 'No sir, that's not true', and you don't know how the jury accept that or don't accept that.

A prolonged exposure to strange, fretting witnesses was not the best preparation for their own appearance in a trial. Far better sometimes was solitude or the comparatively supportive company of colleagues in some private place.

Conversation could be fraught. Like every other professional, talkative policemen or women could be accused of tampering with evidence and coaching witnesses, particularly after they had given evidence themselves and learned the questions that were being put in the trials:

What you've got to be very careful of is not to go into the ins and outs of the details of that particular case because there would then be the allegation that the officer is in collusion with the witness. What is bad in my opinion is when that witness then leaves the court, the officer, if the officer hasn't given his evidence, he can't approach the witness to say, 'Are you alright? Are you getting home alright?' Because the immediate allegation is you colluded with that witness to find out what he or she had been asked so that you could then either rebut or answer the same . . .

The inevitable outcome was an occasional awkwardness that beset relations between near-strangers attending unpleasant events in conditions of pseudo-intimacy. Most characteristically (but not with children or the very vulnerable), the police were mute. They were companions little given to talk because talk could be hazardous and strained. It was not remarkable that they frequently slipped away to be alone or to join the more informal, unmuzzled, and entertaining gossip of their colleagues in the canteen or 'police room': 'I would probably spend most of my time either in the canteen . . . or just literally sit outside the court and read the paper.'

They would almost certainly return from time to time to offer news about the progress of the trial, to check the doings of defendants and defence witnesses, and to seek mutual assurances that all was well (Victim 28 talked about a police officer coming 'in now and again . . . and he said, "nothing's happening yet, we will get back to you as soon as we know"'). Police detachment was not well-defended: after all, as an officer said, 'When a witness rushes out in tears and there's no-one else to help, you may talk'. And their stiffness would melt altogether when the more harrowing cases were before them. In February 1990, for example, after a 16-year-old victim of gross indecency (Victim 12) had been cross-examined quite intensely, the officers in the case were visibly upset, asking, 'Did they give her a hard time?' 'Did they ask sexual questions?' 'It's because of that that people won't come back here as witnesses. It's terrible!'

Over three-quarters of the witnesses in the Smith and Raine sample called the police helpful.[60] Yet the witnesses I interviewed did complain of some neglect: they were characteristically presented with a statement to read on arrival at court, and were then left to hours of dejected waiting either alone ('he just gave us our statements [and left]') or in the company of an officer who was mostly silent (Victim 7 said his officer 'didn't talk a lot'). Again and again witnesses said, as Victim 6 did, 'I saw the officer in charge and he just told me to sit down on a bench and wait.'

Counsel

Under the 'cab-rank rule', barristers were not supposed to refuse a brief unless they were themselves too busy to take new work[61] or the case fell outside their competence or was too poorly remunerated.[62] They could appear interchangeably for defence and prosecution (one said, 'I switch from one day to another') and, appearing interchangeably, they depressed the conflicts that could otherwise have ruptured relations amongst themselves. They were no embattled groups of crime-fighters or defendant's champions locked into their different roles and institutions. They showed instead a general good humour, a distance, and a disinterestedness. Theirs was a willingness to co-operate with opponents with whom they might appear again and again in different roles. A general collegiality of the Bar appeared to transcend the enmities of individual 'fights'.[63]

Yet there was also an inevitable specialization. Some barristers had elected not even to appear on the CPS list of eligible prosecutors, and others were deemed too inexperienced, junior, or inept to be included. Some had become professionally associated with defence or

---

[60] Raine and Smith, *The Victim/Witness in Court Project*, 13.

[61] See R. White, *The Administration of Justice* (Oxford, Blackwell, 1985), 71.

[62] See General Council of the Bar, *Code of Conduct for the Bar of England and Wales* (London, 1989), 13.4.1a.

[63] See M. Hilbery, *Duty and Art in Advocacy* (London, Stevens, 1946), 21.

prosecution work and found that those briefing them had imposed a specialization. They were typed by clerks of chambers: one said, 'It's really how things go, because clerks see you as a prosecutor and they seem to direct you in that way.' Some few were thought to have very particular skills in prosecuting frauds or rapes or child abuse cases.[64] Indeed, entire sets of chambers could become identified with defence or prosecution, finding themselves being briefed quite heavily by one or the other side ('Chambers are self-selecting to a degree', said a CPS law clerk). Sets of chambers sometimes became, in effect, twinned with particular solicitors' practices or CPS branches (a CPS law clerk said, 'We really go on basically who we know. We see counsel doing various types of case').

Defence and prosecution were regarded as quite unlike one another in their relations and commitments. Defence counsel represented solicitors as their professional clients and defendants as their personal, identifiable lay clients, and they were expected to promote their interests "fearlessly and by all proper and lawful means'.[65] Defence counsel were called officers of the Court: they were not supposed to put matters that were not in their instructions or which they could not prove. But neither were they obliged to disclose information that could damage their client's case. Theirs was a professedly partisan and personalized role. Most defence counsel asserted privately that they believed most of their clients to be guilty but, unless their clients disclosed their guilt directly, it remained their job to represent them as best they could, whatever their judgment might be about the truth or falsity of the defence or the moral character of the defendant.[66] They could always skirt the more delicate problems of a client's guilt through indirectness, circumlocution, and elision. And the intercession of a solicitor provided a useful obstacle to open confrontation between barrister and defendant. Indeed, as Lucia Zedner observed, solicitors acted as a 'useful barrier to communication, preventing fatal admissions of guilt or of evidence pointing to guilt'.

Defence counsel were required to be hostile to prosecution witnesses inside the courtroom. They were belligerents whose job was to serve their clients by attacking the standing, credibility, and evidence

---

[64] See J. Morgan and L. Zedner, 'Child Victims in the Criminal Justice System', paper delivered at the British Criminology Conference, Univ. of York, July 1991, 17.

[65] General Council of the Bar, *Code of Conduct*, 13.4.1c.

[66] See *Archbold: Pleading, Evidence and Practice in Criminal Cases* (London, Sweet and Maxwell, 1988), 556.

of those who testified against them: 'The further he can go destroying the prosecution's story, the better are his chances from beginning to end.' Indeed, techniques of questioning in cross-examination stayed much the same whether a counsel defended or prosecuted, transforming the victim into a formal equivalent of the defendant for purposes of cross-examination: in rape cases, for example, they 'obviously put her in the difficult position of almost a defendant, because she *is* on the defensive, saying, "No, I didn't consent".' They were indifferent to prosecution witnesses outside the courtroom, having no commerce with them at all. In one instance, a victim who approached a defence counsel was told roundly, 'I can't talk to you. I'm not your counsel.' And that was that. It was not surprising that only 25 per cent of the witnesses in the Raine and Smith sample who had testified pronounced defence counsel to be 'helpful' or 'sensitive' and 21 per cent called them 'concerned'.

Prosecution was different. I have already observed that crimes in law are portrayed not as offences against individuals as private and independent beings but as offences against the community as a corporate or metaphysical entity. Two hundred years ago, Blackstone claimed that 'public wrongs, or crimes and misdemeanours, are a breach and violation of the public rights and duties due to the whole community, in its social aggregate capacity . . . since besides the wrong done the individual, they strike at the very being of society'.[67] That is a doctrine still strongly held. Victims have no standing in law.[68] It was not their personal rights that were vindicated in prosecutions. They were, in effect, a precondition for the perpetration of crime, the people who must be harmed because the community as an abstraction cannot suffer tangible harm. They were required to aid the prosecution of crime by testifying to what they had seen and heard; but it was not their wrongs that were expressly vindicated in the court (the relatives of a murder victim were reported to have said of an Old Bailey case, '*Our* trial, in which we felt the most vital participants, was not *ours* at all'[69]). Spencer remarked that 'the victim of a crime still does not officially exist. In sharp contrast to some other

---

[67] W. Blackstone, *Commentaries on the Laws of England* (Oxford, Clarendon Press, 1778), iv. 5.

[68] See J. Shapland, in European Committee on Crime Problems, '*Memorandum on the Victim and the Criminal Justice System*', *Report of the Select Committee of Experts on the Victim and the Criminal and Social Policy* (Strasbourg, Council of Europe, 1983), 7.

[69] Quoted in J. Abrahams, 'Victims of the Court', *Guardian*, 13 July 1988.

European States,[70] where the victim has a right to be made a party to the prosecution, in England a public prosecution is a duel between the State and the accused.'[71] Indeed, in England there has been a marked hostility to the proposal that 'victim impact statements' should form part of the sentencing process. The pain and losses incurred by the victim are not directly material. The result, some would claim, is that victims have been robbed of their property in conflict by a usurping State.[72]

Prosecutors appearing in Wood Green adhered universally to the principle that they were officers of the Court, ministers of justice[73] as they put it, representing the State and not the victim. Acting for the State, counsel were not obliged to secure a conviction at all costs. It was understood that they should 'prosecute fairly'.[74] It was said that there were no victories and no defeats for the prosecution. One counsel remarked:

> If he is prosecuting he is also a minister of justice and therefore he has got to be overtly fair, and must present the facts. If it comes to his knowledge that evidence is available that would exonerate the defendant he has to admit it. You have an extra duty whereas, when you are defending, you have no duty at all to ask questions or even to bring them to the court's light, if they could be damaging to your client's case.

Prosecutors were conscious of the risks of seeming partisan, or bridging the gulf between professional and civilian, and, most important, of 'coaching'. I explained in Chapter 2 that all advocates were considered masters of a dangerous knowledge, not only about the particular case but about cases in general, knowledge that could spoil the lay witness's naive recollection of events. Their conversation could influence how testimony was prepared, evidence given, and questions fielded. It could undermine the trial itself.

At first glance, the result appeared to subject victims and prosecution witnesses to a cluster of inviolable proscriptions and taboos (one barrister said, 'Witnesses are not prosecution counsel's responsibility

[70] See M. Joutsen, *The Role of the Victim of Crime in European Criminal Justice Systems (Helsinki, HEUNI, 1987)*.

[71] J. Spencer, 'Help Victims and Beat Crime', *The Times*, 5 Mar. 1986.

[72] See e.g. S. Schafer, The Victim and his Criminal (New York, Random House, 1968), and N. Christie, 'Conflicts as Property', Foundation Lecture, Centre for Criminological Studies, University of Sheffield, 1976.

[73] The phrase appears in W. Boulton, *A Guide to Conduct and Etiquette at the Bar* (London, Butterworth, 1975), 74, and in D. Napley, *The Technique of Persuasion* (London, Sweet and Maxwell, 1983).   [74] White, *The Administration of Justice*, 72.

because there are dangers and laws against prosecution counsel talking to his own witnesses. It is a rule of the Bar'). Prosecutors 'did not regard [themselves] as appearing for a party'.[75] They had no constitutional responsibility for victims: one said, 'A distressed witnesses is none of my business . . . the police will look after prosecution witnesses.' And another said, 'In the Crown Court I would expect the police officer to be in attendance and to round up the witnesses for me.' They would not interview victims: 'We never interview witnesses. The only interview we would have would be the officer in the case.' They assigned victims no special standing: 'I tend not to speak to the witness. I tend to appear that I'm presenting the Crown's case, and all that the victim or the witness is, in fact, is another witness.' Prosecuting counsel, said a senior official working for the branch Crown prosecutor, would pretend that the victim was not there. Any major communications would be conducted mediately through the officer in the case: a policeman said, 'It's all done through the officers.'

During the busier times of the day, before trials and during adjournments, counsel were almost always to be seen in public space. It was there that they would wait, reading briefs, conversing languidly with one another, bantering with court clerks or engaging in more hurried consultations with the officers in the case, law clerks, and defence lawyers. They did have access to their own robing room or mess, but theirs was a public role in the courtroom, consultation rooms, and the waiting areas. They were not accustomed to being retiring.

Victims and prosecution witnesses also haunted public space, and prosecutors found their proximity unsettling. I shall return to the management of relations in space in Chapter 6, but it is impossible not to touch on them at this point. It should be noted that even to be seen with victims was thought reprehensible: 'Nobody should see you walking around with witnesses.' Some would simply not recognize them at all, transforming them into unpersons: 'I don't ever talk to witnesses. . . . I wouldn't even say good morning. It's hard to avoid being rude. But I am not there as their friend. I am there to do a job.' Indeed, the language used was that of contamination and defilement. The branch Crown prosecutor said:

It's contrary to the ethics of the Bar to talk to prosecution witnesses. The first time they will talk to their witnesses is when they're examining in chief.

---

[75] General Council of the Bar, *Code of Conduct*, 25.1.

It is important that they should not give evidence that is *tainted* by anything other than the evidence in statements made by the witnesses. The aim of the prosecution is to get the court the evidence as it happened. [*emphasis added*]

Because it was difficult to ostracize victims altogether, some counsel would resort to stratagems that simultaneously signalled a recognition of their presence and a reluctance to come nearer physically and symbolically. They might nod from a distance sufficient to inhibit speech, or turn to another user to convey messages about the ambivalence of the situation: one would tell police officers, 'Look, point me out and explain that I'm not being unfriendly but it's simply the rule that we can't discuss the evidence now.' Again, they might make use of little rehearsed formulas: 'I think it's not uncommon to say, "good morning, hello, I am prosecuting this case, my name is ——, I'm afraid I can't talk to you. You'll forgive me, this is not rudeness, this is a convention.' When more had to be said, it was gingerly, with the consent of the defence, and only when it touched on safe and approved matters such as securing an agreement to a 'bind-over'. Counsel were told by their professional body, the Bar Council:

In criminal cases a barrister may not discuss the case with or in the presence of potential witnesses of a non-expert character . . . save in exceptional circumstances, which require the careful exercise of a barrister's judgment and discretion.[76]

Victims were not expected to understand that they were in a state of innocence that had to be preserved from the dangers of improper knowledge. The police and expert witnesses were a little different (although expert witnesses were few enough at Wood Green, apart from general practitioners and hospital casualty officers testifying about injuries in assault cases). Conversation with *them* was less likely to be misconstructed by defendants and defence counsel. They were taken to be knowing, aware of invisible boundaries, proof against an epistemological Fall. They could be approached about practical matters of administration, they could relay information to lay witnesses, but, even so, counsel were guarded. After all, expert witnesses were witnesses too.

At stake, one may surmise, were more than quite well-founded fears about dangerous out-bursts in the courtroom and about know-

---

[76] *Code of Conduct*, 23.4.

ledge leaking outside the court to confound trials. The Bar has its traditions whose observance, like that of many other established conventions, has become consequential in itself. Observance formed part of 'a positive pattern'[77] that signified a willingness to be seen to defer to the moral authority of the Bar. It showed one to be a principled, upright, aware member of the group. If lawyers were to be seen breaching a convention in public, what else might they not do? They were at risk of being considered indifferent to the good opinion of colleagues, as unworthy of trust. And trust between colleagues was a prime good in the difficult and volatile world of the Court, where it was all too easy to misbehave, and where so much was at stake. Simmel once argued that 'our modern life is based to a larger extent that is usually realized upon the faith in the honesty of the other . . . We base our gravest decisions on a complex system of conceptions, most of which presuppose the confidence that we will not be betrayed.'[78] It was part of being a professional lawyer that one exercised impeccable self-control. In short, it seemed, a barrister did not, and *should* not, talk to witnesses before a case or behave rudely during the conduct of a trial.

Like the police and other users, counsel enforced a sharp separation between themselves as professionals who handled problems as mundane work and those troubled people, the clients, witnesses, and quarry, whose problems they handled. Freidson once observed: 'In the course of defining and classifying the universe which they claim needs their services, all control agencies in effect become responsible for drawing clearer lines than in fact exist in everyday life . . .'[79] Rapid, repetitive, and morally taxing work demanded that counsel reified their materials: there were, in effect, standard, cardboard judges, counsel, defendants, and witnesses who could not be assumed to have a life and sensibilities independent of the practical purposes of a trial. Any erosion of those separations and categorizations would engender confusion and anguish. Just as gynaecologists and undertakers make human bodies thing-like, so lawyers redefined and diminished their witnesses. They distanced themselves symbolically and emotionally from the distress of their own and opposing witnesses.

---

[77] M. Douglas, *Purity and Danger* (London, Routledge and Kegan Paul, 1966), 38.

[78] G. Simmel, quoted in P. Manning, 'Police Lying', *Urban Life and Culture*, 3(3) (Oct. 1974), 284.

[79] E. Freidson, 'Disability as Social Deviance', in E. Rubington and M. Weinberg (eds.), *Deviance* (New York, Macmillan, 1968), 118.

Trials could be cruel, and it was counsel who were the perpetrators of that cruelty (one experienced lawyer remarked after a bout of cross-examination, 'It's a dreadful business. We do have to be brutal'). Those who dwelt too much on the pain of the lay witness would not last long as effective advocates. Far easier was a detachment that reduced relations to the simplicity of questioner and questioned, of subject and object: 'I have the view that you have got to be at total arm's length from the witnesses because you are there to present a case.' No counsel I met claimed to have been disarmed or put off their stroke by the tears or anger of a witness undergoing interrogation. On the contrary: such afflictions were universally held to be the unpleasant but necessary consequence of cross-examination. To avoid them, to become overly nice about a witness's feelings, would impair performance and betray a client. Professional effectiveness demanded a measured show of indifference. Witnesses had to be transformed so that unpleasant things could be done to them, and it was disquieting to be reminded that things could be otherwise.

Yet it was once again the case that there could never be a complete translation of prosecution witnesses into untouchables. The taboos and conventions *were* violated. To be sure, some counsel were firm enough, even abrupt, as they told prosecution and other witnesses that they would not speak to them. I saw barristers simply turn their backs on witnesses. But most found it difficult to be uncivil. The courtliness of the Bar that I described in Chapter 2 was so pervasive that it could not dissipate entirely when counsel were approached by strangers and witnesses in public space. There was usually at least a residual and wary politeness. I have remarked how a number of prosecutors introduced themselves before removing themselves to a distance. Others even became quite attentive. One remarked that neglect of the victim was less a matter of convention or ethics than 'a question of how much people can be bothered'. He continued:

It's important—you can't sit down and mother them—the victims—I mean the alleged victims, but it's important to sit down, not to sit down, but to always make sure they know who *you* are, so they at least feel some security about who to run to in a crisis . . . such as . . . witness interference.

But even so, he maintained, he was ever-prudent, not touching on evidence in conversation. Attentiveness was, he said, a matter of manner rather than content.

There were barristers who behaved in quite untoward ways. One I observed being almost loquacious as he lolled conversationally besides a victim on a bench outside the courtroom, showing him his statement and suggesting that he should have a cup of tea. He observed that he would not hesitate to talk to prosecution witnesses if there was no discussion of evidence. Most attentive of all was a woman barrister who was positively solicitous in her dealings with a young female victim of indecency (Victim 19). She explained to the young victim and her parents that the trial had been delayed for the sentencing of defendants from an earlier case. She praised the victim for her performance in the box after cross-examination, saying, 'You did very well indeed. I've seen plenty of adults not doing as well as that!' She was to say later in interview that she would normally adhere to the convention of not talking to witnesses but that she felt sympathy for them as they waited: 'Hanging around [is] I feel very often depressing, feelings will come out and I make some polite inconsequential chit-chat and apologise for the delay and try to put myself out.'

It was difficult to account for such variation. It appeared in minor differences between the collective beliefs and practices of sets of chambers. Those most adamant about such matters as not conversing with victims called themselves 'conservative', and they were most loyal to Bar tradition, but I spoke to no-one at all who advocated abandoning the symbolic and functional gulf between witness and advocate. Counsel seemed generally incurious about the issue themselves: discrepancies in the treatment of victims appeared to be a slight matter that they did not discuss.

Variation was ingrained in a freelance profession that required the emergence of strong, independent, and personable advocates who were confident enough to perform with few props alone before a critical audience. In minor Class 4 cases, certainly, they were part of no large team, and they were obliged to take decisions alone and quickly. Some, indeed, had developed quite pronounced idiosyncrasies in their playing of public parts. Being 'colourful' or a 'character' (providing it was not that of a fool or a bully) was no bad thing in winning audiences, and it was easier to step into a role that had become a little exaggerated. Many counsel attending Wood Green claimed to attach little importance to the creation of dramatic effect, but their craft was an ineluctably histrionic one and their performances were quite clearly staged. After all, no conversation in everyday life would ever be conducted with the volume, diction, force, and vocabulary of a routine cross-examination. Barristers were thus at once individual and collective, conventional and unconventional, constrained and unconstrained. Like other users, many infringed the rules on occasion, there always being good secondary rules to cite in justification. Even those professing never to talk to victims could unbend and shed detachment in the presence of exceptional pathos: it was difficult to be churlish to a young female victim waiting anxiously to be interrogated about her sexual conduct. Counsel often deviated in little matters, and a discreet conversation with a deserving victim was just such a tolerated deviation.

If we consider that for every maxim of conduct we can think of a situation to which it does not apply or in which it can be overruled by a superior maxim; if we consider that unmitigated adherence to principle is regarded as vice or at least folly . . . then it is clear that all efforts to live by an internally consistent scheme of interpretation are necessarily doomed to fail.[80]

One clear influence was a history of acting for the defence. Defence counsel were accustomed to meeting lay clients, and they sometimes exported habits from the one role to the other: one lawyer said, "As a defence barrister I spend a lot of time with my witnesses and I tend to try and do the same, within the limits, with the prosecution witnesses.' It may be supposed that confirmed prosecutors would have done otherwise.

Many witnesses detested cross-examination so much that they reacted viscerally: Victim 20 said, 'I was ill. I collapsed in the witness-box . . . you could tell I was shaking, I was going to pass out, but they didn't offer me a chair or anything. I really wanted to sit down. I could feel myself going, I was hanging on to the table.' And Victim 4, a child, said, 'I just wanted it to finish.' Witnesses felt bullied ('He looked at me like this! He was trying to intimidate me, he was'). They felt traduced: Victim 5 said that the defence counsel had 'twisted it all around, like if I said something, he'd accuse me of lying'. It was as if they had been put on trial themselves: Victim 16 said, 'I felt *I* was trying to prove my innocence in all this. *I* was the victim!' and Victim 18 said, 'I felt embarrassed and really hurt because I felt I was on trial.' Witnesses tended to detest the defence lawyers who had inflicted all that discomfort: Victim 17 said, 'I

---

[80] E. Bittner, 'Radicalism and the Organization of Radical Movements', *American Sociological Review*, 28(6) (Dec. 1963), 934.

would say she [defence counsel] was totally aggressive. I think she was waiting for me to make a mistake because she could see I was nervous.'

It is not remarkable that witnesses were more satisfied with the manner in which they had been examined in chief by the prosecution. After all, prosecutors were attempting to coax 'their' witnesses into producing a cogent story that was favourable to their own case.[81] Victim 18 said the prosecutor was 'dead nice, the other one [defence counsel] was dead rude'. Sixty-seven per cent of the witnesses who had testified in the Raine and Smith sample of Wood Green witnesses called the prosecution 'helpful', fifty per cent 'sensitive', fifty-eight per cent 'concerned', and seventy-one per cent 'patient'.

But prosecutors did steer their witnesses forcibly and peremptorily on occasion, telling them to modulate their delivery ('Now pause, because I can see the shorthand writer's already starting to give up'), adhere to what was thought relevant ('You're volunteering lots of information that I'm not asking questions about'), abstain from commentary ('I'm not asking you to judge what she was doing, I'm asking you to say whether you remember she was there'), and cut short evidence that flouted the hearsay rule[82] ('What she saw you can't say. What we're interested in is what you saw. Let me ask the questions'). Witnesses did not always feel that they had been able to recount their own history as they would have liked: Victim 18, a victim of assault, said:

I wanted to say how I felt and what it's done to my life. I mean, there's one thing I've got to face, and that's she's ruined my life . . . And I just wanted to tell them what I'd been through. . . . [The court wasn't interested] and I don't think that's right. They should listen to the effect it has on people.

Witnesses could not understand why they were so shunned by the lawyers whom they supposed to act for them.[83] Victim 26 complained that 'we have never been spoken to by a prosecution lawyer since the case started, on *our* case. It's *our* evidence that will put that man away'. Victim 16 was nonplussed by the news that there was to

---

[81] See D. Barnard, *The Criminal Court in Action* (London, Butterworth, 1974), 80.

[82] See D. McBarnet, 'Victim in the Box', in W. Chambliss (ed.), *Criminal Law in Action* (New York, Wiley, 1984), 329.

[83] The same has been reported for prosecution witnesses appearing in the Belfast Crown Court. See Jackson *et al.*, 'Called to Court: A Public View of Criminal Justice in Northern Ireland', 7.5.

be a request for her defendant to be bound over to keep the peace: 'because I was injured and because it frightened me and he was so abusive and aggressive, I thought, "why should he?" You know. I'd taken time off work, got braved up for it.' She would have liked to consult the prosecuting lawyer but 'I wasn't allowed to speak to her [counsel] because you're not allowed to speak to them before. I don't know why.'

Other Users

The CPS, police, and counsel were the main groups that had significant dealings with prosecution witnesses. Also present in court, possessing their own private territories, recognized as users and attending the chief clerk's meetings, but almost entirely inconsequential to victims, were the custody staff, probation service, and others more marginal still, the shorthand writers and the defence solicitors and their clerks.

Custody officers were seconded for periods of a year from Brixton Prison to guard and produce defendants. They were effectively invisible, confined chiefly in the subterranean parts of the courthouse, only to surface, *deus ex machina*, in the dock with their charges when trials began. They were wholly segregated from the public world, of no significance to witnesses and victims. I shall show how such segregation was maintained in Chapter 6.

Probation officers serviced defendants and defence counsel, 'put[ting] sticking plaster on any social problems that arise with defendants during the day'. They had continual dealings with the other users, the clerks, ushers, defence counsel, and police, and they were at once circumspect and co-operative, part of the 'team effort': 'We may be the best of friends although we've got to keep in our own corners.' Like the police, they were to be seen in the courtrooms where they reported on defendants for sentencing purposes ('My job is to bring the sentencers and the probation service together'), in the common areas of the courthouse searching for clients, and in their own quarters, where they consulted with defendants and counsel. They shared space with the public, and their casual manner with defence counsel and staff identified them as insiders to be approached for help by civilians. If they had contact with prosecution witnesses it was not of their choosing, an accidental encounter, perhaps, or the result of misjudgment by the civilian. Very typically, they would politely deflect the prosecution witnesses who approached them.

It was defendants, not victims, who were their business. They were not paid to attend to victims and prosecution witnesses. They had clear, structured affiliations in the conflicts of the courthouse, and to have truck with those involved in prosecutions would muddle their public role and create doubts in the minds of their clients and the lawyers who represented them. So it was that, however compassionate their private sentiments might be sometimes, they did not intervene to assist the puzzled or lost victim. On one occasion, for instance, it was learned that the illness of a judge required all the participants in a trial to be dismissed for the day. A probation officer remarked sympathetically that the victim, who was sitting rigid and ignorant outside the courtroom, would be the 'last to know'. But he did not himself inform the victim about what was afoot.

Conclusion

This chapter has been a catalogue of the staff and work of a courthouse, and it has established a little of the special character of the witness as a practical entity that arose in that work. Joanna Shapland once wrote that 'the victim is a non-person in the eyes of the professional participants'.[84] Yet victims were more than that. Non-persons are in large measure invisible and lacking in influence, but victims were taken to have an influence that might on occasion almost be described as baneful. They stirred things up around them. The great, central driving conflict of the Court transformed them into diffuse sources of difficulty and danger for all staff and users. They threatened the conduct of cases. They threatened the appearance of neutrality so carefully cultivated by staff. They threatened the studied competence of counsel. They were awkward companions for the police. In sum, they were used in trials, indeed, they were indispensable to trials, but they were also kept somewhat at bay. Together with others collectively labelled 'the public', the defendants, spectators, support teams and friends and relations of the belligerents, they were thrust to a distance, never fully trusted, denied knowledge about much of what transpired, relegated to the safe, outer margins of the Court's social organization. Victims were outsiders. That was a most fundamental distinction. The Court's social world was divided firmly between those who were professional and those who were not,

---

[84] 'Victim Assistance and the Criminal Justice System', paper delivered to the 33rd International Course in Criminology, Vancouver, Mar. 1983, 8.

between familiars and strangers, the trustworthy and the untrustworthy, the knowing and the unknowing.

Now that I have mustered the staff one by one, described their work and shown how it affected prosecution witnesses, I am in a position to analyse how their relations were organized socially within the confines of the courthouse, and that is the task of the next chapter.

5. Insiders and Outsiders

Three chapters have turned on the conflicts and working practices of the trial. In this short bridging chapter, I shall look at those same processes through a different lens to explain how they engendered a particular social world, a world founded on the preservation of safety and privacy, a world that fitted into the physical space that I shall describe in the next chapter. With some little exaggeration perhaps, the organization of the Crown Court centre at Wood Green may be likened to an array of concentric rings whose character was shaped by the workings of opposition and attraction. Opposition flowed from the dangers, antagonisms, secretiveness, and contaminations of the adversarial system, and attraction from the bonds of those who had to work closely together in conditions of trust. Together they plotted a gradient of zones of trust whose outer reaches were open to all but whose inner recesses were restricted indeed. And to complicate matters further, within two of those zones, there were lesser contours and lines of differentiation that kept people and agencies apart.

Judges: The First Circle

There were people who could not and should not meet, hear, or see one another except under the tightest control, and they were kept apart. Quite emphatically segregated from the rest were the judiciary, the judges of law, and jurors, the judges of fact, and it was the judiciary who were clearly the most august, sacred, and protected of all. One judge remarked on how, in some courtrooms, 'The judge is half-way to the ceiling: very terrifying, very remote, almost throned His Majesty.' He continued:

There has been a long tradition of keeping the judge apart . . . there is a philosophical fear of keeping the judge absolutely separate from the party that he is asked to judge. He is always brought in through a separate entrance; doesn't talk to the parties except formally and in open court; goes away at the end and leaves them to sort out their own messes.

The resident judge and a small, fluctuating group of senior colleagues were at the very epicentre of the Crown Court at Wood Green and, apart from the managed occasions when they ventured into open court, they were insulated socially and physically. Only a few special insiders could penetrate their enclave. Unregulated meetings with counsel could probably be managed well enough. ('If it is counsel you will immediately know who they are and they will know who you are . . . you tend to pick up immediately who the chaps are. They look like counsel. They will probably be wearing their bands. . . . They know where to put their Chinese wall, they are used to doing it.') Unregulated meetings with court users were not wholly welcome because judges wished to appear independent of the partisans.[1] But unregulated meetings with the 'public' with defendants, witnesses, and jurors, were to be avoided. They might well lead to physical danger, embarrassment, importuning, or exposure to improper knowledge: 'You might have your mind contaminated by having heard what [another] is talking about in the wrong setting.' Judges were less fearful of assault than of being compromised: 'Segregation is important because otherwise odd bods would approach you and ask "Why isn't my case making better progress?"'

Judges engaged in fateful deliberations, they were at the heart of the conflicts of the adversarial system, and many of those embroiled in trials would have liked to influence or molest them. They had to be segregated, protected by a watchful staff in their courtrooms, chambers, and dining-room, and shielded by walls, doors, coded locks, and dedicated lifts. They were awarded the greatest privacy of all.

Within an enclave in the building's core, the judges would work and meet. Talk in chambers would generally dwell on the affairs of the Court, the courtroom, and the profession, assistant recorders and recorders perhaps coming to solicit the advice of established colleagues about listings, the probable lengths of trials, and procedure. Counsel would seek indications. Those 'backstage' relations were comparatively informal. Judges tended to address one another by first name. Counsel, ushers, and clerks would call them 'Your Honour' in court but 'Judge' in chambers (and, exceptionally, when counsel and judge knew one another well, judges might address counsel by first name: 'You talk to them as you would outside'). Counsel no longer called each other their 'learned friends' but acquired personal names.

Talk at luncheon, like talk at high table, tended not only to be about 'shop' but about wider and lighter matters. Judging is a

---

[1] See A. Ashworth *et al.*, *Sentencing in the Crown Court* (Occasional paper No. 10, Oxford, Centre for Criminological Research, 1984), 38.

difficult and solitary business ('There is the very real risk of being very lonely . . . you need to be a bit remote, you can't be one of the boys') and such meetings could become important, especially to the newer judges. Without them, the judges might have acquired little consciousness of themselves as a group. After all, one judge's knowledge of another was necessarily imperfect and often second-hand, based perhaps on written articles (one of the Court's judge's *dicta* were reported from time to time and he would write letters to the editors of newspapers[2]) and colleagues' own reports. Administrative staff and users were almost invariably too distant and respectful to gossip about one judge's actions to another. And the outcome was that, as a judge said, 'You never see a judge in action, you [only] see him at lunch as a friend.' It was when the court adjourned for luncheon that colleagues established themselves quite obviously as a collectivity, and such a gathering could become quite intimate and influential in a small court.[3] A sense of community and a distinctive style arose as those presiding in the six courtrooms at Wood Green met together each day and talked, their conversation being led by the resident judge. One judge said:

A classic large court would be . . . There the atmosphere is different. You can't hold one conversation at lunch. You tend to be isolated off as a group. You may not talk too much to the resident judge. With only six of us round the table here you can't fail to talk to him. [Such conversation is helpful] for a number of reasons. One is that you need to know how other people work and how they are thinking. It helps you and stops you doing what used to be the very bad habit in old one-judge courts of developing idiosyncrasies that you don't have the opportunity of noticing. A judge who comes into lunch and says, 'Guess what I did this morning?'—he's done something rather outrageous and the others say, 'What!? You can't have done that!' It's very valuable.

Judges thus inhabited two distinct and connected worlds, moving back and forth between an inner, relatively unbuttoned world beyond the public gaze and the outer, visible, and formal world of the courtroom. One of the newer judges said of the transition from private space to the courtroom: 'There is a very definite tightening up because you are playing in public.' And a more senior colleague remarked:

[2] See e.g. the letter from His Honour Judge Finney urging probation officers to adopt a more punitive stance. *The Times*, 22 Feb. 1990.
[3] See Ashworth *et al.*, *Sentencing in the Crown Court*, 36.

It is perfectly obvious that the degree of informality that one would permit oneself when sitting in court is very much less than when one's living one's private life or one's life in chambers. I mean one can speak to counsel, if counsel come to visit you in chambers about something, you can obviously speak to them in different terms than you would in court. And that applies even more so with members of the public who . . . are entitled to expect and to receive a certain level of formality and, as it were, *gravitas*, when one is dealing with important issues in their lives in public.

Resident judges do much to shape the private quality of a Court. The resident judge at Wood Green was well-liked, known to court staff and some users by an affectionate nickname. Those who had frequent dealings with him, senior probation staff, listing officers and the chief clerk, considered him to be unusually 'consultative'. Unlike some other resident judges, who were grand enough to insist on discussing local affairs only with the heads of criminal-justice agencies based physically outside the courthouse, he tended to discuss those matters directly and informally with the staff present in his court.

About him and his colleagues hovered a group of insiders, the ushers, clerks, the chief clerk, the listing officer, and the senior probation officer, who had privileged access to their quarters. The judges seemed to find their relations with that second circle of staff congenial. For practical purposes, the circle stood for the Court itself, and it translated Wood Green into a place that was itself thought congenial. One judge said that the Court 'has a particular character behind the scenes in that it is a very happy ship and a very well run one. It is a much nicer place to work than some other Courts I won't name.'

The judges' proper sphere remained inside their chambers and the courtroom. Although the resident judge would sometimes tour the court offices at the end of the day, he was inevitably a shadowy and awesome figure. Like Kafka's soldiers on the Great Wall, to whom the Emperor was remote, there were staff who were never obliged to go into courtrooms and chambers, and to them judges were distant indeed, glimpsed only at the Christmas party perhaps, and known largely at second hand and through gossip.

The 'Team': The Second Circle

The court staff and users attached to the Court formed a relatively small and stable population. Many had joined the Court at its very inception in 1980 (the senior probation officer remarked: 'I've grown up with some of the people. Some of the judges were young barristers when I started'). They would meet day after day in conditions of intimacy and interdependence, and it was inevitable that they appeared to stand fixed and familiar against the larger tide of anonymous counsel, police officers, and public that swirled all around them each day. In a potentially dangerous and unsettled place, a place full of strangers, insiders had a special regard for one another. They were relatively well-known, reliable, and close; calm and trusted; fellow professionals who shared a history and were unlikely to abuse trust. They offered a tacit promise of mutual aid. Out of the running contrasts between insider and outsider there grew a sense of unity and friendliness that transcended some of the structured antagonisms of the trial[4] (a probation officer observed, 'It's a shame to think that in a place where such nasty things happen, people can be so happy working here').

Yet it was also the case that the Court's resident users and administrators all stood in an ambiguous and sometimes tenuous relationship one to another. They were members of agencies and institutions representing different and sometimes contradictory interests in the criminal-justice system. On the one hand, it was apparent that they could not be readily collapsed into a single team with an identical purpose. On the other hand, they did recognize a commonality and familiarity that marked them off from the rest.[5] Simmel argued that 'there probably exists no social unit in which convergent and divergent currents among its members are not inseparably woven'.[6] It was just so with members of the second circle. Like segments of the wider world of the Court itself, they kept apart and came together in a pattern that was both intricate and loosely coupled. They were, as were their American counterparts, 'responsive to one another, while still

---

[4] D. McBarnet argued, 'The fact that courts . . . are not just legal institutions but the daily work-places of policemen, lawyers, clerks of court, leads to the development of stereotypes, networks of shared understandings, alliances of alleged adversaries'; *Conviction: Law, the State and the Construction of Justice* (London, Macmillan, 1981), 4. And see J. Eisenstein and H. Jacob, *Felony Justice* (Boston, Little, Brown, 1977), 24–7.

[5] See D. Neubauer, who says of the American courts that 'the police, the prosecutor, the judge, and the defense attorney are tied together in executing their tasks, but at the same time they have differing perspectives on how these tasks should be executed'; *Criminal Justice in Middle America* (Morristown, NJ, General Learning Press, 1974), 13.

[6] G. Simmel, *Conflict* and *The Web of Group Affiliations* (New York, Free Press of Glencoe, 1964), 15.

maintaining independent identities and some evidence of physical or logical separateness'.[7]

The members of that second circle were not uniformly and firmly connected. Some had the wispiest of relations, coming together very infrequently, meeting perhaps only at Christmas parties. They might have had no need to come together. A secretary working in the probation department, for instance, would have had no practical purpose in knowing the ushers. Other resident users in the courthouse might have been better acquainted, but their contacts were still focused and constrained. Formal opponents would almost never visit another's office or work-place. It was only those who did not and would not compromise one another who visited and, between them, there was some 'popping in', as Willmott and Young would have described it.[8] The listing officer used to take his morning coffee with the probation officers, for example.

Insiders would have had little to do with another's superiors, those who took the policy decisions that affected the content and style of work. When I began research in 1989, for example, the local heads of different agencies did not generally know one another by face or name, and the relations between their staff were necessarily somewhat more attenuated in consequence. They were not necessarily conversant, and did not wish to be conversant, with one others' problems, histories, and objectives. Their arrangements for communication and the exchange of information were, as a more general report put it, 'patchy and variable'.[9] Very senior staff of the CPS, for instance, did not believe themselves to be part of the Court's system and administrative structure,[10] were lodged in separate buildings at a remove from the courthouse itself, and did not participate in the chief clerk's meetings (although they *were* represented by a more junior colleague based in the courthouse). They were, they declared, 'interested in the content but not in the venue of trials'.

Users vied with one another for resources, and for time in the

---

[7] J. Hagan *et al.*, 'Ceremonial Justice: Crime and Punishment in a Loosely Coupled System', *Social Forces*, 58(2) (Dec. 1979), 508.

[8] See M. Young and P. Willmott, *Family and Kinship in East London* (London, Routledge and Kegan Paul, 1957).

[9] Lord Chancellor's Dept., *Working Group on Pre-Trial Issues: Report*, Nov. 1990, 135.

[10] It should be remembered that cases at the Crown Court centre were but a part of the responsibility of the Wood Green branch of the CPS. I was reminded by the resident judge that most CPS staff never come near the Crown Court. They are involved not only in the preparation of cases for magistrates' courts but also for other Crown Court centres.

courtroom above all (a CPS law clerk said, 'We're very badly co-ordinated and in competition with one another. We're in competition with the listing office'). They worked frequently in a state of uncertainty and confusion, unsure of one another's movements in a place where movements were often obscure (almost every day court clerks would be asked, 'What's happening? What's going on?' and they would reply, 'Nobody knows what's happening. I don't know myself. . . . Everything's in a complete mess'). There were barriers and boundaries around their core activities. They kept secrets from one another (it would not do for a police officer to overhear a conference between a probation officer and client, or for a probation officer to leaf through papers in the CPS office).

Yet relations were amicable outside those offices, apart from those caches of confidential information, and away from the private consultations. They centred freely on discussions of general or neutral matters, of holidays, families, and sport. They were renewed daily in myriad meetings in the public areas, courtrooms, and offices (a CPS assistant principal law clerk remarked, 'We do get to know [other staff] by coming down here every day really. Most of my staff, I would say, know most of the Court staff. . . . I think I know most of them here but it does take a while to get to know them'). They were co-ordinated by the chief clerk, who was expected to 'make decisions which [were] consistent, reconciling the needs of various groups who [had] conflicting objectives'.[11] They constituted a division of labour in which lesser conflicts worked to achieve a greater good. It was a state that Durkheim would have called organic solidarity.[12]

Such a muting of antagonism was not, perhaps, very surprising. What should be noted about these insiders of the second circle was that they believed themselves to be servicing trials rather than engaged as active combatants: the administrators professed a scrupulous neutrality and the attached users a remoteness from the core conflicts of the Court. Counsel might be fighters but probation officers were not. They were 'not really in a trial. We never go along except perhaps to see the seriousness of a trial.'

There was no one phrase or name used to capture that sense of a loosely structured working collegiality, although 'family spirit' and 'team' and 'one of us' were employed. Perhaps the very absence of a single, agreed vocabulary signified the fundamental tenuousness of a

[11] Lord Chancellor's Dept., *The Crown Court Review* (London, 1990), i. 22.
[12] See E. Durkheim, *The Division of Labour in Society* (Glencoe, Ill., Free Press, 1960).

collectivity constructed around semi-independent groupings and an inescapable conflict.[13]

Membership as an insider was associated with enforceable claims to recognition. It was achieved principally by working exclusively inside the courthouse and that, in turn, was marked by the right to use an office, a right that was bestowed by the Lord Chancellor's Department. It was signified by an unchallenged right to move freely in private space and to sit in portions of the courtroom denied the public[14] (only those called officers of the court were allowed so to sit), by invitations to annual Christmas parties, by the use of first names and other linked symbols of intimacy.

Yet there were clear exceptions: the fact of a press office set firmly inside the courthouse did not convert a stream of temporary agency reporters into insiders, for example. New journalists tended to be repelled when they tried to break into the family. They were, after all, attempting to reach one of the insiders' covers, knowledge about trials. They were potentially dangerous because they sought to make public what insiders were expected zealously to protect. One young woman reporter complained of the reluctance of court officials and police officers to confide the names and addresses of protagonists in trials, and names were vital to one who sold stories to local newspapers on the basis of local interest. Another was refused information, became the subject of critical gossip, and found that his liberal offers to buy drinks in the local public house were spurned by ushers and clerks who were suspicious of his motives. Insiders preferred their own company, insisting that trust could not be bought. One secretary working in the probation department said of the reporter's predecessor:

[He] had been here such a long time, about ten years, I knew him. He got his information from all over the building, and he knew how to get information, but because he had such close contact with Probation, the agency, X at the [press] agency, is telling all these others to come into Probation. We've cut it completely. We can't tell them.'

Membership as an insider was thus most evident in a person's ease of access to knowledge about the Court's affairs. Who could be told

---

[13] Neither was there agreed terminology to describe other features of the Court's world: e.g. the *claques* who attended some defendant had no single title. They were 'followers', 'supporters', or the 'supporters' team'.

[14] When the police were very exceptionally asked to clear the courtroom, it would only be the public areas that were cleared. Sitting elsewhere signified that was one was an insider who posed no threat to good order.

what and when was quite critical in a world marked by suspicion and physical barriers to communication. The possession of secrets defined the insider. That has always been part of their significance. Outsiders were denied all unnecessary knowledge about the Court's people, proceedings, and cases. They were not to know more than was good for them. (One security officer said of outsiders, 'They ask, "any interesting cases going on?" We don't give them any information whatsoever. We just tell them we know nothing about the cases. All we have is a name.') But news moved quickly and effectively *between* insiders. Its passage could be almost subliminal on occasion, so finely tuned were members of the family to one another's nuances of expression. What must have seemed incomprehensible to the stranger, and cloudy enough to a professional visiting from the larger world, was sometimes quite transparent to intimates. It is, after all, a mark of a member's knowledge that much is unspoken and taken for granted, that it is composed of what Garfinkel once called ' "seen but unnoticed", expected, background features'[15] (a probation officer said, 'It's only when you've been here a year or two that you are fully aware'). Sitting in court on one occasion, for example, I was told by a probation officer about an imminent change of plea that was being signalled by 'smiles and winks amongst those who know'.

Links between members were made and renewed by a working population that seemed forever to be physically on the move within the courthouse. Many of the staff and users were peripatetic, wandering purposefully or casually between the courtrooms, public spaces, and offices, carrying messages, lists, and documents, and 'keeping an eye on things'. In those wanderings and patrollings, there were frequent opportunities to exchange information and gossip. They would see and stop and greet each other, identifying fellow members and marking their consciousness of a shared social world within the larger and looser mass of strangers around them. (Simmel observed, 'The unity of society . . . is directly realized by its own elements because these elements are themselves conscious and synthesizing units.'[16])

There were clear features of the inner topography of the courthouse that structured such seemingly chance encounters: the reception desk was a 'natural' stopping-point, not unlike the parish pump,

---

[15] H. Garfinkel, *Studies in Ethnomethodology*, (Englewood Cliffs, NJ, Prentice-Hall, 1967), 36.

[16] G. Simmel, 'How Is Society Possible?' In D. Levine (ed.), *Georg Simmel on Individuality and Social Forms* (Chicago, Univ. of Chicago Press, 1971), 7.

for example, and the receptionist herself was privy to much of what happened. More particularly, perhaps, static conversational clusters would emerge at fixed points in the daily cycle. They would form about the main entrance to the courthouse each morning as police, probation officers, security staff, and receptionist surveyed those entering the building and talked together all the while. They would form in the courtrooms as people waited for things to happen, for trials to begin, for counsel to come out of the judges' chambers, for witnesses and police officers to appear, for consultations between defendants and counsel to end. I have observed that one of the most distinctive characteristics of a courthouse is the long periods of dead time in which staff concentrated together had to divert themselves. Insiders were signified by those who were included in such gossiping knots.

What separated the family or team from others at the fringes was a vigilance or mistrust. If their internal relations were loose and ambiguous, dealings over the boundary separating insiders from outsiders were more wary still. I have already described how no police officer, probation officer, clerk, or usher would talk candidly with members of the 'public', the jurors, defendants, spectators, and witnesses who could have improper motives, partisan interests, and prurient minds, and whose memories were not to be sullied.

I have reported, too, how some members of the public came to court to affirm their innocence or to be sentenced, and how others came to redress their wrongs or see the wrongs of others being righted. They often came with strong feelings that were prone to erupt,[17] feelings that were no part of the professional's experience of the Court, and they posed problems of management. Security staff and police officers responded by repeatedly moving about the courthouse to forestall angry and distressed victims, defendants, and supporters. They positioned themselves in courtrooms or on the stairways, studying the reactions of those who might create disorder. They were cautious lest, as a resident police officer put it, 'things get out of hand. Sometimes you get too many people in court supporting one defendant.' Disorder was more often latent than actual, but such vigilance could not but seal absolutely the distinction between civilian and professional. The public was different. It was prone to break down and become emotional. It could threaten the studied impartial-

[17] On 8 May 1992, at another Court, for example, a man involved in proceedings climbed on to the roof the Royal Courts of Justice and threw slates down onto the cars of judges below. See *The Times*, 9 May 1992.

ity of the insider. And it had no recognized right to know more than a little about trials and procedures. It was to be watched and controlled, not trusted.

Members of the family had recurrent dealings with another group, the outside professionals who did not work solely at the Court, the occupants of the third circle, and those dealings were less guarded than with civilians. One CPS law clerk remarked: 'Ironically with the defence counsel, we're perfectly at ease. There doesn't seem to be an adversarial tension. With witnesses and obviously defendants, there is that.' All professionals were supposed to be governed by an overarching discipline, that was part of being a professional, and they would gossip freely about matters that could never be discussed with civilians. But it was understood that the outside professional was not really 'one of us', was not incorporated in the Court's special web of dependencies, and could be expected to have no sentiment about its relations. Insiders were still a little cautious and hesitant, and information was still controlled in the presence of the fleeting police officers, solicitors, and counsel who came to wage conflict. Insiders had a slight but pervasive fear of manipulation, of being used. The situational exigencies of the adversarial process could not disappear. One probation officer talked of the dangers of solicitors' clerks 'tr[ying] to abuse the system, or be[ing] unprofessional'. His colleague remarked how 'lawyers are devious. It's part of their practice really. Well, not devious as such but indirect or selective in what they say.' And he said of the police:

Most probation officers, probably all probation officers, would be wary about exactly what they talked about to the police and the way in which they discussed it. Really, by virtue of the fact that we have a sort of confidential relationship with the client and therefore we do not loosely talk about him to anybody. You may, of course, if you know police officers quite well, exchange a little bit of banter about a particular sort of chap you know because he's so well known. But you tend not to convey too much to the police. There is a sort of distance in a way because the police will sometimes ask personal questions, like 'Where is so and so living now?' Sometimes they know you know.

Outside Professionals: The Third Circle

The third circle was composed of the police officers, solicitors, and counsel who came in and out of court to despatch their cases but were not sentimentally or practically members of its organization. Few of the third circle were embedded in the social fabric of the Crown Court at Wood Green. They did not really need to know very much about the Court to get on with the business at hand. Defence solicitors' clerks, for instance, would act as the agents of solicitors proper. They were delegated a large number of cases, three or four working in the Court on a regular footing. But their informal relations with the Court staff of the second circle tended to be slight. Only one, a former police officer, was known, and he would join some of the conversational huddles that dotted the inner landscape of the courthouse. His colleagues were unattached. One who had practised in the Court for years frequented only the courtrooms and the public spaces of the courthouse, never the special room set aside for solicitors. She had not known that such a room existed and would not have used it anyway. She had put down no roots.

In much the same fashion, many counsel formed only the most casual acquaintance with the social world outside the listing office, the courtroom, and the 'barristers' mess' ('As to how much we liaise with the administration, we don't at all . . . we come in and we come out'). They did find the staff helpful and some they could call by name, but their work would remain much the same wherever they were. For most practical purposes, a Class 4 burglary case in the third-tier courts at Snaresbrook or Acton would not be very different from a burglary case in Wood Green (the chief clerk of a set of barristers' chambers in the Temple said, 'It's just Court, basically'). When counsel rose to address the court, especially, they claimed to lose a sense of what was distinctive about their setting. They could have been in any Crown Court centre in the country (one observed, 'Once you . . . have the attention of the jury, you are speaking to the jury. It doesn't matter if you are in a field dungeon or where you are. You see, you get sort of impervious to your surroundings as you concentrate'. And a second said, 'It's me, the witness and the judge and I see very few other people.'

Counsel, solicitors, and officers in the case tended to see only those spaces, places, and staff that bore on their purposes. For instance, they could not, did not, and did not care to see the jury waiting areas, the shorthand writers' room, or the chief clerk's office. Before April 1990 and the move to the *Palais de Justice*, what counsel *did* see was courtrooms with poor acoustics, a canteen in which different people were jumbled precariously together ('You are surrounded by danger: there are witnesses, you have no idea who is there, witnesses, jurors, all sorts of things'), the listing office, dull corridors, and a poky robing room ('You don't even have enough room to sit down and so some work in some peace and quiet, which is something which everyone should have').

They were concerned about immediate problems of eavesdropping, discomfort, security, diversion, and privacy in a spartan building, and it was those problems that coalesced roughly into their working knowledge of Wood Green as a centre. They called the Court the Bunker because of their familiarity with its mass of dreary internal spaces, and 'the passageways [and] the canteen' especially. They pronounced on its friendliness ('They are all very cheerful and very helpful,' one said, and another remarked, 'The staff are very nice. They know me by face if not by name. I know some of the ushers by face. That's all'). They talked about its shabbiness ('The Bunker [is] a ghastly building'). They could narrate typical experiences to be had there: there were supposed to be Wood Green juries, Wood Green defendants, and Wood Green judges. A mess folklore had developed to elaborate the Court's dreadful physical character (one barrister said, 'It's horrible, a terrible place. As you know [it] was burned down . . . and I think what happened each time they tried to rebuild it someone tried again. . . . it was before my time. I'm only going on what I was told there'.[18])

A few members of the third circle would find themselves attending the Court with relative frequency, growing to know and be known by staff, identified not only by name but sometimes by nickname. They could become *habitués*. One police officer said simply of the Court, 'It is a place that's familiar to me'. The *habitués* were able, if they wished, to cross the boundary and advance a little into the second circle. All that seemed to be demanded of them was a regularity of attendance at the Court, an understanding of the limits that defined relations, and an appearance of trustworthiness, friendliness, and courtesy. It was counsel who were especially prone to straddle the boundaries. They could be witty and entertaining (after all, talking agreeably was a necessary professional accomplishment), and

[18] It had never burnt down in its short history, but there had been some disorder at the time of the notorious Broadwater Farm disturbances of 1985 in which a police officer was killed. Broadwater Farm, the Crown Court centre, and the office building in which the CPS was housed were all neighbours. They formed a trio of imposing structures in an otherwise flat and uninteresting urban area.

those who allowed themselves to become approachable by lingering in public space could soon be absorbed in the little pockets of people who gossiped as the mornings wore on. A court clerk reflected:

When we are in court, there is a degree of banter that goes on between ourselves and the barristers. . . . they become familiar faces, you have a bit of banter with them. . . . Of course, some of them are extremely pleasant, others are more formal, but like everywhere you go they form a spectrum of the more stiff and starchy ones to the other extreme, and you would respond to it.

A barrister said, in his turn, 'When I go there, there's not a clerk, telephonist, shorthand writer, usher, that I don't know. . . . I do feel as if I fit in there, which is nice. My first-ever trial—two, nearly three years ago—was actually at Wood Green. . . . [then] about April last year, these briefs started coming in and they've come in a lot, and I've been much more there than anywhere else.' Yet barristers could never be considered complete members of the second circle. They had independent lives and loyalties. It was considered difficult to incorporate them further, to entice them to join court committees such as the chief clerk's meeting (one member of the CPS suggested that the question in mind was 'Will I get paid?'). Another barrister said, 'They're all very cheerful and very helpful . . . I would feel at home there, because I have been there several times, but I wouldn't consider myself part of the Wood Green establishment.'

The 'Public': The Fourth Circle

I have already described the public, who were not really a public at all but an uneasy agglomerate of spectators (there were perhaps two or three men who came to the Court every day for diversion); jurors before they were sequestered in their own quarters, defendants on bail, defence and prosecution witnesses, supporters, families, and friends.

Only one group within that agglomerate was marked out for special recognition and segregation, and that was the jury, the 'judges of the facts of a case'. It was supposed that jurors should not arrive with prejudicial knowledge, nor should their minds become contaminated in the courthouse itself. They were required on induction to 'say if you know anyone in the trial, a barrister or a defendant. It's no good going halfway through a trial and then the trial folds.' Before April

1990, they were forced to eat promiscuously with others in the Bunker and they would again be warned that 'there is only one canteen—everyone eats there, defendants, barristers. Not the judges! It's very important not to discuss your case in the canteen.' After April 1990, protection against taint was assured as jurors were closeted in their special quarters in the *Palais de Justice*.

The rest of the public came and went in their multitudes, part of the nameless crowd of the courts, not distinguished from one another by clothing or insignia but very different in dress and demeanour from the professionals, considered hardly memorable apart from a few notorious local families. They had no recognized stake in the Court, no great knowledge of its language,[19] topography, or inhabitants, and no reputation for trustworthiness. (New jurors being inducted into the Court were told, 'Don't leave any valuables around. We don't only have barristers and jurors but quite a few villains as well!') The public tended characteristically to enter the courthouse as strangers[20] and would then proceed to wait dejectedly on the benches or in the canteen, at a remove from insiders, smoking, talking to companions perhaps, or in morose seclusion. After all, in the main, it was their problems that were about to be exposed or reanimated painfully and in public. In a sense, they represented the emotional and disorderly in crime[21] and public life that the very orderliness of the Court was designed to balance.[22]

Recall that the average length of trials at Wood Green was a mere five hours. Many trials ended on the very day they began. It was uncommon for members of the inner circles to have prolonged relations with the public. The police might do so, but the frequency of their contacts with the victim and prosecution witnesses declined after the first encounter, and by the time of trial they could be near-strangers to one another again.[23] Counsel would characteristically see

---

[19] See P. Goodrich, *Languages of Law* (London, Weidenfeld and Nicolson, 1990), 222.

[20] Joanna Shapland said: 'They will be nervous, unsure and, above all, confused. Many of the difficulties that victims face in court are due to the fact that they are strangers whereas many of the people with whom they deal—the professionals—are certainly not strangers in that environment'; 'Victims and Court Services', paper given to Victim Support Conference, Warwick University, 8 July 1989, 1.

[21] See M. Wiener, *Reconstructing the Criminal* (Cambridge, Cambridge Univ. Press, 1990), 49.

[22] J. Brown remarked that 'over and above the provision of functional space . . . the building generates imagery and can operate as a symbol of order in itself'; 'A General Survey', *Architects' Journal*, 18 June 1980, 1193.

defendants and witnesses only on the day of the trial itself. Users and administrative staff had too little time and too great a stake in the preservation of professional distance to be more than perfunctorily courteous in their response to the public. On one exceptional occasion only did I hear a young woman defence counsel confide passionately that she hoped that her client would be acquitted, but such a show of feeling was uncommon. More usual was the remark made by an experienced probation officer about his clients, 'you are offering friendship, certainly, and understanding, but you are not going to get too involved and they know that and pick that up very quickly. You are there for the day. I imagine I'm quickly forgotten by people. I certainly quickly forget the clients.'

The experiences of the public were affected accordingly. The public felt themselves to be members of an outer circle at the very margins of the Court. Victim 5's mother said of it all: 'There are so many people walking about, and you don't know who's who or what's happening . . . you're just left.' The boundary between the public and professionals was the greatest of all, the Court's social world being divided firmly between those who were professional and those who were not, between familiars and strangers, the trustworthy, the knowing and the unknowing. It was in this sense that the distinction between outsiders and insiders was the most fundamental feature of the social organization of the courthouse. It marked a chasm which could not be crossed.

Conclusion

The four circles were an insider's map of trust, privacy, and safety, and the outermost circle was populated by those who were thought to be the most faceless, unreliable, ephemeral, and volatile of all, the public who had to be kept apart from the rest. The circles were not only social and symbolic: they framed administrative action and they were marked out in physical space. Let me now turn to the manner in which they were embedded in the very architecture of the courthouse.

---

[23] See J. Shapland *et al.*, Victims in the Criminal Justice System (Aldershot, Gower, 1985); M. Tuck and P. Southgate, *Ethnic Minorities, Crime and Policing* (London, HMSO, 1981); and M. Maguire and T. Bennett, *Burglary in a Dwelling: The Offence, the Offender and the Victim*, (London, Heinemann, 1982).

6. Space

'Who and what interferes with what and whom, to what
extent, when and how, are significant questions that the
urban designer now has to ask himself. (S. Chermayeff and
C. Alexander, *Community and Privacy*)

The Court formed a world spread out in space, and its contours and
divisions were refracted in the built design of the courthouse that
contained it. Indeed, it is a little difficult to write of container and
contained as things apart. The Court and courthouse were importantly one. Read aright, the courthouse was an icon or map of social
organization. The very arrangement of physical space in the Crown
Court centre confirmed identities, segregated groups, and managed
relations. It is ever so with architecture. Evans observed of the classi-
cal architecture of prisons, another segment of the criminal-justice
system, 'These buildings, with their proliferating components and
patterned plans, were to map the location of staff and inmates, guide
their movements and mediate the transactions between them. . . . it
was always architecture that fixed the shape of experience.'[1] The
social and the architectural were also joined in the courthouse, and
this had profound consequences for the experiences of prosecution
witnesses.

The Court as a Spatial Order

The first chapter reported how the Crown Court centre had occupied two courthouses during its lifetime. The Bunker was the first, a
'crash' court in a utilitarian and temporary building that was planned
in January 1977 and opened in 1980. It had been thought that
building the *Palais de Justice* was a difficult undertaking that would
take a long while to complete: the architect observed, 'Somebody . . .
decided it was very difficult to knock four courts quickly into the old
building and it would be easier and quicker to spend a million
pounds on building another special, purpose-built piece at the side
which, in the long term, could form part of the larger complex.' The

[1] R. Evans, *The Fabrication of Virtue; English Prison Architecture 1750–1840* (Cambridge,
Cambridge Univ. Press, 1982), 6.

purpose-built piece was, said the building's project manager, 'designed as a box which they were going to just temporarily get people in'. The temporary building was temporary for a long time. A court clerk introducing it to new jurors in 1990, observed it was 'temporary ten years ago'. The building was devoid of ornamentation apart from the indispensable royal coat of arms above the entrance and the judges' bench (pl. 6.1).

PL. 6.1. *The Entrance to the Bunker*

A court clerk called it 'a disgusting building, really'. Barristers and users were even more scathing, describing it variously as 'appalling', 'the pits', 'grotesque', 'terrible' and 'ghastly'. They bemoaned the state of the lavatories and the absence of quiet spaces for study and consultation. They complained about the absence of privacy:

It is very overcrowded there. I suppose it is a classic example of a court which really needs new and better facilities. . . . we were doing a very long affray at Wood Green . . . and there was an adjournment half way through the afternoon, and so we went into the gents' toilet, a number of us, and we were discussing the case, then suddenly one of them said, 'Ssh' [and the] cubicle opened, and out came a juror!

Witnesses were unimpressed. One victim described the Bunker as 'an old building with just one long corridor, some courts downstairs, and some courts upstairs'. In retrospect, revisiting the Bunker, the Court's senior probation officer observed. 'I felt ashamed of the place, its inconveniences and lack of character, a feeling I had not consciously sensed during the ten years we were in residence.'

The Bunker courthouse was a small, square, plain building with sides approximately 30 metres long, set on three floors, with a ground surface area of some 1,000 square metres and a total floor area thrice that.[2] It was supposed originally to become used as an administrative adjunct of the far larger *Palais de Justice* when that was completed: 'They would gut that building and turn it into the offices for that Court, so it was designed like a building that they could rip the guts out of.' Plate 6.2 shows the two courthouses side by side, the one utilitarian, the other fantastic, resembling as a judge put it, 'the Starship Enterprise sitting on a girls' school'.

PL. 6.2. *The Bunker and the* Palais de Justice

The Bunker's inner spaces were correspondingly austere. Six utilitarian courtrooms were surrounded by meagre, cramped, and 'confused' spaces in which staff, users and the public were forever 'bumping into one another'. (A barrister said, 'The building is unusual because there's no proper accommodation for counsel and you have to be rather careful if you're going to deal with a case that you're not overheard.') Space could be regarded as confused when it

[2] I am grateful to Mina Moshkeri of the LSE Drawing Office for preparing the detailed plans of the 2 courthouses and the courtroom.

was 'shared by too many people to permit natural, unconscious self-policing',[3] and the most confused space of all was the canteen. There were no separate dining rooms for staff, jurors, barristers, and public, and it was a consequence that different groups could find themselves in dangerous proximity.[4] Yet a dense population and frequent encounters also gave birth to a sense of sociable intimacy. A court clerk said on the eve of the move to the new courthouse, 'This building is spartan but quite cosy in one sense and that's what we are all frightened we are going to lose.' Later, after the move, a member of the security staff looked back to the Bunker and said, 'You had a far friendlier atmosphere because you were thrown together.' I shall deal with all these matters towards the end of this chapter.

The temporary Bunker and the permanent *Palais de Justice* had been planned by architects of the Property Services Agency in 1977. They were both early and pioneering. Work on the *Palais de Justice* was to be fed into a meticulously detailed and continually revised *vade mecum*, *The Crown and County Courts Standards and Design Guide*, first produced in 1985 and hereafter called *The Guide*. *The Guide* was produced by a standing committee of court administrators and users, and it reflected the experience gained at Wood Green and elsewhere. Further guidance and direction were secured by a Court Standards Working Party that would visit new buildings after some six months of use to discover how their inhabitants responded to the special spaces that had been created for them: 'You get all the feedback from the Chief Clerk and the clerks that run it, and the judges and everybody else, so we know for the next time. . . . Now the people who are very difficult to get hold of are, of course, the public.' There were consultations with users and administrators as the work progressed.[5] It will be noted that both buildings, the simple and the elaborate, embodied the insiders' map of the social world with all its preoccupations about safety and confidentiality. The courthouses were intended to do away with the disorder and embarrassment that

---

[3] A. Coleman, *Utopia on Trial: Vision and Reality in Planned Housing* (London, Hilary Shipman, 1985), 45.

[4] A Central Office of Information poster displayed in the Bunker and publicizing the new courthouse made much of the fact that 'the façade of the old Woodall House will be retained but everything else will be new, providing, in particular, separate dining facilities for each group of court user i.e. Judge and Justices, Members of the Bar, Jurors in addition to a public dining-room for the use of witnesses and members of the public'.

[5] The architect talked about 'presentations [being] made and shown to rather large groups of people'.

could arise in confrontations between groups of volatile people.[6] After all, as the Management Support Division of the Lord Chancellor's Department reported in 1990, 'The Crown Court by its nature attracts a number of undesirables, some bearing grudges against the Judiciary, police or staff and any perceived lack of security affords opportunities for these people to inflict harm and damage.'[7] There were dangers. The most confidential conversations took place in the courthouses. There were people who would find it compromising to be near one another. And the result was that even the more rudimentary of the two buildings, the bleak Bunker, represented an attempt to put architecture to work in the management of behaviour.

From the first, there was a careful manipulation of the symbolic meanings and physical properties of space. The twin buildings of the Crown Court centre at Wood Green, the little and the grand, were placed next to one another, far back from a busy road in their own landscaped terrain, in the kind of frontier space that Lawrence called a 'transition zone between the public world (the outside, social, profane) and the private world (the inside, personal, sacred)'.[8] After April 1990, especially, those who set out for the centre were quite obviously forced to quit the everyday world as they approached the new courthouse along a path of distinctive pale bricks and past lawns and shrubs:

The provision of an external space between the public footway and the Courthouse is essential. At the scale of the individual user, its crossing allows time to prepare for the forthcoming experience prior to the tension point of the entrance threshold. Change of level, enclosure, view, orientation, surface texture and architectural incident can all contribute towards a successful solution.[9]

[6] Before the founding of the Crown Court and the recent wave of courthouse construction, courts had been sited in buildings that incorporated a lesser preoccupation with control. The former Essex Quarter and Borough Sessions and Court of Assize, for instance, had been housed in Chelmsford shire-hall where, it was reported, 'in the early days, it was necessary to escort two of the four judges to court via the single public staircase through the milling throng. Even after adaptations were carried out it was never possible completely to segregate the judges, jurors and prisoners from other court users. There were no dining facilities and problems arose when jurors, witnesses and sometimes defendants chose to use the same public house or restaurants'; 'Chelmsford Crown Court in Focus', *Your Court*, (2(5) (June/July 1987), 4.

[7] Lord Chancellor's Dept., *The Crown Court Review* (London, 1990), 51.

[8] R. Lawrence, 'Connotation of Transition Spaces Outside the Dwelling', *Design Studies*, 2(4) (Oct. 1981), 203.

[9] Unnamed, undated, unattributed document prepared by the Property Services Agency, p. 13.

Courthouses are amongst the few pieces of consciously grand architecture still being designed (the project manager of the *Palais de Justice* reflected, 'There are very few buildings we build with civic pride these days. . . . There are almost no public buildings anymore. The nearest you get to a public building is shopping malls.') And they are one of the very few structures intended to transact important ceremonial business.[10] Their very appearance is devised to impart a sense of their central place in public affairs. The Property Services Agency argued that 'the designer must be aware that visual imagery is important. Dignity, calm, stability and humanity are all qualities which should be associated with Courthouses and must somehow be interpreted into the design.'

It was thus entirely by design that the new *Palais de Justice* that lay before the visitor was an imposing building with turrets, pinnacles, and *flèches*. Plate 6.3, a photograph of an architect's model, shows how it was intended to loom large and high over its surroundings. The courthouse had five complex, tapering floors that reached 34 metres above ground, and another floor, containing the cells, below ground. The building itself had a ground-floor surface area of 3,000 square metres and a total floor area of 11,574 square metres.[11] Apart from the Alexandra Palace (a people's pleasure palace), a Victorian pumping station, and the dishevelled Bruce Castle further down the road, it was probably the only piece of distinguished monumental architecture in the Borough of Haringey. It was enclosed by a grand Victorian Gothic façade 'that seems to have come from a fairy tale',[12] a façade some 70 metres long that marked it out as a special place. It worked, as a whole generation of Crown Court courthouses were supposed to work, to 'engender a feeling of awe and respect in the public. . . . The design were [*sic*] to put the fear of God into the ungodly . . .'[13]

---

[10] Sumner argued that the criminal-justice system is 'the setting for one of the most powerful symbolic rituals in any society, where good is marked off from evil'; 'Reflections on a Sociological Theory of Criminal Justice Systems;, in C. Sumner (ed.), *Censure, Politics and Criminal Justice* (Milton Keynes, Open Univ. Press, 1990), 47.

[11] *Wood Green Crown Court* (London, Laing, 1989), 5. Even so, it was a fairly modest edifice, a reaction to earlier and much larger courthouses. Its architect remarked that 'times change. When the Wood Green Court was being designed there was a point of view that the courts that had been built in the previous generation were too big, there were too many courts in one building, and they were too difficult to administer. The notion at that time was for 4–6 courts. Since then, things have changed yet again.'

[12] A. Sheehan, 'Court in a Pint Pot', *Building Today*, 5 April 1990, 26.

[13] Property Services Agency, 'Designs for Judgement', *Construction*, 66 (Sept. 1988), 29.

PL. 6.3. *An Architect's Model of the* Palais de Justice

It was in this fashion that space and matter were displayed to make it clear that going to Court was no ordinary event. Plate 6.3 again shows how there was to be a considerable symbolic passage, a passage that was emphasized first on approaching the courthouse and again at its very threshold (its project manager observed 'the judges see the [building] as something to reinforce their control'). The Court did indeed impose control on the public as soon as they entered its doorway. No one was supposed to go in or out without passing staffed checkpoints at a single entrance (Pl. 6.4). Visitors were to be scrutinized, their possessions searched and their cameras and tape-recorders very probably removed. In the *Palais de Justice*, the Court's authority would be reinforced as visitors passed the windows of an internal guardhouse, the security staff's quarters, that looked out on all those who went by (a member of the security staff remarked of it that 'we have a far better control'); by a prominent reception desk where uniformed staff tended to cluster and eye new-comers; and by a third line of control, the door and offices of the police 'law and order unit', set a few yards further on.

Pl. 6.4. *The Entrance to the* Palais de Justice

The newly entered incomer would then be fed into a series of distinct and secure areas that were part of a most elaborate machinery of control. There was osmosis. Each of the Court's social circles were protected against the circles further out; each occupied a designated territory sealed from the rest, a territory known as a 'circulation system'; and each was restricted in the movements of its members from one piece of terrain to another. Each circulation system was a little world with its own discrete entrances and exits, stairways, corridors, and rooms. Each was insulated against the others by more or less visible barriers. The less visible barriers were supplied by the signs that were not there and the information that was not given, by absences and silences, by the locked doors marked 'private' that indicated to the outsider nothing of what lay beyond. They were found in a proliferation of transitional or 'liminal spaces', the corridors and culs-de-sac set before private places, which proclaimed to the public that they were, in effect, about to enter a reserved area in which they could have no proper business (Plates 6.5 and 6.6 show such culs-de-sac in the Bunker and the *Palais de Justice*).

The project manager called those spaces 'semi-private', and remarked, 'Barristers [and others] do like their rooms tucked away a little bit so that you like to put them down a corridor, so someone would feeling uneasy walking that corridor unless they knew they

PL. 6.5. *A Transitional Space in the Bunker*

PL. 6.6. *A Transitional Space in the* Palais de Justice

were a barrister. . . . Most people would think, 'Oh, it's only for bar-risters' and they wouldn't go down there.' Visible barriers were offered by the edges and boundaries[14] that barred people's move-ments, concealed spaces, and prevented sight and hearing: 'People that use these buildings actually only see a quarter of them. Just the

[14] See M. Lavin, 'Boundaries in the Built Environment: Concepts and Examples', *Man-Environment Systems*, 11(5, 6) (1981), 195–206.

bits they use. So they've got no idea what goes in the rest.' I shall deal with some of those matters in turn.

Fig. 6.1[15] shows the courthouse to be a collection of different, restricted places[16] in which different groups waited and worked until the time came to meet on common ground. It was only in the court-room that members of the four circles converged for judgment,[17] and they converged under the most tightly regulated conditions.

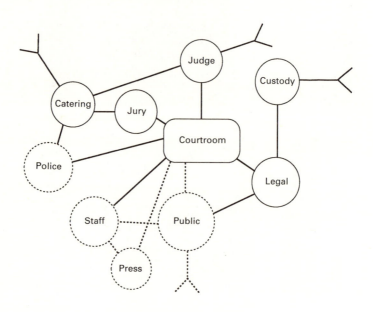

FIG. 6.1. *Worlds in Space*

Space in the Bunker

Circulation Systems

I shall explore what Evans called the 'latent powers of architecture'[18] by focusing principally on their effects in the rudimentary Bunker. I

---

[15] This figure is based on one displayed in the unpublished, unattributed PSA document quoted above.

[16] See D. Canter, *The Psychology of Place* (London, Architectural Press, 1977), 118.

[17] See W. Sobel, 'When the Bench Puts its Case Before Architects', *AIA Journal*, 58(2) (Oct. 1972), 25.

[18] Evans, *The Fabrication of Virtue*, 6.

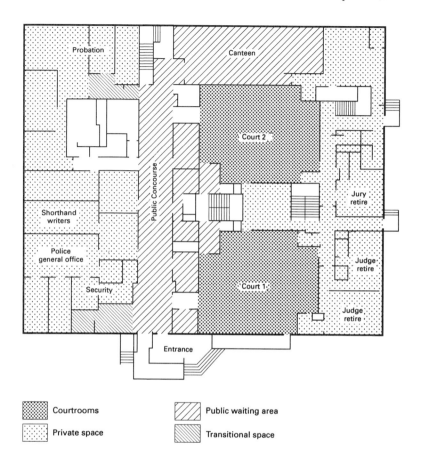

FIG. 6.2. *Space in the Bunker*

shall then proceed to discuss the changes wrought by the more sophisticated design of the *Palais de Justice*. The two buildings did very much the same work. Both defined, segregated, and controlled populations, and their chief instrument was the circulation system. Let me begin with that first (see Fig. 6.2).

Architects and administrators distinguished four parallel universes and set them down in a collection of Chinese boxes that intersected only in the courtroom. The architect superintending the *Palais de Justice* project called it 'four buildings in one'. In a more modern and

elaborate courthouse, each of those universes would be equipped
with all the trappings of a free and independent structure: lifts, passages, entrances, and places to meet, wash, and eat[19] (*The Guide* stipu-
lated that jurors should be provided with everything they need inside
their own circulation area). Each would be insulated against the rest
by guards, walls, alarms, emergency lighting, escape doors, and locks.
The architect described the system thus:

> Firstly there is the obvious segregation of the defendant. He's in custody and
> for security reasons you've just got to segregate him and keep him away. So
> the defendant's in straightforward segregation. The judges obviously, because
> of the pressure on the judges, they are completely separate. . . . Juries are on
> a separate circulation of their own. . . . the day they come into the court, on
> the first day of being a juror, they are a member of the public, they go to a
> point and say, 'I'm on a jury today' and hand in their jury summons, and
> from that moment on they are transformed into jurors and not members of
> the public. . . . We've ended up with four circulation patterns, the fourth
> being the public . . . Now the public are the barristers, the solicitors, the
> probation service, witnesses, family of the defendant, it could be anybody,
> and there is a very limited attempt at segregating that.

Members of those different universes were, in effect, secluded and
stored in their own safe quarters without any need to incommode,
embarrass, or frighten one another. They were kept apart, the better
to confront one another in the courtroom when the time came.
There could, after all, be numerous difficulties and dangers if they
were permitted to meet prematurely and for any length of time.[20]
Segregation emphasized and preserved a system of structured differentiation: it reinforced the symbolic boundaries between groups, prevented them from merging or colliding, and consolidated their
ranking in a hierarchy built on privacy.[21]

---

[19] Older buildings could often not be so described. The public areas of London's
only second-tier Crown Court centre, the Old Bailey, had no canteen, no telephone,
and few places to wait. See *The Independent*, 14 July 1989.

[20] See B. Schwartz, 'The Social Psychology of Privacy', *American Journal of Sociology*,
73 (May 1968), 742.

[21] In so doing, it resembled the social and spatial system of privacy described by A.
Lindesmith and A. Strauss: 'Privacy may be conceptualized as a series of concentric
circles. The inner circle is forbidden to all trespassers. One's trusted intimates may
enter into the second circle, and so on, as one moves to the outer circles that are
accessible to all. This spatial symbolism is actually embodied in the architecture of
dwellings, houses of worship, and public buildings, and in the rules permitting or forbidding entry into various rooms'; *Social Psychology* (New York, Holt, Rinehart and
Winston, 1968), 333–4.

Most private and secure were the judges, jurors, and defendants, hidden away in complex spaces within the deepest recesses of the building; least secure were the public, who were assigned relatively uncomplicated, large, and exposed areas in the 'central core or axis from which most non-judicial functions of the Court building radiate'.[22] The Court's project manager said that the public areas were made 'as simple as possible' because they were to be used by people who 'don't use the building every day. They most probably visit it once in a lifetime.' Abutting the public circulation area were the courtrooms and the 'private and semi-private accommodation occupied by LCD [Lord Chancellor's Department] and Non LCD staff and Probation, Custody Visits and refreshment facilities',[23] facilities known colloquially as the 'canteen'. The public circulation area was a place of waiting, milling, and meeting open to everyone who could pass the security checkpoint. It was also an important thoroughfare for users, staff, and public as they went about their journeyings from place to place, and I shall discuss the problems they faced below.

Home Territories

Brown remarked generally how 'each [Court] occupant tends to draw strict boundaries round his own sphere of operations with unspoken hostilities emanating from the participants'.[24] Staff, users, and judiciary were distinguished by their occupancy of special private spaces, spaces I shall call 'home territories', that lay within the larger circulation areas. A home territory may be defined as a 'private retreat for some special group',[25] and the very right to retire to such a place signified that one was an insider and not an outsider confined to the public realm.

It was chiefly within their own home territories that people felt safe, engaged in 'unsanctioned performances',[26] stored secret data, and discussed confidential matters. A home territory was a piece of 'defensible space'[27] marked off from the rest by physical or token boundaries; a place in which one could exercise some personal control over who could enter and what could be done; a place, in short,

---

[22] *The Guide*, 10.1.

[23] Ibid.

[24] J. Brown, 'A General Survey', *Architects' Journal*, 18 June 1980, 1197.

[25] S. Cavan, *Liquor License: An Ethnography of Bar Behavior* (Chicago, Aldine, 1966), 205.

[26] S. Lyman and M. Scott, 'Territoriality: A Neglected Sociological Dimension', *Social Problems*, 15(2) (1967), 66.

[27] See O. Newman, *Defensible Space* (London, Architectural Press, 1973).

distinguished by the authority, exclusiveness, and interest that owner-
ship confers. To be in a home territory was to be away from
strangers and with one's own. It was there, in their 'mess', that barristers could relax, gossip, dress, and read, untouched by defendants,
jurors, and the public; court staff could unbend as they worked and
conversed with one another; probation officers could prepare and
discuss reports in 'visual and aural privacy'[28] ('In the office, it doesn't
matter what I say in this office, nobody is going to hear, hopefully no
juror will come through that outer door, so this is a little private
here,' said one probation officer); and the police could 'assemble and
rest'.[29] A CPS law clerk said of her general office, the 'CPS room',
'You know there aren't going to be jurors walking past, bumping
into you, so you don't have to watch what you are talking about.'

The home territory was a place where one was not strenuously on
show or unusually vigilant. A security guard remarked that his room
in the Bunker, although small, 'is our withdrawal room, our little
space, where we can relax and be ourselves'. (It may now be seen
how great was the concession he had made when, on a rare occasion, he allowed an outsider, a distressed witness, into that 'little
space' and gave her a cup of tea.)

The personal and private meanings of a home territory were often
proclaimed by the kettles, plants, ornaments, and pictures that people
conventionally use to mark informal spaces in a formal institution[30]
(a member of the security staff observed with satisfaction, 'We have a
kettle and a fridge. We are comfortable'). The police, probation officers, security and administrative staff had made their rooms especially homely. They were full, self-conscious insiders who were on
more or less fixed attachment to the Court, the probation officers in
many cases regarding their posting as the final phase of their careers.

Not all staff wished or needed to domesticate their quarters, others
considered that they had a better base elsewhere, and others still
found their courthouse quarters flawed. On one level, the issue
seemed to turn generally on the relations between the user and the
Court and, more precisely, on the stability of the user's group,
the frequency of its use of different kinds of space, its cycle of work
activity, and the existence of a rival home territory. A number of
people tended to make only the most perfunctory visits to their

offices and rooms in the courthouse, working in the public parts of the building when they were busy and deserting it when they were not. The shorthand writers, for example, had not made their quarters particularly welcoming or habitable (some preferred to retreat into other uninhabited rooms because they wished to smoke and could not do so in their own place), and the solicitors' room and press room were very little used.

Again, the CPS law clerks were largely new, young, and shifting in population, assigned to court work for a while before learning other skills, and their social world was based elsewhere, in a large office block several hundred yards away from the Court. They sometimes felt uneasy in the presence of their seniors in the one undifferentiated space of the 'CPS room' (one said that 'it's a bit uncomfortable if your boss is there'). The 'CPS room' in the courthouse was itself indifferently domesticated in consequence. It was no one's home, being, as a law clerk put it, 'not particularly personalized—it's got a few little pictures on the wall, a few jokes and things like that, but they've been there for ages'.

On another level, the adequacy of private space turned on its privacy, freedom, and safety. A good home territory was sealed against unwelcome intrusion. It was not incursions from other professionals which were feared: they posed little threat to freedom or confidentiality. It was insiders, not the public, who came to the CPS room, for instance, and they were defined as innocuous: a senior official said, 'Anybody who comes into my office tends to be police officers or counsel, you don't have to guard yourself.' Very similarly, the security staff liked their new quarters in the *Palais de Justice*:

It is more cut off from the public, a better environment. They would have to come right through to find us. The only reason they are going to come to this end is to go to the canteen or to read the list. We are better shielded . . . [we come here] just to get peace for a few minutes, to unwind. We like to see the staff . . . the staff know where we are. To the public we are cut off. I would say we are well situated.

But other home territories (the police 'law and order suite', for example) neighboured public space, were accessible to the public, and were, indeed, designed to be visited by the public. They could

---

[30] For a discussion of territorial markers, see E. Goffman, *Relations in Public* (London, Allen Lane, 1971), 41.

be penetrated by outsiders[31] who made warranted enquiries and
'unwarranted intrusions',[32] their seclusion was less than sure, and
they worked less well for staff in consequence. Even the better-
shielded places could be breached sometimes: a juror had once accidentally wandered into the probation offices in the Bunker and
overheard counsel discussing a client's 'antecedents', the defendant's
history of convictions and penalties. That was a most damaging piece
of knowledge to reach a jury.

Maps

The geographical distribution of home territories carefully mapped
all the complex, tense, and conflicting relations of the court organization itself. For example, *The Guide* placed the 'CPS room' 'on non-
LCD staff circulation with good access to courts and near Police
Liaison Suite',[33] but the room was sited well away from the probation offices. Above all, geography plotted the looseness of the connections binding the parts of a court together. Like the God of Bishop
Berkeley, it was only in the mind of the architect that the simultane-
ous relations and existence of all the parallel universes and their
component private spaces were held together. Users, staff, and public
were effectively separate and blind. To them, the courthouse did not
really operate as a whole, as one, simple, internally functioning
entity, but as four different buildings. Its project manager remarked:

The skin holds the whole thing together, but those units have got to work
well as separate units, and it's no good saying, 'I've got a subtle relationship
between the judges' rooms and the public space', as no one ever sees the
subtle relationship That's not what you've got to worry about. What you've
got to worry about is all the judges' accommodation having one sort of relationship, and then all the public can have another one. . . . You tend to
design the [different spaces] as the whole and then, as the whole design gets
together, you pull them out and treat them separately, and then push them
back in again.

Those severed spaces were arrayed on a continuum from the unambiguously public to the very private: the building project manager
observed, 'There is a hierarchy and we've got a great chart that
shows all those relations.'

[31] See N. Felipe and R. Sommer, 'Invasions of Personal Space', *Social Problems*,
14(2) (1966).
[32] Lyman and Scott; 'Territoriality', 72.   [33] *The Guide*, 8.4a.

Witnesses, supporters, spectators, and bailed defendants[34] were the most public of all, for they had no home territory. That was one of the senses in which they *were* the public. They were obliged to congregate in full view in the entrance, concourse, and waiting areas, and I shall discuss the behaviour that revolved around them at length below.

The security staff and the police were at the mouth of the courthouse, maintaining 'visual control' over that public, representing what the police officer in charge called 'a presence at the front entrance', and lending symbolic and physical support to one another. The project manager said, 'You still traditionally try to keep the police near the main entrance with the security staff and, thinking of Wood Green, the security staff are one side and the police are on the other. There is that sort of link.' The police and security staff did indeed have just such a link, which turned on their dual and allied responsibility for controlling the public. The senior member of the security staff said:

We have a wonderful liaison with the police. I can't say enough about the co-operation we have with the Metropolitan Police force here. It has always been a wonderful relationship. We help and support each other.

The rooms of the police and security staff were stationed so that the public could be surveyed and, *pari passu*, the public could see something of them too. The security staff were visible but they were also somewhat physically inaccessible in their large-windowed observation post stuck at the very end of the courthouse, away from the main direction of the public flow, and the public rarely intruded on them.

It was the police private space that was not very private at all. Design forced civilians to move past the law-and-order suite as they penetrated the courthouse; 'They wander in with their letters in their hand, wanting to know what to do, where to go.' A permeable suite, repeatedly visited by strangers, was not a secure home territory. A police officer said, 'I am always careful what I say because you never know who is in the office. They could be witnesses, defence solicitors, and counsel. You never know who is in there. You always have to be careful.'

---

[34] It was only remanded defendants who were treated as sufficiently distinct to be awarded their own circulation system. The defendant on bail was, for practical architectural purposes, simply another member of the public: 'When you actually define people as defendants, they would normally be coming out of the custody area under a certain amount of control,' said the architect.

A little further along the continuum were the territories of those who had frequent dealings with the public world of witnesses, lawyers, and bailed defendants, and who were, indeed, deemed administratively to be members of the public themselves, barristers, probation, CPS, and police. They were allotted what was called 'public accommodation' that 'usually flows out of those main areas so you get those rooms coming off the concourse somewhere'. The public nature of that public accommodation was somewhat ambiguous and confused, reflecting the administrative and architectural relegation of quite diverse and sometimes antagonistic groups to one residual category. The problem of jumbling so many different people together was acknowledged by administrators and architects, but there were physical limits to the number of separate circulation systems that could be incorporated within a single shell. The project manager of the *Palais de Justice* observed, 'There's never been the intention [of further dividing the public]. What we've tried to avoid is a separate circulation for witnesses, because we've already got four segregated circulations, the thought of a fifth!'

Some public accommodation *was* public enough, although it was also importantly private. It was expected that defendants should be able to go to the probation offices and prosecution witnesses to the police liaison suite, but informal, internal arrangements were also made to control the behaviour and movements of outsiders when they did gain access to those rooms. In both the Bunker and the *Palais de Justice*, the most private recesses of the police liaison suite were blocked off by a desk swung half-way across the room. The desk was used quite deliberately to delineate a portion of the suite that belonged only to the officers working in the building. It was a barrier not only to civilians but also to visiting officers, the officers 'in the case', who outnumbered the resident police and promised to swamp them. Unless they were checked, it was feared that they would appropriate whatever space remained, take over its modest desk space, use its few chairs and telephones: 'They'd be everywhere, using your typewriters and everything.'

The probation offices also had their own public area in miniature, an inner waiting-room with chairs and admonitory pamphlets about AIDS and legal aid, that was emphatically different in use and meaning from the probation officers' own rooms ranged around it.

Other 'public' users' rooms (the barristers' robing rooms and the 'CPS room', for instance) were designed to be accessible to certain preferred groups only, to visiting professionals of the second and third circles, and most emphatically not to 'civilians'. In them there was confidential talk and unbuttoned behaviour that should never be displayed before civilians, and the rooms made no internal provision for outsiders at all. Witnesses, jurors, defendants, and supporters had no place in the barristers' mess and the CPS room. Signs that identified those rooms to visiting professionals also warned the public off. Transitional, semi-private approaches and sets of double doors were installed to make the approaching public uneasy. Civilians would have had no welcome if they actually had succeeded in entering: it would have been made quite evident that they were in the wrong place.

Yet further along the continuum was the listing office, the one part of the administrative organization (outside the courtroom) whose staff engaged in frequent relations with visiting professionals, the barristers who sought to discuss 'fixtures' with court staff. It led off the public concourse, but it did so through blank, unmarked doors that kept civilians at bay. It was professionals alone who were supposed to know or discover their way there. The project manager remarked that 'the listing office was 'the only office which is on the interface' between the administration and the public. Together with the semi-private public accommodation of the barristers, CPS, probation staff, and police, 'they are thought of as being half-way between the LCD office staff and the public, and they tend to be on the plan half-way between the two as well'.

The 'LCD staff', the administrators, court clerks, and ushers, were hidden in a private world behind locked doors bearing no sign other than 'Private', away from the public concourse, and invisible to the rest: 'You tend to push it away towards the judges' areas . . .' *The Guide* placed the clerks and ushers in their own closed circulation system near the judges but, unlike the judges, they were required to transverse public space to enter the courtrooms where they worked. And most private of all, behind doors with special locks, were the judges, remanded defendants, and jurors.

Public Space

The Concourse and Waiting Areas

Public space was where civilians were to be found, in the concourse and waiting areas, the canteen and the courtroom, and I shall deal with each area in turn. Staff and users, but not the jurors and judiciary, were obliged to criss-cross public space as they moved between their places of work and their home territories. To be sure, they did sometimes manage to improvise short cuts through the inner circulation areas. (One security guard talked about how, in the new building, 'We can go several ways: up the main staircase, up the lift shafts, the judges' lift, the fire escape. We have a choice of probably five methods of getting somewhere.' And they were helped in doing so. The courthouse project manager stated 'you do try and make sure that there are ways for the court people to move that aren't through the public spaces.') The working lives of professionals were punctuated by alternations between the privacy of their own quarters, the semi-privacy of the inner circulation areas, and the visibility and exposure of the public areas. They experienced and managed those alternations in diverse ways.

I have remarked how public space had its hazards for insiders. There was no physical protection to be had there, and it was only demeanour, stagecraft, and the presence of colleagues that offered a shield from unwanted overtures. Insiders tended generally to respond by adopting a sternness or vacancy of face. They would look abstracted or keenly purposeful. They would stiffen their body, lower their voice, and look warily about them as they moved about. (A court clerk remarked on how 'it's like being in an exam and being outside the exam', and a probation officer said of the Bunker, 'In this particular building you have got to be on your guard, certainly, so it will be soft-voiced conversation.')

The project manager of the *Palais de Justice* observed, 'We are always conscious that the office people don't like walking through public spaces to get to other offices or to get into the courts because they, in fact, can feel very vulnerable.' To be sure, differences between areas were not absolute. The character of the public and the private was contingent, depending in part on the actual and threatened presence of strange civilians and in part on the presence of professional adversaries. Privacy was not wholly a property of space itself. Thus, although counsel sometimes called their mess a 'sanctuary', saying they felt 'most at ease in the barristers' mess because there you can actually let your hair down', they would also say: 'You have to be careful what you talk about sometimes because your opponent might be there or someone you don't want to talk to.' There was an abiding fear of inadvertent leaks.

From time to time, public space itself would be empty of civilians and then, for practical purposes, it was treated as an unprotected extension of private space. But the risks remained, and staff and users continued to use it gingerly. Much preferable was a home territory or a shielded inner circulation area. A shorthand writer said of her movements in public space, 'I'm always apprehensive. I don't know what to be saying. I've never been told whether to speak to them or not. . . . I make a quick exit just in case . . . we have a small staff common room where I would normally go.'

Insiders made varying use of public space, and their behaviour hinged on a number of matters: their occupational role (were they engaged in direct, practical work with the public?); the wearing of special clothing (were they dressed in the distinctive and recognizable uniform of clerk, counsel, police officer or usher?); and confidence (had they a professional history of managing troublesome and ambiguous situations, were they adept at handling what Skolnick once called 'symbolic assailants'?[35]). I shall consider those matters one by one.

There were people who were sealed from almost all unregulated contact with the public. Indeed, the system of circulation areas was designed precisely to save them from venturing into public space. Custody staff, jurors, and judges were cordoned off during the working day. (Jurors were instructed not to leave the 'jury lounge' unless told to do so. And, within that space, I was told, they segregated themselves jury by jury, scrupulously avoiding discussion of their cases with jurors from other trials.) Whatever intelligence those sealed-in people might have about public space would be secured principally through intermediaries. A judge remarked: 'Everybody involved officially in the Court, police officers, lawyers, are all under duty to report any irregularity which they observe, and they very frequently do report such irregularities.' Reports would not only centre on irregularities. In one instance, the same judge was concerned about the plight of a very young victim, Victim 12, who was waiting nervously outside the courtroom for her turn to testify. He asked his court clerk to enquire whether she might not be put in a special place 'with some toffees'. Outside the working day, judges and others might sally out to meet staff. The resident judge made it a practice to do so ('I in fact try to get round the General Office after court hours and speak to the staff there . . . [There are] not many civilians

---

[35] See J. Skolnick, *Justice Without Trial* (New York, John Wiley, 1966).

in the General Office anyway'). One judge was to be seen in public space with especial frequency after the move of the *Palais de Justice* in the spring of 1990: 'It's a new Court, and I don't know where things are, and it's interesting.'

There were those, like court clerks, secretaries, and ushers, whose prime sphere of work was outside public space but who were never-theless obliged to journey within it. The diagram of the courtroom (Fig. 6.3) shows how they, unlike the jury, judge, and defendant, had no restricted circulation into which they could move. They had to make their way through public space, and they took it that they had no proper business there. They had no policing role there ('We are not really responsible for what goes on outside the court', said an

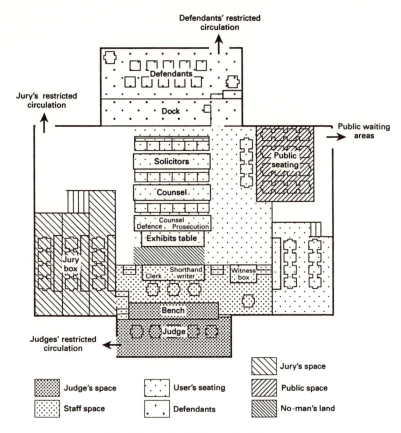

FIG. 6.3. *A Typical Crown Court Courtroom*

usher). They acted as if they were travellers hurrying to private places elsewhere inside the courthouse, and they avoided looking as if they were open to approach. A secretary working in the back regions said of herself, 'I just go straight through', and a shorthand writer observed, 'I usually just try to keep my head up and walk on.' Such non-combatants might well greet other insiders, and they would be relaxed enough when no civilian was present, but they were reluctant to linger or make themselves accessible to outsiders.

I explained in Chapter 4 that the Court staff defined themselves as neutrals with no major duties in the public arena and no wish to become embroiled in the conflicts of the trial. A Court clerk observed, 'You don't have contact with witnesses or people of that nature. . . . We could be approached but we don't go to them.' They would censor conversation with outsiders. There could be no discussion of cases or protagonists: 'Sometimes it puts you on the spot because you've got to draw the line on how much you can listen to and say, "Stop there. I cannot give you any advice" . . . You can say, "Nice weather" or this, that and the other. Anything to do with the case, absolutely taboo!' Overly curious questioners would not be answered but challenged.

Whilst all insiders saw outsiders as problems, those who believed they had no business in public space had less need to scrutinize the civilians who were to be found there; they had to make fewer judgments for purposes of practical action; and they had to make no finely detailed inventory of what they saw (indeed, looking hard and suspiciously at civilians could be constructed as unnecessarily belligerent). What those disengaged professionals sought chiefly was an avoidance of contact. They tried to pass uneventfully through what was tantamount to a sea of undifferentiated strangers. A secretary remarked, 'If we are coming in or out, we just make our way through them.' Whilst probation officers, police officers, and security staff could apply a rough-and-ready stereotype to the public, the 'LCD staff', secretaries, and other non-combatants were unable to do so with any fluency. A court clerk, who moved through public space fairly smartly, refusing to dawdle ('I haven't got time anyway'), said of the public, 'We don't even know who they are sometimes. People wander in and out.' Very similarly, an usher said he would leave his courtroom only to 'call on the defendant and the witnesses'. He could recognize 'a juror out of place' (and jurors were his responsibility after all) but, 'apart from that, it's just hit and miss really'. The secretary's identification of strangers in public space was also weak: 'They can say they belong to the Court, but they could be anybody.' Perhaps that very lack of discriminatory capacity amplified risks for the disengaged and underscored how necessary it was to appear detached.

On the other hand, there were those who had practical work to do in the concourse area, the security staff, police, and probation officers, and they tended not to rush through public space. Doings there *were* palpably their business, and they idled purposively instead. They were alert and suspicious in that idling, staring about them and never visibly at ease in a place full of such potentially difficult people[36] (a police officer remarked, 'My professional eye is trained . . . one never knows where trouble is coming from', and a security guard said, 'You are never really relaxed on a security job'). Police officers might allow themselves to seem approachable but, again, 'If the question was a little bit pointed, I would say, "who are you?"' If they asked some very searching question, it immediately rings an alarm.' Such engaged, attentive professionals could at least make some sense of what they saw. That was their job. Rather than seeing a buzzing confusion, a mass without distinction, they recognized the little cues that betrayed the identities of salient groups, and they acquired assurance from such a power to interpret their environment. A security guard said:

This only comes from experience, I can spot the juror coming in in the morning, on a Monday morning, just by their general appearance and their demeanour. . . . They're not certain of where they're going, they're usually clutching their pink form in their hand . . . Their dress in most cases. We get a tee shirt, but it's usually the dress you can pick your jurors out. . . . We know the barristers, most of them. Most of them that come in here we know whether they're defence or prosecution. We know most of the younger barristers do defence work, most of the older barristers do prosecution work.'

Similarly a probation officer, prowling the corridors in his quest for young, black defendants to divert from custody, continuously decoded the scene that lay before him. On one occasion, he declared that people in the entrance area were 'probably on my side' because they were consulting the publicly displayed lists for their names. His was an informed eye that continually supplied structure and detail to the passing scene:

[36] A police officer remarked, 'One of the problems with this building [the Bunker] [is that] there is no segregation. Even in the dining room everybody mixes when they shouldn't, victims, jurors, counsel.'

I'm matching in my mind what I see with the court list. Remember we are targeting the 17–21 age group and we're targeting the blacks within that group, and you can't tell the colour of someone from a form. You've got to look and see and sometimes the name is a giveaway but not always. . . . If you have worked here a year or so, you know who people are . . . Let's get the jury out of the way. I'm not too clear on jury people because they change and they're ordinary . . . Other people . . . I would survey a corridor and try to work out who everyone is, mostly of course they are cases like floaters waiting to come on, or cases accumulating as it were, people coming in joining a party. . . . I've got my court list, after all, I will try and match the court list to the huddles outside.

Observe that these professionals were attuned by experience and purpose to recognize only a very particular range of identities. The security guard could recognize jurors, the probation officer claimed that he could not (but then he had no pressing need to do so.) Signs abounded if one wished to look for them, and the most potent of all was dress. In the main, insiders wore suits, robes, or uniforms and outsiders did not. Insiders tended to seem at ease in a familiar setting, outsiders did not. Insiders were well-kempt, outsiders generally were not. There were other signs: plainclothes police officers could be recognized by their air of assurance, their blue cardboard wallet files, their suits, and their polythene bags of exhibits; CPS law clerks by the piles of papers that they were forever toting about; defence barristers by the pink ribbons around their white briefs and prosecutors by their white ribbons around green briefs; the listing officer by his clipboard; and so it went on.

Relations between knowing insiders and others about them were once again contingent, reflecting the shifting positions and preoccupations of the adversarial process. Let me return to the example of probation officers. Probation officer would not court chance meetings if they were abroad on a particular errand or were searching for particular people ('If I'm working on two or three things, I would probably avoid eye contact'). But if they were idling purposively in the courthouse, they would be curious about those about them. ('If I'm just on a prowl then I would probably go for eye contact. I would try and work out who's there.') They might talk inconsequentially with a waiting defendant: 'I would have a conversation with him— not on the case, I would make that quite clear.' But they were loath to become involved in talk with members of the prosecution entourage ('I wouldn't necessarily want to get into conversation with the prosecution people and the witnesses'). They could, as I remarked in Chapter 4, be hesitant in discussing defendants with the police (and police officers would be hesitant in return; one officer said, 'It's still a guarded conversation'). They were professionally reticent about gossiping with counsel who had come to court to prosecute, less reticent with defence counsel, and in that, too, their relations were contingent because the prosecutor of one day would be the defence of the next.

Counsel were also required to spend long periods in the public areas. It was there that they hoped to meet their lay clients, the defendants, and their professional clients, the solicitors and members of the CPS. They were often in difficulty. Since their briefs were frequently delivered only hours before the trial itself, counsel tended not to know defendants and witnesses other than by name. ('When one prosecutes, you don't see the victims of the offence until you actually call them as witnesses. I mean, I don't know anything about them other than what I read about them in the papers.') Defence counsel (and, indeed, the prosecution) could not speak to prosecution witnesses, but they had to undertake the delicate feat of locating defendants rapidly in the midst of a mass of anonymous civilians. They were to be seen striding up and down the public areas, particularly in the Bunker, viewing the civilians, calling out the name of their lay client in stentorian tones, but simultaneously trying to avoid the eye of those about them. They attempted to make contact by voice but not by gaze. 'Mr A' or 'Leroy Jones' they would call out, rather like schoolmasters calling a roll. They might go up to likely civilians, asking them if they were the solicitors or defendants they were seeking ('You're not from B?').

Counsel might not even recognize their opponent. A barrister said, 'Counsel sign themselves in with the usher, and the usher keeps a list, then you find out who it is. If you know the person, all well and good. If you don't, you just shout around a bit.' Resort could be made to the tannoy that was operated by the receptionist, and 'prosecution [or defence] counsel' or 'all parties' 'in the case of C [or D or E]' would reverberate twice around the courthouse (on one occasion, remarked an usher, 'all parties' were summoned to a courtroom because 'counsel wanted to meet each other instead of pacing up and down, not recognizing each other').

All those attempts to find partners were freighted with problems. Counsel were enjoined to maintain a symbolic and physical distance from the very people they moved amongst, not knowing who was civilian and who professional; whether they were neutral, quarry, or adversary: 'One is very wary of going up to anybody unless you know who they are and secondly of speaking in a public place', said one counsel. Anyone dressed as a civilian was a potential problem: 'In a court like Wood Green is at the moment [in the Bunker], where everybody gets thrown together, you've got to be very, very careful about what you say.' It was uniforms and robes that reassured the apprehensive lawyer. One so dressed would be a professional, not a civilian, an insider, not an outsider, and less threatening in proportion. Strange counsel, for example, were no peril:

I would certainly say, 'Good morning'. I often start up conversations with them, because I would see them as safe people to talk to. . . . People wearing the uniform of barristers, so to speak, are obvious. You know who is in your case, either because they are in your case or because you know they're not. In either case, they happen to be people that you need to be less guarded with than others. . . . Ushers and clerks too . . . I certainly would feel perfectly comfortable speaking to anybody whom, about which conversation, no one could place a kind of hostile interpretation on. So that would include officers of the court, the solicitors, the solicitors for the other side, the CPS.

There was a third group, the professionals who frequented public space but lacked training or useful experience in managing the dangerous and awkward, and they could find it intimidating to be so adrift. Unlike the probation, police, counsel, and security staff, there were users who would have had nothing to do with defendant and their supporters, knew little of them, and believed that they could not easily pacify them in an altercation. A number of the more junior CPS staff, for instance, were young women who were not well enough versed in the strategic interaction of the criminal-justice system to defuse potentially difficult encounters. And defendants could be quite 'cocky'. The CPS representatives did not, as a senior colleague remarked about herself, 'make a point of lingering'. Neither were they anxious to make direct overtures to strangers. They might instead turn to others more seasoned than they to intercede for them. One law clerk said that she was reluctant to stand out in public space when searching for witnesses: 'It can be quite sensitive because, say, the defendant's family might be sat outside and the witnesses might be sat outside, and it's not very nice to go out and start to call people's names out . . . so what we do is get the police officers, "Could you put me in the right direction?"' Even a senior member of the CPS staff professed occasionally to have misgivings when she was servicing assault cases.

Clusters in Space

Every morning, and on the mornings of those days when new trials began, Mondays and Wednesdays in particular, masses of users and the public would enter the courthouse and assemble in the one central public 'concourse' of the Bunker. By 10 a.m. there could be forty or more people crowded fretfully together in an area measuring some 23 by 3.5 metres (see Pl. 6.7). Beginning as an undifferentiated crowd, a stellar cloud, as it were, they would pass through a series of balletic movements that separated and concentrated them into groupings crystallizing around the twin poles of the trial. In time, they would come to form the nuclei of little social worlds whose populations shifted as members came in and out of the courtrooms and the courthouse. Uncertain at the beginning, it was only after a few long hours at court that those members came to know enough of the geography of the courthouse to move straight through the concourse to their appointed positions in the canteen or the rough vicinity of a courtroom.

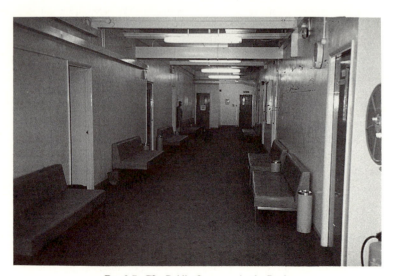

PL. 6.7. *The Public Concourse in the Bunker*

There was a cycle.[37] At about 9.30 every morning, the courtrooms would be locked, the waiting areas would be thinly populated, and the principal groups to be seen were security staff, resident police officers, and a very few early barristers. There might be but three or four people in the public concourse. Within another 15 minutes, that number would double. Then, as 10 a.m. approached, it would double and double again, swollen with the different groups that fed it punctually and predictably each day: counsel and police arriving between 9.30 and 10 a.m., counsel carrying square bags containing copies of *Archbold* and courtroom attire, police officers carrying transparent bags of evidence; shorthand writers coming at about 9.40; he law clerks marching in a crocodile along Lordship Lane to enter at 9.45; jurors arriving at 10 a.m.; and the bulk of witnesses, probation officers, and defendants coming a little later.

It took little more than a quarter of an hour for the public concourse to overflow with people urgently attempting to find one another: counsel sought their opponents; defence counsel sought solicitors and defendants; police officers sought prosecution witnesses; prosecution witnesses sought the police; CPS law clerks sought the police and witnesses; defence counsel sought probation officers; prosecution counsel sought CPS law clerks; and witnesses sought one another. They were, in effect, struggling to give birth to a constellation of teams or groupings, and most began the day unknown to one another.

Counsel, police officers, CPS law clerks, and prosecution witnesses could at least converge on the police room in their quest for one another. But many meetings were achieved clumsily. Although clothing and uniform played a part in symbolizing identity, it was specific individuals that were hunted amongst the many. Although the tannoy played its part, and counsel, solicitors, civilians, and police officers could be summoned to courtrooms or the reception desk, it was still occasionally difficult to discern one's own particular target in a mass of expectant people. Although it might be helpful to call names out loud to the public at large, much in the manner of the boy with the plant in *Hellzapoppin*, many counsel would call for long periods without apparent reward.

Counsel, law clerks, and police officers were, of course, all past masters at rapid and efficient choreography. They brought about the

---

[37] I shall discuss more of the unfolding of events in time in the next chapter.

transition from chaos to organization in different courthouses throughout the South-Eastern circuit every working day, arranging meetings mechanically and in set sequence, conferring in turn with law clerks or solicitors about papers; counsel about pleas; police officers about witnesses; and defendants themselves, perhaps the last to be met, for a hurried consultation in the canteen or public space.

Barristers and police officers, like all professionals, had a care for their stomachs. Those who arrived early to prosecute would first have breakfast at court, reading their papers. They would then seek out their opponent to discover whether the trial was effective or not, and whether there was news of witnesses and courtrooms, 'and then you go and see your officer to see if you've got all your witnesses'. Those who made it a practice to arrive later would go to the courtroom itself:

There's a pretty good drill which you follow if you are marked at a particular time at a particular court, the thing is easy because you go to that court, you see, and meet up outside the court. But if you're not marked up for a particular time, you are what is called 'floating'; what you first of all do is, if you are defending, you see your client and your solicitors, and if you are prosecuting you see the police to make sure your witnesses are there. There will then come a point and so, if you are defending, you will probably tannoy and get everyone to come to reception. If you are prosecuting, you go to the police room and find out if everyone is there, but in due course you tannoy for your opposite number to come and meet you at reception.

I described in Chapter 4 how police officers would meet their witnesses, gather them together, and keep them in a safe place, in a consultation room if they were vulnerable, in a waiting area or the canteen if they were not, and would then return periodically like sheepdogs to ensure that none had strayed. So too with the law clerks. They would work according to recipe. They had to: order had to be imposed in very short time:

We drop our files off, we go down to the police room and check that all our police officers are there; if there are any private witnesses, then we will ask the police officers, 'do you have the witnesses here?' If they do, we give them their [expenses] forms there and then. Otherwise, during the day, we will be asking police officers, 'Are they here?' and we will give them their forms . . . We have to deal with the barristers, if they have any problems, we have to take them up to the room, give them instructions.

Those involved in such work were assisted by others. Security staff, ushers, and the receptionist pointed civilians towards their special stations. Jurors, for instance, would be told to go their own 'lounge' because 'otherwise people won't know where to find you'. Defendants in 'fixtures' often positioned themselves near the courtroom to which they had been assigned in the lists that bore their names. Ushers would parade with clipboards outside their courtrooms, noting counsel ('I check that counsel are there, find out what the length of time the case is going to be, whether it's going to be effective as a trial . . .'). There was self-segregation as different groups of civilians distanced themselves from one another about the courtroom doors.

It was remarkable that most of the teams required for trial did manage to assemble, and within a few minutes only. Disorder usually gave way to order, a pattern emerging as people found one another; transformed themselves into clusters[38] centred, in the case of defendants, around barristers and, in the case of victims and prosecution witnesses, around police officers; and moved off together towards the canteen, the few dark and dingy consultation rooms, or the areas fringing the courtrooms.

The Canteen in the Bunker

One place to which the newly formed huddles might go was the canteen. Certainly the more experienced knew that to be in Court was to wait, and they would head there as soon as they had completed the preparatory work of the morning. Barristers, arriving early, would eat breakfast. Police officers would colonize tables. The canteen in the Bunker was regarded by some as quite cheap (staff had discounts) and the food was thought to be good. However, what did distinguish the canteen, above all, was a collapse of the enforced segregation of the circulation systems. The canteen was where everyone met promiscuously: bailed defendants before they were arraigned, jurors, witnesses, staff, users, and spectators. It was confused space where no one was clearly in possession or control and meanings were unclear.

The staff and users loathed that confusion. They were thrust into the midst of strangers who might harm them physically and compromise them professionally, who might eavesdrop on their conversation and be open to eavesdropping themselves. (A CPS officer said, 'You don't know who's who and jurors can overhear you. We could get

---

[38] Goffman defined a cluster as 'a set of persons physically close together and facially oriented to one another, their backs towards those who are not participants'; *Behavior in Public Places*, 100.

into real trouble.') In short, all the careful controls of architecture collapsed spectacularly in the canteen. The canteen was, as a barrister put it, 'dangerous'. One of his colleagues talked of

> That ghastly court in Wood Green where you all mingle in the restaurant which is absolutely outrageous. You are in a queue with a juror behind you and a witness in front. It is open to the most frightful abuse, both manufactured abuse and deliberate abuse.

From time to time, counsel would report to a judge that they had been in the proximity of jurors at lunchtime, and the judge would reply wistfully, 'I know. I hope things will be better in the new building.'

A number of solutions were devised to confront the problems of eating, drinking, talking, and being together in such a confused and small space that measured but 14.5 by 5 metres. There was one table reserved for staff, and it offered the limited protection of a semi-private territory marked off in public space. A few staff would gather there. But the risks remained: the tables were not set very far apart and, worse, the man or woman next to one in a queue for food or drink might be a defendant, juror, or victim, and that was an uncomfortable notion indeed. (A barrister said, 'It is crucial that there should be segregation. It is embarrassing. If you are in a queue for your beans and mash and you see a chap you've just called a liar, it is terribly embarrassing.') Civilians would be warned about the risks. A counsel told a witness, 'Because this court has only one canteen, the person sitting next to you could be a juror and they could overhear what you say. Don't talk about the case.' Jurors themselves would be warned on induction that 'there is only one canteen—everyone eats there, defendants, barristers. Not the judges! It's very important not to discuss your case in the canteen.' And then there was *de facto* or *de jure* exclusion: flight or banishment.

Flight occurred when those who could retreat to the safety of home territories did so. Secretaries talked of how they would 'get something and bring it back in here [their home territory]'. A shorthand writer said, 'The canteen's totally unpopular because it's not right that you have staff mixing with defence. I get a coffee and get out quickly.' Banishment occurred when, as a matter of course, defendants were released on bail during adjournments on the express condition that they did not enter the canteen ('an additional condition of bail—which anyone familiar with Wood Green will know—is that during short adjournments the defendant must not go into the canteen. Things will be different after March'). A judge called the canteen 'the great curse here'.

More interesting, perhaps, was the tendency for self-segregation to emerge as 'spontaneously' inside the canteen as it did outside. People would enter, look about them, and gauge the composition of the population using the canteen. It was easy to do. Gowns and uniforms fixed the numbers of users and staff. On occasion, one or other of the Court's two broad significant groups, insiders and outsiders, would manage to appropriate the canteen temporarily as its own semi-private space. Such possession would make the other side feel uncomfortable. On days before outsiders had learned their place in the organization of the trial and the internal geography of the courthouse, it would be insiders who arrived first to lay claim to the canteen. There could be something of a competition for space on other days. Just as communities are supposed to 'tip' when 'their' territory has been settled by a critical mass of outsiders,[39] so police officers and counsel could colonize public space, driving others out. At 11.15 one morning in February 1990, for instance, there were 46 people to be seen in the public space of the courthouse: 26 were in the concourse, and they were all civilians; 20 were in the canteen, and they were all lawyers and police officers. When such a state of monopsony obtained, outsiders would make a retreat to the only available place of safety, the concourse: 'The canteen's always full of lawyers and policemen . . . I got a coffee and come back out again', said one witness, Victim 6.

Prosecution Witnesses in Public Space

Prosecution witnesses in waiting occupied vaguely differentiated tracts of public space in the concourse, corridors (see Pl. 6.8, a picture of the public parts of the third floor) and half-landings of the Bunker. I have explained how they were defined as outsiders who could compromise all but police officers and CPS law clerks. They might be approached by hesitant counsel playing complicated distancing games, but they certainly could not put questions back to them. They were excluded from the courtroom itself until they had given evidence (indeed, it was a routine procedure for ushers to challenge strange civilians sitting in the public parts of the courtroom: 'If

---

[39] See O. Newman, *Community of Interest* (Garden City, NY, Anchor, 1981), 40.

PL. 6.8. *The Third Floor of the Bunker*

you're a witness, you should wait outside'). Usually knowing little about what would befall them, their situation having left their control,[40] they would tend to stay limpet-like in view of the doors of their allotted courtroom until the time came for them to be called to testify.

There were no specific waiting areas marked out around particular courtrooms. There were, instead, areas to which were appended pairs of courtrooms. Prosecution witnesses were packed into those loosely defined spaces, spaces that also housed their adversaries, the defendants and support teams whose fate they were about to affect, whose character they intended to discredit, and whose conflicts they were about to revive.[41] Defendants could be a threatening presence. Victim 13 said, 'He was out there, he was downstairs. The first time we came, everywhere I moved, he'd move like this, staring me out.' Victim 20, involved in an affray case, recalled how the defendant and his family 'caused us grief today. My sister is short-tempered and his sister was giving her mouth, pretending to throw up. They just wanted to work her up.' And Victim 26 said, 'I don't agree that a man charged with violence, that he should be given bail, and be allowed to walk around in full view of the witnesses.'

Prosecution witnesses tended to feel structurally isolated (Victim 5's mother talked about 'people going in and out and you're just left').

---

[40] See R. Ericson and P. Baranek, *The Ordering of Justice: A Study of Accused Persons as Dependants in the Criminal Process* (Toronto, Univ. of Toronto Press, 1982), 180.

[41] See J. Jackson *et al.*, 'Called to Court: Lay Perceptions of Criminal Justice in Northern Ireland', unpublished paper, 5.25.

They often retreated into themselves; smoking incessantly if they were smokers; looking down at the ground, trying to appear at once unobtrusive but visible enough to the ushers who might summon them at any moment; avoiding eye contact and conversation with strangers (a Home Office leaflet distributed to some, but not all,[42] witnesses announced, 'It is much better not to talk to anyone about the evidence you will be giving'[43]). They would talk only to companions, if companions there were. (Victim 20 said, 'If I had been on my own, I wouldn't have been able to cope. My mum and dad are getting a divorce. My dad was outside and my mum was here, but I felt closer because they were near me.')

The Archipelago

So it was that an archipelago appeared to mark out in space the people and associations of the adversarial process, a tableau vivant of the social organization of the trial itself. An initial flux resolved itself into a mass of waiting clusters ready for trials, negotiations about trials, and news of trials. The clusters in which victims and prosecution witnesses found themselves were structurally the simplest of all. In the main, they consisted of no more than a witness or two with their supporters, a police officer sporadically in attendance (sometimes crouching in front of them), and a law clerk even more sporadically in attendance, concerned to check their continuing presence. Defence clusters characteristically congregated around the conspicuous, robed figure of counsel. Each would be surrounded by an invisible cordon sanitaire recognizable to those who knew the belligerents by face or could read the ecology of a courthouse (a detective constable said, for example, 'You can usually tell who [the defendant's supporters] are . . . by the fact that they are sitting and the defendant's talking away to them—family, friends'). It was a cordon sanitaire that inhibited people from overly menacing or disturbing one another. Figuratively and physically, people kept their distance.

Just as in the canteen, members of one cluster tended to acknowledge the rights conferred by another's prior occupation of space. They would place themselves at a safe and obvious remove, signalling that they had recognized how conflict, coalition, and secrecy

---

[42] According to J. Raine and R. Smith, 29.9% of witnesses in the 7-court sample and 44.7% of the Wood Green subsample remembered having received the leaflet; *The Victim/Witness in Court Project: Report of the Research Programme* (Oct. 1991), 11.

[43] *Witness in Court* (London, HMSO, 1988).

had carved public space into a mosaic of lesser, semi-private domains centred chiefly on the benches arrayed along the walls. In those domains, there could and should be half-confidential conversations and shows of emotion. Members of clusters organized themselves, in short, to accomplish what Goffman called 'conventional engagement closure', acting as if they were physically cut off from the rest.[44] Prosecutors and police officers would never sit or stand near defendants and their counsel. Defence counsel would never sit or stand near victims and their followers. They would extend 'civil inattention'[45] to one another, manifesting an ostentatious lack of interest in the other's doings.[46] In conversation, they would employ the *sotto voce* tone described by the senior probation officer as 'corridor conversation'. The result was that the groups, so repelled and separated, became a latticework spread across the courthouse. Goffman described the matter generally when he wrote of 'spacing': 'the tendency for units of participation in the situation . . . to distribute themselves co-operatively in the available space so as physically to facilitate conventional closure'.[47]

In the spaces between the clusters, some solitary people would sit in silence, looking at newspapers or at space, avoiding the eyes of passers-by, refraining from listening to others' talk, looking, as Goffman used to put it, 'away'. They would seek to exploit whatever crevices and opportunities the modest architecture of the Court might offer, trying to carve a little privacy out of public space. For example, attempts at discreet conversations were conducted on the unhooded telephone (see Pl. 6.7) by dragging the cord as far as it could go, the callers muffling their voices and retreating round the corner into the small half-corridor that led to the public lavatories.

The Courtroom in the Bunker

Plates 6.9 and 6.10 show that a courtroom in the Bunker was probably as spartan as a Crown Court courtroom could be (see Fig. 6.3) without surrendering its capacity to house trials and orchestrate

[44] *Behavior in Public Places: Notes on the Social Organization of Gatherings* (New York, Free Press, 1963), 156.

[45] See Goffman, *Relations in Public*, 209.

[46] D. Maynard observed how, in the American court, people refrained from 'looking directly at the participants, spacing themselves so as not to intrude aurally on the discussion'; *Inside Plea Bargaining: The Language of Negotiation* (New York, Plenum, 1984), 37–8.

[47] Goffman, *Behavior in Public Places*, 161.

PL. 6.9. *A Courtroom in the Bunker*

PL. 6.10. *A Courtroom in the Bunker*

behaviour. Its inner acoustics were poor: an abundance of hard and obtruding surfaces seemed to prevent sound travelling very far or clearly. Its outer acoustics were poor: noises that should have been excluded intruded instead, interrupting proceedings and bringing about complaint. The blaring tannoy, supposed to be heard only in spaces outside, forced its clamour into the courtrooms, requiring judges and counsel to ask witnesses to repeat themselves ('I can't hear what you're saying. This building echoes,' said one judge to a witness in the aftermath of an outburst from the tannoy). Prominent air-conditioning ducts (see Pl. 6.10) rattled and murmured on hot days. The courtroom was visually harsh and unrelenting, light pouring down from neon strips and bouncing off the pale walls. A court clerk called it 'this awful strip-lightning'. The heating and cooling systems were inadequate. Another court clerk would tell new jurors, 'Things here aren't very good. Some rooms are very hot. Others are cold.' Yet the work was done and, and in retrospect, poor acoustics and a lack of visual pomposity were actually thought by users to have their benefits for those who came to trial.

A courtroom was the terminal where major groups left their protected areas to converge and confront one another.[48] It was where they imploded, 'the focal point of the Courthouse where all the parties in a case come together'.[49] It was, in this manner, an extrusion of the building's surrounding sealed circulation systems, neither public nor private but a kind of fortified marcher area where total segregation was permitted to lapse but only under the most controlled conditions. Architecturally, it was an 'intermediate' place:

> The requirement that some of the participants (Judge, Jury, Defendant and others) should not meet all together other than within the Courtroom creates the need for independent and segregated circulation from respective rooms to specific areas within the Courtroom. These segregated circulation requirements must be maintained on all projects.[50]

The diagram of a typical courtroom shows how the different, clearly demarcated spaces of the architect's and administrator's four groupings protruded into the courtroom itself. Just as in the world outside, so in the courtroom: jurors, judges, users, defendants, and public had their separate, reserved places marked by visible and invisible frontiers and stringently policed by ushers and clerks. Note that the public included victims and alleged victims who were, again, given no special area or segregation from their adversaries. They were not recognized as a distinct grouping with special interests.[51]

Court staff were concerned always about people out of place, and the ushers and court clerk, whose territory the courtroom was, would

---

[48] See D. Dunster, 'Entering the System', *Architects' Journal*, 188(39) (28 Sept. 1988), 54.
[49] *The Guide*, amendment 13, Apr. 1989.
[50] Ibid., amendment 15, Sept. 1989.
[51] There is a planning lag of about 7 years in courthouse design. Both the Bunker and the *Palais de Justice* were old-fashioned by the time they were erected. The newest generation of courthouses (e.g. at Woolwich) makes provision for a special witness room which has its own dedicated entrance to a shielded witness-box. But, for the rest, those witnesses who were not 'special', the public still consisted of a hodgepodge of unlike elements.

eye and question all those who seemed to be acting improperly or whose identity was infirm (I was repeatedly asked to give an account of myself at first). They would ensure that witnesses were not in the courtroom unless they had been released. They would ensure that defendants were in their place in the dock when the trial began (although, in kindly fashion, defendants on bail were usually allowed to sit in the public area with their family and supporters until the very last moment).

'There is', remarked a professional article on courtroom design, 'a concern in court for the security of judge and jury.'[52] No group could (or actually did) encroach on another's space: judges were never to be seen in the well of a courtroom, counsel never entered the dock, jurors remained in their box, the public did not wander outside their enclosure.[53] When counsel moved, they moved vertically rather than diagonally or horizontally (the project manager observed, 'That's how they make their gesture really. It's an "up and down"'). And the seating of the 'counsels' row' was designed appropriately for an abundance of quiet 'up and down' movements but few movements outside the row itself. Counsels' rootedness was supported by the ushers, solicitors, CPS law clerks, and police officers who acted as porters and messengers, carrying papers and objects about the courtroom on their behalf.[54]

Lying between counsels' row and the clerk's and shorthand writer's table was one of the chief frontier territories, not very obvious to outsiders, but known to insiders as 'no-man's-land'. It was where a number of critical lines of sight crossed: between the jury and witness, witness and counsel, judge and counsel, and judge and defendant. No one would go into no-man's-land when the Court was sitting. On one dramatic occasion, a shorthand writer returned to the courtroom to ask the usher to retrieve her handbag. Trying not to obstruct those vital lines of sight, the usher made her way theatrically towards the clerks' table, crawling on hands and knees behind the witness-box and in front of the bench. 'Don't do that again!' she mouthed in a stage whisper.

On another level, the courtroom was quite deliberately insulated

[52] 'PSA on Court', *Building*, 241 (28 Aug. 1981), 24.

[53] See G. Stimson, 'Viewpoint: Place and Space in Sociological Fieldwork', *Sociological Review*, 34(3) (Aug. 1986), 649.

[54] In Canada, by contrast, ushers played no such role, and counsel were forever moving about within the well of the court.

from its environment. The only formal communication with the wider body of the courthouse was conducted by the ushers, the staff responsible for policing the frontier between the courtroom and the territory beyond, the court clerk on a discreet 'whisper telephone', and the jury bailiff and listing officer who weaved in and out to inspect the progress of cases. The courtroom was sealed visually: only the smallest of spyholes in the doors allowed those in public space to see what might be happening within. There were no windows or other reminders of activity without (although judges were to insist on some daylight being fed into the courtrooms of the *Palais de Justice*. When that light did enter obliquely and through a frosted glass panel (Pl. 6.11), barristers greeted their little glimpse of a larger world with evident joy).

PL. 6.11. *Architect's Model of a Courtroom in the* Palais de Justice

The courtroom was sealed socially, by ushers who physically barred the entrances when important matters, such as sentences and summings-up, were in train. It was sealed by marked shifts in the deportment and demeanour of those who entered and left, the conventional signs of respect for a special place. Only exceptionally (when very young child witnesses were being interrogated) would counsel and judges remove their wigs ('Hats off, gentlemen!' a clerk might call on a judge's instructions), although I myself never observed such a relaxation of convention despite attending a number of trials at which youthful witnesses testified. It was sealed by a formality of language that was markedly more stiff and courtly than the speech of corridor, chambers, or home territory. It was sealed aurally by continual attempts to prevent external sounds obtruding into the courtroom.[55] Ushers were sometimes sent to the corridors or the jury rooms when juries became too boisterous or argumentative.

In the Bunker, those attempts tended to be fruitless indeed: a judge remarked to a witness during the course of a trial in 1989, 'It's very difficult to hear in these rooms. they're temporary. They've been temporary for eight years, and their acoustics are very bad.' At the very entrance to the courtroom there was a pair of double doors (called a 'sound lobby'). The lobby was supposed not only to keep unwanted sounds out 'to insulate the courtroom from public waiting area noise',[56] but also, again, to signal the importance of the transition, another symbolic passage, that was to be made when people left the relatively chaotic world of the public spaces and concourse for the more sacred, orderly, and solemn place within.

Inside the courtroom itself, people sat in rigid spatial relation to one another, a relation fixed by tradition[57] and practical utility. *The Guide* laid down:

Within the Courtroom a specific and well defined relationship must be maintained between the various participants. Both sight lines, distance and audio requirements dictate a courtroom layout which has been agreed . . . It has been found that attempts by individual designers to 'improve' this layout have rarely been successful . . .[58]

Every seat and prop had its place and use. The project manager of the *Palais de Justice* remarked: 'When we get a new architect who says, "I can sort these courtrooms out", we say, "Now, be very careful that you don't move any seats because you may well not understand every implication of why that seat is exactly where it is".' So standardized were the underlying formal arrangements of a

---

[55] *The Guide* is replete (see esp. B5/4) with instructions about how to reduce noise in courtrooms. Duct-work, air conditioning systems, and the like were all designed to exclude sound.

[56] Ibid. 1.1b.

[57] The unpublished PSA booklet talked of how 'the relationships of individuals within the Courthouse has become well established over the years' (p. 16).

[58] *The Guide.*

courtroom, so general the recipe knowledge governing the practices enacted within it, that many professionals claimed to become indifferent to the peculiarities of the particular courtroom (a barrister observed blithely, 'It is the same judge in the end and the same advocate'). It was as if they worked in the same archetypal space over and over again, throughout the length and breadth of the circuit. Another barrister remarked of the Bunker and its courtrooms, 'Once a case gets going at the old Wood Green Court, you don't think, "Oh dear! This is awful!" You just get on with it. Once the issue was joined as it were, you just block all of that out.'

In the middle of a room more or less square was an arena where counsel were set down, visible and audible to the major participants arrayed as blocks all around them. It was an arena for the staging of spectacles imbued with what the Property Services Agency, the agency that designed the courthouse, called 'a sense of drama'[59] (although spectacle was inevitably somewhat threadbare in the Bunker). At two ends, confronting one another, sat the defendant and the judge. The defendant was there to be scrutinized, his demeanour and expressions being read by judge and jury as a running text on what was said about him. The project manager of the *Palais de Justice* remarked that judges "do like to be able to able judge [the defendants'] reactions to the things that are going on'.

Lines of sight were deliberately installed not only to allow the judge to 'maintain full control of proceedings'[60] but also to be shown to be in full control. Just like the God of Judgment in the paintings or a medieval monarch in his court,[61] the judge could see all. The judicial bench was raised to impress. The project manager continued:

You're emphasizing the role of the judge in complete control of everybody else. He's in the position where he can see any bit of paper moved about. He can see anybody come in. It's his court and he controls it.

Judges sat on a high elevation which gave them distance, authority,[62] and a commanding view. Yet it must also be noted that they were not *that* high in Wood Green. The courtrooms were regarded as comparatively informal, embodying but one conception of the proper relation between judge and judged. The bench was set lower than

---

[59] 'Designs for Judgement', *Construction*, 66 (Sept. 1988), 30.

[60] *The Guide*, amendment 7, Mar. 1988.

[61] Upon whom the judge in a courtroom must have been modelled.

[62] See E. Hall, 'Silent Assumptions in Social Communication', in R. Gutman (ed.), *People and Buildings* (New York, Basic Books, 1972), 143.

those in older and newer courtrooms (but not in the very newest of the courtrooms-to-be). In some other places, remarked a judge, 'the judge, jury, the defendant and counsel are at [such] an enormous height above the floor, you could in fact play tennis underneath without interfering'. Not all the judges agreed on the desirability of a low bench. Some protested that 'the modern court with nearly everything on a level, and with everyone being able to see everybody has very considerable drawbacks'. A judge said:

You need to be a little way up. It's still stage management. I think having the judge down on the ground is not a good idea. I think psychologically, from the point of view of the people below, authority does increase a little with height. You need to be a bit remote. You can't be one of the boys. You cannot avoid people coming and going in court but, in so far as it approaches a level, then they are appallingly distracting. Also, physically, it is easier to see and think a bit over the heads particularly when you have a chap in the dock behind everybody, you can see him without interruption.

It seemed that architects, judges, and administrators could never quite fix the correct balance between formality and informality, dignity and intimidation. The height of the judicial bench has moved up and down with fashion, the most recent design being taller than those of the Bunker and the *Palais de Justice*, and counsel, defendants, jurors, and witnesses have been obliged to rise with it.[63] The project manager of the *Palais de Justice* observed:

The judge has now gone up again, the jury are going up again, and it's becoming much more of a well, and so you increase the height and you actually begin to fix the people even more than you did before in their roles. Because you have lots of steps and barriers, they are even more segregated into their roles and positions.

That relative lack of differentiation of height in the Wood Green courtrooms seemed to be accompanied by a lessening of the apparent status and role differentials of the diverse groups in the courthouse. It reinforced the Court's reputation for friendliness, 'cosiness' (a word much used in the Bunker), and informality. Perhaps that is what another judge meant when he said of the Bunker, 'The building is a

[63] Although, as I write, in June 1992, the most recent model of all English courtrooms (set out in a mock-courtroom in Teddington) contained a judge's bench that had once again been reduced in height, leading to a lowering of all other features and furniture ('Mock-up Courtroom at Teddington: Changes upon Re-construction of Large Courtroom', Lord Chancellor's Dept., n.d.).

very unpleasant place but the courts are quite intimate in a way. . . .
I did appear here a year before I was appointed: perhaps it's not so
pleasant when you're down below, but certainly I feel it's quite intimate here.' And counsel, ushers, staff, and clerks concurred. A combination of a dense population, frequent meetings in compact space,
low staff turnover, and informal design amplified a marked sense of
Gemeinschaft. A security guard reflected: 'I have always called it the
family feeling at Wood Green . . . Wood Green has always been a
very friendly place. The barristers love coming here.'

Counsel had no sight of the defendant: their backs were to him,
and they argued about him almost as if he were absent.[64] The project manager said, 'The defendant is a rather strange person who sits
at the back as a viewer who is then brought on to the stage when he
has to give evidence. . . . It's a strange relationship, that, until he
becomes a witness, he's not actually there. They're talking about him
but he's at the back there.' A defendant would often be discussed as
if he were not present. He would not be allowed to speak 'for himself' unless it was in the witness-box, and even then in guarded fashion. On the contrary. If he sought to speak from the dock, the judge
might remind him, as one judge did remind a defendant, 'You must
keep silent and if you don't remain silent I'll send you down and I'll
think seriously about your bail.' Again, when a defendant's
'antecedents' were discussed, doubts and difficulties about neutral
matters that might easily have been resolved by direct recourse to the
defendant were resolved instead by protracted and sometimes desultory consultations between professionals. Although the defendant was
in a better position to say whether or not he was in employment, or
was still married, it was not he who was consulted but the
'antecedents' officer or the probation officer. It was quite evident that
the important relations in the courtroom had been appropriated by
professionals.[65]

On another side of the courtroom sat miscellaneous users, the probation and police officers whose right to a reserved part of the courtroom confirmed their standing as insiders (when Victim Support
eventually moved into the Court and the courthouse, and was given

[64] Ericson and Baranek observed of the defendant in the Canadian courtroom:
'Rather than being an active adversary, he sits there mute while the crown attorney
and his own lawyer talk around him . . . treating him like a dependent child who is to
be seen and not heard' (*The Ordering of Justice*, 181).

[65] See N. Christie, 'Conflicts as Property', Foundation Lecture, Centre for
Criminological Studies, Univ. of Sheffield, 1976.

its own office in the *Palais de Justice*, its members too were allowed to sit in that special space). The users' space was not unlike an embassy or diplomatic enclave. It was a privileged area set down at a distance from the home territory for the purpose of conducting business with others similarly placed.

Adjoining the users were the 'public' in their own part, a rag-bag collection of defendants' supporters, victims, witnesses, visiting school and college students, and spectators: a collection of uneasy fellows. Victims and alleged victims had no special area of their own in the courtroom. They had no special place in law. Both courtrooms had been planned some years before, at a time when victims and witnesses had not been considered a separate group with separate needs.[66] At Wood Green, victims and prosecution witnesses were spectators to the trials that transformed them into the witnesses of transgressions against an incorporeal commonwealth. Like the defendants, theirs was a strange relation that gave them significance only when they were in the box to testify. And even when they *were* in the box, they were obliged to stand, underscoring the authority of the Court and the judge who personified it, the judge who sat in his chair above the rest.[67]

Unless they were to be witnesses, the public could come and go as they pleased. They were in the courtroom but not quite fully of it. When the juror, barrister, witness, or defendant coughed, an usher might bring them a glass of water. There was no such relief for members of the public (including journalists and police officers). And confronting them, in their own space, unreachable except by gesture, were the jury (and that was to cause concern in the administrative quarters where alarm was expressed about 'jury nobbling' and intimidation by confederates of the defendant).[68]

[66] The architect remarked in 1989, 'From the LCD's point of view, it's changed dramatically over the last three to four years. Before then, they would have said they had a problem at the Old Bailey over witnesses being intimidated and jurors being intimidated, but no where else. And I think that, I can't pinpoint it, but three or four years ago [things changed and] now every judge asks us. "What are you doing about victims? What are you doing about witnesses?" ' The new mock-up courtroom at Teddington contains a 'witness waiting room [that] leads directly into the courtroom close to the witness stand'; 'Mock-up Courtroom at Teddington'.

[67] For the significance of standing and sitting, witness-boxes and judicial benches, see Stimson, Place and Space in Sociological Fieldwork', 647.

[68] See G. Ridout, 'Concern for Fair Trials Prompts Costly Changes in Court Design', *Building*, 31 Mar. 1989, p. 9. The design of the most recent generation of courtrooms now expressly emphasizes security and prevents defendants from leaving the dock (a 'moat' is placed before them) and from observing and being observed by

In the main arena, near the judge, shorthand writer, and prosecution counsel, was the box that raised witnesses up high to be visible and audible to judge, counsel, jury, and defendant. I have shown how trials pivoted on evidence, the knowledge brought in from the outer world by witnesses whose credit and credibility were to be judged. Witnesses did not have their faces turned towards the 'public', for it was not the public who were required to study their demeanour.[69] They faced the judge, jury, and counsel. Witnesses were also seen by defendants, and defendants could see them: 'He was just looking straight at me,' said Victim 11 (witness intimidation was not a matter that affected courtroom design).

It was their examination by all those people that made the witness-box the true focal point of the courtroom and, indeed, of the Court itself. It transformed the prosecution witness from a mere anyone waiting relatively anonymous and neglected in the wings to a named someone on whom the entire attention of the Court was turned for a while, a someone whose every characteristic could be interrogated publicly. Instead of contact being avoided, it was now courted eagerly and aggressively. Instead of being ignored, the witness was now sought. Together with the defendant, the prosecution witness formed the fleeting epicentre of the courthouse. A barrister said:

In a sense, the formality of the courtroom is there by design to reduce in most people's minds the presence of the barristers and the judge to a sort of static thing, and that [*sic*] the real players, the people that come to life in it, are the witnesses, be they the defendant or the prosecution witnesses . . .

The Palais de Justice

I have explained that the Crown Court centre at Wood Green was one of the new wave of projects that followed in the wake of the Beeching Report. That wave must have been one of the largest programmes of monumental building since the pyramids. It was certainly taken by some to be the 'last major contribution by central government to Britain's city centres'.[70] There was to be massive

the public. The public and jury are also denied sight of one another, being separated by 'obscured sightlines' and barriers: 'public benches are . . . diagonally opposite and some distance from the jury box, sparing jurors the risk of being intimidated by spectators'; T. Daw, 'New Court Makes Security a Priority', *The Times*, 27 May 1992.

[69] See J. Hazard, 'Furniture Arrangement as a Symbol of Judicial Roles', *ETC: A Review of General Semantics*, 19(2) (July 1962), 182.

[70] M. Spring, 'Courting Favour', *Building*, 249 (6 Dec. 1985), 30.

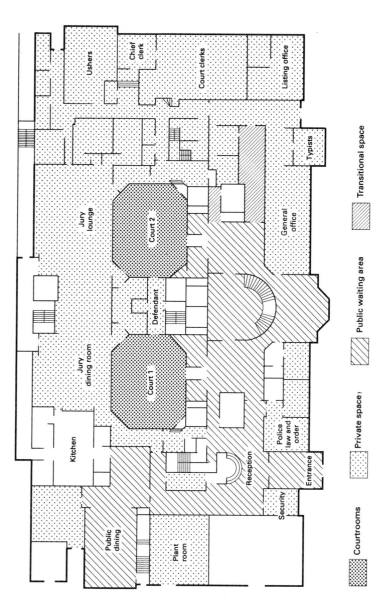

FIG. 6.4. *The Ground Floor of the Palais de Justice*

Courtrooms

Private space

Public waiting area

Transitional space

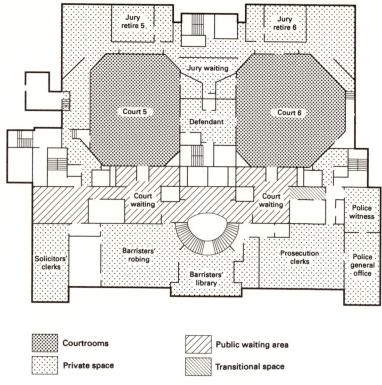

FIG. 6.5. *Second Floor of the* Palais de Justice

construction across the face of England and Wales. The Head of the Criminal Court Division of the Lord Chancellor's Department was reported to have said, 'We have had to deal with the country as a whole from scratch.'[71] A total of nearly 200 projects was contemplated, entailing some 500 courtrooms at £1,000,000 each.[72]

Four inconsistent themes predominated. Courthouses were intended to be well-constructed pieces of grand architecture on 'prominent sites'.[73] They were built to impress, to be dignified and imposing, inspiring awe, not to be mistaken for other, more secular and prosaic large buildings such as office blocks or shopping

[71] 'New Courts for Old', *Your Court*, 1(1) (Oct./Nov. 1985), 11.
[72] See 'The Week', *Building*, 31 Mar. 1989, 9.
[73] PSA, *Building for Justice* (London, 1989), 2.

centres.[74] The Property Services Agency wrote that it was 'creating a civic presence which reflects the majesty of the court and commands respect for the legal process'.[75] At the same time, courthouses were supposed not to be frightening. On the contrary, they should be reassuring buildings that did not cow the public.[76] There was a 'requirement that new court buildings should be less formal than traditional courts, which many members of the public find intimidating'.[77] They were thus to be at once 'serene and dignified' yet 'a good deal less forbidding and more humane than [their] predecessors.'[78] The structures of the new courthouses were complicated solutions to the threat of terrorist attack, jury intimidation, and attacks on judges and juries (in the new Queen Elizabeth II Law Courts at Birmingham, for instance, 'security now is intensive in court buildings and the days of easy access are long gone'.[79] The Law Courts were reported to have 13 separate staircases.) Courthouses were thus intricately figured to keep populations apart and safe, and the complexity of their internal labyrinths limited the architect's freedom[80] and drove the costs of building higher and higher.[81] Yet, lastly, those same inner spaces were also intended to appear simple so that members of the public did not lose themselves, become anxious and confused[82] or escape surveillance.

The New Courthouse at Wood Green

The *Palais de Justice* was planned as a ten-court centre,[83] and it too was required to be dignified and informal, simple and complex. Plans

[74] See 'Designs for Judgement', 29.   [75] Ibid.
[76] See D. Hawkes, 'Legal History', *Architects' Journal*, 7 May 1986, 5. Of the new centre at Southampton, it was said: 'The interior design combines a dignified appearance with a friendly and relaxed atmosphere'; 'Crown and County Courts Southampton', *Brick Bulletin*, summer 1988, 4.
[77] 'Law Courts: Peterborough Crown Court', *Tubular Structures*, 47 (Jan. 1989), 2.
[78] 'Law Courts in Maidstone', *Concrete Quarterly*, 148 (Jan.-Mar. 1986), 14.
[79] M. Booth, 'Queen Elizabeth II Law Courts, Birmingham', *Construction*, 66 (Sept. 1988), 33.
[80] PSA, *Building for Justice*, 2.
[81] See 'The Week', *Building*, 31 Mar. 1989, 9.
[82] In the Crown Court at Nottingham, for instance, 'the planning arrangement evolved is simple and easily understandable for visitors to the new building'; T. Williams, 'Nottingham Crown Court', *Construction*,66 (Sept. 1988), 35.
[83] At first, and for the time being, 3 of those courtrooms were set aside for the use of the County Court and 1 for the Patent Court. According to the resident judge, the provision of courtrooms had overtaken the anticipated increase in the numbers of criminal cases. It seemed quite possible, 2 years later, that those 4 courtrooms would be devoted to criminal trials.

for the new building, some five times the size of the Bunker, projected fairly precise numbers of users, staff, and civilians. Thus it was supposed that the Court could house a maximum of 100 members of the public, 10 judges, 26 ushers and security staff, 45 barristers, 35 police officers, 57 court staff, 60 witnesses, 24 defendants in custody, and 35 on bail.[84]

The *Palais de Justice* was an innovation. It was inserted inside the carapace of what had been the old Royal Masonic Institution for Boys,[85] originally built in 1865[86] and designed by Edwin Pearce as a building 'of plain handsome character without meretricious ornament . . . [and] faced with white Suffolk bricks'.[87] In the 1970s, first the Haringey Council and then the Lord Chancellor's Department sought to demolish what had become known as Woodall House, but there were protests from local conservation groups; the PSA 'recognized the civic importance of the building and . . . decided that the façade and the chapel should be retained and the new Crown Court should be built within them, with three new floors rising above the original skyline'.[88] Five pairs of courtrooms were to rise up in a tapering structure that resembled a monstrous mansard roof, a roof that 'echoe[d] the original craggy Gothic form'.[89] It was, wrote the resident Judge, 'a very large, very complex, very modern building inserted into and over three sides of the shell of the old Woodall House'.[90] The design within was sympathetic to the design without: the project manager talked about 'keeping the quality, the feeling of the outside building, but not just aping Victoriana inside'.

It was inescapable that Wood Green should be described as old-fashioned as soon as it was finished ('Every one that we build is out of date'). It was small and informal. It articulated conceptions of planning that were at least seven years old, and the criminal-justice

[84] Management Services Branch, Court Accommodation Section, *Schedule of Requirements: Wood Green Courthouse* (Lord Chancellor's Dept., Jan. 1977).

[85] It was to pass through incarnations as a training college in 1903 and an office block, first for a gas company in 1931 and then for the Eastern Gas Board in 1948, before becoming a Crown Court.

[86] Interestingly enough, the senior probation officer's father had been a pupil at the Institution.

[87] Original specifications quoted by Judge McMullan in a history, 'Wood Green Crown Court', prepared for the Lord Chancellor on the Crown Court's formal opening in 1990.

[88] PSA press release, 'Property Services Agency Builds Wood Green Crown Court', 15 Mar. 1990.

[89] Spring, 'Courting Favour', 31.

[90] Judge McMullan, Wood Green Crown Court'.

system had evolved fast during those seven years. Victim Support and the politics of victims had come to prominence during that time. The project manager remarked in 1989, the year before it was opened, 'Wood Green is past now.' Like all the buildings of its generation, the *Palais de Justice* had not been planned with the special needs of victims in mind (there were no segregated circulation areas or waiting-rooms for defendants and witnesses, for example), but it was a large enough building to possess the surplus space that could be turned over to victims and prosecution witnesses when the time came. The project manager reflected: 'By luck there were rooms about that [Victim Support] have been able to use. It wasn't planned in that way . . .'

First Impressions

For a while, and particularly before the *Palais de Justice* opened in April 1990, there were flurries of anticipation and expectation amongst the staff working in the Bunker. Recall that the staff and users had seen the new building rising up grandly before them from the start. 'Things will be better in the new building,' counsel would be told when they complained. There were anxieties, too, that a new, large, and imposing building would undermine *Gemeinschaft*. A CPS law clerk talked of how she hoped the *Palais de Justice* would not lose the 'cosiness' of the Bunker.

The new building was awesome by design, something remarkable, and it prompted responses that revealed a little of the spectator who beheld it. Take users and staff. Those who worked in the same courthouse every day tended to invest themselves in its appearance. It became a working extension of their material selves, a statement made in physical form about the importance of who they were and what they did. They were made visibly proud (and sometimes a little abashed) by what was being constructed so slowly before their eyes. A CPS law clerk called it a cathedral. They wanted to show it off to visiting users: said an usher to a barrister, 'It'll stop all you counsel saying horrible things about Wood Green!' 'We never really complained,' the counsel replied. When an usher was told that the Lord Chancellor would formally open the building in July, he observed, 'Very boring! They could have asked [Prince] Charles. The Lord Chancellor! Very boring!'

They showed impatience with the delays in moving (completion was supposed to have taken place much earlier, in June 1989), and rumours circulated that the Lord Chancellor's Department had run out of money and did not wish to incur the more expensive fuel and power bills of a larger building during the winter and before the new financial year. More accurate stories were told about last-minute alterations to the dangerously low ornamental banisters on the grand staircase: it was feared that people might rush out of Court and plummet to their death. Staff worried that they had not been consulted about the design, that they knew too little of the courthouse's inner topography, and that they might not be able to cope smoothly when the courthouse eventually did open.

Ushers, for instance, would be obliged to know every little space and route in the Court, and yet they had given only thirty minutes' viewing by March. They knew that the circulation systems were more complicated and comprehensive than the Bunker. The courthouse would need some scouting. One usher had managed to find a small map of the *Palais de Justice*, and had studied it avidly, but he feared that that would not be enough.

When they did begin their move, in a week left fallow towards the end of March, staff conferred anxiously about new locations and connections, pacing the building out before it began business, exploring each others' rooms, and asking, 'How will I find you?' There was a new geography to be grasped, and insiders felt themselves temporarily and awkwardly to be outsiders, strangers in their own world, having none of the intuitive knowledge of relations and places that had to be mastered if they were to be truly insiders again, in charge of the complicated transactions of a Crown Court. Ushers were to be seen tripping and stumbling under unaccustomed courtroom barriers as they left the judges' bench to return to their seats. They got lost. They found themselves walking much further. A probation secretary declared that she did not know where to go for the lists. Deductions and judgments had to be made about the working logic of the building. Thus an usher could be heard reasoning, as he stood outside a courtroom, 'This is Court 1 so Court 2 must be on the other side'. The sergeant in charge of the police attached to the Court stood as if on point duty on the first day, directing newcomers to their destinations.

Staff and users found that the new building gave them added significance. They declared with pleasure, 'It *looks* like a court now.' One usher said, 'I love it. I think it's fantastic!' In part, the courthouse was welcomed because, in contrast to the Bunker, it was such a dramatically effective setting for actor and activity. People could not fail to become consequential on such a consequential stage. The courthouse was also welcomed because it was an instrument designed expressly to serve insiders' ends. Spaces in the new courthouse were not, like those in the Bunker, simply odd bits and pieces of makeshift architecture that were intended later to be converted into offices (although the *Palais de Justice* had its difficulties. Many of its interior shapes had been dictated by the Victorian architect of a school, not by a contemporary architect of courthouses).

Spaces worked together as a machine supposed to achieve quite specific purposes: the regulation of contamination, compromise, and attack. Controls were tighter, more elaborate, and more durable than those of the Bunker. Each floor was divided into four segregated circulation systems, each with its own colour code and meeting only in the courtroom (a probation officer, being give a tour of the new building, said of the jury lounge, 'I don't expect I'll ever come back here again'). There was a clearer delineation of insiders and outsiders.[91] There was less confused space. Counsel and jurors had their own separate canteens (although other users, defendants, staff, and witnesses did not.) Situated identities were clearer. The chief clerk, in a nice phrase, called the building 'self-regulating'. Spaces were designed for surveillance. And there were other subtle controls devised to pacify the frustrated and angry. The building was, as the anonymous PSA design guide put it, 'psychologically supportive to the emotionally excited user'. There was 'visual interest' to divert the waiting public. There were more soothing horizontal lines than aggressive vertical lines,[92] more calming pinks, lilacs, and greys than 'angry' oranges and reds.[93] Lighting was gentle. Landscaping was 'soft'. Public spaces were simple and comforting.

Counsel were more blasé. After all, they were accustomed to such places, to the new courthouses at Snaresbrook and Acton and Maidstone, and they had no permanent attachment to the building as a place or as a home territory. And, when they were at work,

---

[91] See M. Lavin, 'Boundaries in the Built Environment: Concepts and Examples', Man-Environment Systems, 11(5, 6) (1981), 199.

[92] The architect said, 'There was a document produced many years ago called "Pattern Language" . . . that [discussed] dealing with people in stressful situations and how they should be considered. . . . We tried to develop as much placidness as we could . . . [There was] colour, also the way one deals internal surfaces. You find a lot of horizontal stripes on the wall which give a sense of flowing continuity.'

[93] Although it should be noted that the insides of the lifts were an angry custard yellow.

courts tended to be all one to them. Waiting for trials to begin, getting lost as other insiders got lost, sometimes nervous, they tried to find amusing things to say, and they admired and mocked the building in equal measure. One counsel called it a 'very splendid building'; another told a court clerk 'it's a lovely place'; and a third observed: that it was 'very nice! It's a step up from the dump over the road.' They liked the oblique reminder of daylight that filtered into the courtroom. One barrister informed the court clerk that he had toured the building and thought, 'This is certainly much better than the old one!' He said of the small courts on the ground floor that 'I felt I should ask for a gin and tonic', and of the building as a whole that it resembled the Starship Enterprise ('All you need is Lieutenant Uhuro sitting there'). One barrister likened the courthouse to a crematorium chapel and another to a French château.

Witness and victims reacted much as they were supposed to react. The courthouse conferred a dignity and solemnity on a difficult experience: 'I'd say it was impressive,' said Victim 32. 'I mean, let's face it, when you come into places like this, you should be slightly awed. It's a serious business.' They seemed to have expected a traditional building that might have been celebrated by an Edgar Lustgarten, and the newness of the Court pleased them. They called the courthouse 'very nice'. Victim 30 said, 'I was rather impressed by the architecture. I must say it's more modern than I would expect. I like the architecture and the way it's been done outside. No, it's more modern than I would have expected. Because one has the image of the Old Bailey and that sort of thing. So it's quite user-friendly, I think.' Victim 31 said, 'It's a nice building. It's been very well laid out.' But he lamented the absence of a special circulation area for prosecution witnesses: 'They do need more places where they can actually keep the defendants away, or keep the witnesses out of the way of the defendant and vice versa.'

Scale

Let me describe only a few of the most important influences exerted by the design of the *Palais de Justice*.[94] Most of the influences stemmed from size. The new courthouse was much bigger than the

---

[94] I shall not examine a number of matters. Although the *Palais de Justice* was a much grander and more ornate building, many of its structures were formally similar to those already described in the discussion of the Bunker, and there is little profit in recapitulating fundamentally similar points.

Bunker. During my period of observation there, between April and July 1990, the three County Court courtrooms and one Patent courtroom were not sitting, leaving three floors of the building only in intense use. Yet those three floors were still some two-and-a-half times larger than the Bunker. Staff, users, and civilians found themselves regularly having to cover greater distances. An usher reflected: 'The amount of walking we have to do is considerably greater, partly because of the bigness of the building (this one's much bigger than the other,) and partly because we don't have the same access from A to B as we used to have. There is a lot more running around to do.'

Business and communication slowed down. Judges' chambers were no longer all on the same floor as their courtrooms, and it took time for judges to move from the one place to the other (one judge remarked in court. 'The trouble with this lovely new building is it takes far longer to get around than in the other one'). It took more time for jury bailiffs, listing officers, and probation staff to move to their destinations. It took more time for juries to leave their area for the courtrooms. (And some unorthodox expedients were mooted as a result. For instance, it was proposed informally in one court that jurors should wait in the retiring room whilst counsel made submissions, instead of following the normal practice of returning to their own lounge far away.)

Low Densities in a Complex Structure

Before the move, it had been a pronounced feature of the Bunker that staff, users, and civilians jostled one another repeatedly in the crowded corridors, offices, and concourse. They had been physically near one another, separated by token boundaries, and constricted in their movements. They could visit neighbouring home territories with ease. Spatial controls had been inconsistent, enabling disparate populations to meet where there were weaknesses and crevices in the formal system of closed circulation. Such a relatively high frequency of contact in a small space had created and strengthened relations, mapped out social worlds, and generated a diffuse sense of intimacy, called by insiders 'a family feeling'. That was to change. The population of the Crown Court centre looked appreciably more sparse when it was consigned to the vast new building. The *Palais de Justice* reduced the sheer volume of associations.

A larger, more lavish building had room to spare. Home territories were no longer bleak and utilitarian, as they had been in the Bunker, but generous sets of handsome rooms. The shorthand writers, for instance, appeared to have what was tantamount to a private apartment towards the top of the building, composed of a room each, a kitchen, and a little washroom. The CPS was given two rooms, and the problem that junior law clerks had complained of in the Bunker, the omnipresence of senior staff in a single space, disappeared: instead of 'a very small room with one phone and about two chairs for eight people' there were now two rooms, one for senior and one for junior staff. Junior staff planned to use their room more heavily because 'they'll breathe on us less'. They talked of domesticating it with a refrigerator and kettles in a manner never attempted in the Bunker.

Home territories seemed to assume much greater importance in a large building where it was bothersome to travel far, where private space was unusually appealing, and where, owing to a change of contract, the public canteen was thought to have declined in attractiveness. A new caterer had been commissioned to service the canteen in the *Palais de Justice*, and staff and users were almost uniformly critical of the food and prices (the automatic vending machine in the canteen demanded 40p for a cup of coffee and 35p for a cup of tea.) Insiders inspected the new place and did not like what they saw. One, a clerk, walked in on the first day, looked round, and smartly left again, never to return. They tended to retreat into their own spaces and provide for themselves instead, leaving the canteen to outsiders in the main part and to shorthand writers in possession of the staff table. A not untypical comment was that of a police officer after his first visit to the canteen: 'I don't think much of the canteen next door. I took one look at it and ugh! I wouldn't be surprised if the old police room upstairs hasn't got a kettle.' Like Goldthorpe and Lockwood's 'affluent worker',[95] staff and users became rather more 'privatized' in consequence. They began to lead a less public life. A police officer remarked, 'I don't see probation as much as I did. I don't go in and out of their office as much as I did.' And a denizen of that office, aloft in her third-floor room, remarked, 'You are completely out of touch with everything. You don't see anybody. . . . We don't see nearly as much of [the staff] as we did before.'[96] So it was

---

[95] See J. Goldthorpe, D. Lockwood, F. Bechhofer, and J. Platt, *The Affluent Worker* (Cambridge, Cambridge Univ. Press, 1968).

[96] That was gradually to change over time. Two years later, Geoff Spain was to reflect: 'Any danger of remoteness was soon countered by staff making contact with colleagues elsewhere in the *Palais*, while other sections regularly find an excuse to find the probation office on the third floor.'

that the *Palais de Justice* appeared to encourage stronger bonds *within* the little worlds of the Crown Court but eroded some of the bonds *between* them.

After the transition, staff and users professed to see less of one another, to lose touch with one another, and to learn less about one another's daily affairs. A visiting barrister, one who had always been on the borderline between the second and third circles, reflected that the Bunker had been 'a very friendly court' but that 'now you don't see so many people about. One is surprised that there are so few people around.' And, very similarly, a court clerk remarked to a probation officer in the first week after the move, 'We don't see people for days. It's not like the old Court. We haven't seen the ushers for a week.' Insiders seemed to be busier as they transacted duties that now took more time in a larger place. An usher reflected:

We said this morning when I saw X [another usher], I met him in the corridor here, and we sort of shook hands because we hadn't seen each other for such a long time. Before, in the other Court, we used to come in half an hour early anyway for our own convenience, sit down and have a jaw and a cup of something and, you know, generally prepare ourselves for the day, and then get cracking. . . . But now we find that although we still get in at half past eight, which I mean our time is really nine, we get in at half past eight and we start on the job because there is so much more to do because of the walking . . .

It was not a uniform experience. The impact of a lower population density was less pronounced on those officials who had always had a private space of their own, as the chief clerk had done, or who were exceptionally mobile, as the police sergeant in residence was. But others found that sociability became attenuated as they were scattered more thinly in space, and such attenuation could seem like loneliness. (A security guard said, 'staff-wise, there isn't the contact in a building this size amongst the staff . . . I can't see the family feeling occurring in this building because it is too large.') Those who worked in the deepest recesses of the new Court (in the archives, for instance), or who were physically immobile, began to feel marooned. Clerks and ushers, tied to their courtrooms, could no longer make brief social calls on others as they had once done in the Bunker: said a clerk, 'You haven't got the proximity. I used to pop into the probation office and the police on a daily basis. Now, because of the sheer physical size, you don't do that.' Court staff may have imported much of the social world of the Bunker with them when they moved, but 'anyone who joins now would never get that build-up of friend-ship and closeness'.

Congested, noisy, and bustling offices were replaced by a greater number of rooms laid out in larger areas of space and housing only a few people. The *Palais de Justice* seemed to be quieter, emptier, and less gregarious. A member of the listing staff said: 'As far as the staff are concerned, they are very spread out which probably makes it less friendly, because, whereas before we had all the office virtually in the same room, now they are all in different rooms, which does in a sense make it less friendly.' One person, who had been accustomed to working in a room set in one of the busiest parts of the Bunker, now discovered herself to be quite on her own:

In the old Court we all felt part of a family, but here we've lost that feeling. People are either leaving or sick. I don't have the contact with people I used to. It's just 'Good morning' and they're on their way . . . I don't see so many people. The barristers used to chat, although there was never any con-tact with them. We're in a much larger building with a shortage of staff . . . I feel a bit isolated . . . There's been such a difference. I thought it would be much nicer.

Such spatial attenuation was reinforced by a more emphatic segre-gation of circulation systems. It had become much more difficult to move about the building because places were firmly closed against one another. Barriers had fewer gaps. There was less confused space and more dedicated space (jurors and barristers now had their own separate canteens). There were more walls and more locks. An usher told me, 'It's a lot of leg work. We've found that there are no short cuts between places. We've tried to find them but they don't exist.' Similarly, a clerk said, 'There are more locked doors, digital locks, it all makes it more difficult to get about.' Where once it had been pos-sible for different worlds to meet in the structurally weak areas of the Bunker, they were now firmly disconnected in the *Palais de Justice*. Groups were kept apart, sometimes to their regret. A particularly sociable barrister reflected:

It's very formal. We're all separated from one another. It used to be a happy family court, but it's not so much any more. Everyone's separated from one another. You don't meet people. In the old canteen, you had opportunities to meet people and you could have a chat and break down suspicions. But I suppose a bit of anonymity is a good thing.

The effects of densities and controls worked unevenly. They cer-tainly transformed the new courthouse into a less threatening place.

Segregation kept some opponents at bay (although defendants and prosecution witnesses remained together as before). Surveillance was easier, because the new building lacked many of the blind bends and crannies where people might hide. A security guard said, 'You don't seem to have people lurking. If they are lurking, they are in a confined public area.' Public space was less frequently crowded, and it lost some of its hazards in consequence. Indeed, the courthouse often seemed empty, and being empty, its public parts could be treated ·as the unshielded projections of private space in which insiders could be less guarded. A CPS law clerk said, 'It is easier to stand outside the courtroom and discuss things in public space, should it not warrant having a conference in the CPS room, than it was in the old building. Because in the old building, 90 per cent of the time, you had to go to the CPS room just because there was no space.'

Those insiders who were particularly concerned about managing encounters with outsiders welcomed the pacifying effects of the new building. A lower density of associations seemed to reduce friction. A CPS law clerk said, 'There's no uncomfortable social situation', and a secretary talked of how 'you hardly see any of the public'. Insiders believed that relations between members of the public were themselves less tense. One police officer was concerned that his colleagues would be more distant from one another in crisis, but he was comforted that potentially volatile civilians were also more distant: 'I think it is a more user-friendly building. It tends to spread people out instead of crowding them all together. It is more calming.' And his colleague, a security guard, remarked of the contrast between the Bunker and the *Palais de Justice*: 'Everybody had to be condensed in that rabbit hutch down there. The restaurants—the jury have got their own, the barristers. Security and control-wise, it is a far better project.'

Dispersals

The new structure of space did not only thin people out, it also distributed them quickly and efficiently. Instead of the promiscuous, noisy milling that used to characterize the public concourse of the Bunker, populations entered and were dispersed, and they were dispersed by design. The courthouse's project manager remarked:

Most people have an anxiety to find out what court they are on and to go and sit near that court, because the anxiety is to be close to the doors of that court so that there is no chance of them missing their turn. . . . You do want to locate the waiting spaces close to the courts. The people will then congregate round those waiting spaces.'

The entrance and reception area of the *Palais de Justice* were quite evidently supposed to look as if they led on to more spacious and enticing areas elsewhere. They contained little of visual interest to detain the newcomer. There were no chairs or benches on which to sit and wait. They were not planned as places to tarry: people were supposed to move smoothly on to their appointed places outside courtrooms (the public concourse of another new courthouse, the Crown Court centre at Truro, was described by its architects as 'a linear route which connects two waiting spaces'.[97]

Before the new building opened, the chief clerk explained that there were to be very few large waiting areas in the *Palais de Justice*: people would enter, go to the reception desk, and advance rapidly to the multitude of small areas adjoining specific courtrooms, areas that were intended to separate and diffuse otherwise antagonistic groups. (The architect said, 'One tries to create space and opportunities for people to get away from it. There is a central staircase and people can mill round or look into the central waiting space for the courtroom. If they don't like the look of someone there, they don't have to go in to use it. There are other spaces where people can move around and not to be forced to face stressful situations.') And so it came to be. People entered, very often forearmed by the police with the number of the court to which they should go, wandered around within the reception area, getting their bearings, and then moved on. *The Guide* described the reception area as a place 'contiguous to court entrance lobby and circulation' with a 'high throughput' whose occupancy would be 'transitory'.[98]

At 10 a.m. on the first Monday in the new courthouse, there were but ten people in the reception area when there would have been forty in the public concourse of the Bunker. The receptionist pronounced. 'It's amazing! I was really quite worried, but they all disappeared quite quickly. They came in and went on almost immediately.' There was no congestion, no throng, no atmosphere of a hiring fair in which everyone waited to be noticed. Civilians and users distributed themselves throughout the courthouse, reconstructing the archipelago as clusters gathered in twos and threes outside

---

[97] E. Evans and D. Shalev, 'Concourse and Staircase', *Architects' Journal*, 188(39), Sept. 1988), 83. [98] 10.1b.

the courtrooms. A security guard said at the end of the first week, 'I'm doing my rounds. This building swallows 'em up! Swallows 'em up!'

The New Archipelago

A new archipelago of huddles was then to be seen fringing the court-room doors, as people waited for cases to begin or news to be released. They sat for long periods, as they had sat in the Bunker, next to their adversaries, in a kind of frosty silence, awarding one another civil attention, and under strain (the father of Victim 18 remarked, 'You're more tired sitting around here than if you've done a day's work'). To be sure, the courtroom doors *were* flanked by sound-proof consultation rooms supposedly for civilians and users alike, rooms intended to segregate the nervous and the frightened (see Pl. 6.12). The architect observed: 'There are two spaces outside the courtrooms; one is described as an interview room and one is described as a witness room.' But those rooms were monopolized, when used at all, by police officers and counsel (they could indeed, on occasion, become appropriated as storage rooms for exhibits).

PL. 6.12. *Entrance to a Courtroom in the* Palais de Justice

Witnesses were in a state of enforced passivity, a kind of depen-dency, and not having been told they could hide themselves in the consultation rooms, they did not feel emboldened to do so. The only civilians who entered the rooms were defendants who were taken there by counsel for consultation. (One prosecutor said, 'Oh, these little consultation rooms are very useful indeed. You use these when speaking to your client, and that's very good, or if you are for the prosecution, you have all sorts of matters to sort out.') The rooms were not labelled, their purpose was not made clear to an outsider, and civilians remained firmly outside them.[99]

Outside each of the six courtrooms in the morning there might be but four or five people, clearly separated into clusters of defence or prosecution witnesses.[100] The practice of accomplishing conventional closure through spatial distance was retained in the *Palais de Justice*, as it was in every Crown Court centre in the country. Some prosecution witnesses chose to hide themselves in the liminal spaces outside the lavatories or on the more anonymous staircase landings rather than confront defendants.[101] Victim 32 was one who so hid himself, saying of the defendant, 'He knows I'm a prosecuting witness against him. He's just been giving me dirty looks ever since, every time I see him. I think they could have kept him in the court or in another room away from me so that he cannot try and intimidate me at all.' Counsel still gingerly prospected space, gauged who had established themselves in the waiting areas, and positioned themselves safely. They would sit outside the courtroom if no one else was there. They might closet themselves in their mess or in a consultation room. If they were heavily outnumbered, they sometimes stood on the landing of the grand staircase or sat outside a different courtroom altogether, as if engaged in another case.

Outside the Doors

Waiting, nervously, confined to their space, witnesses would scan the courtroom doors for indications of what might be happening within. The double doors and sound lobby worked to exclude the witness physically and symbolically. They were a boundary indeed. Witnesses knew very little indeed of what was going on inside the courtroom. They were estranged by acts by commission, so that their minds

---

[99] An official of the Lord Chancellor's Dept. who had visited the new building commented on how 'appalling' the 'signing' there was.

[100] Some 43% of the witnesses at Wood Green in the Raine and Smith study reported waiting in the same area as the defendant.

[101] McDonald wrote of how, in America, the victim is also 'left to wait in the halls or some drab room to which the defendant whom he is accusing has free access'; 'Criminal Justice and the Victim', in W. McDonald (ed.), *Criminal Justice and the Victim* (Beverly Hills, Calif., Sage, 1976), 19–20.

should not be corrupted, and by acts of omission, because no one apart from the police took it upon themselves to inform them about what occurred. Police officers were, after all, professionals who were given some access to the courtroom. They knew what could and could not be done, and they were not sent automatically into exile as civilians were.

Until the actual trial itself began, officers in the case tended to wait in court, gossiping amongst themselves and talking to the prosecution and members of the CPS. It was, after all, 'their' case, and they had a proprietorial interest in its fate. From time to time, they would venture outside to convey something of what had transpired to the attendant civilians, saying, for instance, 'I don't know what's happening today. I'll let you know as soon as you're required. Things are being held up as usual.' But those communications were not only occasional but generally meagre, vague, and fragmentary. (Victim 23 said, 'They didn't really give it in sort of detail. We found we got little snippets saying, you know, we knew roughly what was going on'; and Victim 24 said, 'They did say they were going to get this fellow from a prison but I don't know where.') It was the father of Victim 18, again, who remarked, 'You sit outside and you don't know what's going on.' Trials might falter or make progress but the witnesses were told little.

Identifications

A dispersed population of small, discrete clusters sitting outside specific courtrooms eased the problems of identification that had plagued professionals in the public concourse of the Bunker. It was as if people were neatly laid out for purposes of classification. Two or three men and women reading statements in the company of counsel could not but be defendants and defence witnesses awaiting trial in the adjoining courtroom. The other huddle, perhaps gathered around a police officer, could not but be prosecution witnesses. One of those who needed to make identifications was the usher:

Now, each court has its own public area; I think there is more chance of getting to know the witnesses and anybody else coming into the case. . . . In the old Court, you had a common public area to more or less four courts, because the people waiting on the ground floor were probably waiting for courts 1, 2, 3, and 4 because there was no waiting area as such to speak of on the middle floor. But here you do get to see the people connected with your court . . .

Acoustics

The new courtrooms were splendid and beautiful, but I shall not dwell minutely on the impact of their appearance and spatial organization.[102] Despite their grandeur, much of the behaviour enacted within them was not very different from before. Indeed, some underlying features of design were constant, furniture in the courtrooms of both buildings being regarded as low and informal. It was, in any event, the case that counsel and judges professed generally to be oblivious to setting, working as if they were in any courtroom anywhere in the land ('It doesn't affect how you do it at all'). But they did note a change in acoustics. Let me concentrate on that one change because it is a good illustration of how design can affect conduct.

In the Bunker, it will be recalled, witnesses had forever to be reminded that they should speak more loudly, their delivery being repeatedly interrupted by admonitions from lawyers, judges, and shorthand writers. Acoustics in the *Palais de Justice* were different. Care had been taken with every salient physical feature: outside noises were excluded by 'sound lobbies', internal noises were controlled with the use of thick walls, unobtrusive ducts, soft and absorbent surfaces, 'whisper telephones', and 'cross-talk attenuators'. It was not difficult, said the project manager, 'to control courtrooms acoustically'. Architectural journalists on a press tour were told that there was a 'deliberately dead sound'. It was as if there was a loudspeaker in front of counsel, thought an usher.

Unexpectedly, the semi-privacy of the poor acoustics in the Bunker had given way to a kind of aural transparency. The whispered conferences and *sotto voce* asides that would have been generally inaudible in the Bunker were now quite loud and distinct. Conventional enclosures were no longer effective at all. People were revealed as they had not been revealed before. (A barrister told a court clerk, 'The acoustics aren't that good. I had a case here weeks ago and my client was muttering things about the judge, you know, the usual judge things, and the judge heard every word!' The clerk replied, 'You mean the acoustics are very good!') There had to be a much tighter

---

[102] There were some idiosyncrasies. The witness-box, for instance, appeared to be back-to-front, and witnesses had to perform a curious and ungainly movement to enter and leave it. An usher remarked, 'You can shake hands with the judge as you go into the witness-box and I think that's wrong.' It does not seem particularly useful to enlarge on such minute differences between the courtrooms in the two buildings.

discipline (a CPS law clerk advised a lawyer: 'The acoustics are very good, so be careful when you're talking').

Counsel rapidly ascertained how very good the acoustics were in the *Palais de Justice*, and, after some precautionary work ('The acoustics appear to be good in this court but nevertheless could you direct your answers to the back of the court?'), they largely ceased to interrupt the delivery of testimony. Witnesses were thus subject to much less interference as they tried to cope with public interrogation. (A shorthand writer remarked that she couldn't 'complain at all' and a court clerk described the acoustics as 'brilliant. I think only once the judge asked somebody to "Please speak up", and that was counsel. I mean you can hear them because the acoustics are so good, and it's nice and quiet and people don't have to shout.')

Conclusion

Everything that happened within the confines of the courthouse was affected by the insiders' abiding preoccupation with the conflict, danger, and threat to confidentiality represented by outsiders. The courthouse itself was constructed to work as a great engine of social control. Groupings were separated; knowledge was protected; compromising encounters were prevented; and vulnerable groups (apart from those designated members of the public) were shielded. The building's principal mechanism was a system of circulation areas that diffracted and isolated the four different social worlds recognized by architects and administrators. People were kept apart until they met in the courtroom, and they met there under stern control. The circulation areas were arrayed in a hierarchy of privacy and security, the innermost protecting judge, jury, and defendant in custody. Dotting them were the home territories of staff and users, the bounded private territories in which people could escape for a while from the rigours of a formal role in a public place. And all about them were the disquieting open areas in which the public milled.

In the least secure, least private, most accessible of all the circulation areas were to be found that same 'public', a miscellany of unlike groups obliged to share a common space until trials came to a resolution. Prosecution witnesses and victims were taken to be members of the public, and their experience of the inner topography of a courthouse was marked by segregation, regulation, and direction as they were shunted into waiting areas abutting the courtroom and then into the courtroom itself. The public had not been reached or consulted when the courthouse had been planned, and their fears and preoccupations had not been inscribed in its design. There was a symmetry and a dialectic: design refracting social organization, and social organization reinforcing design. It was as if architecture proclaimed that outsiders must indeed be disquieting if such elaborate measures were required to control them. The Court's physical structure was thus a transcription of its social structure, the one reproducing the other.[103] In all this, prosecution witnesses themselves were problematic and marginal, and they occupied the margins of the courthouse, excluded from its private regions and knowledge. Victim 32 remarked:

We were in a foreign land sort of thing. . . . You're just waiting around. You don't know what's going to happen next. . . . With these people going through, you don't know if they've got anything to do with you, whether they're on your side or what. It's that lack of understanding about what the process is and who's who in the game.

[103] Architecture did regulate, constrain, and limit what could be done and who could go where and see what. Members of the public could not, and did not, wander freely around the custody area or in the jury lounge. Defendants did not visit judges in chambers. But design (and social structure) did not quite determine behaviour: at the margins, there remained opportunities for a creative use of space and for some resistance to control. Thus the most sociable barristers, the barristers who had enjoyed conversing with administrators and others users in the past, chose often not to use their own sheltered mess in the *Palais de Justice*, but instead went to the public canteen or the public waiting areas in their search for diverting gossip.

7. Time in the Court

'I should have brought a newspaper. I should have brought *War and Peace*. (One witness to another)

Processes in the Court were stretched out in time. All processes are so stretched. And the organization of time affected the management and experience of the prosecution witness. Two forms of temporal experience met in the Court. One was cyclical, and that was the temporal structure familiar to the professionals and users. It was complex and convoluted, composed of many interlocking and repeated cycles. If it were ever to be represented pictorially, it might resemble a piece of rococo tracery with its many curls and flourishes. The other form was linear, and that was the time known to the civilian. Linear time did not appear to be especially complex, although it could be confusing enough because of its open horizons. Neither did it seem repetitive. Let me deal with cyclical time first.

Cyclical Time and the Professional

The work of large organizations is co-ordinated by timetables devised to bring people together at fixed points and for fixed periods.[1] Such schedules tend to be robust in bureaucracies,[2] and exceptionally so when they bring many strangers together to perform complicated, consequential, and sometimes distasteful activities. In substantial bureaucracies, the endogenous will prevail. Schedules are characteristically imposed without a show of formal attention to external conditions, to rain, heat, snow, strikes, and coups. Such organizations will have their own inner social and physical environment that appears blind to variations of condition and climate in the wider world. So it was in the Court. There was a common starting-time for courtroom business at 10.15 and again at 2.00 every single working day. Civilians, users, and professionals, were all expected to be in a state of readiness at those times, converging at a single point from across

[1] See S. de Grazia, *Of Time, Work, and Leisure* (New York, Doubleday Anchor, 1972), 8.
[2] See B. Adam, *Time and Social Theory* (Cambridge, Polity Press, 1990), 106.

the country and sometimes, indeed, from countries overseas. They were to be ready whatever else might happen. In one instance, in April 1990, when a defendant and all his witnesses had not appeared because they had been caught up in a well-publicized coup in Nigeria, the judge remarked tartly, and perhaps half-seriously, 'Nothing's happened in Nigeria as far as I know.' The will of the Court was supposed to be sovereign, enforceable by bench warrants against civilians and complaints against professionals. (Of course, as judges and administrators knew very well, it was difficult to contend with adverse weather, epidemics, and other contingencies, but a pretence of sovereignty was important. As I have argued, judges had little power to start trials. All they could do, most of the time, was acquiesce and sometimes grumble.)

The work of the Court was shaped by a series of intersecting temporal cycles. The largest and the flattest were the judicial sitting and the season. The sitting was little more than a token matter at Wood Green. There were four sittings, Hilary (in 1990, 11 January to 11 April), Easter (24 April to 25 May), Trinity (5 June to 31 July), and Michaelmas (1 October to 21 December), but the Crown Court at Wood Green actually worked throughout most of the year. The seasonal cycle was somewhat outside the Court's control. It was held to be rather more difficult to gather professionals and civilians together at Easter and in the summer, and unusual efforts had to be exerted to counteract the effects of holidays and leave. Towards the end of May 1990, for example, during what a probation officer called the 'silly season', only four courts were sitting. The Wood Green listing officer claimed, 'It gets more and more difficult in the summer months because everyone wants to go on holiday.'

Yet it will be seen from Fig. 7.1 that the Court did actually manage to keep most courtrooms busy throughout most of the year. There was not a marked fluctuation in the volume of cases disposed of. A member of the listing staff observed: 'Obviously there is more leave to be taken into account and perhaps the warned lists aren't quite as long as we would normally like, but we still manage to keep the courts going.'

A third major cycle was formed by the availability of judicial time. It will be recalled that the Court's judiciary was composed of a small, stable core of judges allocated for some eight months every year, a larger number of judges on circuit allocated for some two months every year, and a group of recorders and assistant recorders who

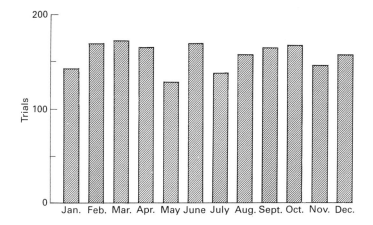

FIG. 7.1. *Trials Dealt With in 1989*

were inserted in the spaces between. The business of each year was constructed like a gigantic jigsaw puzzle, said a senior official in the circuit's administration: 'You sort of put it all down on the table and work it all out and fit in with requirements elsewhere, and then the odd weeks are filled by recorders and assistant recorders.'

The availability of judges shaped the listing of cases. The listing officer could not always assign cases to a judge or recorder who was attached to the Court for only a short space or who was about to leave. Recorders would very rarely be allotted long cases. In 1989, as a result, 37 days were lost officially because of a 'lack of judiciary' and 31 days were 'short' as a consequence of 'judges last day'. There were periodic peaks and troughs in the numbers of judicial days lost (see Fig. 7.2).

A fourth, intersecting cycle was the pattern of the week, and that was the prime framework of activity in the Court. Just as in everyday life, there was a 'weekly rhythm . . . each day [having] its own physiognomy'.[3] Two distinct pulses moved through the week, affecting everyone in the Court. The first was at the very beginning, Monday being the busiest and most difficult of days. The senior probation officer called Mondays 'fidgety'. Masses of new jurors, 80 strong, would troop in to the Court on Mondays, many of them confused about what to do and where to go, the only time that they would be

---

[3] P. Sorokin and C. Berger, *Time-Budgets of Human Behavior* (Cambridge, Mass., Harvard Univ. Press, 1939), 84.

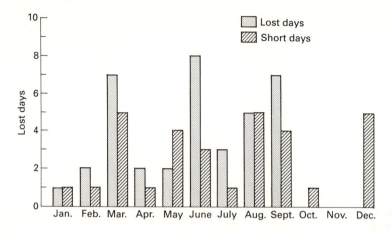

Fig. 7.2. *Days Lost and Short in 1989*

so exposed in public. New fixtures would characteristically begin on Mondays, assembling defendants, witnesses, and counsel unfamiliar to one another and the Court itself. Monday mornings were a time of milling and confusion as the casts caught up in the different trials struggled to find one another. The throng in the concourse of the Bunker was always at its largest then, and staff would be extraordinarily busy as they sought to impose order on disorder. A security officer reflected, 'This is when you have to be on your toes, on a Monday morning, when things are beginning to start off, all the new cases.' Social organization and knowledge would be at their most fragmented. Said an usher to a custody officer in February 1990, 'Have you heard anything about anyone?' and the officer replied, 'No. It's a real Monday here.'

Tuesdays were quieter as Mondays' trials passed into their second day, becoming what were known as 'part-heards'. Jurors, civilians, and professionals would by then have learned where to go, jurors being hidden in their own circulation system. A number of prosecution witnesses would already have given evidence and been dismissed. There were fewer people to be seen in the common parts of the courthouse.

Since trials characteristically lasted no longer than two days (recall that the average length of a trial at Wood Green was five hours), Wednesdays would typically repeat in miniature the pattern of Mondays, being a new beginning in the middle of the week. And

Thursdays were another Tuesday, with few new trials and a number of 'part-heards'.

People were assumed to have settled down by the end of the week. A barrister told a jury: 'Members of the jury, you may have sat before on trials at Wood Green. This being a Friday, I suspect you have.' There were almost no new trials on Fridays because they would have lacked much prospect of continuity. The listing officer said, 'I am reluctant to start trials on a Friday . . . it is not popular with either judges or counsel . . . because of the two-day break in between.' A jury sitting on a Friday trial might be placed under pressure to return a verdict before the weekend, having otherwise to retain complicated matters in their minds or even to return on a Saturday. A senior member of the circuit administration stated, 'It is very costly if they are out overnight and the Court has to open up on Saturday but, secondly, it is very important that the jury shouldn't be seen rushing their verdict.' It was preferable occasionally to discharge juries for an entire day rather than require them to retire on a Friday. Fridays were thus set aside principally as a time for appeals and applications, freeing Mondays for the next round of new trials and the start of a new weekly cycle.

Court work had its precedence. Sentences and pleas were often to be heard before trials themselves. Trials already started, the 'part-heards', took priority over new trials, and 'fixtures' were placed ahead of other trials and of 'floaters' in particular. The pattern of a day's business was itself then cyclical (see Figs. 7.3, 7.4).

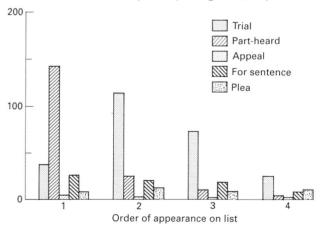

FIG. 7.3. *Order on Lists, February–May 1990*

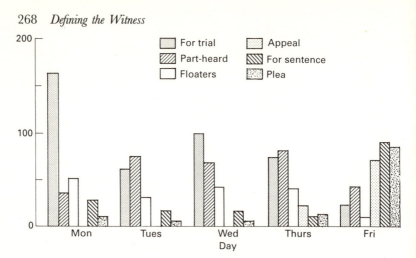

Fig. 7.4. *Some Actions by Days of the Week, February–June 1990*

A week was thus clearly plotted out, and every week would have looked very much the same, enforcing a concomitant pattern and pace of work on staff and users. A CPS clerk reflected:

Mondays is always a busy day because you have got pleas on a Friday and all the courts have finished their cases so you have got all new trials starting on the Monday, which are very often five or six of what we call fixtures, but we also have a back-up in case anything goes wrong. . . . Wednesday is what we call another fixture day. In actual fact, they fix two or three cases for the middle of the week.

There was a standard repetition of phases and parts of phases within most of the trials themselves. One small burglary or assault case could look very much the same as any other. Its conclusion and course might not be wholly foreseeable, and there could be some apprehension about the verdict (after all, juries were unfathomable and there were surprises and 'ambushes'), but its constituents were familiar enough. Juries would be sworn with set oaths and told, rote-like, about the role of counsel and judges, the character of evidence, the burden of proof, and the bare outlines of the events that would have to be proved in court. They would be presented with evidence from victims, prosecution witnesses, and police officers in set order, and after much the same dither about the availability of witnesses and documents. Examination-in-chief would try to coax a recitation of a known, recorded proof out of key witnesses. Cross-examination would try to unravel that proof, the same repertoire of accusatory and sceptical questions being levelled again and again. In short, there were stereotyped patterns within patterns, formulae within formulae. It is hardly remarkable that counsel said repeatedly that they were indifferent to the unique particulars of the courtroom and the Court. They were working with what Schutz called stock recipes and 'cookbook' knowledge[4] that carried them through trials day after day in court after court, often with only the briefest of preparation and with the sparsest of information about a case and its protagonists. Cases began to grow alike with repetition. Their very ritualization imposed a strong, levelling template that reduced the appearance of variation.[5] Cyclical time thus emphasized the insiders' sense of similar experiences reiterating themselves regularly and in successions:[6] counsel, judges, police officers, and administrators passing again and again through the formally similar beginnings, middles, and ends of trials that moved in similar waves through similar weeks.[7] And they would find themselves passing through the same events together, becoming transformed into a group with a shared experience of time, a generation in microcosm. In one court, the court clerk might be seen conversing dejectedly to the shorthand writer in an otherwise empty room, nothing much appearing to happen, time hanging heavily. In the adjoining court, there could be collective excitement at an unexpected verdict, or a sudden outburst.[8]

To be sure, cyclical time could only be known probabilistically. There was no certainty that events *would* repeat themselves in minute detail (and there was an abundant sense of the risks and hazards of the world of the Court). It was only inference that made events seem constrained. The future remained free until it became a past reduced by experience to a re-enactment of the old and familiar.[9] But the

[4] See A. Schutz, 'The Problem of Rationality in the Social World', in *Collected Papers* (The Hague, Martinus Nijhoff, 1962), ii. 73–4.

[5] See P. Fraisse, *The Psychology of Time* (London, Eyre and Spottiswoode, 1964), 169.

[6] It must, however, be stated that lawyers tend not to reduce all the features of cases and trials to formula. Each trial also represents a unique combination of complicated parts that can never be reduced simply to stereotype. Lawyers are reluctant to generalize beyond the particular.

[7] See R. Jackall, *Moral Mazes: The World of Corporate Managers* (New York, Oxford Univ. Press, 1988), 5.

[8] See J. Eisenstein and H. Jacob, *Felony Justice* (Boston, Little, Brown, 1977), 43.

[9] P. Baert, for instance, trying to reconstitute a Meadian philosophy of time, observed that 'people are bound to live in the present. They are eternal imprisoners of the present, in that their experiencing is for ever in a "now". I can, for example,

collective sense of professionals was one of time rotating in ways that were understood and manageable.

Linear Time and the Civilian

It was different for 'civilians'. They saw the professional's cyclical time as linear, and in that difference there resided another source of social separation. Professionals and civilians did not live in quite the same temporal universe. They shared clock time and the local time of the Court, but their experience of the overall patterning of time divided them. Sixty-two per cent of the Raine and Smith sample of Wood Green witnesses had never been to court before.[10] For them, testifying was a new experience that might well never be repeated. There was no reserve of formulaic knowledge upon which they could draw and no easy anticipation of the future. Going to court was not, as Husserl put it, a matter of applying the common sense of 'I can do it again'. Each phase of their experience was novel, to be negotiated afresh and with an uncertain outcome. Young argued that 'the cyclical keeps things the same by reproducing the past and the linear makes things different by introducing novelty'.[11]

The professional's cycle of repetitive tasks was seen by the civilian as a straight and sometimes incomprehensible trail of staggered processes that lurched back and forth between quiescence and vigorous movement. It was a trail marked by what has been called the 'calm and crisis' alternation of temporal rhythms.[12] Months would pass without any discernible change, months when witnesses were not witnesses in any significant sense, only to be interrupted by accelerated activity in which being a witness was very significant indeed.

Trials took shape step by step. After the first rush and flurry of activity surrounding the crime and its discovery, the making of reports and giving of statements, it took, on average, what could only have been seen by civilians as three comparatively uneventful months

---

imagine experiencing something in the future, but necessarily that experiencing, that act of the imagination, is in the present'; *Time, Self and Social Being* (Aldershot, Avebury, 1992), 77.

[10] J. Raine and R. Smith, *The Victim/Witness in Court Project: Report of the Research Programme* (Oct. 1991), 9.

[11] M. Young, *The Metronomic Society* (London, Thames and Hudson, 1988), 4.

[12] See K. Starkey, 'Time and Work: A Psychological Perspective', in P. Blyton *et al.* (eds.), *Time, Work and Organization* (London, Routledge, 1989), 47.

for offences to be translated into cases heard by magistrates and a further four months for those cases to be committed for trial in the Crown Court at Wood Green.[13] Crisis thus gave way to a period of inactivity for the civilian, a period that was often experienced as neglect.[14] Victim 13 said, 'I never saw anyone for months', and Victim 23 remarked, 'Once a few months go by, you just think it's forgotten.'

I explained how cases committed to the Crown Court would automatically be placed on a 'warned list' sent to defence solicitors and the CPS. The warned list for the week beginning 23 April 1990, for example, was dispatched in the afternoon of 28 March: it contained the names of 69 cases for trial, 4 cases for sentence, 3 for plea, and 2 appeals. Receiving that list, solicitors, CPS staff, and police Crime Support Units were told the names of listing office staff who would 'help with your problems', who need 'to know your availability', and 'will help you plan your Bail Applications Appeals and Sentences'. They were told that 'you should expect cases to be listed within 4–6 weeks from the date of committal', and that 'it is therefore important that cases are fully prepared and ready for trial'. Users so alerted were expected to ascertain the state of readiness of their case and the availability of civilian, expert, and police witnesses: a member of the listing staff said. 'The CPS have responsibility of checking the witness leave for the prosecution, and obviously any problems with the witness leave, from the defence side, will be notified to us by the solicitor.'

There could then follow another long silence until the Court issued its 'provisional list' of the next day's business. Such was the uncertainty of one day's cases that the next day's lists were inevitably compiled with little time to spare. Some cases would abort or go short every day, some were delayed and some dragged on. Until very near the end of the working day, it would not be plain which courts and judges could take new cases. Only the court clerks, sitting in the courtrooms and closely watching the progress of each trial, could predict the pattern of the next day's business. The listing officer said, 'The court clerks are meant to come and tell me at lunchtime how they see the case going and whether it is expected to finish, and it's

[13] The actual average figure for all the 2,335 defendants committed for trial in 1989 was 16.06 weeks. Under 77(1) of the Supreme Court Act 1981, trials were not supposed to begin until after 14 days from the date of committal and not later than 8 weeks from that date.

[14] See J. Morgan and L. Zedner, *Child Victims: Crime, Impact, and Criminal Justice* (Oxford, Clarendon Press, 1992), 107 ff.

on that that I base the list.' And the provisional list would be succeeded by yet another list, the 'final' list, towards the end of the Court's day at 4 pm:

> By the end of the day, it's too late to change it because the courts don't rise normally until about 4.15, but the list has to be finalized before 4 o'clock. So in fact, once they've given me their estimates at lunchtime, unless something major happens in court, they don't bother to disturb me again. I just do the list from that information.

Lists would be 'faxed' or 'teleprinted' to the Court's linked chambers, to room 6 in the Royal Courts of Justice, to the CPS, the police crime support units, and defence solicitors, to warn counsel and to notify witnesses. Receiving their lists (and the lists of all other Crown Court centres), chambers' clerks, solicitors, and CPS officers would engage instantly in bouts of energetic activity,[15] vying with one another to secure the services of barristers for the following day ('We're only a little satellite out here competing with the big courts in London,' said an officer of the branch CPS at Wood Green). Counsel already briefed could quite possibly be embroiled in cases elsewhere (some 60 per cent would be so committed), and rapid consultations would have to ensue with barristers' clerks about the eligibility of alternatives:

> I haven't had a confirm on Z for B in Court 4. Does that mean it's confirmed? [Name is offered as a substitute]. Mr C? Have you got anyone else? Yes? How old is he? Well it might not be the same Mr C then. We might be alright. It's a conviction appeal. Have you anyone else? I've got a floater, that's all, but I want to look for a 2 first. . . . She's not a 2 is she? I've had this trouble before, because I took her and she wasn't a 2. The floater is D and [the brief's] at X Field Court.

It was that uncertainty and indefiniteness of trials that brought about the formulaic conduct of cases (Schutz once remarked, 'The ideal of everyday knowledge is not certainly . . . but just likelihood'.[16]) When most briefs were received at short notice, sometimes, indeed, being collected at the Court itself on the morning of the trial, there was almost no time at all for independent enquiry, prolonged thought, or an original approach by counsel. Cases had to be trans-

---

[15] On the occasion I witnessed the CPS liaising with barristers' clerks, the entire business for 6 courts was despatched in 50 minutes.

[16] 'The Problem of Rationality in the Social World', 73.

lated rapidly into set forms that could propel barristers through the trial stage by stage.[17]

Witnesses themselves had also to be warned at only a few hours' notice, being roused by telephone in the first instance and then, if necessary, by personal calls at work or at home in the evening. It was defence solicitors who mobilized defence witnesses:

I explain the difficulties and say do they mind ringing me or alternatively can the defendant notify them. We just try to set something up so that we can notify everybody and sort everything out. Failing that, I would in fact deliver something myself. They are all local people.

And police and civilian witnesses would be warned by the police. If telephone calls during the day failed, it was the practice of the crime support unit attached to Wood Green to send officers on foot to witnesses' homes at about 7.30 at night, and again, if necessary, on the morning of the trial itself (the branch Crown prosecutor talked about 'a very tense time with police rushing and contacting witnesses'). A civilian working in the crime support unit asserted that the 'latest you can normally catch the CPS is about quarter to six', and the consequent gap between the working schedules of the two agencies almost always left the CPS, counsel, and Court uncertain about the preparedness of trials until the very moment they were supposed to start. It was that gap which brought about the anxious milling that so bedevilled the opening phases of a trial.

What, for witnesses, had appeared to be a long lull was thus punctured by sudden and urgent activity, and it is not remarkable that they were sometimes bewildered by the abruptness of the lurch that heralded their appearance in Court. Victim 2, for instance, had waited a year before learning that he was to become a witness on the very day of the trial itself:

They tried to contact me this morning. Evidently, they went to my friends at eight o'clock this morning rather than where I work. By chance, I happened to phone my work and my flatmate left a message, and that's the only chance I had to find out. It said I had to be at Court by ten o'clock and I was on my way to Milton Keynes then, which was a long way away. This was quarter past nine. I hadn't got a clue [what it was all about]. I didn't even know what case it was or anything.

[17] There were, of course, exceptions; e.g. some barristers clearly visited the scenes of alleged offences to form their own independent appreciation of what might have happened, but they were always at risk of not actually being able to appear on the day itself, and many acquired briefs too late to take any such action.

[18] See J. Roth, *Timetables*, (Indianapolis, Bobbs-Merrill, 1963).

It could indeed be difficult to recapture the initial sense of crisis that had infused the crime and its reporting to the police. Victim 24 said:

They asked us to make a statement [eighteen months ago] and then I think it may have been six or eight weeks ago I had the police coming up and saying be ready for court and then on the evening they said it was cancelled. I think this has happened three or four times, and finally I had a phone call last Thursday night to say it would be to come here on Friday and we just sat Friday. I mean, at the time, you think, well I felt that these people should be [prosecuted] and all that and I was ready to be a witness but then after a few months, it seems a bit, what you see and all that, it just doesn't seem worthwhile really.

A bench-mark was passed in that final warning.[18] It defined the onset of a new and distinct phase in the witness's career. Before, the witness had been a quondam bystander or victim, a person whose memories of a crime were perhaps fading and whose very victimization could be of declining significance to identity. Now, it was sure that he or she was about to become something new, a prosecution witness testifying in court before judge and jury. Most witnesses had had no previous knowledge of courts, and they did not always understand what would be demanded of them. There was a measure of anxiety. Victim 5 said simply: 'I don't understand the workings of the Court.'

In effect, the bystander-victim-witness had crossed a temporal boundary[19] and undergone a status passage to become, however briefly, a new sort of person. Most status passages are orderly, rehearsed, advertised, and assisted.[20] It was otherwise for the witness. Going to court was a disordered experience for which there could only have been slight preparation. The bulk of witnesses had not been witnesses before and might never be witnesses again. Few had had contact with a victims support scheme.[21] Most had not even received a copy of the *Witness in Court* leaflet prepared jointly by Victim Support and the Home Office and intended to brief witnesses about their court appearance.[22] They had tended to lose touch with

[19] See E. Zerubavel, *Patterns of Time in Hospital Life* (Chicago, Univ. of Chicago Press, 1979), 2.

[20] See B. Glaser and A. Strauss, *Status Passage* (London, Routledge and Kegan Paul, 1971).

[21] 78.3% of the Raine and Smith sample of Wood Green witnesses had had no prior contact with such a scheme.

[22] 44.7% of the Wood Green sample in Raine and Smith's report claimed to have received this leaflet.

the police officers 'in the case'. The full meanings and problems entailed in becoming a witness could not, then, be grasped initially, but evolved as the situation itself evolved, *emergent* properties of a process.[23] Victim 32 said:

Having never attended court in any capacity, it's all a new experience. The fact that you are not on home ground—if you're on home ground, you're immediately one step in advance, aren't you, but the fact that you are coming into foreign territory is even more confusing.

In many routine status passages, others, more knowledgeable, help the initiates through the sometimes bewildering changes that befall them. Anselm Strauss called such guides 'status coaches':

A coaching relationship exists if someone seeks to move someone else along a series of steps, when those steps are not entirely institutionalized and invariant, and when the learner is not entirely clear about their sequences (although the coach is). . . . The general features of the coaching relationship flow from the learner's need for guidance as he moves, step by step. He needs guidance not merely because in the conventional sense he needs someone to teach him skills, but because some very surprising things are happening to him that require explanation.[24]

Until the coming of the Victim in Court project, there were no effective coaches to ease witnesses through their status passage. On the contrary: for the many reasons I have given, witnesses tended to be shunned. Their most frequent complaint was: 'Someone should tell us what's happening.' Victim 10, for instance, talked about how he was 'pissed off waiting and nothing happening, and no one came up to me'.

The Wobbliness of Temporal Structures

If matters were difficult and confusing for the embryonic witness, they were made even more confusing by the precarious character of the temporal structures that patterned the work of the Court. Perfect trials in a perfect court would have started promptly at 10.15, as they were supposed to do, and then moved effortlessly through their various stages until they culminated in a verdict. Participants would have been able to predict and anticipate what was to come, making appropriate adjustments stage by stage. Schedules in the Crown

---

[23] See F. Davis, *Passage Through Crisis* (Indianapolis, Bobbs-Merrill, 1963), 10.
[24] *Mirrors and Masks* (New York, Free Press, 1959), 110.

Court at Wood Green were not perfect. They were unsteady and frail, difficult to start and sometimes difficult to sustain. The Branch Crown Prosecutor talked of 'cliffhangers . . . there are so many imponderables about the way a case will develop'.

Timetables were prey to delay, interference, and uncertainty. Until the very brink of a trial, professionals could never know quite what was afoot, whether, for example, witnesses, counsel, defendants, and officers *were* actually in the courthouse building as they were supposed to be; whether papers and indictments were in good order; whether, indeed, the trial would be a fight or go short. Beginnings always seemed to be enveloped in a fog of half-knowledge, guesses, and intimations. The typical exclamation to be heard on a Monday or a Wednesday morning was: 'Nobody knows what's happening.'

Consider the problems. It was difficult to muster the people necessary for the mounting of a trial: the counsel, judge, defendant, and witnesses. All the problems of the wider world bore down on the Court to prevent people meeting as they should. Defendants, jurors, and witnesses could fall ill, become pregnant, or lose the will to attend.[25] They might not appear because of coups abroad (there was a coup in Nigeria in April 1990 during the time of my research), rail strikes at home (there was just such a strike in July 1989), epidemics, or inclement weather. Defendants could be lost in the labyrinth of the prison system (a judge remarked of the failure to produce a prisoner 'for reasons of bureaucracy', 'It's beginning to sound like the Ottoman Empire'); police officers and defendants could be embroiled in other trials in courts elsewhere; the witnesses could be delayed by problems of traffic and transport (there were high winds, for instance, in February 1990 that prevented a number of witnesses reaching the Court). Nearly 9 per cent of adjournments in the Crown Court as a whole were caused by 'witness-related problems'.[26] Judges were themselves sometimes unable to preside over trials because they had fallen sick (on eleven occasions in 1989). They might not have been able to take a new trial because it fell on their last day at the Court (31 days were so affected in 1989) or because they were on leave and could not be replaced (17 days were so affected).

---

[25] e.g. in June 1989, considerable press attention was turned on a circuit judge who jailed a witness who refused to give evidence against her former boyfriend; see *Guardian*, 21 June 1989.

[26] Lord Chancellor's Dept., *Working Group on Pre-Trial Issues: Report* (Nov. 1990), 97.

Even when the full cast of a trial *were* assembled, the case would frequently go 'short' because the defendant elected to plead guilty. There were guilty pleas in 51 per cent or 819 of the 1,613 trials conducted at Wood Green in 1989. (More generally, a survey of twenty Crown Court centres conducted in May 1990 found that 67 per cent of listed trials were ineffective, 32 per cent being cancelled by late changes of plea.)[27] Indeed, it will be recalled that the Wood Green listing officer's patent system of double listings and floaters was conducted precisely in the expectation that most cases would fail to become 'fights'. It obliged three separate groups to race one another in their preparations for trial and, much like a steeplechase, two of the groups *had* to fall. Only a third of listed trials could be viable at any one time. It was, said a member of the listing office, 'a gamble that pays off'.

Even when trials *were* successfully launched, their course and coherence could be complicated by parallel trials under way in the same courtroom at the same time. I described in Chapter 3 how a jury was deliberating on another case as Grey himself was being tried, and how a plea was heard to fill empty time, the cases alternating with one another in the same courtroom, jostling one another for courtroom space and the judge's attention.

Waiting and Testifying

Timetables often faltered, leading to breaks and delays and the making of recurrent, complicated decisions about how the Court's resources could best be deployed. Staff and users continually enquired of one another whether or not schedules were effective, had stalled, or had a prospect of being resumed. The jury bailiff and listing officer, counsel, CPS law clerks, probation officers, and police officers were to be seen cruising round and round the courthouse at the beginning of every morning and afternoon, visiting the different courtrooms, trying to discover whether, where, and when they might be obliged to act in a trial. But there remained the ever-present possibility that they would simply fall idle. Just as in other organizations, a complexity of structure was attended by an abundance of enforced waiting.[28]

The prime imperative in the Crown Court at Wood Green, as in

[27] Ibid., 129.
[28] See W. Moore, *Man, Time and Society* (New York, Wiley, 1963), ch. 2.

the Crown Court everywhere,[29] was 'to ensure the expeditious disposal of cases by making full use of the courtrooms and judicial time available'.[30] Judges would hear trials if there was a trial to be heard; but if there was none, there was almost always something else for them to do, their time being filled with pleas, bail applications, applications for bench warrants, and applications to break fixtures. They were not often left without employment.

Others depended on the cases in which they played a part. Trials were collective ventures which carried everyone along, and it was impossible to proceed without a complete cast. There could be no work for the prosecutor or the defence, for professional and civilian witnesses, until a defendant had been produced. All would have to wait, although their waiting might take place in different parts of the courthouse. Indeed, professionals spend much of their professional life waiting. Mastering the ability to wait was almost as useful as acquiring the arts of advocacy or detection. A barrister summarized his career in a desultory conversation with a court clerk in the Bunker, 'You come to the Bar, you dress up in fancy dress, and you sit around.'

Counsel read newspapers and briefs. They gossiped. They amused themselves at cards. They could do little other. There was small prospect of 'making full use' of *their* professional time in the courthouse. Yet, in other matters, barristers also had their precedence. When listing issues were discussed, for instance, 'counsels' convenience' ranked high, signifying the importance of the professional in the allocation of time.

Within trials themselves, there was an uneven allocation of busy and dead time to the various participants. Not everyone was equally engaged. Judges had to be present throughout. So too did counsel and, for the most part, ushers, court clerks, and shorthand writers (although there were periods when they were not needed or could slip away). The defendant almost invariably sat and surveyed his trial from beginning to end. Juries heard much, but they were not exposed to certain deliberations about the admissibility of evidence and other matters affecting the kind of knowledge which could prop-

[29] Court staff in the Crown Court at large were reported to 'consider . . . that their prime objective was to provide sufficient work for judges and so ensure the full use of court resources'; Lord Chancellor's Det., *Working Group on Pre-Trial Issues: Report*, 92.

[30] Lord Chancellor's Dept., *The Crown Court: A Guide to Good Practice for the Courts* (London, HMSO, 1990), 8.

erly be brought before them. And the few spectators and the rare journalist were allowed to remain throughout most of the court's business.

Witnesses themselves experienced their appearance at court as a dramatically alternating sequence: prolonged inactivity first, then a hectic spurt of activity, a slump back into inactivity, a climax in the witness-box, and then rapid anticlimax. But their time was spent chiefly in unproductive waiting, and the time of different witnesses was ranked. Expert witnesses, almost entirely hospital casualty doctors and general practitioners, were held to be busy men and women whose time was valuable and who should not be detained. They might exceptionally be allowed to testify first, in violation of the lawyers' temporal 'order of common sense' and before civilian witnesses (a prosecutor announced on one occasion, 'Normally I would call the [victim] 'first but I shall call the doctor first because he is a busy man and will want to get away'). More frequently, expert evidence would be 'agreed' and read out, freeing doctors from the obligation to testify orally at all. In one very typical instance, a recorder instructed the jury, 'We have devised a system whereby, if evidence is not contested by either side, in order to save time and money, the evidence can be read out in court. Doctors are especially busy.'

The time of civilian and police witnesses was not so valuable. They had to wait. Police officers complained that the apparently endless waiting was one of the most tedious features of their work. Judges and court staff were not uncommonly sympathetic to the plight of witnesses;[31] efforts might be made to speed trials along; counsel would be reminded of the civilians' plight; but witnesses necessarily came last in a ranking of importance. There was a hierarchy in the distribution and use of the Court's time, just as there was in its space and social circles. The lowlier a person in the social order of the Court, the longer the time such a one spent waiting. The situation at Wood Green was not much different from that in America, where:

In some courts, . . . all parties whose cases are scheduled to be heard on a particular day are instructed to be present at its beginning when the judge arrives. This . . . ensures that the judge . . . will not be left with idle time

---

[31] Although, of course, judges would be able to see nothing of them in the public areas; see T. Goriely, 'A Case of Contempt in Court', *Times*, 28 May 1991.

that cannot be put to productive use . . . While this tactic ensures that the judge's valuable time will not be wasted, it also ensures that most parties will be kept waiting for a substantial period of time; some, all day long.'[32]

Indeed, the characteristic experience of *being* a witness was to wait. After what could seem to be a period of frenzy in which witnesses rushed to court, time would slow down again as problems of missing papers, missing witnesses, procedural irregularities, appeals, pleas, sentences, bail applications, and earlier trials were resolved. Witnesses would wait even if there was no longer any apparent need for them to remain. They would wait even after there had been a change of plea.[33] They were, said Justice, 'told to report for duty only at the last moment; left hanging around outside the Court for hours or even days, without any help or explanation'.[34] In Raine and Smith's sample, the witness at Wood Green waited for an average of four-and-a-quarter hours, almost the length of an average Class 4 trial itself. Even one barrister, himself called as a witness in a Crown Court case, recalled: 'I was just left kicking my heels for nearly two days before I was called. It was quite unnecessary for me to be there on that day. The facilities of the Court were very poor.'

Waiting was experienced as time passing slowly[35] although, in retrospect, it often seemed to have passed quickly enough. A period of duration without obvious incident or structure can promote a sense of ennui or listlessness, a loss of grasp on time,[36] an experience of time as *drifting*,[37] and the characteristic expression on civilians' faces was one of dull dejection. I have described how prosecution witnesses read their statements, smoked, conversed disconsolately, or stared into space. There was little else to do. They were uninformed and immobilized, unable to read the cues emitted by insiders, surrounded by purposive people who seemed to know *exactly* what was happening. Witnesses certainly did not know much of what was happening beyond the doors, inside the courtroom, in 'their' cases. Victim 6 reflected, 'I think there should be more information given out. I

---

[32] B. Schwartz, 'Waiting, Exchange, and Power: The Distribution of Time in Social Systems', *American Journal of Sociology*, 79(4) (Jan. 1974), 853.

[33] See J. Jackson *et al.*, 'Called to Court: A Public View of Criminal Justice in Northern Ireland', unpublished typescript, 5.24.

[34] Justice, *Witnesses in the Criminal Courts* (London, Justice, 1986), 1.

[35] See Fraisse, *The Psychology of Time*, 205.

[36] See introduction to Blyton *et al.* (eds.), *Time, Work and Organization*, 7.

[37] See K. Calkins, 'Time: Perspectives, Marking and Styles of Usage', *Social Problems*, 17(4) (spring 1970), 493.

think they should come and tell you more. I just sit here and wait, and that's it.'

In some two-thirds of cases, as I have noted, trials were not fought and witnesses were eventually dismissed. But waiting could also give way to testifying, a process discussed at length in Chapter 2, and testifying had more than one temporal dimension. The average length of time spent in the box by Raine and Smith's sample of prosecution witnesses was 37 minutes. Time so spent was eventful, and eventful time is experienced as more protracted than empty time.[38] It could seem like a very long half-hour: Victims 16 and 34 individually called it 'ages and ages'.

I have also explained how testifying was an attempt to revive and contrast interpretations of time past. It required witnesses to oscillate in thought between a recollection of a distant and perhaps murky experience and a 'refreshed' and vivid memory of reported events perused only minutes before, a memory that was itself edited and now possibly alien.[39] Cross-examined about whether her statement was truthful, Victim 16 could only say, 'I presume so.' If it was in her statement, it must have been so. It was the statement on which witnesses were tested as much as on once-lived experience, and the statement fixed events that had sometimes passed beyond unaided recall (one witness averred, 'I'm sure it was X, because it said in my statement that it was X'). Over and over again, witnesses would protest that they could no longer remember quite what *had* happened. Their inability to testify in particular ways could be described by counsel as a failure of memory rather than as evidence about what may or may not actually have happened ('You don't *remember* Y saying she was taking the video?'). Counsel might ask, as one counsel did ask, 'Would you say that your statement is more likely to be right than your memory of two years ago?'

---

[38] See R. Ornstein, *On the Experience of Time* (Harmondsworth, Penguin, 1969), 103.

[39] The Working Group on Pre-Trial Issues argued that 'the witness's recollection of the incident may fade after a number of weeks and months. The statement will be available, if necessary, to refresh the witness's memory at court. . . . A statement taken at the time gives the witness's account of the incident. Only a "pooled recollection" may be available if the witnesses have had a full opportunity to discuss the case'; *Report*, 26, 27.

Conclusion: Before and After

Any status has duration.[40] Being a prosecution witness was a short-lived, intense, and pregnant experience importantly bounded in time. I have already narrated how, before they testified, witnesses were regarded as the naïve bearers of vital knowledge that should not contaminate or be contaminated. Their associations were to be controlled. They were not to be exposed to the knowing. They should not 'pool their memories' with other witnesses or talk to counsel and staff. They were inextricably bound up in the conflicts of the trial, partisans who could impair others' carefully cultivated appearances of impartiality. They could not enter the courtroom until they testified. They could not learn too much of what took place in the courtroom whilst they waited to testify. They were kept in a state of innocence, apart from insiders, confined to their own space in the public parts of the courthouse. The witness in waiting was a special person indeed, a person to be treated with care.

Having been 'released' (a significant word), witnesses were almost invariably allowed to remain in the courtroom or go as they pleased, and professionals would no longer take a deal of notice of them. They were the carriers of knowledge spent, people whose usefulness was at an end. They could still present a residual danger to those waiting outside, the other witnesses yet to give evidence. They could still embarrass insiders who had just 'slammed' them and who were anxious to defend their show of neutrality and professionalism. Counsel would continue to keep their distance, either by lingering in the courtroom until all civilians had left or else by rushing out ahead of the rest, looking pointedly in front of them, avoiding eye contact and any untoward communication. But after testifying, witnesses began to revert to a commonplace identity in which they were indistinguishable from anyone else.

It was not always an easy transition. The climax of testifying passed abruptly into a successor period that lacked definition, name, organization, and character. There was not much of a role or place for released witnesses. They were, indeed, people known only by their former status.

Witnesses were often angry and discontented after they had testified, bruised from cross-examination and the allegations that had

---

[40] See J. Lewis and A. Weigart, 'The Structures and Meanings of Social Time', in J. Hassard (ed.), *The Sociology of Time* (London, Macmillan, 1990), 90.

been put to them, unhappy that they had not really been allowed to tell their story.[41] The intensity of testifying did not always dissipate immediately, and feelings sometimes remained high as released witnesses stayed to remonstrate and gesture at others who were being examined in their turn (recall the pattern of Grey's trial). More characteristically, they would sweep or creep out of the courtroom and the courthouse. Unless there was a friend or member of the family in attendance, they would be unsupported, unescorted, and without assistance. Certainly, no professionals took it to be their duty to give them comfort or advice, although some exceptionally did show sympathy. Witnesses soon left the building and social world of the Court altogether, their significance, interest, and presence fading fast.

This chapter has completed the diagnosis. Witnesses have been shown to attain their character in a conflict that affects all the relations and processes about them: they are compromising, volatile, too knowing and yet too innocent. They are pushed to the margins of the Court's social world, kept at a distance where their danger can best be averted, and their marginality is built into the physical fabric and temporal structure of the courthouse itself. They are confused and confusing, often distressed, a threat to the insiders who will not and cannot comfort them. When organized comfort did at last come, it came from without, and its provision will be the theme of the remainder of this book.

---

[41] 42% of the Raine and Smith sample of witnesses who testified declared that the experience had been worse than they expected.

Part II

Supporting the Witness

8. The Politics of the Witness

A just society depends on the reporting of crime and the giving of evidence. Victims are central to that process, yet until now they often appear to have been ignored. The criminal justice system should find ways of exploring what is happening to victims and why, and listening to what they have to say. (Lord Windlesham, speaking at the launch of the Victim in Court project, 22 January 1990)

I have described something of the travails of victims and witnesses appearing in the Crown Court. They were quite visible to those who were able to look hard at a population that was kept in some deliberate obscurity.[1] Many of those who worked in the Court, the probation officers, judges, ushers, court clerks, and CPS officers, privately expressed a measure of compassion for the private witness, but I have already explained why it was that those perfectly sympathetic men and women felt themselves restrained from doing much to supply comfort and aid. Multiple problems of time, access, resources, neutrality, collusion, commitment, and embarrassment prevented them from doing so. They had no mandate to adopt prosecution witnesses as clients or dependants, and such a mandate would have been compromising indeed.

Let me now stand back from affairs as they existed in the Crown Court at Wood Green in late 1989 and early 1990, so that I can explain how a project to alleviate the plight of prosecution witnesses came to be established there. To do so, I must move back a few years in time and return to the core of the national politics of victims, the world of Victim Support and central government of the mid-1980s which I discussed in *Helping Victims of Crime*.

The Prosecution Witness as Property and Client

Politically and symbolically, the prosecution witnesses seemed to have no clear, immediate, and effective institutional sponsor within the

---

[1] In discussing work for this book and for its predecessors, I was interested to note that most colleagues' and others' curiosity centred almost exclusively on the lot of the defendant in the criminal trial. Victims and prosecution witnesses were quite out of focus.

criminal-justice system of that time. Sponsorship was lacking in the local world of the Crown Court and in the larger world of the head-quarters organizations administering the criminal-justice system. The staff of those organizations were neither formally antipathetic to the witness (as they had sometimes been to the victim at the birth of Victim Support) nor enthusiastically prepared to come forward as the witness's champion. On the contrary. Witnesses were little considered: they were unproblematic and taken for granted, the 'fodder of the criminal courts' who were barely seen. How could it have been otherwise? It is always difficult to change the standing of groups in the criminal-justice system, and it is harder still to establish new rights. Witnesses themselves were not particularly salient in the practices and deliberations of the agencies. Like all but the victims of rape and domestic violence before the coming of Victim Support, they were marginal, generally unorganized, and isolated, kept at a distance and treated perfunctorily. For most practical purposes, they were unnoticed.[2] Championing them would have seemed to lessen the neutrality and distance vital to so many in the adversarial system, there was no sense of a looming crisis in the trial system,[3] no discernible public clamour to answer, no conspicuous politics of the witness in England and Wales, no politicians, no lobbies, no marches, no national organizations demanding action.[4] Quite typical was an official of the Lord Chancellor's Department who said in 1989:

[2] It is not remarkable, perhaps, that in N. America, as I shall show, the stock epithet for the victim in victimological circles was the 'forgotten party'. Victims came to the fore in the US victims movement principally in their guise as witnesses, and it was then that they probably felt most acutely neglected. See e.g. A. Meade *et al.*, 'Discovery of a Forgotten Party', *Victimology*, 1(3) (Fall 1976), and *Remembering Forgotten Victims* (Sacramento, Calif., Office of the Attorney-General, 1980).

[3] It was, as I shall show below, precisely that conception of an imminent crisis that spurred events on in N. America.

[4] There were, to be sure, groups which had begun to emerge around the experiences of prosecution witnesses. One, most conspicuously, was the rape crisis centre, a group whose politics I discussed briefly in *Helping Victims of Crime*. Another example was the Campaign Against Drinking and Driving (CADD), one of whose aims was 'right of appeal against too lenient sentencing. Victims and their families should have the same rights of appeal as are allowed to convicted criminals'; '9 Ways You Can Help' (Pershore, CADD, n.d.); members of CADD were critical of the decisions sometimes taken by the CPS (one, later a volunteer in the Wood Green Victim in Court Project, had successfully initiated her own private prosecution in the Old Bailey). They were critical of sentencing policy. They criticized the neglect of the witness in drink-driving cases. None of these groups was centred on the prosecution witness *as* prosecution witness. They did not embrace all prosecution witnesses but a very few victims of specific harrowing events. Their aims were to promote wide objectives that ranged well beyond the courts, objectives which reduced testifying to but a part of a larger

We get very few complaints here from witnesses. The odd professional witness will crib because of a listing fault and the time that was wasted at the department or hospital or whatever. But they're fairly rare.

Victim Support

There *was* Victim Support in the mid-1980s, the national association that co-ordinated the affairs of victim support schemes in England and Wales. But, at the beginning, Victim Support had a precise practical relation with victims precisely defined. I narrated in *Helping Victims of Crime* how that association tended at first deliberately to concentrate on 'short-term crisis intervention' in the immediate aftermath of crime, not on the provision of succour that might engross the volunteer and straggle over many months. Such succour, it was argued, would have violated a fundamental principle of good practice, that victims should not be so supported that they were at risk of translating their victimization into a central theme in the manufacture of a new identity. Victim Support was informed by a labelling theory that raised the alarming prospect of people undergoing what might be called 'secondary victimization', the symbolic reorganization of the self around the facts of victimization. Victims should be supported so that they ceased to *be* victims as quickly as possible. It was short-term support that was offered chiefly to the victims of commonplace crime,[5] the very largest group, and the group which the volunteer members of Victim Support were best equipped to help. And those victims of burglary, theft, and minor assault typically lacked a recognized and apprehended offender.[6] Their crimes did not often go to trial at all.

The association's own vade-mecum, the *Members' Handbook*, had it that 'anyone can be a victim of crime and victims should not be regarded as a new "problem group". . . . People should not be encouraged to be "victims" for longer than necessary.'[7] There could

problem. They were part of a different politics altogether. And the groups were generally small and had had indifferent success in attracting sponsorship from the central agencies of the criminal-justice system. One exception, perhaps, was the Women's Royal Voluntary Service, which maintained a presence in some courts, dispensing tea, sympathy, and advice.

[5] See 'Director's Report', *Fifth Annual Report 1984/85* (London, NAVSS, 1985), 10.

[6] e.g. in 1984–5, of the 102,512 referrals made to the 170 victim support schemes of England and Wales, some 75% were burglaries, 11% were victims of other property offences, and 9% the victims of violence; *Fifth Annual; Report 1984/85*.

[7] *NAVSS Members' Handbook* (London, NAVSS, n.d.).

be jeopardy to victim and volunteer alike if support persisted exceptionally for any length of time, and it *did* undoubtedly take time for cases to reach the stage of prosecution. A victim supported during those long, seemingly empty months of waiting might well become artificially frozen in a new and undesirable master status. The volunteer, too, might cease importantly to *be* a volunteer and become another sort of person altogether, a 'quasi-professional'.[8] Volunteers were not support to be 'adjuncts to professional workers. They are ordinary members of the community.'[9]

In time, to be sure, it became possible to extend the reach of Victim Support to the prosecution witness, but there were appreciable constraints as well, and Victim Support did not move immediately. Besides, in the mid-1980s, the association was busy enough campaigning for the funds and patronage that were necessary for its survival, engaging in bouts of structural reorganization, exploring its connections with voluntary and formal bodies at home and overseas, and doing much else that exhausted the time of its small headquarters staff.

The Home Office

The Home Office was the only department of state working on criminal justice[10] that had had significant political dealings with victims and Victim Support. Victim Support had had something of a struggle to transform typifications in the official mind, but by the middle 1980s the victim's claims as a deserving supplicant had been established by careful work. Victims were no longer seen as angry and irrational outsiders with whom it would be hazardous to have a connection. Neither were they simply people whose problems could be put right by a bit of prudent insurance or 'target hardening', whose usefulness lay chiefly in promoting the welfare of offenders, or whose pain could be extinguished by monetary compensation. Victim Support's success (and the success of the 1984 British Crime Survey[11]) was to recast the victim and volunteer as people who not

---

[8] Helen Reeves, National Director of Victim Support, in minutes of evidence taken before the Home Affairs Committee; *Compensation and Support for Victims of Crime* (London, HMSO, 1984), 64.

[9] *Report of the Working Party on Training of Volunteers* (London, NAVSS, n.d.), 2.

[10] The qualification is introduced because the former Dept. of Health and Social Security had had early dealings with Victim Support.

[11] See M. Hough and P. Mayhew, *Taking Account of Crime: Key Findings from the 1984 British Crime Survey* (Home Office Research Study 85, London, HMSO, 1985), ch. 6.

only needed and deserved assistance but would not become new vigilantes if such aid *were* given.

It was as a result of that success that the Home Office assumed financial responsibility for the National Association of Victims Support Schemes (NAVSS), later Victim Support, in 1979, and then more lavishly, firmly, and generally in 1986. Victims, victim support schemes, and their national association had become established as legitimate clients of the Home Office and, once established, the relation was considered more or less permanent: the Home Office continued to care for Victim Support. It believed that the association possessed a responsible and authoritative voice (an official observed towards the end of 1989, 'We are still in large measure responsive to what Victim Support propose and what they identify as problems with the system'). It began to consult the association. It suggested new tasks for the association. Of course, none of this loomed very large besides the endemic problems of mounting crime rates, intermittent civil disorder, and a rackety penal system, but the bond was close and matters affecting victims had begun to affect the Home Office too.

If victims were no longer the institutional pariahs they once had been, the standing of prosecution witnesses was uncertain: *they* had not been subject to much definitional work at all. Universities, polytechnics, and government had little formal knowledge about them. The Home Office had what an official called a 'folk understanding of what the system looks like. It's not very good in terms of plenty of systematic first hand data, but it is quite good at the level of anecdote.' Some staff in the appropriate divisions had undoubtedly begun to sense that matters might be awry. They had been alerted by Joanna Shapland's extraordinarily influential and much-cited work on the passage of victims of violence through the criminal-justice system.[12] They had listened to the beginnings of talk in conferences and seminars. They discussed what were described internally as the poor facilities for victims and witnesses generally at courts, and the confusing nature of the witness order form used when a case was committed to court.

---

[12] See J. Shapland *et al.*, *Victims in the Criminal Justice System* (Aldershot, Gower, 1985). The work that was to be so influential was an earlier, unpublished report commissioned by the Home Office: *The Victim in the Criminal Justice System: Final Report to the Home Office* (Oct. 1981). For a description of Joanna Shapland's impact on policy-making, see *Helping Victims of Crime*, 305–10.

Yet there was more than one difficulty. Chief amongst them was the problem that the constitutional division of labour between departments of State brought it about that Home Office officials had no duty or mandate to attend closely to policies and practices affecting prosecutions and procedures within the Crown Court.[13] The Crown Court was independent of the Home Office, then the ministry of the magistrates' courts, police, prisons, parole, and probation.[14] The Crown Court's responsible department of State was the Lord Chancellor's Department[15] and that department had had little connection with Victim Support.

It would be mistaken to imagine that those departmental mandates were unconditional. They had arisen through custom, convention, and accretion. There were areas of overlap and ambiguity (after all, the Home Office did touch on matters that touched on the Crown Court, being the ministry concerned with the legislation and users that animated the Court's work, and it was accepted that its research capacity was far greater than that available to the Lord Chancellor's Department[16]). Matters of independence, territoriality, and responsibility were akin to any other in the loosely coupled criminal-justice system of England and Wales. They were never quite absolute. Unlike the frontiers between government departments in Canada, where skirmishes, colloquially known as 'turf wars', seemed forever to be fought (sometimes with major casualties), the borders between the Home Office and the Lord Chancellor's Department were comfortably blurred and negotiable, far from jealously policed. Questions about conducting research on foreign terrain appeared remarkably uncontentious, for instance. An official of the Lord Chancellor's Department said:

---

[13] See ibid., esp. ch. 1.

[14] Helen Reeves was to say after the Home Office *had* become involved, 'Politically, there was an issue that the Home Office can't actually get into policies affecting the courts because it's the Lord Chancellor's Department, and they were rather cautious.'

[15] In 1986, a Home Office internal review of measures to aid witnesses noted that 'officials from the Lord Chancellor's Department may wish to comment on developments in relation to the building and refurbishment of Crown Courts, which are the responsibility of the Lord Chancellor'.

[16] It will be recalled that the Home Office Research and Planning Unit had conducted research on the Crown Court without accusations of trespass. See e.g. D. Moxon, *Sentencing Practice in the Crown Court* (Home Office Research Study No. 103, London, HMSO, 1988), and R. Pearce, *Waiting for Crown Court Trial: The Remand Population* (Research and Planning Unit Paper 40, London, Home Office, 1987).

The Home Office's own research group do research into the whole area of the criminal justice system and that would very often cover Crown Courts. And, indeed, we've done research recently into the spread of business between the Crown Court and the magistrates' and they've given us access to magistrates' quite cheerfully. So there is no territorial dispute. Particularly in the criminal justice area, the Home Office has by far the greater research capability . . .

And a Home Office official concurred:

In a formal sense, the Lord Chancellor's Department are responsible for the Crown Courts. There is that split between us and them, the magistrates' and the Crown Court. . . . but, of course, any number of issues which are of deep interest, perhaps of primary interest to the Home Office, do affect the Lord Chancellor's Department, perhaps most notably how cases get to the Crown Court, the whole business of committal, and all that. Given that, there isn't a rigid territorial distinction between the departments, and if we have a function or an interest group or something . . . then there is no reason why we shouldn't be interested or involved.

There was, too, a recognized mandate for the Home Office to proceed in the Government's 1985 White Paper on compensation and support for victims of crime.[17] An inter-departmental steering group on victims had been established under the chairmanship of the Home Office to manage relations between Victim Support and government bodies.[18] In late 1986, it commissioned a piece of internal stock-taking on the position of 'The Victim in Court', and note was taken of the paucity of accommodation in magistrates' courts, the importance of considerate treatment by court staff, the need for an explanatory leaflet for those about to attend court, forthcoming legislative provisions to improve the powers of courts to order compensation, and the problem of 'malicious mitigation' in the magistrates' courts. Moves were taken to explore the utility of video links in trials requiring testimony from the child victims of abuse.[19]

---

[17] *The Government Reply to the First Report from the Home Affairs Committee Session 1984–85 HC 43* (Cmnd. 9457, London, HMSO, 1985), 1. A fuller account of this and other early government actions is given in *Helping Victims of Crime.*

[18] A government member of the group remarked, 'It's designed to try to make sure that, where there is interaction, as there must inevitably be between the volunteers that the NAVSS represent a various unwieldy and apparently unsympathetic government bodies they have to deal with, we can at least be aware of what their actual difficulties are'.

[19] See e.g. the report by M. Weaver in the *Daily Telegraph*, 15 Oct. 1986, 'Easing the Pain of Prosecution'.

Very characteristically, Home Office activity consisted of listing and developing projects and proposals already in train rather than launching bold new measures. It did not seem to be a good time for bold new measures (the White Paper itself had talked quite cautiously about how the Government was anxious to improve the lot of victims 'to the extent that this is possible within the constraints of public expenditure policy and available resources'). And the introduction of many measures would have foundered on the inability of the Home Office to direct almost any criminal-justice agency to do something substantially new. The interdependent independence[20] of the agencies prevented the centre dictating to the periphery in that fashion. Consider one of the problems reviewed in the internal briefing, the poor facilities for victims and witnesses in the magistrates' courts. Magistrates' courts were formally part of Home Office territory but, under the Justice of the Peace Act 1979, the Magistrates' Courts Committees of local authorities were deemed responsible for the provision of magistrates' court accommodation, and 'the question whether facilities should be provided especially for victims in a magistrates' courthouse [was] therefore for the magistrates court committee to decide in consultation with the local authority'.[21] It was sometimes easier to let matters rest.

There was certainly only the curtest mention of the witness in the Home Office's own consolidated statement of policies in train that was published in 1986. *Criminal Justice: A Working Paper* alluded to the victim's right to claim compensation in court, but its sole reference to victims as witnesses was brief and without detailed commitment (it referred only to 'arrangements to ensure that victims receive consideration and advice when interviewed by the police or appearing as witnesses in courts'[22]).

When it is recalled that witnesses were not voicing audible demands, that Victim Support had not yet started to make firm proposals of its own, that the Home Office was very generally 'reactive' rather than 'proactive' in its policy-making, and that fiscal prudence was being urged insistently and continuously by the Government, it will be appreciated how very little inducement there was for the Department to embark unilaterally on a major new spate of policy-making for the prosecution witness in the Crown Court. That would

---

[20] See Rock, *Helping Victims of Crime.* 39.
[21] Letter from C2 Division to NAVSS, 5 Mar. 1987.
[22] *Criminal Justice: A Working Paper*, rev. edn. (London, Home Office, 1986), 36.

have been deemed adventurous, expensive, and almost certainly invasive of another department's territory.

The Lord Chancellor's Department

Constitutionally and administratively, the Crown Court lay uneasily within the sphere governed by the Lord Chancellor's Department. It was not an entirely easy relation because, although those known as 'LCD staff', the administrators, ushers, clerks, listing staff, and others, were clearly under the aegis of the Department, the doctrine of judicial independence was very strong, and judges themselves could not be administered, managed, or regulated in any conventional sense. Judges played the central part in the Crown Court, but they could not be told what to do. Any policies touching on the Crown Court, and on the judge's sphere in particular, had to be devised with exemplary care and diplomacy, and especially at a time when the Lord Chancellor was mooting fundamental changes in the Legal Services Bill, changes that were not held in complete favour by the judiciary.

The Lord Chancellor's Department took it that the Crown Court had to be visibly independent of the accusations, struggles, and factionalism of the adversarial system. The Crown Court furnished a venue and organization for the mounting of trials, but it was not a party or protagonist in those trials. Court staff could not be seen shielding witnesses against the necessary brutality and rigours of inquisition. Neither, more importantly, could they be seen as partisan towards one or other of the parties in contention (the Lord Chancellor warned Victim Support in 1990, 'It is an essential part of the administration of justice that, whatever the pressures, the understandable urge to protect the victim does not lead to unfair treatment of the accused'[23]). If witnesses were ever to receive comfort and support from the Court, it could not be prosecution witnesses alone but all witnesses. An official stated, 'Our customers are defendants as well as witnesses and expert witnesses. *Anybody* who comes into court has to be treated as well as we can manage.'[24] Proposals to aid the prosecution witness alone were thus innately uncongenial to the Department.

[23] Lord Chancellor's Speech to Victim Support AGM, 30 Oct. 1990.

[24] Even the Home Office, the department of state responsible for the magistrates' courts, pronounced in late 1986 that 'the Government's declared intention is to ensure that victims are treated with as much consideration as possible, subject to the over-riding duty of the court to remain impartial and to ensure that the defendant receives a fair trial'; *The Victim in Court: A Progress Report* (C4 Division, Sept. 1986).

Policy officials working in the Lord Chancellor's Department had had to answer no organized representations from prosecution witnesses. They were not formally responsible for witnesses ('We've had to go on saying that witnesses are essentially the responsibility of the parties calling them'). Victim Support had not yet advanced substantially into their terrain, they had no recollection of significant independent dealings with the association (an official said, 'I'm not aware of there having been formal headquarters involvement'), and they knew little of it and its history ('How the NAVSS has developed their procedures, I really don't know'). They had no presentiments about difficulties in the courts. But neither did they have any principled objections to the promotion of policies for witnesses, providing there was no threat to the department's manifest neutrality ('The Lord Chancellor has made it quite clear that the place of the victim in the criminal justice system has been the place of the Cinderella and that it was essential that there should be much more consideration given to the way they were treated'). In the mid-1980s, then, officials were not much moved to move, but were not minded to obstruct others who sought to proceed in a sensible manner. Rather later, towards the end of 1989, one such official reflected:

Our involvement has been driven from outside except . . . for the fact that we have been aware for quite some time that our delivery of services to customers has been rather more impersonal than it might be, so in fact we were coming together quite conveniently. But although we were moving in the direction of trying to put a more human face on it, I doubt that we would have arrived at an NAVSS scheme left to ourselves. But given the wind towards such a scheme being started, then we're obviously very pleased.

The Crown Prosecution Service

There had been quiet deliberations between Victim Support and the staff of the Director of Public Prosecutions before the CPS started work in 1986, and it was made clear that the prosecution's responsibility for witnesses would be restricted. It would be the police who would continue to warn witnesses (and there was talk about the possibility of a leaflet to aid witnesses so warned), but the prosecution would present information about compensation to the courts, and the CPS would assist witnesses to claim expenses (an official of its headquarters organization said, 'We *are* responsible for the payment of witnesses and that sort of thing').

The new CPS was at first also wary about compromising entanglements, about accusations of collusion and coaching. They too wished to advertise their distance from witnesses ('obviously we have certain duties towards witnesses which go so far and no further than that'). They too did not wish to compromise cases. ('We work to the principle that whatever we do with regard to victims and witnesses, we should not be seen to be influencing what they are saying. . . . It should never be in a position where it could be thought that the prosecution are manipulating their witnesses.') They manifested little interest in proposals to aid witnesses, and evinced no manifest enthusiasm about learning of the workings of schemes in North America and elsewhere. Theirs was a studied lack of interest akin to that of the Ontario Crown prosecutors in the late 1970s, who had argued that witnesses were not a party to an action and that outsiders had no business exciting them or interfering with them.[25]

Like the other departments and agencies, the staff of the CPS responded when they were invited to do so, but they did not act first or of their own volition: one official stated that the Service became involved with a new initiative 'quite simply because we received an invitation from Victim Support Schemes to say would we be interested in helping, and the obvious answer was, "Yes, we would"'.

The Terrain

So it was that, because of a reluctance to spend new money, the practical invisibility of the witness, and the scrupulous disinterestedness professed by administrators, users, and agencies, prosecution witnesses met with no ready sponsorship from within the system. People working in and about the Crown Court of the mid-1980s were quite ready to give lukewarm support to new policies and programmes for the prosecution witness, but they were not really ready to initiate very much themselves. Change was inhibited by what a former permanent secretary of the Home Office once called the 'institutional arthritics' of the criminal justice system. It was not until the end of the 1980s, when events seemed, in effect, to be running away with themselves, that users, agencies, and departments really stirred themselves. It was not a major stirring, the ground was well prepared and it did not take very much for those bodies to join in a new initiative.

---

[25] See my *A View from the Shadows*. 175.

It certainly confronted few of the obstacles, doubts, and uncertainties that had plagued the beginnings of Victim Support and which were chronicled in *Helping Victims of Crime*.

Once again, it was Victim Support, a voluntary organization outside the formal criminal justice system, that promoted new policies and programmes for victims. It was to become the prosecution witnesses' champion too, and by 1986 it had what all organizations require to make their mark in the inner circles of the criminal-justice system in England and Wales: trust in a mistrustful world. Victim Support had to work on behalf of the prosecution witness, but it did not find it necessary to mount a great new campaign *ab initio*. The terrain lying before it was already half-colonized.

North America

It had been different in the United States and Canada. There had been few significant victims' organizations to grow outside the boundaries of the criminal-justice systems of those countries. They were born chiefly of a larger and stronger politics of feminism,[26] and they marched with feminism to centre on rape, sexual abuse, sexual assault, and domestic violence. There was no North American voluntary organization for mundane 'ungendered' victims that was at all comparable to Victim Support. Instead, reforms in the treatment of burglary, theft, and assault victims had welled up from within the agencies and institutions of the criminal-justice system itself, and they refracted the practical preoccupations of those organizations.[27] In Canada, for example, it was the police who had been principally responsible for the creation of victim service units that relieved officers of some of the work imposed by victims' distress. In Canada, too, attorneys-general and Crown attorneys had eventually been persuaded to institute programmes to help victims and witnesses appearing in court, and they did so to ease prosecutions.

Very similarly, it was attorneys-general and district attorneys who founded the first victim/witness programmes in the United States, programmes that did some of the work of victims support schemes

[26] There were other groups as well, centred on e.g. arson survivors, victims of 'drink-driving', and the families of murder victims, but they were significantly less powerful. See *A View From the Shadows*, ch. 3.

[27] See P. Rock, 'Governments, Victims and Policies in Two Countries', *British Journal of Criminology*. 28(10 (1988).

[28] See S. Hillenbrand, 'Victim-Witness Programmes', in E. Fattah (ed.), *The Plight of Crime Victims in Modern Society* (Basingstoke, Macmillan, 1989).

but also embraced the victim as witness.[28] Those victim/witness programmes offered more comprehensive information about court
schedules, compensation, and expenses; transportation to and from
court itself; help with baby-sitting; 'property return';[29] and the like.
They assisted the victim-witness, in part, because official fears had it
that the criminal-justice system of North America would be at risk if
they did not do so.[30]

The idea of the forgotten and alienated witness came to the fore in
the 1970s, coaxed into being by talk about another form of 'secondary victimization', that inflicted by the criminal-justice system
itself.[31] It was claimed that witnesses were often forced to make fruitless and repeated journeys, were intimidated and confused, and were
the poorer through lost wages.[32] Witnesses were said to find the
actual experience of appearing and testifying so disagreeable that
they were loath to return.[33] Being loath to return, they would not
report crimes and furnish evidence in future, prosecutions would collapse, and the trial process and the criminal-justice system would be
endangered: 'It is questionable whether providing increased aid to
law enforcement, the courts, and corrections will have maximum
value as long as crime victims refuse to enter the criminal justice system, decline to co-operate with the system once they enter, or are
victimized further in money and time by entrance into the system
proper.'[34] In one survey conducted in 1976, 80 per cent of the prosecutors in Philadelphia were reported to consider the unco-operative
witness a significant problem.[35]

A great wave of projects were founded to save the witness from

---

[29] It had sometimes taken a very long time to return property that would feature as
evidence in trials. Property-return schemes substituted photographic or other records
for the actual property itself.

[30] For a brief general history of the projects, see R. Davis, 'Crime Victims:
Learning How to Help Them', *NIJ Reports*, May/June 1987.

[31] See E. Viano, *Victims and Society* (Washington, DC, Visage, 1976), p. xv.

[32] See R. Knudten *et al.*, *Victims and Witnesses: Their Experiences with Crime and the
Criminal Justice System* (Washington, DC, Law Enforcement Assistance Administration,
US Dept. of Justice, 1977), p. iv.

[33] See F. Cannavale and W. Falcon, *Improving Witness Cooperation* (Washington, DC,
Govt. Printing Office, 1976).

[34] M. Knudten and R. Knudten, 'What Happens to Crime Victims and Witnesses
in the Justice System?' in B. Galaway and J. Hudson (eds.), *Perspectives on Crime Victims*
(St Louis, Mo., Mosby, 1981), 60.

[35] F. Cannavale and W. Falcon, *Witness Cooperation* (Lexington, Mass., D. C. Heath,
1976), 12.

estrangement.[36] Between 1970 and 1977, the Law Enforcement
Assistance Administration of the US Department of Justice spent
$49,300,000 on some 200 victim-witness programmes.[37] By 1990, it
was reported that the number of programmes had multiplied twenty-
five times.[38] Most projects were based in courthouses and were
administered by prosecutors: one directory of 195 American projects
disclosed that 73 per cent (or 142) were set in prosecutors' offices.[39]

Take one particular project, the Brooklyn Victim Witness
Assistance Program,[40] founded in 1975. It offered witnesses a special
lounge with coffee, magazines, telephones, and 'individual working or
reading areas'. Staff provided counselling and practical information
about expenses, compensation and restitution, a 'child care facility',
transportation, taxi vouchers, and subway tokens. A number of witnesses were not summoned automatically to wait in the courthouse at
all, but were placed on a 'standby telephone alert' at home or work
instead. The Program was to become one of a number of agencies
consolidated as the Victim Services Agency in 1978 by Mayor Koch.

In a number of Canadian provinces, programmes mounted by
attorneys-general and Crown attorneys offered what was called 'witness preparation'.[41] There was concern there too about the alienated
witness who threatened the effectiveness of trials,[42] and prosecutors
and their staff undertook to educate witnesses about what lay before
them. In British Columbia, for instance, witnesses would be met by a
worker who could 'explain what will happen in court, give you information about times and dates, help you prepare a victim impact
statement, prepare you for testifying in court, and support you

[36] The first American victim-witness project seems to have been established in 1969
in Yakima, Washington. See A. Roberts, *Helping Crime Victims* (Newbury Park, Calif.,
Sage, 1990), 43. For an account of the growth of projects, see F. Dill, 'Victims, Police,
and Criminal Court Decisions: A Research Note on Witness Participation and Case
Processing', *Victimology*. 6(1–4) (1981), 352–3.
[37] See A. Schneider and P. Schneider, 'Victim Assistance Programs', in Galaway
and Hudson (eds.), *Perspectives on Crime Victims*. 365.
[38] See W. Skogan *et al.*, 'Criminal Victimization', in A. Lurigio *et al.* (eds.(, *Victims of
Crime: Problems, Policies, and Programs* (Newbury Park, Calif., Sage, 1990), 9.
[39] See the Commission on Victim/Witness assistance, *The Victim Advocate* (Chicago,
National District Attorney's Association, 1977).
[40] The following is based on R. Rosenblum and C. Blew, *Victim/Witness Assistance*
(Washington, DC: Law Enforcement Assistance Administration, US Dept. of Justice,
1979), 33 ff.
[41] I am very grateful to Susan Lee for her help in the preparation of this section.
[42] See Ontario Association of Corrections and Criminology, Ottawa Branch, *Report
of the Workshop on Victim/Witness Programs and Services* (Ottawa, 1980), 2.

through the court process'.[43] The Ontario attorney-general's *Vision Statement* remarked: 'When a victim/witness is adequately prepared for the court process . . . [they are] likely to be more confident and cooperative with the court and generally have more confidence in the operation of the criminal justice system.' It was reported in that province that 'the Crown Attorneys' . . . general perception is that the courtroom orientation and improved familiarity with the legal process which witnesses acquire as a result of the Program, produces less nervous, more confident, and better briefed witnesses who are capable of giving stronger, and more credible testimony'.[44]

Victim Support in England and Wales had its own obscure, long-forgotten, first glimmerings of inspiration in the work of a radical American criminologist, Richard Korn. But it may otherwise be described as a domestic response to a domestic British problem. So it was to be with the beginnings of Victim Support's later 'Victim in Court' project. The director and officials of Victim Support had travelled to the United States and Canada and knew of developments there, but they did not consciously emulate what they had seen. The assistant director of Victim Support claimed:

I don't think we've consciously set out to say, 'Let us take the American model and let it be grafted on here'. I think that what we've actually done is build up on the basis of the needs we perceive, how we perceive the [way] the criminal justice system works in this country, and how we could influence that . . .

And Lady Ralphs, the woman who steered the early proposals for the project, remarked:

It was an extremely home-grown project, and it didn't draw on [the American experience.] . . . I mean in America they started with this business of the witnesses being needed in court, being crucial to the judicial system . . . it started in court. Whereas here it started in the homes of the people, and we are taking it into court.

[43] *The Victim Assistance Program* (Vancouver, Ministry of the Attorney-General and Ministry of the Solicitor-General, 1989).

[44] R. R. Ross and Associates, *Victim/Witness Assistance Program User Satisfaction Report* (Ontario, Ministry of the Attorney-General, 1989), 17. Another evaluation of an Ontario scheme proclaimed that 'overall, the Crown Attorneys claim that with the assistance of the V/W Coordinator, their time with the victim/witnesses is more productive. They noted that a prepared and willing witness is a much more effective witness and recalled that prior to the V/W Program they were not always able to see all the witnesses except immediately before court in some instances'; L. Axon, *Preliminary Evaluation of the Etobicoke Court-Based Victim/Witness Project* (Toronto, 1988), 17–18.

The papers of Victim Support themselves confirm the immediate irrelevance of North American victim-witness programmes to an understanding of the origins of the Victim in Court project. Like so much else in the United Kingdom, early work was not immediately informed by models overseas. Yet the North American projects were eventually to exercise a decisive, albeit oblique, influence on the passage of events, and I shall return to them below.

The Growth of Victim Support

Victim Support had grown throughout the 1980s. It had grown in standing, wealth, business, and gravity, and that type of progress is best portrayed graphically. It may be seen from Fig. 8.1 that there had been a steady increase in the number of schemes being founded until the late 1980s, and that that number then began to stabilize at about 350. The volume of police referrals continued to grow unabated, member schemes becoming larger and busier (see Fig. 8.2).

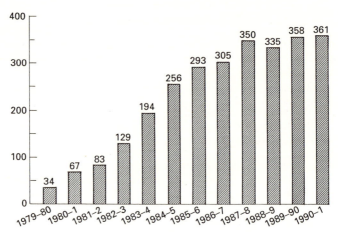

Fig. 8.1. *Growth in the Numbers of Victims Support Schemes, 1979–1991*

Home Office and private funding to the headquarters organization of Victim Support grew, leading to a commensurate increase in staff and activity (see Fig. 8.3). And schemes were beginning to support the victims of more and more serious crimes, the victims that once would have never been referred by the police and whom volunteers would have felt unable and unwilling to help. The police and Home Office had come to trust Victim Support (as they did not universally

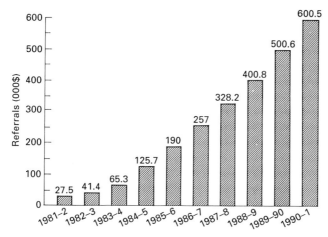

Fig. 8.2. *Referrals to Victims Support Schemes, 1981–1991*

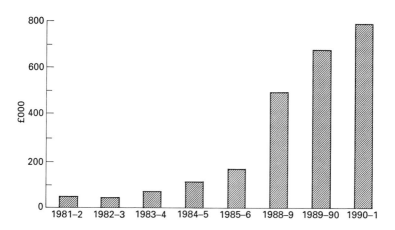

Fig. 8.3. *'National' Victim Support's Income*

trust refuges for battered women and rape crisis centres). The police started to use volunteers and co-ordinators in the training of their own officers. Victim Support itself reached out into areas once considered too difficult and compromising for its volunteers.[45] Between

[45] An undated, unpublished Victim Support briefing paper of the late 1980s talked about how 'a majority of Schemes now have experienced volunteers who are able to work with victims of serious crimes such as rape, and with families of murder victims'.

1987 and 1989, it mounted a demonstration project to assist child victims in Bedfordshire. Racial harassment was the subject of an experimental scheme[46] in Camden, Newham, and Southwark. Murder was the subject of another experiment, an 'action research project' planned by the Victim Support Working Party on Families of Murder Victims, that began work in January 1988: the police referred the relatives of victims of murder and manslaughter to five schemes in Essex, Merseyside, and elsewhere. Towards the latter part of the 1980s, a Victim Support Working Party reported on 'The Victims of Rape and Sexual Assault'. The outcome was that rape victims and the families of homicide victims were seen in ever-larger numbers (by 1990, it was claimed that the police were referring half the reported cases of rape and homicide to the schemes) (see Fig. 8.4). Victim Support's annual report for 1987–8 noted that 'many more victims of violence are now being referred to Victim Support . . . and it is all the more essential for us to acquire greater understanding of their needs and how best to meet them. We are also anxious to extend help to victims not currently reached by our services.'[47] Referrals of other forms of serious crime rose in even greater numbers (Fig. 8.5). And offences defined as serious by Victim

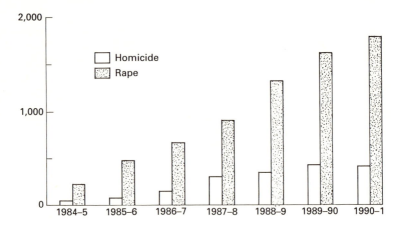

Fig. 8.4. *Referrals of Homicides and Rapes*

[46] See J. Kimber and L. Cooper, *Racial Harassment Project: Final Report* (London, Victim Support, 1991).

[47] *Victim Support Annual Report 1987/88* (London, Victim Support, 1988), 10.

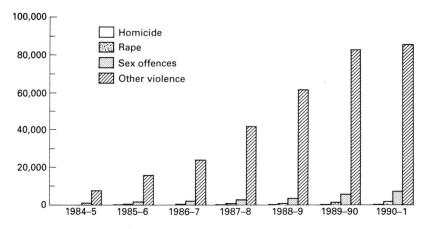

Fig. 8.5. *Serious Crime Referred to Victims Support Schemes*

Support represented a growing proportion of all referrals made to victim support schemes (Fig. 8.6).

It is evident that the very character of victim support was being transformed throughout the 1980s. The undergirding conception of 'short-term crisis intervention' was no longer applicable to a significant fraction of the work being done, and 'quasi-professionals' were beginning to emerge amongst the volunteers. The members of a number of schemes now prided themselves on the extent of their training and skill in counselling. Their labours were centred on the victims of rape, incest, and other major offences who could not be abandoned within hours. It was no longer appropriate to fear that they could foist secondary victimization onto some of the people referred. Quite the reverse. The effects of some forms of crime were so grave that they could persist without any additional signifying work from victim support schemes, and victims might well feel doubly abandoned if they were subjected only to 'short-term crisis intervention' by volunteers.

Supporting victims became more intense and more protracted. Its character changed. In 1991, for the first time, Victim Support began to measure the workload of its member schemes by 'recording the length of contact with victims, as well as the number of cases referred'. In that year of 1990–1, returns submitted by 212 schemes revealed that 12,350 cases were 'active' a month after referral; of those, 9,210 were active after 3 months and, of those, 5,950 were still

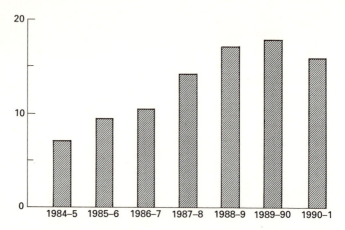

Fig. 8.6. *Serious Crime as Percentage of All Referrals*

in contact six months after referral. It was estimated that 3 per cent of referrals resulted in contact for longer than a month.[48]

Murder, rape, and serious assault *can* culminate in arrest and trial, and volunteers found themselves following their victims to court.[49] They discovered the discontents of the prosecution witness and, no doubt, their discovery was tinted with the peculiarly poignant experiences of the victim of traumatic crime and of rape in particular. Reports returned to local schemes and to Victim Support at the centre, and they were reports about the suffering of the particularly afflicted. A northern scheme wrote to Victim Support in August 1988 about the agonies suffered by a client, the victim of an assault, who was terrified by the presence of the offender's family: 'Although they did not in fact threaten our client verbally, their body language and sudden realization by our client that even if the offender was convicted she was at risk by family and friends absolutely terrified

---

[48] *Victim Support Annual Report, 1990/91* (London, Victim Support, 1991), 16.

[49] Tim Gustafson, the man who was to be Victim Support's co-ordinator of the Victim in Court project declared, 'Work with victims in court has . . . come about as a result of the Association's increased work with victims of serious crime'; 'Court-Based Services to Victims', unpublished paper delivered to Victim Support annual conference, Warwick Univ., 1989. Victim Support's own 'notes for editors' .at the press launch of the Victim/Witness Court Project on 22 Jan. 1990 stated: 'Over the last 10 years Victim Support has expanded its services to include victims of serious crime such as wounding, rape and families of murder victims. Largely as a result of this, trained volunteers have extended to victims to cover the often distressing experience of attending court.'

her.' There was a report from Harrogate Victim Support Scheme about 'a harrowing day' in the Crown Court at York, a day of un-explained adjournments and lengthy delays, of disagreeable encoun-ters with the defendant (the young victim of assault involved 'arrived back in the witnesses' room in tears' after one such meeting), a day that culminated in the case being dismissed without explanation. Victims themselves wrote directly to Victim Support. It was not a deluge. The relevant files at Victim Support are not thick. But it was clear not only that there was discontent and 'unmet need' but that schemes were beginning spontaneously to improvise their own replies to the problems of the victim in court. An early project to help wit-nesses had been established in the new Crown Court at Guildford in 1986. In Harrogate in 1988, the CPS invited the local scheme to aid prosecution witnesses appearing in the local magistrates' court. It was reported that 'a volunteer's presence has been appreciated by most witnesses. Some require no help but are pleased that someone has spoken to them.'[50]

In January 1989, an internal survey disclosed something of the extent to which victim support schemes had become involved with the criminal courts. Of the 139 groups replying, 76 per cent reported that their volunteers had accompanied victims to court (88 to Crown Court and 98 to magistrate's courts); volunteers from 13 per cent of the schemes so involved stated that they 'frequently' accompanied victims to court; and 73 per cent of the schemes had embarked on providing special training for volunteers. It was concluded that 'a surprisingly large number [of groups] are already involved in discussions with their Courts regarding Victim in Court Services issues. However, many groups appear to be still only beginning to face up to the implications of the degree of inter group and agency co-operation required to pro-vide an adequate service to Victims at Court.'[51]

Victim Support has always moved diplomatically and carefully, attempting to avoid the maladroit actions that may so easily be misconstrued in a complex and distrustful criminal-justice system. Its every initiative has been planned, and the planning has been visibly reassuring. The prospect of local schemes moving in unco-ordinated, unrehearsed, and fragmented fashion towards the intricate and suspi-cious world of the courts prompted anxiety in its national office. There was a strange and novel universe of relations, risks, and roles

[50] M. Stableford, 'Going to Court for the First Time', *Victim Support*, 32 (Dec. 1988), 7.
[51] Memorandum, 'The Victim in Court', 5 Jan. 1989.

to master. The assistant director of Victim Support, a former senior probation officer, talked about how 'there is a whole new set of rules that we've got to abide by. There is a whole different training. I mean, if someone were to say something untoward or was seen to be talking to a victim or witness at the wrong time that could throw a two-million-pound case out of the window!' And his colleague, Helen Reeves, the national director, observed:

People [were] going to court with individual cases and they weren't necessarily trained or prepared and they didn't really know what their role was. So it was just happening spontaneously in the normal course of befriending, and it seemed fairly clear that we had to do something formal to test out the logistics and the standards and the type of preparation that was needed.

Victim Support acted.[52] It sought to give order to what was afoot, to regulate the new ventures, and to avoid compromising entanglements. And that effort to regain control over its members was not inopportune. The courts were considered to be an important tract of the landscape which would have had to be scouted and colonized at some time. They were another part of the map to paint red. The assistant director argued, 'For Victim Support not to be involved in courts in the long run would seem to be a huge missing piece of the jigsaw.' The courts were an important, unclaimed portion of the criminal-justice system, a portion inhabited by judges and other men and women of influence whom Victim Support wished to win over to its campaign to transform the treatment of victims, and the initiatives could serve as a kind of bridgehead:

What it really comes down to is that, if you are going to influence criminal justice in the longer run, I don't think you can influence it without being in the courts and being part of—and I use that word with great caution—the administration of justice. In the end, I think one needs to go to have a presence there, especially, it seems to me, in the Crown Court where the judged are, because of the way justice is separated, one's really going to need to be in there . . .

None of this could be done dictatorially. Victim Support could not but tread gingerly in the Crown Court, it had to be politic in its rela-

---

[52] An immediate spur seems to have been those early deliberations in Feb. 1986 with officials of the DPP about the position of the witness and the responsibilities of the new CPS. Victim Support was consulted about drafts of the notice warning prosecution witnesses to attend court, and some part of the later working party's time was devoted to the preparation of a leaflet for witnesses.

tions with government, and it had to treat its own members warily. The association is a federation of local volunteers whose members have conventionally resisted the more obvious attempts to impose central direction from the national office in London.[53] To be sure, the head office did insist on firm standards of accreditation and training (the history of those matters was described in *Helping Victims of Crime*), but it presented itself always as a small, 'co-ordinating' (a much favoured word) body answerable to the schemes. It was best not to command. It was best to be seen responding to initiatives that emanated from below, from the members, and so it was to be with the new ventures in the Courts.

The staff of Victim Support publicly underscored how the impulse to innovate had flowed from the schemes. In time, the man who was to become co-ordinator of the Victim in Court Project was to observe to members of Victim Support at their annual conference: 'As with many issues in Victim Support, this impetus seems to have come from the members themselves. Volunteers and co-ordinators took on the initiative to accompany victims to court and offer them advice and reassurance during the proceedings.'[54] Victim Support declared that it would itself respond to the members' own enterprise by determining needs, establishing standards of practice and training, and discovering ways of generalizing and extending what had been learned. It proceeded in typical manner. Its National Council set up the first of a sequence of committees.

Stage 1: The Victim and Victim Support in Court Working Party

Victim Support initiatives are typically vested in committees, and those committees are always thoughtfully designed. They are calculated to show a care for balance in a factious world; to be faithful in their representation of the different baronies of the criminal-justice system; to incorporate those who might in time have to intercede on the association's behalf; and to include those whose very presence would convey reassurance to important outsiders standing in judgment. They signal responsibility and even-handedness. They enlist those whose aid will be needed. They are, in short, devised to anticipate and manage the

---

[53] It is revealing that Victim Support has always preferred not to use the words 'head office', insisting on 'national office' instead.

[54] Gustafson, 'Court Based Services to Victims'.

problems that are thrown up when a small body manœuvres new ideas before others more powerful than itself.

The first working party was to be chaired by Enid Ralphs, a person who had been something of a power in the world of criminal justice (and particularly in the local world centred on Norwich, where she lived), a woman of unquestioned scrupulousness, a lay magistrate herself and former chairman and vice-president of the Magistrates' Association. Helen Reeves had met her when she was chairman of the Magistrates' Association, at an earlier time when there had been some controversy about whether magistrates could properly be victims support scheme volunteers. The Magistrates' Association, like the judges, had argued that magistrates must be seen to be above conflict, and could not give comfort to one party only in an adversarial system. Lady Ralphs' own view had been that 'you can't come down from the Bench and go over to the other side, it gives the appearance of not being even-handed with all the witnesses'. She was one who could never be portrayed as lacking in balance, judgement, or experience:[55] it would be useful to prepare a report in her name.

On her retirement from the vice-presidency of the Magistrates' Association, Lady Ralphs agreed to work on what was to become the Victim in Court project. She was, she said, 'an enormous supporter of Victim Support, there's no doubt about it. I am very keen on a much closer rapport and understanding between the courts and the scheme.' She had been alert to the issue of the neglected witness when she had been a magistrate, but hers had been something of the alertness of the criminal-justice insiders I have described, a distant, professionally cool alertness tempered by apprehensions about partisanship. 'I'm ashamed to say that really it is with hindsight that I realise [the seriousness of the plight of witnesses] rather than at the time.' She had been 'alert to the issue, but not feeling that it was a great issue'.

Lady Ralphs formed a working party representing the criminal-justice system, a parliament of the professionals, and most of the members stemmed from her own circle of acquaintance in Norfolk. The group consisted finally of a judge from the Crown Court at Norwich, the clerk to the Norwich justices, a London solicitor in private practice, a Norwich barrister, two senior Norwich police officers,

---

[55] She was e.g. to insist later to the working party that 'care should be taken with the use of the term "victim", because of the danger of prematurely implying the guilt of the accused. [She] felt that the word 'complainant' should be used where appropriate'; minutes of the working party meeting, 16 July 1986.

a Norwich probation officer, the head of legal costs at the CPS as an observer, and a Hertfordshire magistrate who was also a member of NAVSS council. It was, Lady Ralphs said, made up of 'trained lawyers and people who really knew their way about', and the actual Victim Support 'input' itself 'was fairly minimal'. It met first at Norfolk police headquarters in May 1986, and it there determined to explore a broad question (how could coming to the adult court[56] 'be made less of an ordeal for the victim of crime?'[57]), a question that resolved itself into three broad areas: 'the victim's preparation for and reception at Court', 'the victim in Court', and 'the victim after Court'.[58]

The working party determined to meet infrequently (it actually met on ten occasions) and to complete its business within a year. It was under pressure,[59] composed of busy people and in competition with developments already unleashed. It was understood that it could not be serviced lavishly by Victim Support.[60] Neither could it commission its own research (the secretary, Martin Wright, noted that 'a full study . . . would obviously require a considerable investment of time by the . . . members, and especially its secretary, and would require separate funding'). It did not intend to undertake a substantial review of the existing research: not only was no money committed to such an end, but the working party's own report would have been published by the time any such review was complete.[61] What the working party *did* do was to solicit accounts of problems experienced by individual victim support schemes, draw on its members' own knowledge, and peruse some of the more readily available writings on witnesses. It consulted those in and about the criminal-justice system about how witnesses were warned, advised, treated, and accommodated. It produced a sheet of background materials 'with special reference to waiting times and unnecessary appearances', a list containing thirteen items, one (presciently) by the Victim Services Agency of New

---

[56] It was agreed that it should only be the work of the adult courts that was considered.

[57] Letter from Helen Reeves, 15 Sept. 1986.

[58] Minutes of the 1st working party meeting, 9 May 1986.

[59] It had been planned originally to circulate a draft report to agencies and influential bodies for comment before revision, but in Oct. 1986 'it was agreed . . . that that would take too long: the working party should proceed straight to the drafting of the report,'; minutes of the meeting of the working party, 20 Oct. 1986.

[60] 'Lady Ralphs drew attention to the fact that NAVSS had not the resources for a large-scale collection of evidence or detailed questionnaire'; ibid., 1 Sept. 1986.

[61] Ibid., 20 Oct. 1986.

York. The judge serving on the working party prepared the core draft of a witness leaflet that was eventually to be adopted by the Home Office for issue by the police. And it produced a report.

In writing that report, members of the working party severally composed statements on matters on which they were expert (Lady Ralphs and the clerk to the Norwich justices prepared the section on courthouse accommodation, for instance, and a police officer and the CPS observer drafted that on pre-trial procedure). The whole was redrafted a number of times and then published in June 1988.[62] It was not, said Lady Ralphs, 'in depth'. But it did have some authority:[63] it bore a distinguished name, and it had been produced by men and women who worked inside the criminal-justice system, were familiar with the system's practices, knew what would be construed as reasonable argument, and could anticipate some of the difficulties that might arise.[64]

The Report

I have described how the working party had not commissioned independent research, delved deeply into existing reports, or systematically taken evidence. Its own report was, in effect, a distillation of the insider's knowledge of witnesses' troubles, peppered with answers to specific enquiries put out by its secretary, and with reports of incidents, ideas, and observations that member schemes had relayed at Victim Support's request (Martin Wright had been instructed to take account of 'suggestions from VS Schemes as appropriate'[65]).

The preamble of *The Victim in Court* narrated how 'Victim Support volunteers who accompany victims to court have drawn attention to the difficulties experienced by victims when they attend court' and how the working party itself had 'examined how a court appearance can be made less of an ordeal'.[66] The report then passed through the stages of becoming a witness, beginning with the difficulties faced by

[62] *The Victim in Court: Report of a Working Party* (London, NAVSS, 1988).

[63] In a lengthy summary of the report, a summary that noted the chairmanship of Lady Ralphs, a clerk to the justices wrote in *The Justice of the Peace* about 'parts of the report [being of] . . . immense value to magistrates' courts (and Crown Courts)'; M. Headen, ;"The Victim in Court": A Working Party Report', *Justice of the Peace*. 19 Nov. 1988, 748.

[64] There was e.g. sustained and effective opposition to the proposal that courts should provide crèches for witnesses' children.

[65] Minutes of meeting of the working party, 4 Dec. 1986.

[66] *The Victim in Court*. 1.

victims before they came to court. It was observed that there was a lack of information about the court, the offence, and the hearing in the notification to attend; and there were unexpected adjournments. The report discussed the difficulties faced by prosecution witnesses in the courthouse itself, touching on the inexplicable shunning of the prosecution witness by counsel and the fear of those victims who had to stay in close proximity to the defendant and his entourage in the courthouse's waiting and dining areas (its recommendation was that there should be separate waiting-rooms for prosecution and defence witnesses). It discussed the experience of testifying, emphasizing (in a direct echo of letters received by the working party) the distractions caused by excessive movement in the public gallery and the need for microphones in the witness-box. It talked generally of how, 'from the moment of entering the court building, many victims find themselves looking for support in a formal context which by its nature evokes apprehensiveness in many individuals.'[67] In all this, it was argued, Victim Support volunteers could be a solace:

They can make unaccustomed circumstances acceptable by explanation, by knowing their way round the building and by being informed about whom to see for further guidance when necessary. Thus they also assist the court. Meticulous preparation is required. . . . In some Schemes, there are new initiatives by which volunteers, trained for court work, are available on a rota basis to assist victims at court. The preparatory discussions for setting up such services have mainly been with the Crown Court, but initiatives should be extended to Magistrates' Courts. A full programme of research and monitoring should be implemented to ensure that the findings of early projects will be of benefit to all Schemes.'[68]

A lengthy section was devoted to the future preparation of volunteers who would be set to comforting witnesses. Advocating an extension of Victim Support into the Crown Court and the magistrates' courts, it enjoined volunteers to observe courthouse procedure and to undergo a rigorous programme of training. Training has always played a pivotal role in Victim Support: it was not only practically useful but it publicly signalled responsibility. Volunteers should learn about the geography and staff of the courts; the role of the victim in the detection of crime and in proceedings as a witness; and the adversarial system and the nature of evidence. Volunteers, it was said, 'should never give legal advice but should know where the

---

[67] Ibid. 19. [68] Ibid.

victim/witness can obtain it'.[69] Neither should evidence be discussed. What victims should be appraised about was court procedure and the forms they will be obliged to complete. They should be warned about the possibility and implications of an acquittal. They should receive emotional support. To make all this possible, Victim Support should itself produce guidelines for the selection and training of volunteers, and appoint a National Training Officer 'to advise local Schemes on training programmes and methods'.[70]

The report was endorsed by Victim Support's National Council in March 1988 and published on 14 June. It was sent to criminal-justice agencies and departments, to the Home Office, the CPS, and the Lord Chancellor's Department. It went to the inter-departmental steering group on victims where it created a little flurry (an official remarked, 'The most active we've been has been fairly recently since Lady Ralph's report came out, making quite a lot of recommendations, all of which we had to go through obviously, in some detail from our own departmental points of view').

The report was received generally by government officials as a piece of uncontroversial good sense, but it did not lead to a galvanic response. Little of the sort did in the government of 1980s. The Lord Chancellor's Department endorsed every proposal but that relating to separate waiting-rooms for prosecution and defence witnesses ('In buildings which are up at the moment it's difficult, and it's not easy to segregate prior to the trial starting, because defendants off bail and the victims are all arriving at court . . . and they are going to be in the vicinity of [their] courtroom until they find their way in a different direction, so it's difficult'). It was considered at the Home Office: an official said, 'Victim Support passed [it] on to us and said, 'What are you going to do about it?' and, as quite often with new claims made upon government, the answer was, 'Well, not an awful lot in a great hurry, but we *will* look at it'. One couldn't say it's been snapped up and acted upon instanter, but then these things aren't.'

Stage 2: Proposals for a Project

It should be noted that there had been other talk in Victim Support about founding an experimental victim-witness project. In 1985–6, at about the very time Victim Support was beginning to establish its

---

[69]   *The Victim in Court.* 28.   [70]   Ibid. 29.

working party, Lord Windlesham, chairman of the Parole Board and a one-time Home Office minister, had been drafting his *Responses to Crime*,[71] an exposition of 'some of the leading issues in criminology and public policy: victims of crime, drugs, juvenile delinquency . . . being among the topics covered'. Lord Windlesham's interest in the broader issues of criminal justice had been prompted by his position on the Parole Board, 'an excellent vantage point to take a wide interest in the criminal justice system generally'.

Much of the book's second chapter touched on the victim's experience of the courts, and it reiterated many of the arguments that had been rehearsed in North America: 'There is nowhere to sit or stand or wait. Unless their presence is required as witnesses, no one pays any attention to victims attending a trial. Their reception varies from indifference at best to discourtesy at worst.'[72] Victims, it was argued, found courts forbidding and disenchanting places to which they were reluctant to return.

Lord Windlesham wrote about what could be done. He narrated the victim's progress 'to the centre of the criminal justice stage, after remaining so long in the wings'[73] in the United Kingdom and United States. He talked of compensation and victim support in England and Wales and of the victim-witness programmes of North America, particularly the work of the Victim Services Agency he had observed in Brooklyn. His inspiration 'came from my visit to Brooklyn. . . . I [had] spent a day in the courts in Brooklyn and met the people concerned with the victim . . . I was attracted by what happened and it seemed to me that this was something that could easily be done here.' He was to write: 'Quite apart from the worthwhile contribution that such measures can make towards countering feelings of alienation experienced by victims caught up in the criminal process as a consequence of crime, more attentive attitudes towards victims and witnesses should encourage the reporting of crimes and a closer co-operation with the enforcement authorities.'[74] He concluded his second chapter by announcing: 'Improved reception arrangements in the courts should be a priority.'[75] Establishing a victim-witness project was, he said, 'indeed something close to my heart'.[76] Some parts of that draft chapter on victims had been discussed with Helen Reeves, who recalled, 'I wrote quite a long letter

---

[71] Lord Windlesham, *Responses to Crime* (Oxford, Clarendon Press, 1987).
[72] Ibid. 27.   [73] Ibid. 34.   [74] Ibid. 37.
[75] Ibid. 61.   [76] Letter, 17 Nov. 1989.

to him . . . which led us to have a conversation about victims and what he might do. . . . I told him that victims in court was one of the issues that we wanted to get into but hadn't actually worked out a way of doing it.'

'A way of doing it' took the guise of a characteristic piece of political choreography in which stimuli were planted and events were enacted to bring about desired outcomes. Lord Windlesham was to float the idea of a project in an article in *The Times* that had been commissioned to foreshadow the publication of *Responses to Crime*. There was, he wrote,

> ample scope for greatly improved reception arrangements in the courts. . . . American experience had underlined the importance of victim/witness reception areas being kept apart . . . [this is] a rare chance for an enterprising charity to fund the provision of experimental victim/witness reception centres in a sample of crown courts.[77]

Lord Windlesham was to act as the 'broker' between Victim Support and the director of just such an 'enterprising charity' who was 'looking around for interesting projects that he could put to the trustees. . . . I spoke to him about this as something he could interest his trustees in and said it was worth a try. He asked who would handle it if they did decide to go ahead, and I explained about the National Association of Victim Support Schemes and said that I thought it would be useful if he were to see their director.' The article in *The Times* was itself not quite as innocent as it may have seemed: it was designed to generate the very 'rare chance' of which Lord Windlesham had written (he had 'already sounded out . . . the first Director of the anonymous charity. I thought this publicity might help him to obtain a favourable decision from the trustees'). Lord Windlesham then arranged a meeting at the Parole Board's offices in September 1987[78] and he recalled, 'we had a lengthy discussion and he was very encouraging and said he would like to consider the project and asked her to prepare a submission'. Helen Reeves herself remembered how she had

---

[77] 'Third Parties the Courts Forgot', 27 Aug. 1987.

[78] 'The more encouraging development since we last spoke . . . is that I have now had a talk with ——. He has shown considerable interest in exploring the possibility of establishing a small number of victim/witness reception centres in Crown Courts following the analysis which I make in *Responses to Crime*', letter to Helen Reeves, 18 August 1987.

actually been quite surprised when [the acquaintance] suddenly sat back and said, 'Now I think we ought to get down to business. I would have thought that a project with, say, three centres and four full-time members of staff and such and such and such . . . We threw up a very quick project proposal . . . We realized suddenly that we could actually do something reasonably substantial.'

Thus it came about that some money was available in principle by the time the working party reported. It was agreed that there should be funding of £40,000 per annum for three years if 'matched funding' could be secured from other sources. A budget was prepared that would have included three local workers and a proportion of a training officer at the national office to support the training of volunteers. The residue would have been allotted to a central committee and to research. But matched funding was not easily obtained. 'It had been made clear to us that neither the Home Office nor the Lord Chancellor's Department would be willing to provide any funding for the court proposals,' said an official of Victim Support. Neither were other private bodies much interested in supporting the project: 'It was for this reason that we went on pressing to get that money from the Home Office.'

Towards the end of 1988, 'while we were still trying to find the matching funding, with limited success', Victim Support and the Home Office held a strategic planning meeting in York,[79] at which the allocation of the 'local-funding budget' was discussed.[80] Said a Home Office official of that meeting:

We took ourselves off for a couple of days to talk about where the organization was going . . . We needed to know how much money we were looking to put in over the next few years. . . . one of the things they were keen to move into was help at court. And I do recall that we saw that as one of the most important and most exciting [projects], that here was one of the things we said that we would go along with and could recognize the importance of.

After much talk, it was agreed that Victim Support could use seven salaries from that local-funding budget for 'co-ordinators', who could be placed in the courts rather than in a conventional victim support scheme. There was to be no Home Office financial support for the research, which would remain a Victim Support matter. Helen Reeves observed, 'The availability of seven co-ordinators

[79] The chairman of Victim Support was John Southgate, the Dean of York.
[80] For the history and significance of that budget, see *Helping Victims of Crime*, ch. 8.

naturally changed the project out of all recognition. We no longer needed to take the salaries of three local staff from the charitable money, but we did need a central project co-ordinator, complete with secretary, and a much more ambitious research budget.' The private foundation was a little reluctant to accept the Home Office money as 'matched funding', but eventually agreed that it could 'account for 50 per cent of the matched funding required'.

So it came about that, at the beginning of 1989, Victim Support returned to the Home Office, its major patron, with a proposal for a two-year demonstration project. The project's aim, it was argued, would be to 'ascertain the role of Victim Support and other relevant agencies in the provision of support services to victims and witnesses attending criminal courts [and] determine the most appropriate method of providing such a service'.[81] Professional research services would be secured to monitor a number of pilot projects set in the magistrates' and Crown Court, but principally in the Crown Court, a central project worker would assist and guide the project areas, and each scheme would employ a court-based project co-ordinator. The Home Office was requested to pay the basic costs of the project staff, and the private foundation would fund the research. It was, said a member of the Home Office Research and Planning Unit, a strange relation, because the money for the research would not come from the Home Office itself, the research design was not an 'RPU matter', and the Home Office could assess what was done only from a distance.

The York meeting led to a commitment of money in principle, but it was a decision without detail and it was to be greeted with some chariness within the department. The officials of one division, protective of Victim Support and attentive to what one member of the working party had said to them, professed concern lest volunteers should find it much more congenial to work in the dramatic ambience, 'regular pattern', and physically dry surroundings of a court. After all, victim support volunteers were often obliged to venture out in poor weather and at night. A Victim in Court project might bleed victim support schemes of their volunteers. It was insisted in consequence that one of the aims of the evaluation would be to ascertain the effect of the project on victim support schemes themselves.

The commitment to spend had been prompted principally by anx-

[81] *Proposals for a Victim Witness Support Two-Year Demonstration Project* (London, Victim Support, Jan. 1989).

ieties about the Home Office's ability to manage within its own sphere. Funding the project would enable the department to regain control over what might otherwise be a rogue initiative by its own client. There was anxiety that the court projects so freely inaugurated by victim support schemes were not constrained by 'any particular requirements or discipline'. There was nervousness about 'the pace at which victim support schemes are developing their activities in court and the scale on which untrained volunteers are apparently being turned loose on the court system'. If Helen Reeves was right, it was said, some 50 per cent of victim support schemes were about to invade the courts. Official funding would enhance Victim Support's capacity to retain authority over its schemes and the department's own capacity to monitor and regulate Victim Support. There was the additional apprehension that, 'knowing Victim Support', a demonstration project would be succeeded by demands for money on a grand scale,[82] and 'it was essential to know what was going on and keep on top of things'.

Stage 3: A New Committee and Victim Support Haringey

Tim Gustafson, formerly working in the secretariat of the Southwark police consultative group, was appointed project co-ordinator in June. In that same month of June, a management committee was established to judge the applications and oversee the scheme, a committee composed quite typically of Lady Ralphs and representatives from the Association of Chief Police Officers, the Association of Chiefs of Probation, the Home Office, the CPS, the Women's Royal Voluntary Service, Victim Support's own national council, and the Lord Chancellor's Department as an observer.[83] It was a committee known as 'the great and the good' in the national office of Victim Support, 'although not to their face'. Members of the new committee were told that the aim of the project was 'to ascertain the role that Victim Support and other relevant agencies may have in the provision of support services to victims and witnesses and attending courts

---

[82] Indeed, the director did say: 'The Home Office knows perfectly well that if the project is successful and if we can show that we are assisting victims . . . then obviously we would be going back to all the departments to say how do we make it nationwide. They know that.'

[83] An official of that Dept. said: 'We want to see how it goes. There could be mishaps with volunteers not knowing the roles of people and overstepping the mark. We must display impartiality, not seen to be siding with one group.'

and to determine the most appropriate method of providing such a service'.[84] It was held that the role of Victim Support within the court 'is to be aware of the needs of victims/witnesses and to respond to these as appropriate'. Paraphrasing the *Victim in Court* report, the committee was told:

Victim Support volunteers can be invaluable companions to the victim. They can make unaccustomed circumstances acceptable by explanation and help familiarise the victim/witness with court procedure and the role of the various participants. They can provide information about the layout of the building and facilities and inform the victims of their rights and responsibilities before, during and after the trial. . . . Victim Support also has a role in responding to the emotional needs of victims/witnesses and this could include dealing with anxiety, confusion, trauma and upset, disappointment and anger.[85]

At very much the same time, in June 1989, the Lord Chancellor's Department and Victim Support had come together to discuss what was in train. It had been made clear that the project was welcome enough to the Department but that its timing was unfortunate. Relations between the Department and the judges of the Crown Court were frail because of impending legal reforms, and it would not do for the Department to become embroiled with the judges about any new matter. The proposal would have to be handled with delicacy. It was agreed that the scheme would be called a pilot project, and that the headquarters of the Lord Chancellor's Department would describe it favourably to circuit and court administrators.[86] Cautious soundings would be taken with the Lord Chancellor and the Deputy Chief Justice before it was decided how much prominence should be awarded to what was proposed. At best, the project might be portrayed as a little local initiative. There was to be regular liaison between the Lord Chancellor's Department and Victim Support to ensure that matters did not go awry. Further, local schemes seeking to make an application would be required to discuss their proposals not only with the chief clerk of the affected Crown Court centre but also with officials in the circuit administration.

It was as a result of that meeting that the management committee

---

[84] Letter from T. Gustafson, 25 Aug. 1989.

[85] *Principles of Victim Support in Court*, n.d.

[86] In the event, the headquarters of the Lord Chancellor's Dept. omitted to inform the chief clerks of affected Crown Court centres that projects were about to be established in their courthouses, leading to a somewhat frosty reception when the scheme was actually launched.

was warned that the Crown Court was 'a new area for Victim Support and we need to ensure that we act at all time with sensitivity and tact'.[87] The committee was further reminded that volunteers should be under discipline: they should not attend court unless they had been trained in court procedure and the rules of evidence; offer legal advice or an opinion on the case; make statements about the impact of the offence upon the victim;[88] play any part in court proceedings; or breach confidentiality.

Fears about the project aborting through a volunteer's clumsiness were, indeed, to pervade the committee's subsequent management of the projects. The very idea of victims having 'rights' was discouraged (a member of the committee remarked forcefully, 'Victims have no rights as victims, only as witnesses', and another reflected that victims' 'rights' would not be recognized by lawyers). There was trepidation about possible allegations of volunteers coaching witnesses. ('It won't be long before a volunteer is called to account about collusion with witnesses,' said a member of the committee. There had, indeed, been some remonstration earlier about the presence of a victim support scheme volunteer in a magistrates' court.) The CPS member observed: 'I think a training element is essential. Of concern to me . . . would be to make sure that nothing is being planned or put forward which will in any shape or form prejudice the case about to take place.' It was decided that it would be best if volunteers did not go into the courtroom in advance of their witnesses: they would then not be at risk of having dangerous knowledge to transmit. They should not attend trials at all unless they were accompanying witnesses. There should be a refusal to supply victim-impact statements to the courts. Separate volunteers should support different witnesses.

The final plank of the new project was a 'data-rich evaluation survey' to be conducted by professional consultant researchers, John Raine and Rena Smith, based at the Public Service Management Centre of Inlogov (the Institute of Local Government Studies of the University of Birmingham). Raine had earlier conducted work on the 'quality of services' delivered in magistrates courts,[89] 'what you call the wallpaper and the smiles, about convenience, waiting times,

---

[87] 'Principles of Victim Support in Court', n.d.

[88] Such 'victim-impact' statements were common enough in N. America but were regarded with some abhorrence by officials in Victim Support and the Home Office, who maintained that they would lead to inconsistencies in the sentencing process and undesirable appeals against sentence.

[89] J. Raine, *Local Justice: Ideals and Realities* (Edinburgh, T. and T. Clark, 1989).

about personal treatment', and the new commission had come as a 'complete accident'. He had been informed that he would be required to

Work with court-based Victim Support services predominantly located in the Crown Court to determine (a) the needs of victims/witnesses in court and how these needs were met by [diverse organizations]; (b) the most efficient and effective means of receiving referrals of victims/witness at Crown Courts . . . (c) the most effective method of providing support and information to victims/witnesses regarding court procedures, the role of court personnel, the process of giving evidence and the sentencing options open to the court, [and] (d) the training needs of the . . . agencies relating to victims experience in court.[90]

The project's dimensions were progressively modified to make it more affordable and useful. By March 1989, it was no longer proposed to establish schemes in the magistrates' courts, and the actual number of Crown Court centres was reduced on grounds of cost (the Home Office had suggested 3–4 centres, the Birmingham team 10, and the compromise was to be 7). It was envisaged that some 15–20 volunteers would be recruited to staff each project, two being available at any one time.[91] Raine's original proposal of January 1989 had talked of 50 interviews with witnesses at each of 10 schemes but, by March, the number of interviews at each centre was enlarged at Home Office instigation, to allow for the tabulation of a larger and more adequate range of variables.

The ensuing proposal envisaged interviews with the administrative staff of the Crown Court centres, a MORI survey of 100 victim-witnesses at each of the 7 centres, and an elaborate compilation of monitoring forms to be completed by the co-ordinators of the new schemes themselves. The victim in court project was conceived by Raine and Smith to be delivering a service, and the research would, in effect, be a piece of consumer research:[92]

In thinking holistically about the initiative which Victim Support has taken to provide on a more comprehensive basis than in the past a support service at court for victim/witness, it is possible to perceive the issues in the context

---

[90] 'Research Brief, Victim Witness Support Demonstration Project'.

[91] T. Gustafson (project co-ordinator), talk given to the 1989 annual conference of Victim Support.

[92] It was a phrasing that was to give rise to some ideological squabbling, with one scheme that disliked the introduction of a market metaphor into a voluntary organization ('If Victim Support was about markets, there wouldn't be any movement. It's about an idea,' it was argued).

of a marketing framework. Although the application of language normally associated with the commercial sector with the work of an organisation like Victim Support might seem strange, we would contend that, in many respects, the introduction by Victim Support of court-based services is not unlike the launch of any new product or service and that, as with all such product or service launches, a number of strategic marketing questions need to be addressed.[93]

Schemes applying for funding were informed that they must agree to co-operate with any assessment that would take place, and, as I shall show, one of the pioneering schemes was thereby automatically disqualified because the resident judge at the Crown Court centre was unwilling to consent to research being conducted in his Court.

Stage 4: Selecting and Managing the Demonstration Projects

The closing date for proposals was eventually fixed as the end of June[94] and, at its very first meeting in August 1989, the management committee had before it nine applications. Two were declared to be flawed, one because the scheme had been unable to obtain the court's permission and the other because it was 'incomplete and did not include written court permission'.[95] The remaining seven, including a proposal from Victim Support Haringey to establish a scheme in the Crown Court at Wood Green, satisfied the criteria laid down by Victim Support, and it had been just seven projects that the plans had envisaged. To the regret of the committee, there was very little actual selecting to be done.

Tottenham and Hornsey Victim Support Scheme (rechristened Victim Support Haringey in September 1988) had been established in the autumn of 1983 by two people, one of whom, Irene Rondell, the Chairman of the Management Committee, remained firmly in control of its organization and work:

In 1982, I was a member of a community centre in Stamford Hill and whilst I was doing my job, a user of that centre entered that building and promptly

[93] 'The Victim/Witness in Court Project Research Progress Report No. 5' (n.d.), 2.
[94] 'Provision of Government Funds for Victim Support Schemes, 1989–90', Victim Support, 6 Apr. 1989.
[95] 1st meeting of Victim/Witness Court Project management committee, 1 Aug. 1989. There was some little dissatisfaction because 1 of those 2 rejected applications had been from Norwich, the home of most of the members of the Victim in Court Working Party. There were to be repeated attempts to substitute Norwich for one of the 7 schemes actually approved.

collapsed in that building. She had been mugged. They all flapped around saying, 'Aren't you lucky, you could have been killed' and made things worse. They were doing the usual things when they were trying to make things better. I went into my office and reflected on what I had seen . . . I realized there wasn't a twenty-four hour emergency service—we found nobody who wanted anything to do with this.

She had been introduced by the police to the founder of the Islington scheme, who 'said everything I had conceptualized was VS. I now had a name.'

Victim Support Haringey and Irene Rondell represented a characteristic fusion of founder and institution, the one symbolically entangled with the other[96] ('it was X and myself that set the whole thing up and I've been involved ever since'). Irene Rondell was like many another founder, an energetic, busy, independent, and commanding person who identified herself strongly with her progeny. She said of herself, 'I can be a fairly forceful character'. The scheme and the woman were importantly one. What was done to the scheme was also done to Irene Rondell. And the scheme had started with a large sum of money ('I raised £250,000 but had to spend it quickly') and an unorthodox model of organization that set it apart from the National Association itself. It was unusual in that Irene Rondell's new and well-endowed scheme relied on part-time paid staff. Most victim support schemes did, after all, insist on the symbolic and practical importance of voluntariness: 'we met quite a lot of objections from National Victims Support. . . . We were told that VS should only have volunteers. They shouldn't have part-time staff. "How can you do things when you're in part-time employment?" and we said, "thank you for your input, we know how to do things, we know how to get money. If other groups need our advice we'll let them have it." From that point we never had any trouble from National. So that is the history of our uneasy relations with National.' The uneasy relations were to continue, affecting the court project itself.

Victim Support Haringey was set in the working-class suburbs of north London and it was one of the busier schemes. In 1989–90 it received 5,739 referrals, of which the vast bulk (3,372) were burglaries and thefts in a dwelling. Typically, and by design, the scheme would soon lose contact with the victims referred to it. It would lose knowledge of victims' careers, their later encounters with the criminal-

---

[96] I have discussed some of these matters in 'The Birth of Organizations', *op. cit.*

justice system, and their experience of the courts.[97] But it was significant that those 5,739 referrals also included 1,123 robberies, 27 rapes, and 2 homicides. *Those* were crimes serious enough to lead members of the scheme to undertake special training in such matters as rape counselling. And, exceptionally, members of the scheme did venture into court. Victims turned witnesses were being given special help and preparation some twelve times a year. One of the scheme's co-ordinators remarked, 'For someone who hasn't been to court before the whole thing is terrifying. So what we like to do is take people to court and sit them down and explain what's going on, so that when they actually go to court they know who all the people are and what they are going to have to do.' Irene Rondell herself had spent some six weeks in 1986 in attending cases at the Old Bailey: 'I would phone up and talk to one of the clerks or something or other and say, "Look, I'm coming in. What can you do for us?".'

There had been a number of inconclusive discussions with the police and others at that time about improving the lot of victims whose cases went to trial: 'Victims of crime were not getting a fair deal from the police, from the courts and from our scheme,' said Irene Rondell. The scheme had an interest in providing more and better information about the progress of cases, about verdicts and sentences,[98] but the imminent arrival of the CPS would affect any arrangements made and 'we couldn't find a suitable system at all, and we dropped it'. Ideas of forming a closer liaison with the courts were suspended until Irene Rondell and other members of Victim Support Haringey attended the annual conference of Victim Support in 1989. One speaker at the conference had been the co-ordinator of the pioneering project in the Crown Court at Guildford:

I chatted to her at length afterwards, asking her about the problem and things like that. Also Paul Gee[99] was with me . . . and we were talking about

[97] Irene Rondell observed: 'Only as and when our victims actually came back to us, and those that we were in long-term contact with, did we ever know anything about the court situations.'

[98] Stephen Okafor, the man later appointed victim-witness support co-ordinator at the Crown Court at Wood Green, was later to trace those beginnings back to 1984: 'This was when the local scheme, the present Victim Support Haringey, began to discuss the possibility of establishing a base for the provision of support and assistance to victim-witness in the Court'; talk given to the CPS London North training weekend, Brighton, 6–7 Apr. 1990.

[99] A police representative o the scheme's management committee who was to play a prominent role in the Victim in Court project at Wood Green.

it and we said . . . we had wanted to do something about this for a long, long time. And they seemed to have achieved it, what we had been talking about. So we arranged to have contact with Guildford. They sent me some information . . . And, again, nothing happened. Our main priority at the time was finding premises, suitable premises. So when National started . . . its initiative, we by then had the build-up over a few years of bits and pieces of information . . . We got the concept in our minds that we would be looking for a volunteer who would start to operate in a very, very small way in the Court. Volunteers in Haringey are basically impossible to get . . . And we also didn't have any new funding situation to look at, any honorarium or anything like that. So, when the National initiative started to come through, it was, in inverted commas, 'a nice bandwagon', to jump on, because it's what we'd wanted to do and had never had the financial resources to look at. So it fell very nicely into place. . . . We whacked in for it.

Victim Support Haringey approached the chief clerk of the Crown Court at Wood Green (who was 'very interested, very supportive') and the branch Crown prosecutor, and both signified their interest in the scheme.[100] But the chief clerk left in April 1989, and it was to be his successor who signed a supporting letter on 11 July 1989, a letter agreeing 'that I would be interested in a victim support scheme operating at Wood Green when the new Courts open'.[101] The new chief clerk had heard nothing about the new scheme apart from the request for a formal consent. Things had actually 'already gone very far' by the time he had taken up his new post.[102]

The Victim in Court project was discussed at a meeting of the management committee of Victim Support Haringey in June 1989, and it was agreed that 'an application to National for funding would be made as we could comply with the criteria set out'.[103] The proposal submitted on 3 July 1989 recounted some of the history of Victim Support Haringey's flirtation with a court-based project: 'It is

---

[100] The branch Crown prosecutor did indeed write to Irene Rondell on 6 July 1989 stating: 'We endorse your aims and objectives. I should be interested in attending any joint agency meeting you may set up to discuss what appears to be an important local initiative.'

[101] It was the chief clerk's view not only that there was space in the *Palais de Justice* but not in the Bunker, but that the introduction of a new project would be best calculated to coincide with all the structural and physical changes that accompanied the move to the new building. It would be but one new beginning amongst many.

[102] Victim Support Haringey's proposal of 3 July 1989 stated: 'The Chief Clerk . . . is fairly new in post and our negotiations have been with his predecessor. He is supportive of the project.'

[103] Minutes of management committee meeting, Victim Support Haringey, 19 June 1989.

now two years since our scheme discussed its development into the courts. As we were aware of a new court building due for the area, we planned to be part of its service and took steps to attain this. . . . The new court building will be opening at the end of this year and this couples nicely with the proposed start of the project.' The scheme had 'received confirming permission when new court opens at end of 1989': a room had been promised in the new courthouse; a co-ordinator would be recruited through press advertisements (retired police officers being the prime target population); and new volunteers would be sought amongst the scheme's own members and through the press.[104] The project itself would provide 'support and information for victims/witnesses attending court': court procedures would be explained; there would be assistance with the completion of claims of expenses and compensation; information would be provided on pleas and results; counselling would be offered before, during, and after court appearance; and there would be a quiet waiting area set aside for witnesses. It was uncertain how victims and witnesses would be contacted: no 'firm referral processes have [yet] been worked out and we would wish to call upon the help and expertise of the National's staff, Guildford etc. to help us complete this'. The scheme promised to train all new volunteers: 'Specialist training will be given—according to guidelines and Agencies requirements.' Important assistance would be provided by the Court's senior probation officer, Geoff Spain, who was also a member of the management committee of Victim Support Haringey, and whose room would adjoin the project's quarters in the new courthouse.

At the beginning of August, the management committee were informed by their vice-chair that the 'application submission . . . has been successfully accepted'.[105] At much the same time, Irene Rondell and members of the six other schemes were warned by the assistant director of Victim Support that the conduct of the project would require great delicacy: 'It is anticipated that we will launch the project in January 1989 [*sic*] and that in the meantime, we would hold fire on both national and local publicity. . . . Having visited the Lord

---

[104] At the meeting of the management steering committee of 13 Dec. 1989, the project co-ordinator reported that Victim Support Haringey proposed to recruit 20–30 volunteers.

[105] According to a letter from Tim Gustafson to Irene Rondell of 4 Aug. 1989, Victim Support Haringey was to be awarded £30,600 for the employment of a Court Project co-ordinator for 27 months, and a 'one-off payment for project expenses' of £1,000.

Chancellor's Department recently, it is evident that we are operating within a sensitive climate.'[106]

By September, it was reported, the job description of the co-ordinator was nearly ready and advertisements were about to be placed in *The Guardian*.[107] In November 1989, Tim Gustafson, the national co-ordinator, conferred with the management committee of Victim Support Haringey. The Court Project was, he said, 'designed to ascertain the needs of victims and witnesses where they were required to attend court'.[108] Training 'would be crucial to ensure the success of the scheme'. It would be 'the big issue. We mustn't be seen talking to two witness, passing between them.' Referrals would 'come from the Police and CPS and [there would be] some self-referrals'. In his turn, Gustafson was told by Geoff Spain that 'the new building would not be operational until March or April'. Spain had already undertaken some of the diplomatic work to prepare the ground for the new scheme. He had conferred with the two chief clerks. He had been very careful 'not to tread on any toes'. A steering group was formed to oversee the project in the short-term (a group destined never to meet) and interviews for the local project co-ordinator would take place on 22 November, the selection committee consisting of Irene Rondell, Geoff Spain, and Tim Gustafson.

Conclusion

Consider what had happened. With some wariness, government departments had consented to mounting a trial project to assist victims and prosecution witnesses attending the Crown Court. The Home Office was to fund the project's staffing costs but not the evaluation research, which would establish its effectiveness. The Lord Chancellor's Department was to afford access to the Crown Court, but it did so only with some nervousness. The witnesses whose cause had been championed by Victim Support were pictured chiefly as the victims or bystanders of various serious crime, and of rape and murder above all, and their needs were deemed to be exceptional in proportion. The Crown Court in which they would appear was depicted as a place fraught with anxiety about problems of collusion,

---

[106]   Letter of 10 Aug. 1989.
[107]   Minutes of management committee meeting, Victim Support Haringey, 11 Sept. 1989.
[108]   Ibid., 20 Nov. 1989.

interference, and coaching; exemplary care would have to be taken with any volunteers who ventured into it. No project would prosper without a great show of attention to training, and training would have to emphasize the dangers that could flow from maladroit action. There should be no victim impact statements, statements of the kind that had become accepted in a number of courts in North America and which listed the suffering and injuries inflicted on the victim as matters to be considered by the judge in sentencing. There should be no movement of volunteers into the courtroom before the witness had testified, no legal advice, and no discussion of the case. *The Lawyer* quoted Tim Gustafson, the project's national co-ordinator, as saying, 'We don't give legal advice or coach or comment on the content of a trial'.[109]

Victim Support Haringey, a large scheme chaired by an independent woman, had toyed for some time with the idea of establishing a project to assist victims and witnesses in court. The invitation to submit proposals from 'National', the headquarters organization of Victim Support, had been regarded as timely enough, but the authorship of what was to be done in Wood Green was claimed firmly by the scheme (at the inaugural meeting of the project's steering group in the Crown Court at Wood Green in February 1990, the vice-chair of Victim Support Haringey was to announce: 'We have been thinking about doing this for years').

There had been negotiations about the project with a chief clerk of the Crown Court at Wood Green, but he had been superseded, and it was to be his successor, a man who had had only the most perfunctory dealings with the proposals, who was actually to administer the Court in which the project would be set. And the Lord Chancellor's Department itself had neglected fully to alert the circuit administration and Crown Court centres about what was afoot.[110] It was not until 6

---

[109] 'Victim Support Set to Help Court Witnesses', 30 Jan. 1990.

[110] Tim Gustafson was to write to project co-ordinators on 15 Sept. 1989: Victim Support had 'received a call from a Circuit Administrator who expressed concern that he had not been informed of the imminent arrival of Victim Support in 2 courts on his circuit. It would appear that in some areas, the lines of communication between Circuit Administrators and Victim Support are not yet fully established. . . . It is essential for us to establish and maintain good relations with court officials from an early stage in this project. Can you ensure that the Circuit Administrator is made fully aware of your scheme's success in receiving funding for a full-time post for work at the court as well as your timetable and plans for establishing the project. In view of the need to step carefully in this sensitive area, it would be expedient to talk to the Chief Clerk about any letter to be sent to the Circuit Administrator.'

June 1990 that the chief clerk was finally told by the Lord Chancellor's Department that he could give the project 'his full backing'.

Although the seven projects were intended to start work in January,[111] the project at Wood Green was obliged to wait on the opening of the *Palais de Justice* in April, and it was delayed in consequence. Irene Rondell herself commented, 'It hasn't really held us up, although National would like to think it's held us up. If anything, it's given us the breathing space we need.' But there was continuing criticism at Victim Support and its project management committee about the slowness of progress at Wood Green and other matters: in October 1989, for instance, one member of that committee observed that Victim Support Haringey was held to be 'less enthusiastic than others . . . It might be a problem for the future.' Victim Support Haringey was to be chivvied,[112] dogged by a project management committee whose members were reminded repeatedly about resentments in Norfolk and about how a project in the Crown Court at Norwich could efficiently fill any void supplied by the abandonment of the Wood Green proposals.

---

[111] And, indeed, the project was launched nationally on 22 Jan. 1990, a month chosen, in part, because the time near Christmas is generally devoid of news, and thus the launch would receive appropriate press attention. Lord Windlesham and Lady Ralphs addressed the press conference in the House of Lords (described by Victim Support as 'the highest court in the country'). The press was told in its invitation that 'Victim Support, the national charity set up to help victims of crime, has become increasingly aware of the problems faced by victims attending court. These may range from the need for basic information about court procedure to fears about being confronted by the offender and anxieties about having to give evidence.' For press reports, see *Mail on Sunday*, 21 Jan. 1990; *Daily Telegraph*, *The Times*, 23, 24 Jan. *The Times* quoted both Lord Windlesham and Helen Reeves talking about the neglect of victims in court.

[112] e.g. in Feb. 1990, the Project management committee at Victim Support was informed that no volunteers had been recruited. 'Against the odds, progress has been made in Haringey . . . [The main problem] appears to be lack of managerial support and supervision.'

9. The Project

If we are successful, then this little child, this experiment at Wood Green will spread right across the country. (Stephen Okafor, 19 March 1990)

In this last chapter, I shall describe the first four months, the opening phases, of the victim-witness project in the Crown Court in Wood Green. I have already laid the ground work of much of what is to come. The social organization of the Court and the embedded rationality of Victim Support were to become fused with the imperatives and presumptions of the Victim in Court Project to engender what appears in retrospect to have been a reasonably clear pattern of development. As in any history, the pattern appeared to the different participants in different guises, each being the moving centre of a distinct world and each conceiving the others to be, as it were, his or her satellites. One's insider was another's outsider, and it is difficult to defend settling on any one centre and declare it absolute.[1] But I shall remain with the Court and its organization as primary, the Court having been my principal framework until now, and I shall deal with the pattern of development as it appeared from within that framework. Let me trace the unfolding of some of its chief features step by step.

---

[1] To those at Victim Support, for instance, it was as if the hub of events was the Project management committee, the separate court projects were satellite bodies, and the Crown Court centres themselves were more remote still. Quite the reverse iconography would have appeared to the chief clerks of the 7 Crown Court centres. To Stephen Okafor, the project's co-ordinator, a man I shall introduce below, it was quite understandable that the Wood Green project was to be seen as the moving centre of affairs. He was eventually to take issue with my general representation of the social world of the Court at Wood Green as a landscape mapped out in defended tiers. He quarrelled particularly with the argument that, as outsiders, the project and its co-ordinator had to be aided by a knowing insider. It is evident that the history of the victim-witness project, like any other history, was 'polysemic', amenable to many interpretations that mirror the positions and interests of the tellers. There is no royal route to the reconciliation of those multiple truths. Rather, it may be presumed that the task of the sociologist is to reconstruct and explain the frameworks in which the truths emerged, whilst, at the same time, treating the frameworks as products of those truths. The very coexistence of such disagreements reinforces the larger point that the history had a complicated phenomenology.

The Co-ordinator

The construction of the project was orderly. It had to be: it was, in effect, a planned attempt to install a strange body in the suspicious and divided world of the Crown Court. Irene Rondell remarked that it was like starting a victims support scheme all over again. It certainly confronted very similar problems of building confidence, connections, and identity, and it was equipped with all the working logic of Victim Support that had been used and proved in Haringey only seven years before.[2]

First a co-ordinator had to be appointed (the works of Victim Support abound with co-ordination and co-ordinators, a legacy from its birth in NACRO,[3] and the Home Office funding that had had the effect of transposing 'co-ordinators' to the projects). The job of the co-ordinator would be to take the project into the Court and superintend its progress; liaise with Victim Support Haringey and 'national' Victim Support and their committees without, and with the Court and its users, agencies, resident judge, and administrators within; recruit, train, and manage volunteers; secure referrals of prosecution witnesses; maintain records of witnesses; and report to the local project management committee.[4] Tim Gustafson said that such a co-ordinator would have to 'get on good relations with all members of staff, and set up a referral system and get a good base for Victim Support'. There would have to be 'a sound knowledge of criminal justice issues', an 'ability to form positive working relations with variety of individuals from different agencies and court personnel', and 'some understanding of the functioning of voluntary-sector organization'.[5]

Interviews for the post were held at the end of November 1989, candidates being subjected to a battery of identical questions about the problems faced by witnesses in court; their own capacity to 'establish good relations with various court users'; and their plans to create a referral system for victims or witnesses, recruit and discipline volunteers, and co-operate with the project's linked programme of research.[6]

---

[2] Okafor, the man who was to become the project's co-ordinator, stated that 'the Wood Green project is to all intents and purposes an extension of Victim Support's established pattern of work into the Crown Courts'.

[3] The National Association for the Care and Resettlement of Offenders; see *Helping Victims of Crime*.

[4] *Induction Programme for Court Based Co-ordinators* (Victim Support, 1989).

[5] Job description for Court Project co-ordinator for Haringey.

[6] Questions for candidates.

One of those interviewed was Stephen Okafor, a trained theologian (he had first attended King's College, London, and had then been awarded a Ph.D. from the University of Leicester); active in Christian welfare organizations and especially in the Nigerian organization, Hour of Freedom, that had coped with the aftermath of that country's civil war; a volunteer member of Camden Victim Support since 1984 ('this is spiritually rewarding for me'[7]); a participant in a six-week course in 'practical and counselling skills for work with victims of crime' offered by Camden Victim Support; and trained in information technology and 'office skills'. He was, noted one of those who selected him, 'highly intelligent', 'very genuine', enthusiastic, and a good listener. He was 'extraordinarily keen', observed another member of the selection committee. Indeed, it was his seemingly boundless energy that was most frequently marked by professionals working in the Court.

On 28 November 1989, Okafor was told formally that he had been appointed co-ordinator and that he was to begin work on 2 January 1990, some three months after his colleagues elsewhere. A member of Victim Support's project management committee remarked that it had been a very long delay in the career of a short-lived programme. Okafor would have but three months to assemble a scheme before the opening of the *Palais de Justice* in April.

Plans and Meetings

By December, Okafor had devised a plan that would steer him through his first month. He would, he thought, begin by meeting Irene Rondell and secure and read all the documents 'on Victim/Witness Court Project, with particular reference to the Wood Green Crown Court Project',[8] 'get to know staff, admin set-up and ethos of Victim Support Haringey', meet the management committee 'to discuss and agree a time schedule for the recruitment and training of Project's volunteer workers'. In the second week, he would acquaint himself with the Court and its catchment area; meet the Court users and administrators; attempt to design a referral system; meet me and the research consultants from the University of

---

[7] 'Volunteer's Report', *Annual Report 1989* (Camden Victim Support, 1989), 9.

[8] 'Victim/Witness Court Project Co-ordination, Wood Green Crown Court, Personal Action Plan for The First Four Weeks', 18 Dec. 1989. In the event, he never did manage to 'secure and read' those documents. They were not passed over to him.

Birmingham; and begin recruiting volunteers. In the third week, he would select volunteers, attend trials at Wood Green, and report to Tim Gustafson. In the last week, he would 'finalize and update arrangements for volunteers' training', discuss the furnishing of his new office in the *Palais de Justice* with the management committee, and begin a six-week period of volunteer training. He would visit the Court one day a week, on Mondays.

In short, and little by little, he proposed to construct an organization and then work himself, his (as yet incorporeal) project, and his (yet to be appointed) volunteers into the Court and its environment.[9] It would have to be done cautiously: the Court was not an open institution, and there could be resistance to the sudden incursion of a new and untested body (after all, at the beginning, the members of Victim Support were outsiders and strangers to the world of the Court.) It would have to be timed carefully and in sequence: it would not do to recruit volunteers too early, for example. Okafor said, 'This thing has to be properly arranged because we do not want to start off and then lose the enthusiasm of the volunteers before [we have got all] the administrative set up there.'

Interpretations

The plans had their phenomenology. They were multivocal. Okafor was not the only person considering the project's move into the Court. It had a number of spectators, each in an embedded position, each with a practical interest, and each with a limited stock of knowledge.[10] Information about the project was parochial at first, scattered between the pockets of an internally divided social world, thin and undeveloped, subject to little elucidation by those in the headquarters organizations who could be presumed to know about the initiative. Even at a relatively late date, Court administrators had heard nothing from the Lord Chancellor's Department[11] or their col-

---

[9] Stephen Okafor's 'line manager' at Victim Support talked in late Jan. about how Okafor had been 'trying to sort of make himself familiar and them familiar with the idea of the project as well as himself'.

[10] Shapland once remarked that 'there is no central body or service co-ordinating the criminal-justice system. . . . The British criminal-justice system is a loose confederation of independent powers . . . all of which owe no allegiance to each another'; J,. Shapland, 'Producing Change for Victims in the Criminal Justice System: The UK Experience', unpublished paper, 10. On the grand and the minor scale, communication did not travel easily within such a 'system'.

[11] And that, conceded a policy official at the Lord Chancellor's Dept., 'had probably been a mistake'.

leagues in the six Court centres where other projects had been established. (Policy officials *inside* the Lord Chancellor's Department itself heard little about what was stirring in their own Department; an official from another Department commented, 'That's the problem facing Kremlinologists. People inside the Kremlin are the last to hear what's going on.') The chief clerk had not been approached by his colleagues in the other six centres housing projects. The branch Crown prosecutor had heard nothing from officials in Queen Anne Gate or from his colleagues elsewhere.[12] He had not been approached formally about the project. He did not attend the chief clerk's meetings and could not have learned anything from the Court itself. One of his staff declared in January 1990, 'We've come in very late and we've been a little in the dark.'

The Administrators

Knowledge followed acquaintance, purpose, and practice. What was quite big to 'national' Victim Support, Victim Support Haringey, and the members of the project was a smaller matter to almost all the professionals working in the Court and its surrounding criminal-justice system. There were some (solicitors, barristers, junior probation officers, clerical staff, and others) to whom the project would be relatively inconsequential. But there were others who were obliged to take a stance towards it, if only for a while.

Because the project would have to be accommodated in the *Palais de Justice*, it was perhaps of the greatest immediate importance to those actively responsible for supervising the new arrangements, the chief clerk and his staff. At the very least, the chief clerk had to make an administrative judgement about the kind of organization the project would be. He borrowed from models at hand, defining it as yet another small user that would be entitled to a home territory of its own.[13] It would be a partisan user which would act as the agent of

[12] But there *was* a clear presumption that the CPS would 'establish constructive relationships with other institutions responsible for the efficient and effective administration of criminal justice. Co-operation and liaison were and are vital, not only because the CPS has had to establish its own credibility as a new and independent prosecuting authority, but also because we have recognized our potential for giving new impetus to the changes and developments occurring within the criminal justice system as a whole'; CPS, *Annual Report*, 1988–9 (London, HMSO, 1989), 27. In practice, the branch Crown prosecutor was a good friend to the project from the start.

[13] The co-ordinator of the Liverpool project observed, 'The very fact that Victim Support have actually been offered accommodation within Liverpool Crown Court is not lost upon other court users'; N. Canevali at the Victim Support National Conference, Warwick, July 1990.

an external organization as others did (although one that could never be quite as authoritative or substantial as a body formally representing the State). The project would service trials as probation officers and the police did, playing a modest part in a loosely coupled and informal system, largely invisible to the insiders of the first and second circles.[14] The Court's own role would be to assist the project and its staff by providing physical and social space (as it did every other user); it would ease their work in the first trying months; and that would be virtually all. It would not intervene much in their lives. The Court did not intervene much in the life of any user. That would have been unnecessary, unconventional, and compromising. The chief clerk said:

I see the Court's involvement as being fairly minimal, so we can provide [the project] with facilities. But it's an independent thing. I mean it's a counterpart of the probation service but on the other side. I see them as largely running their own show, sort of fitting in.

The Judges

When I dined with the judges in November 1989, only the resident judge was acquainted with the proposal, the project, and the name of Lady Ralphs. That was hardly remarkable: there was no other such project in the South-Eastern circuit and judges would not have met its like elsewhere.[15] More important, perhaps, unless matters went awry, unless witnesses were contaminated and trials were upset, victim-witness support was likely to make very little practical difference to the everyday work of the judiciary. It would unfold out of their sight, beyond their courtrooms and chambers. The project was deemed to be laudable but remote, barely visible, somewhat obscured by the language in which it had been presented ('It seems a shame that, at the end of the twentieth century, charity should have such an odd language'). Judges did not really *need* to know much about it and, indeed, it was not to be the subject of formal discussion

---

[14] And the chief clerk's expectations were shared by other knowledgeable users who would have dealings with the project. The CPS assistant principal law clerk imagined that it would be necessary to 'get the project established but after that it should virtually run itself'.

[15] After all, only a few centres anywhere actually had a project. When the Court's High Court judge (known as its 'red judge'), the Hon. Mr Justice Alliott, paid a ceremonial visit in Apr. 1990, the project was one of the matters pointed out to him as something new, and he expressed marked interest in it. He told a member of the Court, 'This is what my fellow judges will be interested in. They are watching it.'

or decision amongst them ('[I know] only what you have told me and there has been a little bit in the newspapers about it,' said one judge in February 1990). To be sure, as I remarked, the resident judge knew what was afoot. He had encouraged the project from the start; he had given it his consent; he had conferred periodically about its development with his chief clerk and with Geoff Spain; and he was to be one of the first insiders to meet Stephen Okafor. But in all this he was an exception.

Even later, after it had become established, the project would be the subject of no more than modest conversation amongst the judges ('[We do] discuss it from time to time [and] I think everybody agrees it's a good thing,' one judge said). There would be some private trepidation about the project's proliferating committees and the threat that volunteers might offer to trials[16] ('I've heard that the supporter may get too close to the victim and there may be an element of coaching'[17]). Much would depend on the co-ordinator ('It's going to be very much down to Mr Okafor—he seems okay'). He would have to cultivate his relations amongst the inner circle ('I haven't really a clear idea as to how these things ought to be organized [but it rests] I would have thought on the organizer and his willingness to get round and keep the good will flowing, as it were'). But it was also noted that the project already commanded support ('Quite clearly there had been plenty of official interest from the police and CPS . . . it's a matter of policy that they should be keen').

Other Insiders

In December and January, before the move to the new courthouse, victim-witness support could have had very little significance to other insiders. They had certainly been notified about what was to come at a chief clerk's meeting in 1989, before Stephen Okafor had even assumed office, and the response had been warm enough, just as it

---

[16] Other affected insiders confessed to an uncertainty tinged with anxiety: CPS law clerks, for instance, worried about possible allegations of coaching. Like the judges, they generally took it that the project was an amalgam of the commendable, the unknown, and the slightly dangerous.

[17] There was to be but one such potential incident during the time that I had knowledge of the project. At the beginning of Mar. 1991, a shorthand writer alleged that a volunteer had prompted a witness. The allegation created a stir, and an inquiry was conducted by the trial judge, who recalled police and witnesses. It was concluded that no impropriety had taken place: the witness herself was a young girl whose mother had been in the public gallery whilst she was being examined; the mother had been remonstrating with the volunteer who had gestured to her in reply, and that gesture had mistakenly been read as a signal to the witness.

had been in the larger world of the headquarters organizations (the CPS assistant principal law clerk had said, 'Anything to help victims or witnesses, we're glad to help'). Insiders might have been able to ascertain that two successive chief clerks and the resident judge had given formal approval to the scheme, and that Geoff Spain, the senior probation officer, seemed to be acting as some sort of intermediary. But there was not much more to be known.[18] The retiring chief clerk had not even bequeathed his papers on the project.

Quite typical was a senior police officer from the law and order unit who said at the end of November 1989, 'I knew that something was taking place but nobody has explained as yet exactly what it is.' How could it have been otherwise? There was little enough to see or hear, no changes yet visible in the social composition of the Court or the treatment of witnesses, no room yet occupied by a new user, no new group to meet, no problems to gossip about, no preparations to make or responses to rehearse. And other more pressing matters were looming. Above all, there were the upheavals that would accompany the Court's imminent expansion to ten courts and its move to the *Palais de Justice*. Insiders in the early months of 1990 were more preoccupied with planning the bodily transfer of an entire organization than with resolving questions about a small unit that would be appended at a later date.[19]

Many insiders would have few enough practical dealings with the project even after it had been installed. Ushers and court clerks, for instance, were scrupulous about their neutrality, and they avoided any unnecessary involvement with protagonists and the champions of protagonists. *Their* sphere was the courtroom, and that was a place where the volunteer would rarely be expected to go. The project would impinge but little on them. They had goodwill towards it, but they did not expect that they would have to change their behaviour or discover much of what was to come. All would be well, remarked an usher in late February 1990, 'as long as it doesn't interfere with the running of the court. The court must run smoothly at all times. The judge will not tolerate any hold-ups.'

---

[18] Some, indeed, were under the impression that the project was intended principally to assist *defendants*, a mark perhaps of the practical invisibility of the victim and the prosecution witness.

[19] It was, in part, for that reason that the chief clerk deemed it best to defer the opening of the project until it was installed in the *Palais de Justice* in Apr. It would almost certainly meet with the least opposition during the more general structural disruption of that time.

Ushers and court clerks eventually took it that the project would jostle the boundary between the public and private worlds of the courthouse, becoming neither a full insider nor a full outsider. On the one hand, there would be a paid co-ordinator with his own office, a man who was on his way to becoming 'one of us', and in that the project would resemble a conventional user. On the other hand, the project would be serviced by unpaid volunteers who were really little different from the public at large. Project and volunteers were to be treated uncertainly, as if they were on the margins, more akin to the agency reporter than to the probation officer. It was certainly telling that, when they were guided about a courtroom during their training in March 1990, volunteers were told quite firmly by one Court official, the listing officer, 'You are members of the public. As a member of the public you are entitled to sit in these seats. The rest of the court is out of bounds. . . . Those are the public areas you can use.' But it was also inevitable that volunteers were to become increasingly familiar to ushers and clerks and could not always be regarded as mere 'members of the public'.[20] From time to time, indeed, they were allowed to sit in the users' space (an usher told them at the very beginning that should they sit in the courtroom, they were to go to the back so that if the police were instructed to clear the court 'they'll know to leave them alone'). There was to be an enduring ambiguity about quite what identity the project should assume within the structured world of the Court.

Victim Support: Supporting and Supervising

Definitions of the project welled up within Victim Support itself. Just as Stephen Okafor was considering how to manage the project, so the staff of Victim Support were considering how they would assist and manage Okafor. The project was an intensely practical matter for 'national' Victim Support and Victim Support Haringey: it *was* a big thing for them. 'National', in particular, attached significance to the proper management of the new court-based co-ordinators. After all, the project had been initiated quite specifically to restore order and discipline to the drift of Victim Support schemes into the courts. 'Support' and 'supervision' came to describe the principal methods

---

[20] I am grateful to Tim Gustafson for reminding me that, ironically, being members of the public was precisely how Victim Support intended its volunteers to be seen. There was an important symbolism attached to being an outsider, a non-professional, not part of the official body of the Court.

by which Victim Support controlled, helped, and was seen to act responsibly towards the new court-based co-ordinators.[21] And Victim Support, nationally and locally, remained the principal manager of the project: Okafor himself reflected later, 'It is incontrovertibly the case that Victim Support Haringey . . . and Victim Support National remained my primary sources of policy, administrative information, guidance, and management throughout the life-span of the project.'

Victim Support Haringey had undertaken to support and supervise the new co-ordinator, and Okafor was placed formally under his own 'line managers', first Irene Rondell and then Hugh Clark, the vice-chair of the scheme, who would 'induct' him. (Irene Rondell had said, 'It's approximately a six-to-eight-week induction . . . so that he can become very comfortable with Victim Support Haringey.') Okafor would be given advice, 'taken through action plans', and encouraged to visit the other schemes. But the relations with his 'line management' and mother scheme were never to be very close. Initially, and before the opening of the new courthouse, there was to be a connection, because Okafor was housed in 'the Cottage', Victim Support Haringey's own base in a former farrier's yard, and he worked next to the scheme's own co-ordinators and staff. But when he moved just less than a mile to the *Palais de Justice* in April 1990, that relation became attenuated and even a little fraught.

In part, the character of the relation was personal, depending on the interplay between two people, Okafor, the enthusiastic new-comer, and Irene Rondell, the most powerful member of Victim Support Haringey, indeed, the very embodiment of Victim Support Haringey (an outsider once described the scheme as a 'one-Rondell show'). Irene Rondell rather overshadowed the scheme's manage-ment committee and two co-ordinators (a member remarked that one 'should not expect too much of the Committee, they're not very high-powered'). Members of the scheme themselves did not often

[21] It was argued that 'support and supervision of court-based co-ordinators is a cen-tral element in the establishment of effective services to victims and witnesses and, for this reason, it is one of the criteria that project management committees must satisfy as a condition of funding. . . . *Support* is needed because while court-based co-ordina-tors will generally experience a high level of job satisfaction . . . the work can be demanding and stressful. Co-ordinators will need to off-load their emotions and anxi-eties, exchange ideas and look at new ways of solving problems. . . . The aims of *super-vision* are to establish the worker's accountability to the organization, to assist in their professional development and to maintain a high standard of service delivery. Each court-based co-ordinator has a designated supervisor'; 'Victim-Witness Court Project Information', 1 (May 1990), 4.

meet formally or hold annual general meetings. A small Court Project subcommittee eventually founded by the management committee was never actually to meet, being rapidly superseded. It was Irene Rondell who largely controlled the scheme and the project, and she had to do so by fiat on occasion (Okafor was later to tell volunteers in training, 'The project is almost entirely managed by Irene'). It was, therefore, not surprising that she suffered the dilemmas of one who was formidably powerful and busy.[22] She could not always respond promptly to everything that came before her. She could not always attend meetings. She did not attend the new Court steering committee when that was constituted (a committee I shall discuss below), although her failure to do so was intended partly to allow others to grow big in her absence ('I just didn't have the time to do that and . . . also I can be a fairly forceful character and I felt too much of me would be going into that. [My absence would] allow Stephen to establish his authority and his character and his personality'). She retained responsibility for decisions about administrative and financial matters, about the release of funds and the printing of posters and leaflets, but she could not always be found; she was often engaged elsewhere,[23] and that irked an energetic Stephen Okafor who was ever straining to move matters forward (he liked 'planning and getting on with things').

The relation had a territorial character: Victim Support Haringey claimed the project as its own. Administratively, said Irene Rondell, the court project was to be regarded as an arm of Victim Support Haringey, and the person who administered it would be treated as a deputy co-ordinator working for the scheme (Okafor himself roundly declared that he had no desire to be so treated, although he *did* recognize that he was taken to be 'really an employee of the [scheme's] management committee [who will] tell me the kind of arrangements that are available'). The new committees managing the project were to become defined as subcommittees of the management committee

[22] Irene Rondell was employed by Community Industry, 'a national provider of training and work experience for young people with special needs and unemployed adults' (*Annual Report 1989*, Community Industry) established in 1972 by the National Association of Youth Clubs. Like other such posts in charitable organizations, it was a most taxing position.
[23] I remarked how, by the end of Jan., Irene Rondell decided to delegate her supporting and supervisory duties to the scheme's vice-chair, an amiable man who was perhaps not quite as large or strong as she. Because she was 'so busy, I have invited Hugh Clarke to step in for me', she announced. But she was to resume those duties again after a short while.

of Victim Support Haringey. 'National' Victim Support was to look askance at early leaflets and posters that identified the Victim in Court Project as 'a project of Victim Support Haringey'. (After all, it was alleged, other victim support schemes were also supposed to refer their witnesses to the project. 'It *isn't* a service of Victim Support Haringey,' said one of those administering the projects at 'National' Victim Support.) Those working most closely with the court project mused that it might be best if the project detached itself altogether from Victim Support Haringey in the long run.[24]

There was to be a structural problem. It is perhaps unremarkable that the victim support scheme was sometimes represented as greater than its new progeny, the court project. It was more substantial, more senior, and more permanent: a member of its management committee announced: 'We are an established victim support scheme, this is only a demonstration project, and we mustn't forget that, although it may change in time.' It was a consequence that the project seemed slighted from time to time. It did not bulk large in the everyday life of the Cottage. The two co-ordinators at Victim Support Haringey certainly did not take it to be their business to sustain the court-based project. On the contrary: they treated it as an independent entity. One co-ordinator remarked of Okafor, 'He has a separate Management and it will be to all intents and purposes a separate project.' The scheme's co-ordinators went but infrequently to the Court, and when Okafor himself came to the Cottage, said a co-ordinator, it would be but 'once a month, only to say "Hello"'. Links were loose, knowledge was tenuous, and interest was slight. Even in May, towards the end of the first phase of the project, a scheme co-ordinator observed flatly of the success of the court-based project, 'I don't have enough information about it to say if it is or if it isn't [successful].'

A member of the management committee of Victim Support Haringey was to observe in June 1990, 'There is animosity. I am

---

[24] And, indeed, that is precisely what did eventually happen in early 1992. It was to be announced at a meeting of the Court Project steering committee on 12 Mar. that the project was to become both independent and permanent. Victim Support Haringey was to write that it was 'realized that a single scheme was stretched to provide adequate support and supervision. This has been accepted by National Office who are arranging a different management structure for London compared to the rest of the Courts'; 'Victim Support Haringey and the Court Project', *End of Court Project and Start of Court Programme* (Victim-Witness Support, Wood Green Crown Court, 1992), 8.

monitoring it. . . . I'm not at all happy with the vibes I'm picking up
from the Cottage towards the Court Project. . . . I certainly didn't
anticipate the lack of co-operation between the co-ordinators and the
victim support team and the co-ordinator of the court project. I find
that very disappointing. One of the things we had hoped for, which
hasn't happened, was that all three co-ordinators would become
interchangeable at various given points, so that when Stephen wants
to go away on leave, we wouldn't consider closing the project down.'
But no such system of substitutability emerged (and Okafor had himself never hoped for it): 'It just seem incredible that liaison isn't happening. . . .'

Relations within the triangle of 'National' Victim Support, Victim
Support Haringey, and the Court Project were to remain unsettled
throughout the early stage of the project's life. Okafor felt uncomfortable about being in such a cockpit, about 'National' 'going through
me and Irene going through me'. He wished there could be direct
confrontation instead. Letters of complaint did indeed pass back and
forth, telephones rang, special meetings were held. The national project co-ordinator, Tim Gustafson, repeatedly acted as messenger
between national and local committees. He mediated, advised, and
directed (but always with tact). He should have acted as a 'liaison'
but was becoming obliged to work as a 'manager', thought one
observer. Increasingly involved in the workings of the project and in
the external relations of Victim Support Haringey, Gustafson came
to attract some little opprobrium himself. It was said by a member of
the management committee of Victim Support Haringey of one
round of talks that 'he [and the chairman of the national steering
committee] demanded meetings . . . which I felt was particularly use-
less and a complete waste of time, but it allowed them to express
their authority and, if that made them happy, then I sent two people
away happy.' The Wood Green project was 'taking a larger part of
[Gustafson's] time than we would have wished', said a member of
the Project steering committee at 'National'.

Questions of the effective support and supervision of Stephen
Okafor loomed large at meetings of the national Project steering
committee.[25] The structure of the Wood Green project was perhaps

[25] e.g. the minutes of the meeting of the Victim-Witness Project management committee of 14 Mar. 1990 record that 'concern was still expressed about Haringey,
where it was felt that the support and supervision structure for the court based co-
ordinator was not adequate'.

more frequently and anxiously debated than that of any other. After all, it was argued, if it did indeed prove defective, it could always be replaced by another project waiting in the slips at Norwich.

The Patron

Whilst Irene Rondell and Victim Support Haringey remained constitutionally Stephen Okafor's manager, it was Geoff Spain, the senior probation officer and member of the management committee of Haringey Victim Support, a man based at once in the Court and in the scheme, a bridge,[26] who came to advise and befriend Stephen Okafor, act as his chief mentor and patron,[27] and become his supporter *de facto*.[28] The phrase Okafor himself employed to describe Spain was 'shop-floor supporter'.

Spain was to be Okafor's neighbour in the new courthouse and his first source of information about the practices and customs of the Court centre.[29] Not only did Spain counsel Okafor about how he should proceed, he also served as his guide in the strange terrain of the Court at Wood Green, gave him help in kind, commended him to insiders, and, at the very first, provided him with information about forthcoming cases. Okafor reported to the management committee of Haringey Victim Support, 'The probation service is the people who're helping us out'.

I described in *Helping Victims of Crime* how the loosely coupled organizations of the criminal-justice system of England and Wales are bound together by chains of patron–client relations that stand for inter-organizational structure, construct identities, confirm each other's trustworthiness, impose controls, establish webs of dependency, and create reciprocal obligations. At the very outset, little can

---

[26] He not only acted as a bridge between the victim support scheme and the project, but also between the national Court Project steering committee (on which his chief probation officer served) and the local world of the project. Victim Support Haringey's application to Victim Support had stated that he would be 'requesting of his Chief a few hours each week to assist in the supervision of the project'.

[27] There was to be one another important mentor who acted from without the courthouse—Paul Gee, the police representative on the management committee of Victim Support Haringey and its co-founder. Okafor said of him: 'He was not only very co-operative but also discharged his tasks very professionally and very effectively'.

[28] Tim Gustafson's formal evaluation of the project reported that 'the Senior Probation Officer at Wood Green Crown Court, who is also a member of Haringey Management Committee, was also helpful, though this induction was not formalized'; *Evaluation of Court Project. Area: Wood Green, London.*

[29] It should be noted, however, that Okafor had had experience of supporting victims in court as a volunteer of Victim Support Camden.

be accomplished by any outsider who lacks effective patronage, and it was to be Spain who acted as Okafor's principal patron. Spain was to write, 'My association with the experiment [was] rather more vivid than I had expected. My involvement . . . has been part managerial, by virtue of my Victim Support committee membership, and part shop-floor support.'[30]

Spain was one of the chief peripatetic users, resident in the courthouse and known to the professionals. He was unusually well-liked and trusted, and he had it in his gift to translate Stephen Okafor into 'a friend of ours',[31] a near-insider who could be trusted in his turn.[32] He could take Okafor into the inner recesses of the Court and introduce him to significant insiders (although 'not too many at first', he said). Okafor remarked at the very beginning 'I would very much want him to introduce me to the CPS and all the other court users', and that is precisely what Spain did. He escorted him into the inner circle.

Okafor reflected afterwards: 'I decided what I wanted and sought the help and support of whoever could help', and, from time to time, Spain acted as Okafor's herald: 'Geoff was there and he went in before me and actually explains quite a lot to them.' Spain introduced him to the assistant principal law clerk of the CPS, a woman based in the courthouse herself, who would be indispensable to any effective witness referral system.[33] He introduced him to the security staff and to the law clerks (who nevertheless remained confused about quite what the project would do). On 17 January he introduced him to the resident Judge, the man with the greatest symbolic influence of all, and there was some talk between them about the

---

[30] 'Victim/Witness Support and Probation Service', in *End of Court Project and Start of Court Programme*. 24.

[31] At one point, in early Feb., a member of the court staff had been heard to say of Okafor, 'In a few months, he'll just be one of us'. That was precisely what Spain had wanted to happen.

[32] Okafor's position was enhanced by the proposal to allot the Victim in Court Project its own room in the *Palais de Justice*. The possession of his own home territory signified that he had the makings of an insider.

[33] His introduction was timely and useful. Like the Lord Chancellor's Dept. the headquarters organization of the CPS appeared to have neglected to inform the branch Crown prosecutor about what was about to stir in the Crown Court. Loose-coupling does not only distinguish relations between the different agencies of the criminal-justice system, it also colours relations *within* them. The course of the project was to be bedevilled by lapses and breaks in the flow of information between the parts of the system. Perhaps it was because the project was but a minor matter, not worth concentrated attention in the headquarters organizations.

need for boundaries and the risk of interfering with witnesses. He introduced him to the chief clerk, the man of the greatest practical consequence.

In all that work, Spain tried simultaneously to depict Okafor as one both near and apart. It was as if Okafor were a reliable man, one whom he could vouchsafe,[34] but also one who should really not be taken for a member or ally of the probation department. The goal was to present Okafor as a new and independent user in the Court, not as a dependent. He would have to 'stand on his own feet when he was ready'. After all, the probation team was aligned with the defendant, not with the victim or prosecution witnesses, and ambiguities could arise if there was no secure symbolic distance between itself and the new scheme.[35] Spain observed that the new office in the *Palais de Justice* 'is close enough for me to help but not too close to be confused with probation. We wouldn't want to be seen with two hats.'[36] And that separation is precisely what happened: Okafor became independent enough after the first critical weeks.

Committees

Those preliminary introductions and meetings bore fruit at a rapid succession of meetings, and first at a special meeting between Court users and Haringey Victim Support on 22 January 1990. It was Geoff Spain who, again, paved the way. He had floated the idea of a meeting because the users and the scheme would have closely to collaborate, because 'Stephen Okafor is anxious to meet CPS rep to introduce himself', and because it was imperative to form a 'steering group' of some five people to assume general control over the future course of the project.[37] Actually present at that meeting were to be

---

[34] It is significant that, as a result of that chaperonage, by the beginning of Feb. 1990, Okafor was beginning to be called by a nickname, 'old Stephen', by insiders.

[35] It is perhaps a little ironic that Spain's involvement with victim support arose from the convention that the management committees of victim support schemes should be clearly balanced, containing in its probation members the representatives of the offender as well as police and others as representatives of the prosecution.

[36] And there were to be some resulting reservations about Okafor's frequent presence in the probation offices and, later, his use of probation papers for the purpose of location witnesses. It was considered not quite right that the prosecution witness's supporter should be so visible in the home territory of the defendant's ally.

[37] Those proposed were Irene Rondell, Tim Gustafson, a representative of the CPS, a local police representative, and himself.

two officers of the branch Crown prosecutor's office, five police officers, Irene Rondell, Geoff Spain, and the scheme's two co-ordinators. Okafor was introduced and he recounted his history, his knowledge of Haringey (he had once lived behind Hornsey police station), and the conception, aims, and timetable of the project.

The users and the Court (in the person of Geoff Spain) affirmed their support: the CPS announced that it would be 'most anxious to be part of any steering group'; the police said they were 'happy to agree to participate', they were 'fully supportive'; and the Crown Court itself was reported to give 'warm support'. Spain said, 'It's a team approach at the Crown Court. Stephen will have to be seen as part of the team. He should probably be on the chief clerk's committee.' Okafor's translation of himself into an insider was proceeding apace, but it had not yet been completed, as I shall show. It was not easy to break into the inner circle.

Thereafter, the users and Court represented in that meeting continued to give running symbolic and material support to the project, and they did so in the way of the Crown Court, pragmatically and discreetly.[38] Assistance was to be given but it was never to be formalized: 'Things would fall into Stephen's lap if he tried.' One of those users was to tell Okafor towards the end of February 1990, 'I would see how much you can get away with without asking too many questions, providing people don't go over their budget.' And another advised, 'You should get in with the police staff. They're not going to raise any problems about a few sheets of paper [if their photocopying machines are used] . . . in the first year you can let a lot of your expenses get absorbed in the police budget.' In effect, Okafor was being told, the oblique and the understated would work best in the negotiated order of the Court. Things should be done by making use of informal networks. But that was not quite how the project was to evolve.

The Steering Committee

The project was to be propelled by formal committees instead. I have explained how, in the world of Victim Support, committees undertake symbolic work to reassure potential critics and spectators

---

[38] e.g. The Lord Chancellor's Dept. subsidized the project by charging no rent for the offices or costs for the telephone and other services, but it was not be a declared, written arrangement. The CPS offered the project 2 manual typewriters 'that we inherited from the Yard and a spare electric typewriter with a screen'.

about the character of a new enterprise. It was just so with the Victim in Court Project. Committees would move it along, affirm its respectability, draw powerful outsiders in, and, said Irene Rondell, make 'people feel that they own it, not that it's something that's imposed on them'. It was thought that a shell of committees would confer an appearance of solidity, structure, and scale on the frail project within (Weick once observed that members of organizations 'act as if they have environments, create the appearance of environments, or simulate environments for the sake of getting on with their business'[39]). There was to be a multiplicity of committees. Rondell told the 22 January meeting:

I can't reiterate strongly enough the need to set up a steering group. We need to know now that [the project's] going to operate on a day-to-day basis, who'll it be accountable to, and who to turn to when problems arise. I'd like to see the formation of the steering group as quickly as possible. I suggest that the steering group should be no more than that, responsible for setting up and directing the project. After that it would be an advisory group . . . There should split off from that a subcommittee which would meet every six to seven weeks and liaise with the police.

So it came about that, in the last week of January, Okafor (with Clark and Rondell) worked at organizing the inaugural meeting of an independent Court Project steering committee. Their timing was actually to be propitious: David Waddington, a new Home Secretary and a one-time criminal barrister, a QC and recorder, had seized on the importance of victims and was about to issue his *Victim's Charter* on 22 February, 'European Victims' Day'. He had arrived in the Home Office with an interest in victims and wished to put his own stamp on what was afoot (it was, said an official, all rather 'dramatic and sudden'). The charter itself was a consolidation of events in train, the Home Secretary having supplied the intent and officials the contents. Subtitled 'A Statement of the Rights of Victims of Crime', it was one of a number of such charters created by the Government at the time, and it was 'aimed at the chattering classes and the criminal-justice agencies, not for victims themselves'. The charter declared that the 'Government wishes to do all it can to help the victims of crime', and proceeded to make express mention of the Victim in Court Project: 'in a few courts Victim Support are running projects to

---

[39] K. Weick, 'Enactment Processing in Organizations', in B. Staw and G. Salancik (eds.), *New Directions in Organizational Behavior* (Malabar, Robert E. Krieger, 1982), 278.

identify more fully what special needs victims may have when attending court, and how they can best be met, either by new facilities or by adapting old ones. This is an ambitious project which will take two years to produce results'.[40] The imminent publication of the charter was announced in the press (see *The Times* of 6 and 7 February). Officials in and out of the Court were to take the charter seriously. It was described by a Home Office official as 'a public declaration by Government. It will become management tool to ensure that the services will not lose victims.' The Lord Chancellor himself gave it a wide circulation within the courts,[41] and a member of the Lord Chancellor's Department reflected that it 'makes official backing quite clear. People should not be treated as fodder to be processed through the courts.' The branch CPS had telephoned the assistant principal law clerk working in the courthouse to say that they should be at the meeting of the steering committee: 'Of course we must support it. Haven't you seen today's newspaper?' (Characteristically, Victim Support itself declared that it had had 'no prior warning about the charter'.)

The Court Project Steering Committee

The Court Project steering committee at Wood Green was to consist of some thirty people, including police officers from the three divisions attached to the Court, the CPS assistant principal law clerk, and representatives from diverse victim support schemes and community groups.[42] The committee was quite deliberately intended to be catholic in its membership, a signal of the scale of external support, an advertisement of its respectability (Irene Rondell said on 18 January, 'We've got to come in . . . with what I feel is a reasonably professional image'), a reassurance, a piece of common property.[43] But that dramaturgy was not entirely successful.

---

[40] *The Victim's Charter* (London, Home Office, 1991), 16.

[41] See *Victim Support*, 40 (Dec. 1990).

[42] The size and scale of that committee were not peculiar to Wood Green. The Raine and Smith report shows that all the projects had their large committees: see J. Raine and R. Smith, *The Victim/Witness in Court Project: Report of the Research programme* (Oct. 1991), 32.

[43] The *Interim Training Guidelines* later prepared by Victim Support claimed that 'early consideration should be given to the establishment of an Inter-Agency Steering Committee composed of representatives of court users. Establishing a Steering Committee will help maintain good relations with other court staff and criminal justice agencies and ensures that the commitment of the service and responsibility for its

Thirty people actually looked like a large body to those working in a small court. After all, the Court was a loose confederation of independent powers whose relations were generally negotiated in informal, secluded, and hurried transactions.[44] Large meetings bore the stamp of the outsider, one who did not quite know how to do things. Thirty people were certainly far more numerous than the modest five first mooted by Geoff Spain.[45] Such a group seemed out of scale, inflated, and indigestible, a rash of gigantic bureaucracy, no part of the way in which a small user should behave. One of the insiders involved with the development of the project considered that it would appear more of a public meeting than the inauguration of a steering group: it 'had all got a bit out of hand'. Indeed, insiders were quite unaccustomed to public meetings or to the public itself being at large in their inner reaches. They asked, 'what are all those people doing in our court?' One senior administrator remarked:

I wonder really if it's necessary to have so many people involved. It seems to be a local-authority thing, doesn't it? Government by committee, and the more people involved the better they like it. I wonder if half these bodies are really necessary . . . if at the end of the day, by having them all in that full-scale committee, you are going to achieve much.

The very first meeting of the Court Project steering committee gathered on 12 February, its members arrayed somewhat stiffly and self-consciously around one of the larger courtrooms.[46] It was told

---

development is shared amongst all agencies working within the court. In addition, a Steering Committee establishes the service's accountability to the court'; *Victim/ Witness Court Project: Interim Training Guidelines* (Victim Support, Sept. 1990), 13. See also T. Gustafson, 'Court Training', *Victim Support*, 41 (Mar. 1991), 14.

[44] Indeed, a senior administrator was to say of the construction of the project as a whole, 'It should be kept as a low-key exercise, between individuals.'

[45] They were equivalent in size to over half the total complement of the Court's own part- and full-time staff.

[46] In the event, those attending were to be 2 police officers from Tottenham police division; 1 police officer from Hornsey police division; the branch Crown prosecutor and one of his staff; a representative of Victim Support London; Geoff Spain; Stephen Okafor; a Church community representative; a member of Haringey social services; a police officer member of the management committee of Haringey Victim Support; the vice-chair of Haringey Victim Support; the resident judge; a member of a local Afro-Caribbean project; a local magistrate and his wife, members of the management committee of Enfield Victim Support; a representative of Barnet Victim Support; Tim Gustafson from Victim Support; and myself. Another 12 were invited but did not attend, including the chief clerk who tendered his apologies. The minutes of the meeting itself expressed the hope that the steering committee would be enlarged further to include 'the Court Clerk, barristers and a local law society'.

what had become by now the well-rehearsed truths about the project. Tim Gustafson was there to narrate something of the history of the Victim in Court initiative, its origins in the Ralphs report, its support by private charity and the Home Office, and its launch by David Windlesham 'in the highest court in the land, the House of Lords'. The structure of the project would be much the same as that of a conventional victim support scheme, and its object (said Hugh Clark) would be 'to give victims and witnesses some emotional support and to explain the Court layout and procedures'.[47] The project would not give succour to defence witnesses (Gustafson said, 'We could not turn away distressed people of either side but in a planned sense we cannot seek to look out for defence witnesses').

The National Association 'had given guidelines as to the most appropriate methods of supporting victims'. At least thirty volunteers would be needed to 'operate on a rota basis', working three or four at a time, after they had been 'given some basic training in serious sexual-assault counselling'. Witness referrals would be a problem: there would have to be an effective system of securing early referrals, and any such system would require the co-operation of the police and the CPS.

Subcommittees were proposed and founded,[48] one centred on witness referrals (to be composed of Stephen Okafor, the branch Crown prosecutor,[49] a detective chief inspector, and the police member of the management committee of Haringey Victim Support) and another on the training of volunteers.[50] There might well have been other subcommittees on finance and on the identification of witnesses' needs, but the resident judge interjected, 'Do you actually need a subcommittee for that?' and it was concluded that perhaps, after all, no more committees *were* necessary.

[47] Wood Green Crown Court Victim/Witness Project steering group, minutes of meeting of 12 Feb. 1990.
[48] The resident judge asked, 'How many subcommittees do you have in mind?' and was told 'Perhaps two, that is the very minimum'. 'Quite,' said the resident judge.
[49] The branch Crown prosecutor stated publicly 'I'm very much in favour of this scheme. If there's anything I can do to help with referrals and with training . . . We have a lot of experience at the rough end of it.' He was to be co-opted on to the 2 subcommittees.
[50] Those 'proliferating subcommittees' were also to occasion some anxiety amongst insiders, and insider members tried to reduce their number and the frequency of their meetings.

Somewhat to the relief of insiders, structural expansion was checked at that point.[51]

The Referral Policy Subcommittee

The matter of advance referrals was to exercise Okafor. It had been flagged as a problem by Victim Support.[52] It had been cited expressly in his job description as a task to organize. Referrals had to be secured methodically and in advance. Okafor's own experience as a volunteer in other welfare organizations had been that 'people tend to move into themselves in times of crisis . . . rather than get out there to seek help and assistance'. Yet referrals were not to be easily secured throughout the initial phases of the project.

The referral policy subcommittee met first on 21 February in the offices of the CPS (an important sign of the diffusion of institutional patronage). It was attended by the branch Crown prosecutor, a detective chief inspector, the police member and secretary of the management committee of Haringey Victim Support, the CPS assistant principal law clerk, a co-ordinator from Haringey Victim Support, and Stephen Okafor.

The CPS estimated that there were some 600 witnesses attending the Crown Court at Wood Green each month, 2–3 a case, perhaps 30 a day (although many were held to be embroiled in shoplifting cases with insignificant numbers of private witnesses). Of that multitude, only the prosecution witnesses should be supported: after all, said the branch Crown prosecutor, the principal source of support for a suspect was a lawyer and 'we can't be all things to all men' (that 'we' should be noted). It was the police who would filter cases initially, because they were the sole agency with adequate prior knowledge of witnesses ('We're the only one who can identify needs,' they declared). They would make 'selective referrals'[53] to the project, 'targeting rather than [giving] blanket cover'. Police crime support

---

[51] The threatened proliferation of committees arose, in part, at Gustafson's suggestion. The project at Wood Green was rather behind the others in its development, and Gustafson used other models, and particularly that at Newcastle, as a guide to what should be done there. The objection to the growth of structures was peculiar to Wood Green, almost certainly reflecting its small scale and comparative informality.

[52] Indeed, the first experimental victims scheme in Kingswood had failed for want of an adequate referrals policy. See *Helping Victims of Crime*, ch. 3.

[53] It had been just thus in the early days of Victim Support: the police selected those whom they would forward to victim support schemes. Later, and after trust had been established, it was conceded that there should be 'automatic referrals' of all reported crimes to the schemes. Control over referrals was to be contested for some time.

units would also distribute special leaflets advertising the project at the time witnesses were 'early warned' some three weeks before the trial itself. The CPS might subsequently provide supplementary information and make occasional direct referrals to the project: 'When we know about witnesses we will be able to contact.'

In the event, as I shall argue, neither the police nor the CPS did prove to be a significant source of referrals during the first four months of the project's life. Special leaflets were indeed sent, but no witness came forward in response to them (although witnesses did start to present themselves after the fieldwork for this research had been completed). No one professed to understand why the new system should have been so unsuccessful. It was conjectured that witnesses remained indifferent to the prospect of attending court until the very eve of the trial. It was thought that the crime support units might actually have omitted to send leaflets, although checks by the detective chief inspector sitting on the subcommittee disclosed otherwise. The CPS referred two cases in four months.

Prior warning did not work at first, witnesses were not forthcoming, and Okafor was obliged to rely on a complementary stratagem, identified initially and somewhat disparagingly as 'touting for business', that was later to be taken as a model for other schemes. I shall return to it below.

The Steering Subcommittee on Training and Recruitment

The second subcommittee met some five days after the first, and again in the offices of the branch Crown prosecutor. It consisted of two members of the CPS, Paul Gee, the police member of the management committee of Victim Support Haringey, and Stephen Okafor.

Okafor revealed how few people had applied to become volunteers. Only 10–12 applicants would actually be interviewed in March, and those appointed would enter an immediate 3–4 day training programme. It would all be a bit difficult, because such a small number of volunteers could easily feel overwhelmed and, said Stephen Okafor, 'I can't ask too much of volunteers. They *are* volunteers. We should be careful and allow them to provide voluntary service to the extent they want to do it.' Numbers might later increase. It was certainly intended that there should be continuous and repeated recruitment and training thereafter.[54]

[54] One later stratagem was to prove more successful. Social work students at Middlesex Polytechnic were given practical work placements in the project (not unlike

Recruiting Volunteers

Victim Support Haringey's application to Victim Support had talked of using the press in its recruitment of volunteers (Irene Rondell said, 'The local press has always been very kind to us'), and articles duly appeared in local newspapers at the beginning of February 1990.[55] It was reported that the Crown Court at Wood Green was the only court in London to house one of the new projects that were intended to help victims 'overcome the ordeal of appearing in court'. The project would 'provide a service to explain court layout and procedure and give emotional support', and readers were invited to 'give justice a hand' by serving as volunteers. Advertisements were published at the end of January.[56] Stephen Okafor was interviewed on local radio. The Court and its scheme were shown on regional television.

Tim Gustafson had fixed on 15 to 20 volunteers as the proper number for each project.[57] Stephen Okafor had hoped for 30.[58] A member of the steering subcommittee on training and recruitment talked about 'the magic number of 40 that is the target number that will get this project going'. But the first wave of recruitment was to be disappointingly small, securing only 11 applications. The applicants were to be described to the steering subcommittee on training and recruitment as 'basically retired people': they 'looked alright but quite elderly'. Okafor reflected, 'I don't really want them to be like that but that's what we've got at present. We wanted young and old, black and white, but at the moment we haven't got that.' It was always feared that it would be so in Haringey,[59] a borough with a small middle class and a shifting population[60] (Irene Rondell had

the Bristol Univ. students who worked in the first victim support scheme in the mid-1970s).

[55] Identical articles on 'victims of crime to get help in court' appeared in the *Tottenham and Wood Green Journal* and *Hornsey Journal* of 1 Feb. 1990.

[56] The advertisement sought volunteers who would help 'witnesses overcome nerves and give practical support' (*Tottenham and Wood Green Journal*, 21 Jan. 1990).

[57] Speech at the 1989 conference of Victim Support and at the 1989 annual conference of Victim Support Northern Ireland.

[58] That was certainly the kind of figure reached elsewhere. See e.g. the article on the project in the Crown Court at Maidstone in *The Times*, 24 Jan. 1990.

[59] The vice-chair of Victim Support Haringey had hoped that the Victim in Court Project would attract volunteers from a larger and rather different area than that associated with the victim support scheme. Haringey had always been difficult as a recruiting ground.

[60] See M. Gill and R. Mawby, *Volunteers in the Criminal Justice System* (Milton Keynes, Open Univ. Press, 1990), and W. Skogan, *Disorder and Decline* (New York, Free Press, 1990), 130.

observed that 'volunteers in Haringey are basically impossible to get.
. . . You won't get volunteers crawling out of the woodwork for this').

Stephen Okafor had hoped to select people who could 'provide
information and assistance with practical issues such as explaining
court layout and procedure and identifying the needs and entitlements
of victim/witnesses; . . . provide emotional support and assistance to
victim/witnesses who attend court; [and] give practical information
about the trial or role of the victim/witness'.[61] Volunteers would
evince a 'caring and supportive attitude', be willing to provide 'support
and assistance', have an 'ability to communicate well and form good
working relationships with victim/witnesses, other court users and outside agencies', be able to work independently and in a team, and give
at least a day a month to the project. They would not have a criminal
record (just as in any victim support scheme, the police checked the
antecedents of applicants). Neither would they have applied for what a
police officer called 'funny reasons'. There was no need of 'the occasional weirdo whose motives you can't work out'. Interviews were held
in early March, the whole being conducted by Irene Rondell with
Geoff Spain, Stephen Okafor, and Paul Gee of the management committee of Victim Support Haringey. So large had been the number
sought, so few and unexceptionable were the people who had
applied,[62] that all 11 applicants were appointed. A member of the
interview panel recalled:

They weren't interviews because we weren't summing people up as to
whether they were suitable. That had already been done. We were told by
Stephen that these were people who had answered the advert. It wasn't any
sort of interview. It was a formality. I think the first was an interview and
the rest we greeted formally. We were very grateful to them for turning out
and offering their services . . . They seemed to be very good-quality people.
I thought they were a most competent group of volunteers. No doubts at all.

Those appointed were white (11), predominantly middle-aged and
elderly (9) women (10). They were people whose lives had intersected
significantly and memorably with the courts and the criminal-justice
system at some stage in the past; were now all retired or unemployed
and searching for voluntary work,[63] had seen the project described in

---

[61] 'Position Specification, Victim Witness Support Volunteer'.

[62] Indeed, it was to be reported to the recruitment, training and referral subcommittee meeting of 24 Apr. 1990 that there were insufficient volunteers to service the
scheme.

[63] Three had had experience as victim support volunteers.

a newspaper, and took an application to be the logical next step in their lives.

Consider the biographies of some of the volunteers. One, 'Mac', had been an usher and then a member of the listing staff at Wood Green soon after the foundation of the Court in 1980, and he recalled how happy he had been as a member of the 'team': 'It was an extremely happy set-up, extremely well-run.' He had retired in 1983 but could not 'accept retirement. I must do work all the time.' He had seen the scheme described first on television and 'then in the local paper . . . so I phoned Stephen'. A second applicant had been a magistrates' court clerk and 'I saw it in the local paper and I sent my letter here . . . I have the experience. I thought, "well, I know what the court is like and what fears the witnesses have", so I felt I should do something. . . . I could afford to do once a month.' A third, Emma, had been a solicitor's clerk who had seen the harrowing of prosecution witnesses: 'At the Old Bailey especially, you get lots of rape cases. [There was one case in particular] when the victim had come to sit near me and I had to say, "I am sorry I can't talk to you" and she was very distressed. . . . I always used to say, "Oh thank God, it wasn't me. I couldn't cope". So I think you need somebody to cope, to help you cope.' But she had also taken pleasure in her work as a clerk: 'I enjoyed it . . . so I thought, well, it was no use me getting a voluntary job that I wasn't going to like. It would have defeated the object. I would have been more miserable. So I said I would try this.' A fourth had been through a difficult divorce in the courts ('When I think about it, when I came out, I hadn't got a voice . . . I thought it was quite simple, you know, it wasn't violence or crime, but all the same.' The project had sounded 'interesting and satisfying really'. A fifth had trained as a store detective but had found how reluctant she was to work at prosecuting and testifying ('It turned out if I take someone to court, it had to be my name and [I] didn't like that idea, that I had to give my name and where where live'). But she had not lost her fascination with criminal justice, being 'always interested in cases', and 'would like the court work'. Another (who was not to stay) had trained for the law but had not completed her course. She had always 'done voluntary work of some kind', having worked in a Citizen's Advice Bureau, and she was now employed by a solicitor. They were members of a group that could be described as retired professionals or as professionals *manqués*, people who wished, as one put it, 'to do something useful in my retirement', able simultaneously to comprehend the problems of witnesses and yet to retain a distance from the conflict and anguish of the trial.

There was to be another, smaller group of two who found it difficult to maintain such a distance. The intersection between their lives, the courts, and victimization was to become unbearably poignant on occasion. They had earlier been embroiled as victims in their own Crown Court trials, and entertained what could swell up to become an insupportable strength of fellow feeling with other victims. It would, said one, be difficult to 'keep her feelings out of it'. One of that group had been a direct victim of a serious assault, and she recalled that being a victim had been 'a very frightening experience [that allowed her to] sympathize with victims in court, I know what they're feeling'. The other had been an indirect victim, the mother of a young man killed by a drunk driver, a founder member of CADD (the Campaign Against Drinking and Driving), and she still called herself a victim. She had joined the project 'because I was a victim myself'. She had known

What it's like being in court, to go into court, not sure what was happening or anything. When I was at the Old Bailey I didn't even know where the canteen was or nothing . . . so I thought having someone saying, 'Well look, I know where it is' and to take you straight there. And also when I was in court, seeing the person who committed the crime against me, you know, it aggravated you. And if the person in court here could recognize them quick enough so I could get them out of the way, because it does bring up a lot of anger and hurt in you. . . . I thought [this project] would be a very good idea for someone to be there, especially if the person's alone and they're on their own.

Supporting witnesses was to revive those two volunteers' earlier pain ('I relive my trauma every day,' one said) and they too left the project after a while. Okafor said later of one of them that she had 'serious difficulties in relating to people in court'.

Training

Training was a matter of the first importance. It would methodically draw the volunteers into the project and the Court, introduce them to the topography and etiquette of a special institution, and acquaint them with the needs of a special population. It signalled control and responsibility. It was a check on misbehaviour, blunder, and error.

Tim Gustafson had promised the entire Court and its users assembled as the Court Project steering committee on 12 February, 'We're convinced that training is *very* important. We're aware that courts are sensitive areas and we don't want to send in bungling amateurs.' Amateurishness and bungling could be prevented only by a careful programme of training that had been laid out in a master template[64] under the guidance of the Project management committee at 'national' Victim Support.[65]

Okafor's plans for training the new volunteers followed and adapted that template. The first part of his own projected programme was designed to move through a discussion of 'the unsupported victim witness in court', a section consisting of talks about the 'British criminal-justice system' (to be given by a magistrate member of Victim Support Enfield who was also a member of the Court Project steering committee), the 'role of the police in Crown prosecution', the CPS, 'the place of the victim witness in the criminal-justice system', and the 'legitimate work of the defence and the victim witness'[66] (to be given by a solicitor and a barrister).[67] It would proceed in its second part to 'giving support to victim witnesses in court', dwelling on the origins of the project (Tim Gustafson[68]) and its adoption by Victim Support Haringey (Irene Rondell), the needs of victims (Stephen Okafor), and the provision of

---

[64] The template had recommended 7 sessions: a discussion of Victim Support and its court-based service; an introduction to the criminal-justice system (touching on the presumption of innocence and the prosecution's duty to prove guilt); the range of cases at Crown Court (with an express emphasis on 'the particular needs of victims of serious crime such as sexual assault and child abuse' and 'the needs of families of murder victims'); 'the Crown Court, layout and procedure'; trial at the Crown Court; services to victims and witnesses; and 'further aspects of the trial'. *Training Programme* (Victim Support, n.d.).

[65] Internal Victim Support papers attest to the importance attached to proper preparation. One such paper, *Principles of Victim Support in Court*, talked about how 'the Crown Court is a new area for Victim Support and we need to ensure that we act at all times with sensitivity and tact. Volunteers should be aware of the boundaries within which they can work and in particular follow the limitations which have been agreed with the court.' Another, 'Training Guidelines for Court Based Volunteers', argued that 'the training of volunteers . . . is a crucial element in the provision of a competent court-based service. Victim Support will be coming into contact with a variety of organizations and agencies within the court and we need to establish our credibility at an early stage. Volunteers who are well trained and fully briefed on the aims of the project will play a large part in helping us achieve these goals.'

[66] The phrase was subsequently changed to 'the legitimate duty of prosecution and defence'.

[67] *Court Project Training Programme* (initial draft).

[68] Gustafson had chosen exceptionally to attend the entire programme to acquaint himself with the training of volunteers.

services and counselling (one of Victim Support Haringey's two co-ordinators). The whole would end with sessions on the 'code of conduct for workers' (Tim Gustafson), the 'Wood Green Crown Court layout and rules of procedure' (the chief clerk), and 'co-operating with the research team' (John Raine).[69]

In effect, it was planned to offer volunteers a panoramic vision of a troubled world, a vision that borrowed heavily from Victim Support's own training programme. It is significant that the master programme did not actually mirror the routine work of a small, third-tier Crown Court centre such as Wood Green. One very obvious point of difference was that the programme turned insistently to the needs of those who had suffered the most distressing and difficult crimes of all, the crimes that had first brought numbers of victims support scheme volunteers to court, the crimes that had prompted the writing of the *Victim in Court* report: rape, sexual assault, and murder. The training programme's third model session, in particular, prepared volunteers 'for the full range of cases they are likely to encounter at court including serious crimes such as rape and murder', and it noted that 'the nature of court based work means that volunteers may deal with victims of such crimes from the first day. Trainers will need to involve members of Victim Support who have undertaken training in dealing with victims of sexual assault.' Okafor's draft programme for Wood Green followed closely in the steps of the more general model. It promised that 'training on the subjects of sexual assault, murder and racial harassment will be arranged in the near future'.

Training was conducted over three days in a local Salvation Army Hall in mid-March, and it departed from Okafor's earlier proposals in two important ways. Murder, racial harassment, and rape were to receive an even greater prominence, and there were to be changes in the cast of insiders coming forward to speak. The structural identity, affiliations, and patronage of the new project were beginning to show. No barrister or solicitor helped to train the recruits (it was discovered that lawyers were unwilling to give assistance during the daytime). It was as if there was an emerging, tacit understanding that

---

[69] It was observed by one member of the steering subcommittee on training and recruitment: 'It seems rather a lot to cram into rather a short time—is thirty minutes long enough for counselling and counselling skills?' and by another: 'It's going to be a very intensive two to three days and you can't go into too much. People can only take in so much.'

victim-witness support had become the special property of one battalion of adversaries in the trial system.[70]

Stephen Okafor introduced the project: 'The scheme is brand new,' he said, 'and no one knows quite what will happen. . . . If we are successful, then this little child, this experiment at Wood Green will spread right across the country.' He narrated the history of the project and its network of sponsors, the police, the Lord Chancellor's Department, and 'different agencies in the catchment area'. In all this, the role of the volunteer would be 'to give support and assistance to victims who give evidence in the Crown Court. They find it an alien world, frightening, a strange building.' Training itself would supply 'an opportunity to learn from the experts, because we're not experts yet'.

A procession of experts followed. The first was a magistrate, a member of the management committee of an adjoining victim support scheme. He discussed courts, prosecutors, and prosecutions, and he discussed them as a single enterprise, somewhat conflating the organization of the magistrates' court with that of the Crown Court. He hoped that 'you will be able to sit next to the victim, give them a smile of encouragement when they give evidence, and get them over that hurdle'. It would not be easy. Courts were difficult places and the courtrooms in which volunteers would work were fraught with danger:

You must be very careful . . . You may be reprimanded. You may be ordered to leave the court. You may find that your need is to be with the victim and you're letting the victim down. You've got to be very careful about not signalling to the victim. You have to be careful about how you conduct yourself.

Volunteers asked about what they could say to witnesses, and were told that the victim's representative was the Crown prosecutor (who would mainly be a solicitor) to whom messages could be passed ('There'll always be an usher who can pass the information along to the Crown prosecutor'). It was becoming a little muddled. Tim Gustafson, observing the training programme, intervened with the formulaic Victim Support reply:

The role of the volunteer is practical information about the court and its layout and practical support—tea and sympathy. You can't discuss the evidence, legal advice, the sentence or information like that. You could get defence counsel jumping up and down: practical procedure but not evidence in the case.

[70] Barristers did participate in later training programmes after my fieldwork period.

The next expert was a senior police officer, a member of one the project's subcommittees' who talked of crime and the reporting of crime; of witnesses and the crime support group; of the CPS and committal proceedings in the magistrates' courts; of listings and the warning and summoning of witnesses. He talked about the projected referral system that was not actually to take shape during the time of my field research, a system designed to allow volunteers and witnesses to meet on the eve of the trial.[71]

Next was the branch Crown prosecutor ('another important individual, if he's not the chief man, he's very close to being the chief man at the CPS. They are the people who we're setting to get hold of,' said Okafor). Volunteers were told about the structure and organization of the CPS; about the decision to prosecute ('We are obliged by statute to consider whether a prosecution is in the public interest'); about bail, listings, and the issuing of early warning lists ('We only have the power to persuade, we don't have any say in that, we join a kind of queue'); about the kinds of case that were committed to the Crown Court at Wood Green (there would be no murders and very few rapes); and about the moral and symbolic distance of the prosecution from victims and prosecution witnesses ('We don't operate for the victim. We're not here to try an issue before person A and person B').

Testifying was represented as a wretched experience, an assault on claims to credit and credibility, a reliving of earlier anguish that could leave witnesses feeling desolate ('I get a lot of letters from people who're worried about the fact that they've not been believed. They feel the misery of the initial assault and that no one has believed them'). It was because of the witness's structural isolation and dejection, said the branch Crown prosecutor, 'because of the lack of a victim's friend, that this scheme is so important, it is the one obvious area where there is a gap. . . . I think this scheme is desperately needed.'

---

[71] It was envisaged that the Victim in Court Project would be warned by the Crown Court case warning clerk in the crime support unit ('the person who is responsible for everything that can take place in connection with witnesses'). Volunteers would discuss the trial with the witnesses on the day before: 'The hope is that you will have dealt with all the issues as they arise, whether they can bring sandwiches, the layout of the court.' A volunteer asked, 'Does that mean we can get involved with witnesses before they come to court?' and Okafor replied, 'Yes, there will be rapport established and you will know their needs. You can show them the court layout before.' Such an advanced referral system did not actually come to pass in the first 4 months of the project.

The next expert was an acquaintance of Geoff Spain, a retired court clerk who had worked at the Crown Court for four years, and he spoke for the defence counsel who could not be persuaded to attend themselves. The defence was portrayed as unashamedly partisan: 'It is the task of the defence to minimize or repudiate the evidence given by the prosecution. . . . other people have concerned themselves with the victim. I do not. I shall put the victim under considerable stress, under the greatest amount of pressure.' It must, he said, 'be a most terrifying experience for the victim. It is your job to prepare them for that.' And he was echoed by a police officer serving on the management committee of Victim Support Haringey:

Defence counsel start by being smarmy and then they'll go for the jugular! They'll suddenly say, 'That's not the case is it? I put it to you, you're mistaken.' What they're saying is, 'You're lying through the back teeth. You were a hundred miles away and committing a burglary yourself.' You feel indignant: what right have these people to make me stand up in public and say, 'You're a bloody liar!' And the judge will say, 'Thank you' and you go out feeling, 'They didn't believe me'.

Next, Geoff Spain talked about the role of probation, the Crown Court ('The operation of a Crown Court is a team effort. people work together to achieve the Crown Court project'), and the Victim in Court Project itself:

I have seen out of the corner of my eye that, whilst the defendants have had a hard deal, victims have had a very hard deal, and some victims leave in high dudgeon and some in tears, and it's high time that something was done.

Tim Gustafson returned to catechize volunteers about the pains of victimization and testifying. There would be the initial crime, and that would engender feelings of confusion and anger. Then there would be the early witness warning ('It all comes back again, doesn't it?'). There would be a host of emotional and practical problems ('Am I going to get paid? Who'll look after the children?'). There would be alienation on arrival 'at that posh new court'. There might well be fear of intimidation, anxiety, fear, uncertainty: 'Can I see my evidence? I'm very nervous . . . If I fail, will I be accused of lying? Can I speak to the barrister? Where is the police officer in my case? And all the defendant's friends are whispering. . . . How am I going to find out the verdict?' 'Was it worth it?' asked Tim Gustafson, and the volunteers cried out as one, 'No!' And so ended the first day.

Tim Gustafson resumed the following morning, and he talked once more about the history of the project and its conception in the new work of victim support schemes (volunteers had become involved in 'quite "in-depth" counselling over a longer period [and] they asked "National" how to act in court'). He talked about the administrative organization of the project and its carapace of committees ('The committees allow all these agencies to feel they possess the project as well'); the meaning of the volunteer ('You're here because you want to do it, not because you're paid to do it'); and the hazards of working in court:

Courts are conservative institutions. They're a closed shop. They say, 'Everything's alright. Why are these people interfering?' So that is the importance of training. You're not going to be upsetting people, treading on corns. You're going to do it right.

Gustafson took volunteers through the moral imperatives, the Aims of Conduct,[72] that would bind them in Court: 'It's part of our drive to establish and maintain good relations with the staff at Wood Green.' There was a decalogue that insisted, *inter alia*, that volunteers must be trained; that they should not attend trials 'unless accompanying the victim' ('We don't want the judge, the defence counsel, to see the volunteer going in and out, that's going to give a bad message—defence barristers are going to pull out everything they can and say, "This volunteer is prejudicing the case by informing the victim"'); and that support should consist only of the provision of practical information, not legal advice.

Gustafson was succeeded by Irene Rondell, who talked again about the local history of the project and the scheme, and by Stephen Okafor, who listed the needs of victims and witness (there was the fear of the unknown, the practical needs of child care, the need for elementary information about lengths of time spent waiting and in court, and the need for reassurance).

The volunteers were told about practical skills and problems. They were told about race relations and racism in the criminal-justice system by one who had worked on Victim Support's racial harassment project (the volunteers declared their dissatisfaction with that session. It was patronizing and unwarranted, they said: 'We all know about race relations and I don't think it does any good to stir it up'). They were told about counselling by one of Victim Support Haringey's

[72] *Victim-Witness Court Project: Statement of Aims and Code of Conduct.*

co-ordinators (they were most interested in counselling and wished they could have learned more: 'We don't need the technical knowledge as much as we want to know how to approach people and, if necessary, give them support and comfort'). They were told about rape by the co-ordinator of another scheme who had been trained in rape counselling. Rape was depicted as a devastating crisis, a loss of control, and it generated 'long-term acute stress reaction' that could be reactivated in the witness-box ('It is a true reliving of all the experiences of rape. It is not just a recalling'). Coming to court, the victim of rape would be humiliated before strangers. In supporting rape victims, the co-ordinator said, volunteers would have to deal with their own anger and 'try not to cry with the victim because the victim will then feel obliged to help the helper and will feel that the helper can't cope'. Jane Cooper of Victim Support told the volunteers about helping witnesses and the bereaved in murder cases. Rena Smith talked about the Birmingham evaluation. The listing officer talked about listing, and about the business and organization of the Court ('you will never see murder, arson, or piracy on the high seas. Only three of the judges can try rape. Occasionally I get them from the Old Bailey'). And the volunteers were conducted around the new courthouse, being shown their place in the geography of the building: they were to be confined to their office on the third floor, the public parts within the courtrooms, and the public spaces without ('Please note that all the doors marked private are private. You are confined to the public areas and to your office').

Let me review what had happened. Hugh Clark of Victim Support Haringey had predicted that the training 'will encompass all the particular types of problem that the volunteer/Stephen will face in the Court environment'. In procession, the new recruits had been told about the pains of becoming a witness, the conduct of volunteers, and the onerous disciplines of the courtroom. 'It was an awful lot to be crowded into three days,' said one. The original thrust of the wider politics of witnesses had travelled deep into the organization of the Wood Green project, stamping its impress on images of victims, witnesses, and needs. Local insiders may have insisted that the Court tried only Class 4 offences, but a succession of outside experts had concentrated on three specific offences only, rape, indecent assault, and murder, with the clear implication that that must be useful knowledge to have. The Court in which it was said those dreadful crimes were tried was itself presented as a fierce place; laced with taboos and boundaries, with prohibitions and dangers; policed by vigilant defence counsel and judges ever ready to pounce on impropriety. Volunteers should not move in and out of the courtrooms, make themselves obtrusive, compromise trials, or venture into private space. They should remain quietly in the public areas where they belonged, talking only about innocuous matters. It was concluded later that 'the Code of Conduct was emphasized so much that many volunteers were over cautious when working within court'.[73]

It should be observed, too, that no solicitor or barrister contributed to that first round of training. No solicitor or barrister joined any of the committees or subcommittees of the project.[74] Hugh Clark had asserted that the training programme would draw on 'the help of other agencies that perhaps have encountered difficulties'. Those other agencies were in part the project's patrons, and they could be identified chiefly as Victim Support, the police, and the prosecutors. More distant patrons were the Court administration (the chief clerk attended some of the meetings of the Court steering committee, and the listing officer, the expert on witness matters, came to represent the Court on the referrals steering subcommittee); and, more distantly still, the judiciary (the resident judge did not attend the Court steering committee after the first, but he kept a benevolent eye on the progress of the project[75]).

In all this, the project refracted the structure not only of the Project management steering committee based at Victim Support but also of the larger national politics of the witness. The detached, disinterested, but 'facilitating' role of the Court listing officer mirrored the observer status assumed by the Lord Chancellor's Department's representative on the committee and the stance of the Department itself. The local project's committees and the Project management steering committee contained no counsel and no solicitors, and the Bar and

---

[73] Gustafson, *Evaluation of Court Project*.

[74] This was the general pattern for the other projects, although it should be noted that there were counsel present on the steering committees of the projects at Newcastle and Teesside, and members of the Law Society at Liverpool and Newcastle. The Crown Court at Newcastle was serviced by a small number of barristers occupying a number of sets of chambers only a few yards from the courthouse. Links between the Court and counsel were much closer than in London.

[75] Indeed, he chose to issue a laudatory press release at the time of publication of the Raine and Smith report in Oct. 1991, giving public support to the project at a time when its future funding was uncertain. His conclusion was: 'This scheme must not be allowed to end or decline for lack of money. The Report demonstrates the importance of this work, we hope the money would be available and available soon.'

Law Society were absent from the national politics of the witness too.[76] No judges sat in regular attendance on the project's committees locally or centrally. And on both sets of committees, perhaps somewhat incongruously, were probation officers, the defendant's champions, signalling the balance of a Victim Support that refused to engage in a politics antagonistic to the offender. The administrative alignments and position of the project were there clearly delineated.

Touting for Business[77]

It had been expected that witnesses would be referred by the police, by the CPS and victim support schemes[78] but, in practice, none of those bodies proved to be a significant source of referral during or after the time of my fieldwork. Some 30 per cent of the witnesses seen were referred by a professional agency 'on the day'; over half were contacted by a volunteer in the courthouse; 4 per cent were 'self-referrals' in advance; 2 per cent were referred by local victim support schemes; and only 13 per cent were referred by professional agencies in advance[79] (Okafor concluded a little bitterly that 'fair words are easy enough'). The number of referrals from local victim support schemes was found to be 'surprisingly, very low'.[80] That problem of securing referrals was known to other projects nationally[81] and, indeed, internationally.[82] Witnesses were not referred to

---

[76] It should be remembered, however, that they had been represented in a fashion on Lady Ralphs' working party.

[77] 'Touting for business' was to become common currency, particularly at 'National'.

[78] Minutes of the Victim/Witness in Court Project management committee meeting of 13 Dec. 1989. In practice, for instance, only 22% of the Wood Green witnesses interviewed for the Raine and Smith evaluation recalled having had previous contact with a victim support scheme (*Report of the Research Programme*, 10) and 2% were referred by a scheme (ibid. 38).

[79] Wood Green was unusually high in its use of 'touting for business'. 52% of its referrals were secured in this fashion. The comparable figures for the other experimental courts were 20% at Teesside, 2% at Manchester, 1% at Liverpool, 20% at Preston, 3% at Newcastle, and 3% at Maidstone. Based on J. Raine and R. Smith, *The Victim/Witness in Court Project: Report of the Research Programme* (London, Victim Support, 1991), 38.

[80] Gustafson, *Evaluation of Court Project*.

[81] See, e.g. the article on the project at the Crown Court at Maidstone, *The Times*, 24 Jan. 1990.

[82] See R. Rosenblum and C. Blew, *Victim/Witness Assistance* (Washington DC, US Dept. of Justice, 1979), 47.

the project.[83] Neither did they refer themselves (by 6 June 1990, 800 leaflets were supposed to have been distributed to witnesses, but it was to all to no effect. Okafor told the steering subcommittee, 'We haven't received a single reply. I've asked the volunteers to monitor the position, but we haven't seen a person who's received the leaflet.'[84]) Okafor resented the impotence occasioned by such an enforced and ineffectual reliance on others ('We lose control the moment we send [the leaflets] out,' he said). At an early point, he resolved to take remedial action and outflank the agencies. He would send his own volunteers to track down the elusive prosecution witness and, in doing so, he followed the normal practice of a victim support scheme ('Victim Support . . . has always relied on proactive approach in reaching victims').

Okafor needed names. He was unable to move without advance knowledge, and it was knowledge of a kind that would not be disclosed freely. Only the insider was entrusted with lists of indictments, victims, witnesses, defendants, trials, and courtrooms, and it seemed that Okafor was not quite accepted as an insider when the project began its work on 2 April 1990. Staff of the CPS had certainly declared themselves willing to provide information, but they shied in practice (Okafor was told by one of the law clerks in May that 'he was too busy to help me and there's nothing we can do'). The listing officer was no more eager. He informed the referrals subcommittee in April 1990, 'Stephen is going to ask for a list of witnesses which I'm not going to supply . . . Stephen's also asked me to give copies of the indictment which I've also been instructed not to give.' It was not to be until 6 June, two months after the project had started, that an official at the Lord Chancellor's Department telephoned the chief clerk to declare that he could give the project his 'full backing', and, in his turn, the chief clerk told the listing officer to accord the project what would be, in effect, the accredited status of a full user. That decision of 6 June brought about a galvanic change, but it was not to be until another two months in the future, and Okafor had to devise a referral system in April.

---

[83] Minutes of a meeting of the amalgamated subcommittees of the Victim in Court Project, the general purposes committee, held on 8 Aug. 1990.

[84] He also told the management committee of Victim Support Haringey on 1 June 1990, 'By now I would have expected us to have these forms back but I didn't receive any. So at the end of May we started to monitor the situation by asking the victims if they'd received any forms and the response has been negative so far.'

Okafor turned again to Geoff Spain, his own patron, improbable as such a source of information might appear to be. After 4 p.m. every afternoon, when the final cause list had been issued, he would cross the landing on the third floor to the probation offices and peruse warning lists, committal papers, and indictments (and his presence there created a little *frisson* in the probation team. It was not thought quite proper that one allied to the prosecution witness should examine the papers of the defendants' ally or should be seen in the home territory to which defendants and defence counsel themselves retired[85]). Geoff Spain flagged the cases likely to need support. He reported the location of distressed witnesses seen in his tours of the courthouse.

Access to papers in the probation offices and to the lists enabled Okafor to ascertain who would be the 'officers in the case', the defendants, the victims and prosecution witnesses;[86] which trials had been allotted to which courts or to no courts at all; and the offences that would be tried and how much distress there might be. He could, in brief, learn where volunteers should search, and the condition and names of the people they should look for (after all, the papers supplied rudimentary information about the gender, numbers, and combinations of witnesses). But he lacked the visual detail that was indispensable to his project. Only insiders with their close knowledge of a case could recognize particular faces and identify need. The project could not rid itself of dependence on professional knowledge. It still needed the other users.

Every morning, appropriately primed, volunteers would be dispatched with lists to the public areas abutting the courtrooms. Once there, they would seek out the informed insiders (the police officers, law clerks,[87] sympathetic ushers, and, exceptionally, counsel[88]) who might

---

[85] There is no reason to suppose that Okafor had sight of any confidential information, or that he would have made improper use of it had he done so. The matter was symbolic rather than practical. Yet Spain was still to remark later, 'Office facilities were made available where necessary and possible. There was obvious value in a measure of mutual support in dealing with human crisis. However, respective clients were always segregated from one another to avoid potential conflict of interests and because the two units could never operate as one'; 'Victim/Witness Support and Probation Service', 25.

[86] The CPS also intermittently supplied information about prosecution witnesses.

[87] It was necessary to approach law clerks because they also supplied volunteers with expenses forms to pass on to witnesses.

[88] A notice about the project had been pinned up in counsel's robing-room.

consent to act as their eyes in spying out prosecution witnesses,[89] who could interpret needs[90] (and deserts[91]), and so bring volunteers and witnesses together. Okafor said, 'We go to them first to be able to identify the people we are supposed to be giving support because we do not know them yet.' At the end of April, after the first month of the project's life, he reported to the Court Project Steering Committee:

At present we reach the victim witnesses by touting at the foyer of the different courts every morning between 9.30 and 10.00 a.m. Within this period, we must identify them through the CPS counsel or the police officer in the case, explain the aims of the project, complete necessary forms and/or go to another part of the court building to obtain any required information, explain court procedure, and give emotional support.[92]

A process becoming known coloquially as 'touting for business'[93] was there under construction. It was a difficult process that obliged vol-

[89] Locating witnesses could become a major piece of detective work conducted in a hurry. On one day in June 1990, Okafor was told that a victim in a floater needed attention. He went to the police room looking for the officer in the case but without success. He tried to tannoy the officer but was told by the receptionist to go to the 'CPS room' where he was told the name of the officer; he returned to the receptionist, tannoyed the officer, finally made contact and, together, they set off to find the witness. Securing witnesses required a fine inside knowledge of the Court's workings.

[90] e.g. on 24 April 1990, prosecution counsel told a volunteer that the principal prosecution witness was a businessman and did not need her. On another occasion in June, counsel determined that a witness was a policeman, 'a serving officer and he doesn't need help'. One wonders quite what stereotypy was at work in such rapid assessments of need.

[91] On one occasion in June 1990, police officers intimated that a particular prosecution witness required to help. He was said to be troublesome, involved in the levelling of 'all sorts of allegations' against the police. The volunteer was told that if anything happened she might be called to give evidence herself and she would not like that, 'going into the box'. The volunteer sought Okafor's advice about what she should do and was told that she served the project, not the police, and was not obliged to accept the advice tendered by the police. She concluded that she would be better employed elsewhere with other witnesses. The witness, a Guardian Angel, did in fact assert that he did not want support. He was quite capable of looking after himself. On another occasion, counsel told a volunteer that a witness did not need help because he had been a defendant himself. It was not clear whether the inference to be drawn was that the witness did not *need* or that he did not *deserve* support.

[92] Report of Victim/Witness Support Co-ordinator to the Court Project steering committee, 30 Apr. 1990.

[93] 'Touting for business' was the phrase that eventually became conventional in describing the method adopted at Wood Green. Others had been ventured before. Okafor at one point called his methodology 'making ourselves available in court' (meeting of the Court Project steering group, 12 July 1990). The technique was not very different from the standard Victim Support strategy of 'outreach'.

unteers to move as strangers without distinctive uniform or identification[94] into the delicately figured archipelago of the public areas, accost anonymous members of the public and professionals who had no evident wish to be accosted, who were suspicious of strangers and strangers' motives[95] ('Some people think you are nosey parkers, do-gooders,' said one volunteer), and who sought frequently to seclude themselves in insulated personal territories of their own making. In all this, the relational order of the courthouse was an exaggerated version of Lyn Lofland's world of strangers, a world where there was 'minimal expressivity' and body contact, the signalling of aversion to interaction, the avoidance of eye contact, and a tendency to be inattentive or to flee when accosted.[96]

It was not easy to move about such a world. 'You have to go to identify yourself to someone and say, "Are you counsel or prosecution or defence?" and they don't like it . . . They sort of sneer at you a bit to sort of say, "What do you think you are going to do?"' Volunteers had to make rapid, and at first untutored, guesses about who the prosecution witnesses and others might be ('It's the initial approach, you just don't know who the witnesses are, do you? You could go up to the witnesses for the defence, couldn't you? You don't know who anybody is,' remarked one. 'I just look close and see if I can see a worried face,' said another.)

At first, without their badges, volunteers looked just like any other members of the public[97] ('Nobody notices us and we have to go and make the approach and it's not always easy'). They had to shake off their own anonymity and trespass across what were, in effect, the invisible boundaries erected by each of the members of the archipel-

---

[94] An identity card and badge were to be produced in time, but they were not available for the first several weeks of the project. The card certified that a volunteer was 'an approved Victim Witness Support volunteer based in the Wood Green Crown Court', and informed the reader that 'Victim Witness Support volunteers work from the VWS office . . . They provide emotional and practical support to victim witnesses who attend the Crown Court to give evidence.' Before this, volunteers had no proof to offer of what they were, no means of proclaiming identity in a place where identity was signified quite clearly. One volunteer said, 'I think it would be better if we had something on our shoulders . . . so that the ushers were aware that we were in the building.'

[95] Okafor commented: 'How many times have visiting police officers and counsel mistaken myself and volunteers for a witness or defendant?'

[96] See *A World of Strangers: Order and Action in Urban Public Space* (New York, Basic Books, 1973).

[97] On one occasion in May 1990, a volunteer, Emma Giovanni, was taken by a defendant to be his 'brief', and she proceeded to help him to find his real counsel.

ago. One volunteer said in the middle of May 1990, 'The worst thing is the beginning . . . it's the initial introduction I find the most sensitive.' And another talked of how intrusive she felt, not being at home, invading another's space. And another talked of how intrusive she felt, not being at home, invading another's space. Volunteers could be rebuffed. They could meet with guarded, unhelpful, or flippant answers ('This is nothing to do with me, I'm only here for the beer,' one volunteer was told enigmatically by a police officer. On another occasion, a volunteer reported, 'The defence one [counsel] looked down his nose and didn't want to know'). They were apprehensive about the staff: 'They change, I don't know who they are.' Volunteers, in short, laboured under the handicap of their situationally defined identity: they appeared to be just like any other nameless members of a public who should be avoided in the public space of a courthouse, members who none the less appeared wilfully to flout what Milgram called 'a rule of urban life . . . respect for other people's emotional and social privacy'.[98]

They were assisted in part by the sole volunteer who could not really be defined as a nameless outsider. I have already observed how one of the project's most active volunteers, John McEleney, known as 'Mac', had retired from work at the Court in 1983. An erstwhile insider himself, he may not have known the physical geography of the new courthouse, but he certainly knew its social structure, and he acted as a volunteer guide, a sherpa, for the other recruits, taking them, as he put it, 'under my wing and introducing them to people I know'. On the very first day of the new project's working, he donned his own hand-made badge and announced cheerfully, 'I supposed I'd better wander round and see what's happening in the various courts. Judge X will have a fit when he sees me!' He was at ease in the complex social relations of the Court: he knew its terminology and, indeed, remembered many of its staff by name. He could not be readily objectified as a 'member of the public' by the professionals: 'It seemed to me that my past experience of Court work could be useful to the new project. . . . Initially, few witnesses and people working in or using the Court knew who we were. As a result, most volunteers were a little apprehensive at first.'[99]

---

[98] S. Milgram, 'The Experience of Living in Cities', in J. Helmer and N. Eddington (eds.), *Urbanman: The Psychology of Urban Survival* (New York, Free Press, 1973), 6.

[99] 'A Volunteer's Comment', *End of Court Project and Start of Court Programme Report*. 10.

Okafor used Mac to aid the other, more nervous volunteers in the early days. The two would act in unison, making the first approach to professionals and strangers, and then summoning a volunteer from the wings to take his or her place beside a targeted witness. Some witnesses reported that they found it rather disconcerting to be smothered by such a sudden onset of help. It would have been better to have a little time 'to allow me to get my bearings and sit down and read the report', said one. But volunteers found Mac's role as sherpa helpful: one said, 'I was very nervous about that because I'd never done it before. I don't know the people. With the help of Mac, I was looking for people but I wasn't sure how they would take me.' Mac became a model, his methods being observed by other volunteers as he mapped out the relations around him. (One nervous volunteer remarked, 'I can see who's who, you know. Mac approaches them. But I couldn't do that yet.')

The very first referral stemmed from a choreographed action between the more confident people attached to the project. The peripatetic Geoff Spain had noticed a young girl in distress. Mac then went forward and announced himself to the usher: 'I used to work here. Now I'm back with victim support. I understand there may be a witness who needs help.' And he was told in his turn that there was, indeed, 'a little one who may want help'. The usher went even further and briefed Mac about the case, a case of indecency involving a young girl ('The judge may suggest wigs off in court') in a manner that he would have done with no outsider.

Twenty witnesses were seen in the first eighteen working days[100] (one being referred by the resident judge), and the lineaments of the project began to form. First, the project's work cycle closely followed that of the Court itself, short spurts of frenzied activity being interspersed with long periods of languor. Raine and Smith called the workload of volunteers generally 'patchy', 'partly because of the pattern of business from day to day in the courts'.[101] It will be remembered that the Court was at its very busiest on Mondays and Wednesdays, and the project itself was stirred into complementary action on those days. Between 9.30 and 10.30 on Monday and

---

[100] Report of victim-witness support co-ordinator to the Court Project steering committee, 30 Apr. 1990.

[101] J. Raine and R. Smith, *Research progress Report No. 6* (8 Mar. 1991), 2.

Wednesday mornings were the most energetic times,[102] volunteers fanning out throughout the courthouse in hot pursuit of witnesses. If witnesses were not found early on those days (and they were sometimes thin on the ground), they were generally not found at all. There were only 72 'supports'[103] recorded during the entire first 3 months. Despite the propensity of work to become concentrated at certain times, an average of 6 effective 'supports' a week during the period of the fieldwork, and of 15 a week during the first 19 months of the project, were sufficient to occupy only a small number of volunteers. There were, in effect, periods of involuntary redundancy, of dead time, that were marked by a distinct ennui. Whole days elapsed when nothing memorable at all seemed to happen, when the cry to be heard in the project office was that there was no one to help and no work to be done: 'I'm not needed! It's getting monotonous! I'm going home!' Twenty-seven days between 2 April and 26 June 1990 were thus empty. No witness required support on any Friday during that entire period. There were even four Mondays without 'supports'. Demands for assistance and the density of witnesses waxed and waned unpredictably. Volunteers could be swamped with tasks one morning, only to fall idle the next.

The second pattern was that the number of effective volunteers shrank. Enforced unemployment for long periods left its impact. Hanging around the courthouse and the project office in the hope that a late floater might possibly yield a witness or two was a dispiriting enough way to pass one's time. And there were more particular reasons for shrinkage. Two volunteers left after being trained (one after two hours in the new Court). They had recoiled from the idea and practice of 'touting for business'. Two more left in response to the emotional pitch of the courthouse (one has been assigned less taxing work in the Project office, but she was not to last). Of those few who remained, two (Mac and Emma Giovanni) undertook most of the work (between 3 April and 13 June 1990, they shared over half of the 73 'supports' between them). A third, Ingrid Marsh, undertook 17 per cent of the 'supports', and a fourth, Pat Wilkinson, 13 per cent. Two others were responsible for the remaining 18 per cent. In effect, the project had become centred on the persons of

---

[102] 70% of all 'supports' between 2 Apr. and 26 June 1990 were on Mondays and Wednesdays.

[103] A victim could receive more than 1 'support' over a period of time.

374 *Supporting the Witness*

Okafor and four key volunteers.[104] Mac had known the Court as an insider and Emma Giovanni, the former solicitor's clerk, became a near-insider herself in due course. They soon joined the little conversational huddles that spotted the courthouse. They eventually joined Okafor on the Court Project steering committee as volunteer representatives, becoming even more fully drawn into the social fabric of the project and the Court.

Thirdly, and partly in consequence, the volunteers began to wield the insider's power to interpret their environment, establish the composition of the crowd around them, and discern who was likely to be a prosecution witness. They were consulted and approached by ushers and police. They made direct approaches to the more desolate and dejected figures sitting on the yellow benches in the areas adjoining the courtroom doors. They began, in short, to become close to professionals themselves in action and knowledge.

The volunteers' exchanges with witnesses were characteristically solicitous, formulaic, and perfunctory. After all, they were encounters between strangers in strained circumstances and with little agreed common ground. They were brief (three-quarters of the 'supports' at Wood Green lasted under three hours[105]). Volunteers developed set homilies to manage relations. Mac's litany was, 'You call him, "Your Honour". The CPS rep. will come and give you your expenses form. When you go in there, please speak up, answer as truthfully as you can, and if you don't remember, you don't. Have you seen your statements? No? Well when the police officer comes, he'll give it to you.'

Volunteers might be required to field questions about such matters as the public disclosure of addresses, about expenses ('Do you get paid even if you're not called to give evidence that day?'), about whether witnesses had to adhere rigidly to what they had said in their statements, about whether witnesses could swear on the Koran, and about whether written copies of oaths could be seen in advance. They sometimes escorted victims and witnesses away from the neighbourhood of the defendant and his supporters and towards the canteen or the police room or witness consultation rooms (that marking the beginning of the use of consultation rooms by prosecution witnesses). They gave out forms to claim travelling expenses and compensation. All that constituted instrumental support: 32 per cent of

---

[104] Of those 6 pioneering volunteers, 5 were still involved with the project 2 years later.
[105] Raine and Smith, *Report of the Research programme* (Oct. 1991), 38.

the Wood Green witnesses interviewed for the Birmingham evaluation cited the provision of information as 'what was valued about the projects'.[106]

But the volunteers also accomplished an important work of signification in the wider, growing dramaturgy of criminal justice.[107] They offered what one described as 'a smiling face and just a bit of sympathy, holding their hand, and if they smoke, offer a cigarette quick to calm their nerves. Just to say, "Well, don't worry".' They enacted a gesture. They moved towards witnesses rather than away from them. They acknowledged witnesses rather than slighted them. They were the understanding and informed strangers who exceptionally came forward to put an end to alienation, marginality, and anonymity: 'It was important knowing there was somebody else there, they gave general reassurance all the time. There is a guy there knowing what witnesses are going through. It's nice to have someone aware of that fact,' said Victim 26. The phrase witnesses used repeatedly to describe the volunteer was 'a friendly face':

It was handy, say, like on a plus point, it was definitely handy to have someone there like a friendly face, because like most of the time you come in to these places and all you see is, like, even the people who are supposed to be on your side, they can't actually tell you anything or say anything or talk to you at all. I think that's court procedure. So it's nice to have a bit of a friendly face around you.

Victim 18 reflected, 'They come as a friend basis and it makes that person, the victim, feel a lot better and then they feel safe. I mean had I been here alone I'd have felt uncomfortable, unsafe.' Victim 29 said: 'They make you feel more at ease. I mean you're still going to be nervous, but they make you feel more at ease because they're

---

[106] It will be recalled that volunteers had been expressly instructed to seal themselves off from the doings of the courtroom lest they be accused of coaching, collusion, and contamination. The courtroom was where information about cases was chiefly to be had. It was there that ushers, clerks, counsel, and police officers gossiped about the progress of trials as they waited for news themselves. The outcome was that, locked outside in public space, volunteers were often condemned to share an ignorance with (and indeed of) prosecution witnesses.

[107] See P. Manning, *Police Work* (Cambridge, Mass., MIT Press, 1977), and C. Fischer, 'A Phenomenological Study of Being Criminally Victimized', *Journal of Social Issues*, 40(1) (1984). Joanna Shapland claimed of one group of victims moving through the criminal-justice system that it was symbolic recognition, not monetary compensation or retribution, that was chiefly sought. See J. Shapland *et al.*, *Victims in the Criminal Justice System* (Aldershot, Gower, 1985).

talking about what's going on and what you can do and what you can't do.'

In its first 14 months of its working, the project supported 693 people,[108] 56 per cent being classified as 'victim-witnesses', 29 per cent as witnesses but not victims, and 1 per cent as defence witnesses.[109] A mere 82, or 12 per cent, were 'advance referrals', 20 being 'self-referrals', 4 coming from victim support schemes, 43 from the CPS, and 10 from the police. Of the much larger number 'seen on the day', 407, or 67 per cent, were encountered as a result of 'touting for business', 71 were self-referrals, 43 had been referred by a court official, 20 by the CPS, and 60 by the police. The witnesses supported were white (67.5 per cent), somewhat disproportionately male (57 per cent), and of middling age (16 per cent were under 18 and 2 per cent were over 65), and their cases centred chiefly on the staple Class 4 cases of the Court: assaults (270), robberies (114), thefts and burglaries (98), and indecent assaults (68). There was but one murder case, one attempted murder, one manslaughter, 14 rapes, 2 sexual assaults, and one incest in 14 months: 20 victims of serious offences (under 3 per cent) being supported over this period.

In time, and perhaps inevitably, what had been a makeshift expedient[110] came to be regarded in Wood Green as *the* way to do things, superior to other methods in use elsewhere.[111] The innovative and temporary become conventional. Okafor told the steering subcom-

---

[108] The data in this section are taken from *Court Project Co-ordinator's Report to the Court Project Steering Committee* (July 1991).

[109] In June 1990, Okafor had been called to help a woman in distress, the wife of the 'alleged defendant', who had been upset at being at home when the police made a forced entry with guns, and levelled a gun at her own head. She said it had ruined her life, Okafor reported. Okafor was becoming increasingly uncertain about boundaries, about who victims really were, and whether this particular woman had been a victim of the police. The distinction between victims and defendants was becoming blurred, he remarked.

[110] Okafor observed later: 'Despite strenuous effort [advance referral] never progressed as was anticipated.'

[111] Okafor and Gustafson were to debate the utility of the method employed at the project in the Crown Court at Newcastle. The CPS made use of an LWAC form (list of witnesses to attend court) that laid out the names of prosecution witnesses and enabled the Victim in Court Project to transmit a letter beginning: 'I understand from the Police that you were the victim of a crime and may be required to give evidence at Newcastle Crown Court . . . in the next few weeks. Appearing at court is often a new and unfamiliar experience and our scheme offers a free and confidential service of support and practical advice to witnesses who may be a little unsure about what to expect when they appear. We are not able to discuss evidence, but aim to ease any worries you may have about appearing as a witness . . .' There was both a telephone

mittee in June 1990, 'A direct approach is better.' The once inferior method of 'touting',[112] a method dismissed as 'soliciting' by the resident judge of another Crown Court centre, as 'cold calling' by a police officer, was to be held up as an example of good practice by Victim Support.[113] Okafor was to claim: 'We are operating this multi-faceted approach and that seems to be the best to adopt. If you've got an 85 per cent response, the result is very impressive.' By June 1991, 80 per cent of 'supports' at Wood Green were secured by what were called contacts 'on the day' (and in that, the project's practice was not so very different from that of other users: Okafor himself remarked later, 'Contacting witnesses on the day is part of the tacit aspect of the culture of court procedure'). The Wood Green project had developed its own idiomatic methodology.

Volunteers and a Project in the Social World of the Court

The Project was to 'bed down' in the fashion anticipated by the chief clerk. It became another small user whose staff inconspicuously got on with their work, a project unnoticed by anyone who had no express practical business with them. Members of the new, amalga-

number and a tear-off slip which could be completed by a witness seeking help. The Newcastle project's methodology was commonly regarded as exemplary. It secured about a 20–25% response rate, but Stephen Okafor was to say in mid-June 1990, by the time 'touting for business' had become accepted practice at Wood Green, that such a rate was low and inefficient and that *all* the victims his volunteers contacted 'indicated their willingness to be helped'. Okafor remarked at a meeting of the steering subcommittee in June 1990, 'Our experience is that 96% of victims want support, so I'm very suspicious of that figure of 25%.' One of the Univ. of Birmingham evaluation team, John Raine, observed that no simple referral system had emerged. In retrospect, he said, it had been naïve to imagine that there would be one. Each scheme had developed its own system.

[112] Gustafson told the Court Project steering committee at Victim Support on 13 June 1990: '"Touting"—that's volunteers coming and in and looking for victims.'

[113] Gustafson's formal report to the Court Project steering committee on 12 Dec. 1990 stated of Wood Green: 'The method of advance contact with victim/witnesses is not proving very effective. . . . However, on-the-day contact with victim/witnesses is proving very effective: it appears that people contacted in advance often fail to approach Victim Support for help, but when a volunteer makes direct contact on the day of the case, their assistance is welcomed.' Again, the evaluation team reported in Mar. 1991 that 'the fact that 'on-the-day' referrals/contacts, to date, have accounted for some 89% of Wood Green's work, while the proportion is between 6 and 39% for the other six projects, seems indicative of the *potential* for additional support service that might be provided, if greater emphasis were placed on face-to-face contact system, rather than relying mainly on letter/contact systems and referral procedures involving professional agencies'; Raine and Smith, *Research Progress Report No. 6* (8 Mar. 1991), 3.

mated recruitment training, and referral subcommittee noted towards the end of the first month that 'there was still a lot of ignorance amongst court users about the scheme'.[114]

Knowledge about the project was moulded by the physical and social ecology of the courthouse. Some, moving about in public space, chose not to look at the volunteer as they organized themselves for 'conventional engagement closure'. Counsel, for example, had not been consulted or informed about the project, knew almost nothing of its coming,[115] and observed little of it when it was established. They might be approached by volunteers seeking witnesses, but they were professionally disinclined to peer about them too closely. Indeed, they feared that their opponents would think ill of them if they were seen conferring intimately with members of this new, untried, and possibly partisan group. They preferred to establish their own personal territories, and, once in occupation, they would brood about the case before them and award civil inattention to anyone but the few known and trustworthy professionals around them. If volunteers were seen at all, they were deliberately thrown out of focus, never scrutinized.

Some users and professionals, indeed, most insiders, would see nothing of the Project. The professionals' domain was private space. Above all, those working in the courtroom expected and chose to see little of what unfolded between volunteers and witnesses in the public areas of the courthouse. One court clerk stated, 'It's a bit difficult for me because one only sees with one's own eyes in court . . . and we don't [leave it] very often and we wouldn't particularly look at them anyway.' Judges, too, could see nothing of the scheme from where they sat in their chambers and courtrooms. The project remained invisible and substantially irrelevant to their work, their knowledge being based only on a rare oral or written report.

Administrators were largely satisfied that the project was evolving as it should. They did remain perplexed at the scale and abundance of committees feeding the project in the private reaches of the Court, and they did worry about the practice of 'touting for business' in public

---

[114] Meeting of recruitment, training, and referral policy subcommittee held on 25 Apr. 1990.

[115] There were a few exceptions. Counsel who appeared at other times as assistant recorders had certainly learned about the Project in their capacity as judges.

space. A good project was an inconspicuous project,[116] and volunteers threatened to become rogue elements in a fragile world of fraught relations, a world where any disturbance was undesirable. A senior administrator observed at the end of May 1990, 'I'm a little unhappy about them touting for work around the building, approaching counsel and this sort of thing. I don't think it's the right way to go about it.' The Court was for trained professionals who stayed discreetly within bounds.

There had been concern that users might complain, but there had been no criticism, no scandal, and no friction. The chief clerk remarked at the end of the second month, 'I think they're keeping it very low-key in court, which is fine. I mean, the clerks are aware of its existence, and they're going about their job. But they're not causing any problem.'

Conclusion

Viewed from within the inner regions of the Court, it was to be a while before the project became accepted as yet another small user with its own territory and an unobtrusive part to play in the conduct of affairs. Viewed from without, however, from the public spaces where people waited, the project assumed larger proportions. It gave the Court a reassuring face. It reorganized the experience of victims and witnesses, reduced uncertainty, and acknowledged the presence of those once neglected. Victim 31 said:

He tried to reassure me, which was very nice. And he told me bits about the courtroom and said it is very nerve-wracking, but don't make yourself nervous. Just try and relax. . . . I was very pleased that there was someone around who cared about our feelings, about the way we felt instead of just, 'Okay, fair enough, you're here and thank you, good-bye'.

---

[116] There was to be a continuing and unresolved question about the size and number of signs advertising the Project. Okafor wished for many, large, and obvious signs; the chief clerk did not.

Postscript

> I do not think I would have coped so well without Victim Support. They helped me from the time of the attack right through the ordeal of giving evidence in court. The volunteers tended to be older and really did seem to care. (Sarah, quoted in 'Witnesses See Benefit of Support', *Independent*, 30 October 1991)

The Raine and Smith report was published on 29 October 1991, and its conclusion was that the seven experimental projects had been most successful in meeting the needs of victims and prosecution witnesses attending the Crown Court.[1] Users and administrators were all said to be 'very favourable' and 'any initial concerns about the potential for volunteer actions disrupting court proceedings' were found 'to have been dispelled by the very professional manner in which the volunteers were perceived to have been conducting themselves. Indeed the clear consensus was that the initiative should be continued.'[2] Raine and Smith ended by observing that the service could be provided for around £20,000 to £25,000 a Court centre and, on the assumption that there would be some 80 centres served, recommended that £2,000,000 should be provided to allow Victim Support to continue and enlarge what it had started.

Victim Support adopted the report and it endorsed the recommendation. Its director, Helen Reeves, declared in a press release that Raine and Smith had shown 'that Victim Support can provide a crucial service to the courts', and that 'funding must be found not only to continue it but to develop it to other courts'.

There was a press conference to publicize the Project and the report, a conference chaired again by David Windlesham and attended by officials from the Lord Chancellor's Department, the CPS, and the Home Office, by reporters from *The Independent*, *The Daily Telegraph*, and the BBC, and by young victims who had been supported by the Maidstone project (and it was those victims who received the greatest subsequent journalistic interest). Tim Gustafson recounted how it had 'taken time to convince the agencies that we

---

[1] J. Raine and R. Smith, *The Victim/Witness in Court Project: Report of the Research Programme* (Oct. 1991), 65.

[2] Indeed, it will be recalled that the resident judge at Wood Green publicly proclaimed himself to be part of that consensus.

are not a bunch of bumbling amateurs. We didn't upset one trial. I would wake up with cold sweats worrying about that, but it didn't happen.' And then, just as the Home Office had known he would, Gustafson proceeded to ask the Home Office official for £2,000,000 to translate the project into something more general and permanent. That, after all, was the end to which the entire project and report had tended.

Gustafson received no more reply than 'We're looking at the report. It shows that the scheme works very well, but it will need studying to see whether it needs £2,000,000 from the Home Office . . . There's no immediate answer as to whether £2,000,000 will be available.' But there was to be an answer, and it came within a month. In November 1991, the Home Secretary informed Victim Support that its annual grant was to be increased by £1,600,000 (or 28 per cent) 'to enable you, if you so choose, to maintain the present Victim/Witnesses in Court Schemes and to extend them to other areas'.[3] A month later, in December 1991, Victim Support's Victim/Witness Court Project management committee did indeed resolve to maintain and extend the court programme in up to 30 Crown Court centres.[4] And the Crown Court at Wood Green was confirmed as one of the centres that would house what was now no longer called an experimental project but a 'court programme' under 'direct line management by Victim Support National'.[5]

---

[3] Letter from Home Secretary to John Southgate, Nov. 1991.
[4] Minutes of management committee meeting, 11 Dec. 1991.
[5] Agenda for Wood Green Court Project steering committee, 12 Mar. 1992.

Index